D1503415

Barry M. Moriarty

in association with

David J. Cowen

E. Julian Ford

Nicholas Gajewski

Edward J. Kaiser

Robert E. Leak

C. Donald Liner

Robert M. Sparks

David C. Sweet

Edward J. Taaffe

James O. Wheeler

Industrial Location and Community Development

The University of
North Carolina Press
Chapel Hill

© 1980 The University of North Carolina Press
Manufactured in the United States of America
All rights reserved
Library of Congress Catalog Card Number 79-16029
Cloth edition, ISBN 0-8078-1400-8
Paper edition, ISBN 0-8078-4064-5

Library of Congress Cataloging in Publication Data

Main entry under title:

Industrial location and community development.

   Bibliography: p.
   Includes index.
   1. City planning—United States—Addresses, essays,
lectures. 2. Industry, Location of—United States—Addresses, essays, lectures. 3. Community development,
Urban—United States—Addresses, essays, lectures.
4. Land use, Urban—United States—Addresses, essays,
lectures. I. Moriarty, Barry M. II. Cowen, David J.
HT167.I43   338.973   79-16029
ISBN 0-8078-1400-8
ISBN 0-8078-4064-5 pbk.

To Lorraine:
good friend,
devoted wife, and
dedicated teacher

Contents

x   Contents

Figures

Tables

Preface

This book is an outcome of the American Industrial Development Council's accredited Basic Industrial Development Course (BIDC) conducted at the University of North Carolina in Chapel Hill since 1971. Its purpose is to describe and explain the concepts, materials, and methods designed to make community economic development programs more effective, especially during an era of growing government intervention. Its chapters convey the practical experience and accumulated knowledge of the many professional economic development practitioners, planners, and academicians that have served as instructors in the NCBIDC program. Many of the chapters are the result of the composite expertise of several professionals.

The book's content was determined primarily by four different groups. The American Industrial Development Council's accreditation committee provided an outline of the basic information needed by those who are involved in industrial and economic development. The NCBIDC Steering Committee suggested additional topics and helped to select appropriate lecturers. The BIDC participants, most of whom were private or public industrial, community, or economic developers and planners, suggested many improvements to the program's content over the years. Finally, the BIDC instructors themselves, following proposed topic outlines furnished by the principal author, provided the substantive principles, materials, and techniques considered necessary for the practice of comprehensive industrial or economic development in the United States today.

The overall theme of the book is the problem of how to bring together effectively three different types of decision makers in an area—the industrial land user, represented by the manufacturer searching for a location for his plant; the landowner, represented by the industrial developer; and the community, represented by the planner and other local officials—each of whom is responsible to different interests, to achieve a development outcome that will be satisfactory to all. While other ways in which community economic development can occur are fully recognized, the main thrust of the book is toward the practice of industrial development. The book is divided into five sections. Part 1 focuses on community development and planning principles. Part 2 concentrates on industrial location trends and the plant location search process. Part 3 is devoted to specific regional and community location factors of concern to industrial prospects, part 4 presents sources and methods of financing industrial development undertakings, and part 5 discusses ways of promoting local industrial development.

The introductory chapter was coauthored with James O. Wheeler, professor of economic geography and chairman of the Department of Geography at the University of Georgia. Edward J. Kaiser, professor of city and regional planning at The University of North Carolina at Chapel Hill, authored chapter 3, "Land Use Planning for Industry." Chapter 4, "Government Programs for Industry," was written by Robert M. Sparks, an economic geographer, presently serving as the director of administrative services for the Maryland Department of Economic and Community Development. David J. Cowen, associate professor of economic geography at the University of South Carolina, was coauthor of chapter 5, "Locational Trends in Manufacturing." Edward J. Taaffe, professor of transportation geography at Ohio State University, wrote chapter 7, "Transportation and Industrial Location." Nicholas Gajewski, manager of the Proposal Management Department of Roy F. Weston, Inc., and former economic development analyst for the North Carolina Division of Economic Development, coauthored chapter 10, "The Environment and Industrial Location." C. Donald Liner, associate professor of economics and assistant director of the Institute of Government at The University of North Carolina at Chapel Hill, wrote chapter 11, "Taxation and Industrial Location." Robert E. Leak, whose positions in several development organizations include past president of the American Industrial Development Council, past director of the North Carolina Division of Economic Development, and executive director of the South Carolina State Development Board, assisted in writing chapter 14, "Planning and Organizing for Development." E. Julian Ford, past president of the Southern Industrial Development Council and director of Industrial Development for the Carolina Power and Light Company, also assisted in writing chapter 14. The concluding chapter, "The Systematic Approach to Development," was written by David C. Sweet, an economic geographer who has served as director of Regional Economic Research for Battelle Memorial Institute, director of the Ohio Department of Community and Economic Development and a member of the Ohio Public Utilities Commission. He is presently dean of the College of Urban Affairs, Cleveland State University. In addition to writing chapters 2, 6, 8, 9, 12, and 13 and coauthoring chapters 1, 5, 10, and 14, I have taken nearly unbridled discretion in editing and rewriting the remaining chapters to such a degree that any problems with content or substance have become my responsibility.

Special acknowledgment needs to be made to several individuals for their contributions to this book: to Robert E. Leak for his insistence as chairman of the NCBIDC Steering Committee that the North Carolina program teach not only the concepts of economic development but also the practical day-to-day techniques required by industrial and economic developers; to David G. Basile, chairman of the Department of Geography at The University of North Carolina at Chapel Hill, for his support and assistance in conducting the NCBIDC program and in the production of this book; to Richard Preston and Larry D. Cohick, former chief stewards of the American Industrial Development Council, for their efforts in promoting the NCBIDC; to Richard E. Lonsdale, chairman of the Department of Geography at the University of Nebraska at Lincoln, for without his interest in establishing the NCBIDC this book would never have been written.

For many reasons, I am most indebted to my wife Lorraine, to whom this book is dedicated.

Barry M. Moriarty
Chapel Hill, North Carolina
January 1979

Industrial
Location and
Community
Development

Chapter 1
Introduction

Industry and Development

Industrial activity has long been associated with the concept of development, ever since the oppressive working environment of the Industrial Revolution in Great Britain in the last half of the eighteenth century. The application of technological developments to manufacturing, such as the substitution of the steam engine for water power, has had momentous consequences. Transportation and other innovations created profound new locational possibilities for industry. Monopoly production in one area could be undercut by the transfer of technology to other manufacturing sites. Despite the adverse working environment, the use of child labor, and the often unpleasant living conditions the Industrial Revolution propelled Great Britain to its zenith as a world power.

As industrial technology spread to other countries, including the United States, a continuing and intensifying association built up between industrial activity and economic development. In the United States, early manufacturing was of course concentrated along the East Coast, where, primarily in response to manufacturing growth, the nation's largest urban centers sprang up and began to compete with one another for economic dominance. Eventually New York, because of its accessibility to the continental interior, emerged as the largest city and the country's leading manufacturing center. Since New York could serve the largest market and have access to the widest range of raw materials, it was the most advantageous location for manufacturing. The concentration of industry in New York, and in the other large cities along the Eastern Seaboard, acted as a magnet, attracting both native and immigrant workers to settle and derive their livelihood from the factories. Thus the concentration of industry at one stage set up conditions that would assure an even greater clustering of manufacturing at a later time. This circular growth process, with local variations from city to city, region to region, and industry to industry, was repeated all across the United States.

The repetitive process of urban and industrial growth in the early stages of industrialization has been described and interpreted in some detail by Allan Pred (1966). His simple descriptive model, called the circular and cumulative process of industrialization and urban-size growth, provides valuable insight for industrial developers. Briefly, Pred perceived that a new or expanded industry in a city creates an initial multiplier effect—i.e., a need for additional businesses, services, construction, and transportation to provide for the enlarged industrial labor force (see chapter 2). In turn, the population growth of the city, created by both the industrial labor force and the various new business and service workers (such as doctors, retail merchants, and teachers), increases the threshold level, or the level at which markets in that city grow sufficiently large enough for new industries and businesses to operate economically. For example, during one period, the local urban and regional market may be too small to justify a high capital investment manufacturing plant or a plant that can obtain only a small per-unit profit on its output. But if the population size and hence the local purchasing power are increased, new and larger industry can gain a foothold. The process is thus both circular and cumulative.

Pred recognized a second consequence of the location of new or expanded industry: the enhanced possibility of invention or innovation. As more individuals become involved with the details of the manufacturing process, more efficient production, managerial, and financial arrangements are likely to develop. Inventions and innovations may often involve the creation of new technology whereby a local industry is able to achieve a competitive market advantage, resulting in increased production, additional workers, and new local or regional thresholds. Although the process, sketched here in barest form, cannot apply uniformly and comprehensively to all industries or to all communities, the elements of Pred's descriptive model, stemming from the Industrial Revolution in Great Britain and applied to the United States experience, are frequent but poorly conceived concepts in the thinking of industrial and economic developers about the relationship between industry and community development.

Traditionally, the relationship between industry and development has been described in two somewhat polarized approaches. One, largely reflected in Pred's view, sees the relationship as positive and desirable. Economic development, population growth and prosperity have gone hand in hand. The frontier philosophy, viewing expansion as natural and inevitable and physical resources as inexhaustible, led to aggressive campaigns to stimulate local and regional economies for the increased well-being of society. Government at all levels enacted legislation or created mechanisms and agencies to assure economic expansion, usually through stimulating the industrial sector. At the extreme, every community aspired to be a Detroit, Pittsburgh, Chicago, and New York combined into one grand conurbation.

More recently, the gradual recognition that the population growth rate has slowed dramatically and that resources have become frighteningly scarce and unbearably expensive has forced upon American society a different viewpoint. The frontier outlook has been replaced by a new conservation principle with enormous consequences for all of society, but especially for the modern developer. Faced with scarce resources and stagnating market demand, the industrial, economic, or community developer must be concerned with new dimensions of the development process.

Although it has always been recognized that industrial location decisions have an impact on the local community and region, it is now increasingly apparent that any decision may have both positive and negative impacts. Indeed, whether a given impact is good or bad is often debatable. Even the concept of development takes on different connotations. Some view any growth or expansion of industry as harmful for their locale and wish only that industry would locate in some other place. The modern developer is faced with a tremendous challenge, for both positive and negative impacts must be anticipated from all development decisions. The developer of the past who only took credit for the beneficial impact that new industry had on community development must now be accountable for the harmful impact it may have on society.

The question of quality of life bears directly on the issues with which the professional developer grapples. Unfortunately, the phrase *quality of life* has no precise meaning and is virtually impossible to quantify. A whole series of societal and individual creature comforts are embodied in the concept. Environmentalists, including energy conservationists, are bringing increasing pressure on developers to be concerned about the quality of life in the future as well as in the present. Despite the ambiguity of the concept, quality of life must certainly be considered in industrial development planning and policy.

In order to meet these new challenges and to be able to assess the future impacts of industry on society, the professional developer must be well informed and experienced in both the community economic development and industrial location processes. Both theoretical and applied knowledge is essential. The developer who has only an applied background may be constrained by glaring biases because of the limited number of case studies on which he has worked. Likewise, the armchair developer, steeped only in industrial location or economic development theory, has little grasp of how to apply the theories to a particular practical situation. Clearly, these are two sides of the same coin.

General locational factors transcend any particular case study. One must be aware of principles of locational change and the forces that drive them. General principles, however, never fully explain the impact of industry on development, since it is the human decision that creates the impact. The entrepreneur perceives an opportunity, rightly or wrongly, and thereby effects some change. He may either explicitly or implicitly act partly according to established principles; at the same time some of his motivation may be based on highly personal goals. It is clear that development must be viewed from both sides.

Organization of the Book

The first part of this book focuses upon the community interested in industrial and economic development. The community is the place where the industrial location seeker and the developer come together, each to achieve different goals: the location seeker, to operate a business at a satisfactory profit; and the developer, to promote the economic well-being of the community. The overall interests of the community are represented by the planner, who has yet a different goal: to maintain a financially unencumbered, quality living environment for the community's inhabitants. The first chapter, dealing with the community, concentrates on the development process itself, briefly describing how planning and policy programs can be used to influence the development process. In particular, the chapter examines the process by which community population and economic growth takes place and evaluates planning and policy instruments to direct that growth, specifically input-output analysis. The second chapter emphasizes the role of the land use planner in directing community development, the planning techniques used, and the policy instruments available to exercise control over development. This chapter provides a valuable perspective of the community planner's approach to planning for industrial development in order better to prepare the developer to work more effectively with local planners in creating development policies and guidelines. The final chapter in this section focuses on the policies and programs that have been implemented by federal, state, and local governments to assist developers and communities in their economic development efforts. The chapter reviews the several forces stimulating the steadily increasing government involvement in the field of industrial location and the nature of regulatory intervention by various levels of government during the 1960s and 1970s.

The second part of the book discusses industrial development trends, focusing on the industrial location seeker and the manufacturing firms interested in locating at sites where they are able to operate satisfactorily in a competitive market economy. The first chapter in the section presents a detailed examination of the locational factors evaluated by industrial location seekers in their search for an industrial site and describes how these factors are responsible for the changing manufacturing patterns in different regions of the country and in different areas of the city. The industrial location search process is described at both the regional and the local level. The second chapter in the section underscores the theme by showing how the site selection team of an actual industrial firm evaluated alternative sites. This chapter also presents detailed guidelines on the site selection decision process adopted by numerous firms.

Part 3 consists of five chapters dealing with industrial development factors. This section, as well as the two that follow it, focuses on the industrial or economic developer. The first chapter discusses the effect of freight costs on the location of industry, as well as how an industry's choice of a location may be affected by its accessibility to specific markets, labor, and information. Several methods demonstrate how developers can portray their community's accessibility to specific market areas or material sources. The important and complex effects that freight cost and access exert at a regional level in the location of industry are discussed. The second chapter in this section covers the characteristics of labor forces and the labor requirements of industry and outlines methods for evaluating the availability of a qualified work force in a labor-draw area. The third chapter examines the utility requirements and costs of manufacturing firms and federal legislation controlling industry's waste disposal. It also discusses industry's power and energy resource requirements, how industry has to use different fuels in certain cases, and how government can and has imposed energy conservation measures on industry. The fourth chapter, a companion to the third, examines the impact of the major environmental legislation on industry, particularly its effect on the location of industry. Like other chapters, this one suggests ways for developers to assist manufacturers in dealing with their locational needs. Both chapters are especially informative for those interested in industrial development, since they treat contemporary issues such as energy and environment from a developmental perspective. The last chapter in this section discusses why state and local taxation practices *do not* play a significant role in the industrial location decision, particularly at the regional search level. The numerous studies examined in the chapter support the conclusion that taxes are only a minor cost of the total cost of doing business and, as such, enter into the locational decision only if there is a tax difference between two communities that are equal in all other respects.

The two chapters in part 4 address financial matters. Chapter 12 deals with nongovernment (or private-sector) sources and methods of financing industrial development, presenting the most common ways of securing equity and borrowed funds for industrial firms. The last chapter in this section details the most important public-sector sources and methods of industrial development financing. The chapter describes not only the federal programs available for industrial firms, but also those available to communities that seek to increase their attractiveness as locations for industry. The chapter also surveys various state and local government financing organizations and programs.

The last part of the book discusses strategies for community and regional development. Chapter 14 emphasizes the importance of local preparedness for a successful development program, presents a step-by-step review of the process of selecting and acquiring sites for potential industry, and details the basic community and site information that should be compiled for industrial and business prospects. The final chapter describes some methods that can be used to identify community advantages and disadvantages and appropriate development goals. It also focuses on ways to identify target industries—those that the community may be most likely to attract, at the same time meeting the community's development goals. Community marketing strategies are reviewed, including the community brochure, trade associations and publications, direct-mail campaigns, development trips, and advertising and news releases.

This volume, then, is designed as a contribution to the literature on industrial, economic, and community development, from both a conceptual and an empirical point of view. The book provides the substantive knowledge necessary for successful development decisions. At the same time, it gives specific applied and planning guidelines and suggestions for the day-to-day duties of the professional developer. The book also may be read profitably by students of scholarly disciplines such as economics, geography, planning, political science, and sociology—disciplines concerned with the community. Finally, the book is grounded in the traditional basics of industrial location and economic development as well as aimed toward offering insights into the issues that will increasingly occupy the professional developer in the future.

Part 1

Perspectives on
Community
Development

Chapter 2
Community Population and
Economic Growth

The economic growth and well-being of most communities, whether they are urban settlements, counties, states, or even larger regions, result from the location in those communities of establishments engaged in manufacturing production or in the distribution of goods and services. Except for a few instances in which growth occurs because of the location of military, religious, or political establishments, or enterprises engaged in raw material extraction, most communities owe their growth to the location of production and distribution functions. In general, then, as either the production or the distribution function expands, so also do the population and economic wealth of the community. The purpose of this chapter is to describe the process by which community population and economic growth take place and to examine planning and policy instruments designed to direct this growth.

The Community Growth and Development Process

Economic development analysts designate establishments engaged in manufacturing production and certain types of service activities as the prime determinants of community growth. Although this idea has frequently been attacked for a variety of reasons, it is still considered a viable explanation of population and economic growth (Isard et al. 1960, pp. 194–205). According to this viewpoint, in order for a community to grow, it must manufacture and export goods and services to regions beyond its own area or in some way engage in activities that will bring new money into its own economy. This sector, referred to as the basic sector, in turn supports a nonbasic sector that does not export, but rather supplies goods and services to the establishments and households of employees in the basic sector, as well as to those in its own. Thus, as the basic sector grows, it creates multiplier effects that cause the population and nonbasic sector of the community to grow in an attempt to maintain a state of equilibrium.

Although manufacturing has been the basic activity responsible for much of the economic development in the past, other activities also bring money into a community. Truck and warehouse parks, hotels and motels, and research facilities are readily recognized examples. Less commonly known are those that take advantage of local circumstances. All types of recreation activities, natural history and local-culture museums, crafts centers, and even abandoned mines have been developed and promoted to attract tourists from both within and outside the region. Not to be overlooked are activities that serve the local and regional population but receive a substantial portion of their income from state and federal government transfer payments and grants. Boarding schools, homes and centers for senior citizens, nursing homes, and medical clinics are examples. All such activities increase local employment, only slightly in some cases, but they are nevertheless important, especially in small communities faced with unemployment and out-migration. Because the emphasis here is industrial location, these other impetuses to community development will be given less consideration.

The export-base proposition, along with evidence of how populations and employment increase over time in restricted areas, suggests that the community growth that results from the development of basic industry occurs ideally in six phases (fig. 2.1): (1) the initial equilibrium or stagnation phase, (2) the export manufacturing industry development phase, (3) the ancillary or complementary manufacturing industry development phase, (4) the nonbasic service industry development phase, (5) the social-overhead capital development phase, and (6) the post-equilibrium or stagnation phase.[1] This delineation does not imply that a unique set of events occurs during each phase, but rather that particular events are more prominent during certain phases than others.

The *initial equilibrium or stagnation phase*, as its name implies, represents a period in which the community's output per person, as well as its population and income in constant dollars, is relatively stable. Employment is confined to business firms and institutions that provide the essential goods and services required by the community's inhabitants and manufacturing establishments (if they exist) that have experienced little or no growth for some time. Tax revenues are constant but are sufficient to maintain the existing level of public services. Taxes would have to be increased, however, for any expansion or improvement to take place.

Much of the housing and other building stock is aging, and a small amount of capital is invested in its maintenance and replacement. The social structure of the community is stable, with well-defined social relationships. The phase can last indefinitely unless the community's more innovative inhabitants awaken to a need for development or unless development is stimulated by exogenous private or public forces.

During the *export manufacturing industry development phase* a basic, export-oriented industry moves into the community because its location provides production and transportation costs that allow the firm to operate in a competitive market and realize a satisfactory profit (fig. 2.2). A major consequence of the industry's development is that a number of new employment opportunities are created in the community. Whether the industry will need to attract some employees from areas outside the community depends upon the number of new employment opportunities, the level of local unemployment and underemployment in the skill categories required by the industry, the distance people are willing to com-

Figure   2.1 Community Population and Employment Growth per Total Area

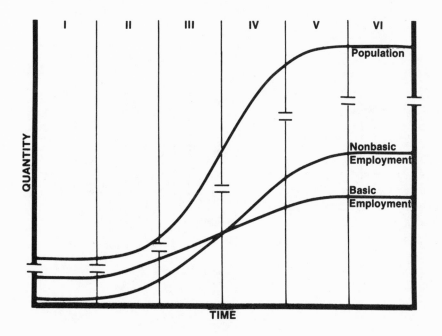

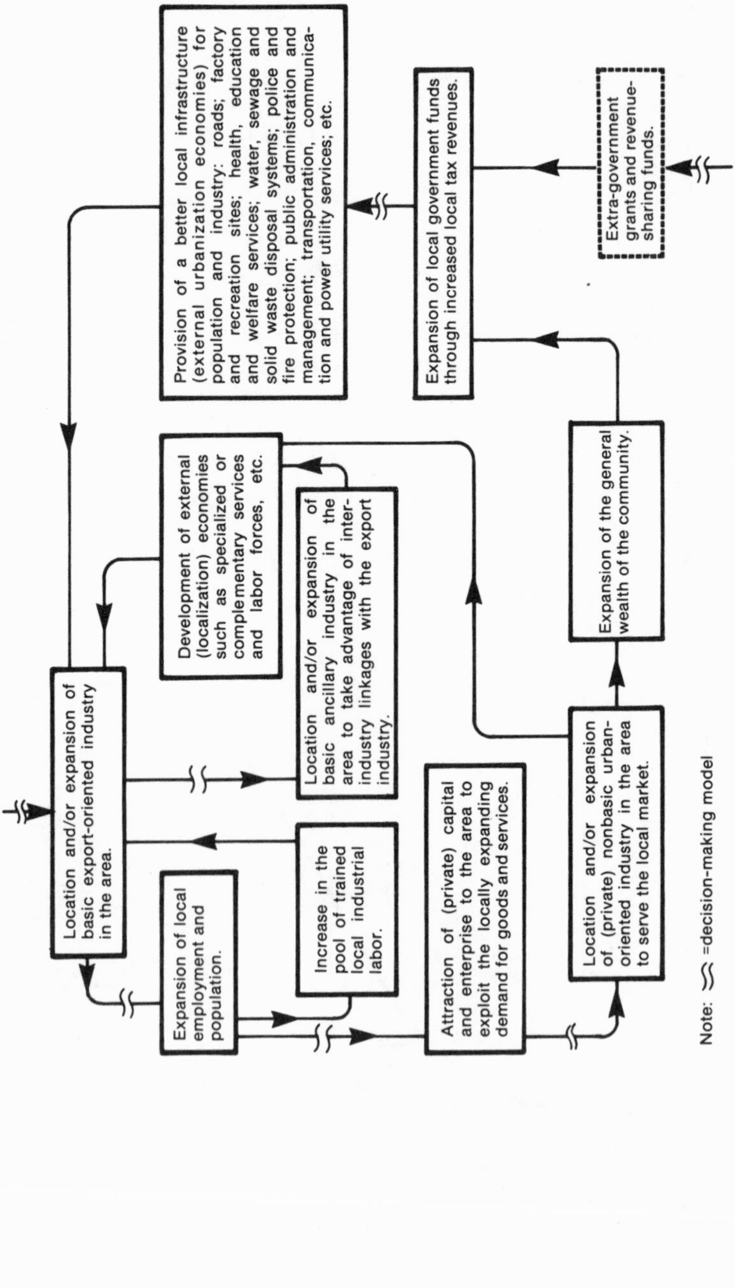

Figure 2.2 General Model of Economic Development

Source: Adapted from Myrdal 1957.

Location and/or expansion of basic export-oriented industry in the area.

Provision of a better local infrastructure (external urbanization economies) for population and industry: roads; factory and recreation sites; health, education and welfare services; water, sewage and solid waste disposal systems; police and fire protection; public administration and management; transportation, communication and power utility services; etc.

Expansion of local government funds through increased local tax revenues.

Extra-government grants and revenue-sharing funds.

Development of external (localization) economies such as specialized or complementary services and labor forces, etc.

Location and/or expansion of basic ancillary industry in the area to take advantage of inter-industry linkages with the export industry.

Expansion of the general wealth of the community.

Expansion of local employment and population.

Increase in the pool of trained local industrial labor.

Attraction of (private) capital and enterprise to the area to exploit the locally expanding demand for goods and services.

Location and/or expansion of (private) nonbasic urban-oriented industry in the area to serve the local market.

Note: ⧗ =decision-making model

mute each day in order to work, and the number of inhabitants who choose to seek new employment. The migration of these workers, along with their families, to the community causes an increase in the local population as well as changes in its social characteristics. A further consequence of the basic industry's locating in the community is that the employees become more skilled in their occupations over time, thus creating a supply of trained workers having higher productivity. The higher productivity lowers unit production costs, and if this saving is passed on to consumers, a greater demand for the industry's products is created. The increased demand enables the industry to expand both its plant facilities and its employment opportunities, taking advantage of internal economies of scale that result from bulk transactions, the standardization of production processes, and the more efficient use of both labor and equipment to produce even lower unit costs.

When the basic export industry becomes large enough to create either internal markets for intermediate products or external localization economies for other industries the community enters the *ancillary manufacturing industry development phase*.[2] At this time one or more basic ancillary industries choose to locate in the area. The ancillary industry may be attracted to the community because of transportation economies, such as in the case where both the ancillary and the export industries use similar raw materials or intermediate products in their manufacturing processes, or where the product or by-product of one industry is a major material input of the other.[3] Another reason for industrial juxtaposition (or linkage) to be established is the production economies that can result from the complementary use of the community's labor force. That is, the ancillary industry may choose to locate in the area because it employs workers possessing skills similar to those employed in the export industry or because the export industry employs only a certain age, sex, skill, or racial group, leaving a labor surplus in other groups that can be hired at low wage scales for tasks to which they are suited. The attraction of ancillary industry to the area improves the external localization economies offered in the community because establishments that provide specialized (maintenance, business, professional, transportation, and communication) services to the industrial sector become increasingly more proficient in providing rapid and reliable service. As a consequence of the improved localization economies, both the export and the ancillary industries may find it profitable to expand production further; or, if the community has established a reputation for the production of particular goods, additional export industries producing similar goods may be attracted to the area. The net effect of the ancillary industry's locating in the area is a continual growth of the local labor force and population.

The *nonbasic service industry development phase* is a direct consequence of the population expansion brought about by the growth of the
basic industries during the two preceding phases. As the population expands, so also does its demand for private goods and services, some of
which are found within the community and some of which are not. When
the aggregate disposable income of the total population rises to a sufficient level, entrepreneurs recognize that the community has become large
enough to create new trade and service areas for additional nonbasic,
community-oriented industries. In some cases the new nonbasic establishments provide the same goods and services found in already existing
establishments that have undergone expansion to the point of satisfactory
returns. In other cases the new establishments provide higher-order goods

Table   2.1. A Summary of Trade-Center Types as Defined by Business Functions

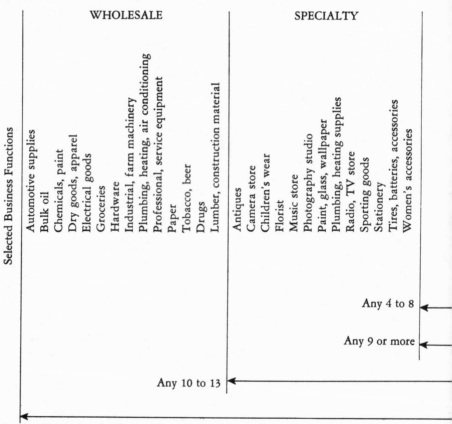

Source: Borchert and Adams 1963, p. 4.

and services that were previously available only in other large communities some distance away (Borchert and Adams 1963; table 2.1). When the demand for these higher-order goods and services reaches certain threshold levels (that is, the minimum number of goods or services that would have to be sold in order for particular establishments to maintain their existence), they make their appearance in the community (Bell 1973; table 2.2). A substantial part of the financing of these industries is usually obtained from outside the community, especially when multi-regional business firms are concerned.[4] One consequence of the growth of the nonbasic, community-oriented sector is the further improvement of the external localization economies offered in the area, making the location even more attractive for the continued expansion of the basic indus-

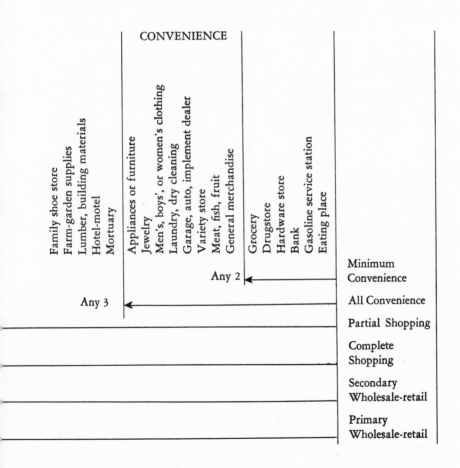

Table   2.2. Population Threshold Sizes and Ranks for Selected Central Goods and Services in Central Iowa, 1960 and 1970

Central good or service	1960 Population threshold	Rank	1970 Population threshold	Rank
Grocery stores	528	1	428	1
Automobile dealers	605	2	752	5
Gasoline service stations	811	3	558	2
Hardware	852	4	1392	16
Banking services	872	5	850	9
Restaurants	887	6	763	6
Physicians	935	7	751	4
Animal husbandry service	1030	8	1234	14
Lumber yards	1037	9	1121	13
Furniture stores	1060	10	1631	19
Fuel oil dealers	1273	11	690	3
Appliance stores	1452	12	7389	35
Dry goods and general merchandise	1614	13	2505	26
Radio and TV repair	1641	14	1902	23
Frozen-food lockers	1656	15	4334	33
Insurance agencies	1668	16	1073	12
Churches	1709	17	1053	11
Beauticians	1775	18	938	10
Taverns	1889	19	830	8
Drugstores	1906	20	1502	18
Railroad terminals	1907	21	2671	27
Dentists	1938	22	1860	22
Automobile repair service	2038	23	1716	20
Veterinarians	2196	24	768	7
Real estate agencies	2436	25	1390	15
Hay, feed, and grain	2740	26	2047	25
Electrical supplies	2770	27	1489	17
Laundromats	2813	28	2779	28
Lawyers	2825	29	1971	24
Dry-cleaning services	3239	30	1746	21
Sporting goods	3416	31	10721	37
Women's apparel	3793	32	3121	29
Electrical repairs	3971	33	3803	32
Farm implement dealers	3975	34	3259	30
Radio and TV sales	4221	35	7031	34
Assembly halls	4309	36	3320	31
Intercity bus terminals	6295	37	12157	38
Hospital services	7596	38	10229	36

Table   2.2   (continued)

Central good or service	1960 Population threshold	Rank	1970 Population threshold	Rank
Stockyards	11829	39	13293	39
Movies	11897	40	16434	40
Men's apparel	21291	41	18068	41

Source: Bell 1973, pp. 122–23.

try sector. Thus, employment in the basic industries may increase (depending upon worker productivity gains) as a result of the savings created by the improved economies. Of greater significance, though, is the substantial increase in employment in the nonbasic industries brought about by growing consumer demand (Morrisset 1958; Ullman, Dacey, and Brodsky 1971; table 2.3). The increased labor requirements of the nonbasic sector generate additional population growth as more families migrate to the community to take advantage of the new employment opportunities. The additional families, in turn, stimulate even greater expansion of the nonbasic sector.[5]

The *social-overhead capital development phase* occurs concomitantly with the growth generated by the implantation of the private basic and nonbasic industries in the community. The development associated with this phase is characterized by the creation by the community's inhabitants of publicly financed nonbasic industries to satisfy a demand for public services that will benefit most of them collectively. The scale of public services provided by the community depends upon its overall wealth, as measured by the total assessed market value of its private and real personal property. The overall wealth, in turn, depends upon the type of basic and nonbasic industries that have located in the area, and it expands in a manner similar to the way employment multiplies in the community. On the other hand, the level of public services demanded multiplies in a fashion similar to the community's population growth. The level to which the services are provided depends primarily upon threshold levels of demand, although somewhat upon the methods by which they are financed —by local taxes, revenue-sharing grants, subsidies, user's fees, or some combination. The public nonbasic industries created are of two types: those providing joint services that can benefit all of the community's inhabitants equally and those providing merit services that benefit specific "qualified" inhabitants of the community. Most joint-service industries are financed almost entirely by local tax revenues and provide the essential services associated with police and fire protection; public administration

Table 2.3. Percentage of Employed Persons Working in Nonbasic Employment by Size of Urban Place

Employment sector	National percentage	Northeast population (in thousands)						
		(10)	(25)	(50)	(100)	(250)	(500)	(1,000)
Mining	0.9	0.0	0.0	0.0	0.0	0.0	0.0	0.0
Construction	6.2	2.4	2.7	3.0	3.4	3.8	4.0	4.2
Durable mfg.	15.9							
Furniture	1.3	0.0	0.1	0.1	0.2	0.3	0.4	0.4
Primary metals	2.6	0.0	0.0	0.1	0.1	0.3	0.5	0.4
Fabricated metals	1.8	0.1	0.1	0.1	0.2	0.5	1.1	1.4
Machinery	2.9	0.1	0.2	0.3	0.5	0.9	1.0	1.0
Electrical mach.	1.8	0.0	0.1	0.1	0.1	0.2	0.7	0.7
Motor vehicles	2.0	0.0	0.0	0.0	0.0	0.1	0.3	0.3
Transport. eq.	1.1	0.0	0.0	0.0	0.0	0.1	0.1	0.2
Other durable	2.4	0.2	0.3	0.4	0.6	1.0	1.3	1.3
Nondurable mfg.	14.2							
Food mfg.	3.0	0.5	0.6	0.8	1.0	1.4	1.8	1.8
Textile mfg.	2.2	0.0	0.0	0.0	0.0	0.0	0.0	0.1
Apparel	2.4	0.0	0.0	0.0	0.1	0.2	0.2	0.2
Printing	2.1	0.5	0.6	0.7	0.8	1.1	1.4	1.4
Chemicals	1.3	0.1	0.1	0.1	0.1	0.3	0.6	0.7
Other nondurable	3.2	0.1	0.1	0.2	0.3	0.6	1.2	1.5
Mfg. not specified	—	0.0	0.0	0.0	0.1	0.1	0.1	0.1
Transport & Util.	9.2							
Railroads	2.9	0.4	0.4	0.4	0.4	0.5	0.7	0.9
Trucking	1.3	0.4	0.4	0.5	0.6	0.8	0.9	1.0
Other trans.	2.0	0.4	0.5	0.5	0.5	0.6	0.8	1.1
Telecom.	1.4	0.5	0.6	0.7	0.7	0.8	0.9	1.1
Utilities	1.6	0.7	0.8	0.8	0.9	1.1	1.3	1.3
Trade	22.6							
Wholesale	4.4	0.9	1.1	1.3	1.6	2.2	2.8	3.0
Food stores	3.5	2.7	2.7	2.7	2.7	2.8	2.8	2.9
Eating	3.6	1.9	2.9	2.0	2.1	2.5	2.8	2.9
Other retail	11.1	7.2	7.5	7.9	8.3	8.9	9.2	9.2
Services	30.8							
Fin. & ins.	4.5	1.5	1.6	1.7	1.9	2.3	2.6	3.0
Business services	1.1	0.2	0.3	0.3	0.4	0.6	0.7	0.7
Repair services	1.6	1.0	1.0	1.0	1.0	1.1	1.2	1.2
Private households	3.3	0.8	0.9	0.9	1.0	1.3	1.4	1.4
Hotels	1.1	0.2	0.2	0.2	0.3	0.4	0.5	0.5
Other pers. svcs.	3.0	1.7	1.9	2.0	2.0	2.0	2.0	2.0
Entertain. & rec.	1.2	0.5	0.5	0.6	0.8	0.8	0.8	0.8

Table   2.3   (continued)

Employment sector	National percentage	Northeast population (in thousands)						
Services (continued)								
Medical svcs.	3.6	1.6	1.7	1.9	2.1	2.5	2.7	2.7
Education	3.9	2.2	2.2	2.3	2.4	2.6	2.6	2.6
Other prof. svcs.	2.2	1.0	1.1	1.2	1.3	1.5	1.6	1.6
Public admin.	5.3	1.7	1.9	2.0	2.2	2.4	2.6	3.0
Total	100.0	31.5	34.1	36.8	40.7	48.6	55.6	58.7

Employment sector	National percentage	South and West population (in thousands)						
		(10)	(25)	(50)	(100)	(250)	(500)	(1,000)
Mining	0.9	0.0	0.0	0.0	0.0	0.0	0.0	0.0
Construction	6.2	4.2	4.4	4.6	5.0	5.7	6.1	6.4
Durable mfg.	15.9							
Furniture	1.3	0.1	0.1	0.1	0.2	0.4	0.5	0.5
Primary metals	2.6	0.0	0.0	0.0	0.0	0.1	0.2	0.3
Fabricated metals	1.8	0.0	0.0	0.1	0.2	0.3	0.4	0.7
Machinery	2.9	0.1	0.1	0.1	0.1	0.2	0.4	0.8
Elec. mach.	1.8	0.0	0.0	0.0	0.0	0.0	0.1	0.2
Motor vehicles	2.0	0.0	0.0	0.0	0.0	0.0	0.1	0.1
Transport. eq.	1.1	0.0	0.0	0.0	0.0	0.0	0.0	0.1
Other durable	2.4	0.1	0.1	0.2	0.3	0.6	0.8	0.8
Nondurable mfg.	14.2							
Food mfg.	3.0	0.7	0.8	0.8	1.0	1.3	2.0	2.7
Textile mfg.	2.2	0.0	0.0	0.0	0.0	0.0	0.0	0.1
Apparel	2.4	0.0	0.0	0.0	0.0	0.2	0.5	0.6
Printing	2.1	0.6	0.7	0.7	0.9	1.1	1.3	1.3
Chemicals	1.3	0.0	0.1	0.1	0.1	0.2	0.4	0.6
Other nondur.	3.2	0.0	0.0	0.1	0.1	0.2	0.5	0.8
Mfg. not specified	—	0.0	0.0	0.0	0.0	0.1	0.1	0.1
Transport & Util.	9.2							
Railroads	2.9	0.3	0.4	0.5	0.7	1.1	1.2	1.5
Trucking	1.3	0.5	0.5	0.6	0.7	0.9	1.0	1.2
Other trans.	2.0	0.5	0.6	0.7	0.8	1.0	1.4	2.1
Telecom.	1.4	0.8	0.8	0.8	0.9	1.0	1.1	1.4
Utilities	1.6	0.8	0.9	0.9	1.0	1.1	1.2	1.4
Trade	22.6							
Wholesale	4.4	1.4	1.6	2.1	2.7	3.8	4.7	5.1
Food stores	3.5	2.7	2.7	2.7	2.7	2.7	2.8	2.8

Table   2.3 (continued)

Employment sector	National percentage	South and West population (in thousands)						
Trade (continued)								
Eating	3.6	2.1	2.2	2.3	2.4	2.7	2.9	3.0
Other retail	11.1	9.0	9.2	9.4	9.9	10.6	10.8	10.8
Services	30.8							
Fin. & ins.	4.5	1.7	1.9	2.1	2.4	3.2	4.1	4.7
Business svcs.	1.1	0.2	0.3	0.3	0.4	0.6	0.7	1.0
Repair svcs.	1.6	1.1	1.2	1.2	1.3	1.5	1.5	1.6
Private hh.	3.3	0.8	0.9	1.1	1.2	1.9	1.9	1.9
Hotels	1.1	0.3	0.4	0.4	0.5	0.8	1.0	1.0
Other pers. svcs.	3.0	2.2	2.2	2.3	2.4	2.5	2.5	2.5
Entertain. & rec.	1.2	0.8	0.8	0.8	0.9	0.9	0.9	1.0
Medical svcs.	3.6	1.5	1.8	2.0	2.2	2.6	2.8	2.8
Education	3.9	2.9	2.9	2.9	2.9	2.8	2.8	2.7
Other prof. svcs.	2.2	1.2	1.2	1.3	1.4	1.6	1.9	1.9
Public admin.	5.3	2.3	2.4	2.5	2.6	3.0	3.2	3.7
Total	100.0	38.9	41.2	43.7	47.9	56.8	64.3	71.0

Source: Morrisset 1958, pp. 50–51.

and management; libraries and museums; water, sewage, and solid-waste-disposal systems; road construction and maintenance; and industrial and recreational park areas. Other joint-service industries, quasi-public in nature but regulated by government agencies, provide communication, transportation, and power utility services for which a user fee is charged. Merit-service industries are those associated with providing health, education, and welfare services to inhabitants of the community who may qualify for them from time to time. Merit industries are financed partially by local taxes and partially by state or national government agencies, which regulate their activities. The physical manifestation of the public and quasi-public nonbasic industries comprises the infrastructure of the community, and this infrastructure, together with the public services offered, creates the level of external urbanization economies provided by the community.[6] As these urbanization economies improve, both the export and the ancillary industries may find it profitable to expand production further, or new basic industries requiring the newly created services may be attracted to the community. In some cases, individual industries may become interested in locating in the community if the community is willing to provide special joint or merit services at little or no cost. Although such costs must be borne by the community's inhabitants in the form of higher taxes or user fees, the net consequence of the growth of the public nonbasic industry sector is the continued growth of the local labor force and population.

The *post-equilibrium or stagnation phase* represents the period in which the community's growth tends to stabilize. Numerous causes can bring the situation about, all of which may result in basic industry plant shutdowns or new plant expansions to take place elsewhere. Sometimes new technologies may render a basic industry's plant, product, or production method obsolete. Or shifts in the location of markets, equipment, parts, raw materials, or energy resources can impose upon a basic industry higher transportation or communication costs than if it were located elsewhere. In still other cases reduced labor force productivity can occur in a basic industry because of the unavailability of required skill levels, the unwillingness of workers to meet normal output quotas, excessive wage and fringe benefit demands, and employee pilfering—any of which can create higher unit production costs. Finally, external localization and urbanization diseconomies may occur in the community. Diseconomies such as traffic congestion; poor transportation, communication, water, sewage, or solid-waste-disposal service; inadequate police and fire protection; or unreliable fuel and energy resource availability can raise unit production costs and place a basic industry's product in poor competition with similar products on the market. Whatever the causes of stagnation, the events that have taken place during the previous phases are apt to produce significant changes in the characteristics and well-being of the community's inhabitants. Depending upon the rate and magnitude of growth, the building stock will be more youthful, the median age of the population younger, the fertility ratio higher, and the dependency ratio lower at the outset of this final period. In addition, the overall educational attainment, the proportion of white-collar workers, family income levels, female labor force participation, and the value and condition of the inhabitants' housing are all affected by the types of basic industries that choose to locate in the community. These industries frequently have a beneficial impact on the social, economic, and environmental quality of the community, but sometimes they may be detrimental to the community's well-being. And, as the period progresses, the community once again tends to experience the conditions that characterized it during the initial equilibrium phase.

Planning Community Economic Development

Because the spending habits of people in an economy are relatively predictable, the number of nonbasic jobs created by the addition of each basic job can be estimated. While this number actually depends upon the complexity of the local economy, it is somewhat related to the size of the local labor force and the wealth of the community's inhabitants (table 2.4). Knowledge of the average nonbasic employment multipliers for communities of different sizes allows an estimate of the new nonbasic jobs resulting from a specific number of new basic jobs to be calculated. For example, in a county of 10,000 to 19,999 inhabitants, 100 new basic jobs would, in time, create 100 new nonbasic jobs, for a total of 200 new jobs.[7] Once the total employment has been estimated, the expected new total population can be forecast. In the United States nearly 40 percent of the total population is in the labor force, so the 200 new jobs would generate a population increase of 500 persons or approximately 166 additional households (since the average household size is nearly 3 persons). This information can be used in land use planning and for projecting increases in the public services. Taking into account the number of available housing vacancies in and near the community, additional new dwelling units (single- and multiple-family houses and apartment buildings) would have to be constructed. Additional commercial floor space would also be required. Approximately 7 classrooms and teachers would be necessary to accommodate the estimated 166 new children of school age at an average of 25 students per classroom (each household includes about 1 school-age child). From the estimate of the number of new workers, people, and dwelling units, additional forecasts for public services and their costs can be made, along with projections of the new tax revenues that can be expected. Calculations can then be made to examine whether the projected revenues are able to pay the projected service costs.

Another method of replicating the community population and economic growth process, which is useful for both planning and evaluating economic development strategies, is input-output analysis (Isard 1951;

Table 2.4. Average Nonbasic Employment Multipliers by County Employment Size-Class

County employment size-class	Average employment multiplier	Employment multiplier range (s.d.)
1,000– 2,999	1.7	1.5–1.9
3,000– 4,999	1.8	1.5–2.0
5,000– 9,999	1.9	1.6–2.1
10,000–19,999	2.0	1.8–2.2
20,000–49,999	2.2	2.0–2.4
50,000 and over	2.2	2.0–2.5

Source: Gadsby 1968.

Leontief 1965), a technique that recognizes that a change in the level of output in one sector of the community's economy will trigger output changes in all other sectors because of the interdependence of all activities. Thus, it provides a method for analyzing economic problems, as well as for projecting the impact of a decrease or increase in economic activity associated with any one or more sectors.

Input-Output, Dollar-Flow Relationships

In order to understand how input-output analysis can be applied to community development planning, the annual dollar-flow relationships between the economic sectors of the state of North Carolina can be used (table 2.5). The numerous sectors have been aggregated into twelve—eleven located within the state and one representing all purchasing and producing sectors located outside the state.[8] The dollar flows represent the value of products or services each industry sold as output to every other industry, government unit, or household within the state or exported outside the state. Similarly, the dollar flows represent the value of products or services purchased as inputs from every sector within the state or imported from outside the state. The sources of inputs and destinations of output are shown in table 2.5.

The first column in table 2.5 (agriculture) shows that the agriculture industry in the state purchased for use as inputs $246 million of products from its own sector within the state and imported $53 million of products from the agriculture sector located outside the state. The state's agriculture industry also purchased $11 million worth of products from the state's mining-construction-stone industries, imported $10 million worth of products from similar industries outside the state, purchased $108 million in products from the state's food and tobacco industries, and imported $26 million worth of products from food and tobacco industries located outside the state. Additional purchases from other industry sectors located both within and outside the state, including payments for labor, rent, profits, and accumulated capital amounted to $1,053 million, paid to the state's value-added sector. The agriculture industry during the year purchased a total of $1,941 million worth of inputs and employed 196,300 workers. Each column in table 2.5 gives the total set of inputs purchased by each sector from both within and outside the state, the number of jobs, and the value of wages, salaries, and other payments that corresponds to the jobs provided.

The dollar flows also account for the fact that what one industry purchases as inputs from a second industry also represents the sales that the second industry makes to the first. The first row in table 2.5 shows that the agriculture sector within the state sold $246 million worth of products to itself. The agriculture sector outside the state sold an additional $53 million to the in-state agriculture industries. The state's agriculture sector made no sales to the mining-construction-stone sector, but the out-of-state agriculture sector sold $2 million worth of products to the state's mining-construction-stone industries. The next set of figures in the row represents $492 million in sales of state agriculture products to local food and tobacco industries and $288 million sold by the out-of-state agriculture sector to the state's food and tobacco industries. The agriculture sector also sold products to other sectors within the state, including $66 million to the final-demand sector, which includes primarily household consumption, but also sales to local and state governments. The out-of-state agriculture sector sold an additional $68 million of products to the state's final-demand sector. However, $15 million of agriculture sales to consumers cannot be allocated to any particular sector because all of the sales or purchases cannot be accounted for. The agriculture sector did export $1,019 million of products outside the state for sale to other industries ($884 million) and final demand ($135 million). The state agriculture sector had total output sales of $1,941 million, which is exactly the same as the total value of all inputs. The dollar-flow table provides for each sector a comprehensive view of the distribution of its output among its purchasers and of the inputs purchased by each sector from its suppliers.

It is of interest to note that the total value of the state's output (including value added) during the year from all sectors was $59,644 million. Of this amount, $17,340 million represents imports, giving the state a gross domestic product of $42,304 million. However, the state exported only $13,381 million in products and services, creating a trade deficit of $3,959 million. With $13,381 million attributed to the state's basic export industry sector, $28,923 million of the gross domestic product can be attributed to its nonbasic industry sector, or approximately 2 out of every 3 dollars.

Input-Output Constant Production Coefficients

For examining industrial development and the analysis of problems dealing with local economies, another type of input-output table, showing constant production coefficients, is preferred (table 2.6). The table shows the cents worth of inputs purchased from each producing sector per dollar of output sold by a particular purchasing sector. The greater the cents worth of input, the greater is the importance of the producing sector as a source of supply, whether it be materials, components, equipment, labor, or some other required input.

For example, the total annual output of North Carolina's agriculture sector was $1,941 million. In order to produce this output it was necessary for the sector to purchase $246 million of local inputs from itself. Hence 12.7 percent of the total value of the output was spent to purchase agricultural inputs such as seeds ($246/$1,941 = .127). In terms of cents worth of input per dollar of output this represents 12.7 cents ($0.127). Table 2.6 shows further that agriculture purchased inputs worth $11 million from the mining-construction-stone industries within the state, or 0.6 percent of the total value of the agriculture output (6 mills, $0.006). Similar calculations reveal that for every dollar value of output the agriculture sector imported 17.8 cents ($0.178) worth of inputs from outside the state and paid 54.3 cents ($0.543) in wages, salaries, rent, and other costs associated with the value-added sector.

The cents worth of input per dollar of output expended outside the state reveals the high reliance of some sectors on imported products and services. The final-demand sector, for example, purchased over half the value of its inputs ($0.540) from outside the state. Approximately one-third of the value of all inputs used by the mining-construction-stone sector ($0.336), the textiles-apparel sector ($0.359), the paper-chemicals-leather sector ($0.338), and the metals-machinery-equipment sector ($0.363) were imported. The agriculture ($0.178), wholesale-retail trade ($0.154), and services ($0.168) sectors were the least dependent on imported inputs. Obviously, the former sectors are less closely linked to their suppliers than the latter ones. This observation suggests some development strategies.

Determining Projections

The dollar-flow relationships and constant production coefficients can be used to project the consequences of changes in the levels of production and consumption. The projections may be in the form of sector changes in value added; value of imports or exports; employment; population; industrial, commercial, residential, or public land use; tax revenues; or government expenditures for services.

Assume that the constant production coefficients remain stable for some period of time and that there is an increased export demand for $1 billion of North Carolina's products, distributed proportionately across all sectors (an increase of approximately 7.5 percent). What impact will this increase have on the economy of the state? How many new basic jobs are likely to be directly generated, and how many new nonbasic jobs are likely to be indirectly generated? To meet this export demand the agriculture sector would have to purchase an additional $76 million of in-

Table   2.5. Input-Output (Dollar Flow) Relationships
(in millions of dollars)

SECTOR Producing (Output)	Purchasing (Input)					
	Agriculture	Mining -Construction -Stone	Food -Tobacco	Textiles -Apparel	Wood Products	Paper -Chemicals -Leather
Agriculture	246	*	492	82	6	*
	(53)a	(2)	(288)	(388)	(1)	(*)
Mining-Construction	11	51	3	13	4	11
-Stone	(10)	(154)	(10)	(23)	(3)	(17)
Food-Tobacco	108	*	614	1	*	3
	(26)	(*)	(327)	(2)	(*)	(6)
Textiles-Apparel	1	*	*	741	24	2
	(10)	(2)	(1)	(831)	(19)	(7)
Wood Products	1	55	*	*	164	24
	(*)b	(39)	(*)	(*)	(110)	(11)
Paper-Chemicals	37	1	45	375	46	82
-Leather	(74)	(102)	(122)	(612)	(38)	(366)
Metals-Machinery	*	71	*	3	12	0
-Equipment	(24)	(275)	(37)	(28)	(42)	(25)
Transportation						
-Communications	11	27	19	49	9	23
-Utilities	(23)	(63)	(47)	(79)	(29)	(49)
Wholesale-Retail	28	84	20	68	14	13
Trade	(25)	(72)	(35)	(113)	(24)	(26)
Services	37	67	126	92	25	47
	(100)	(74)	(88)	(82)	(35)	(41)
Imports	345	783	955	2,158	301	548
Value Added	1,053	1,128	1,367	2,400	639	827
Total Value (Inputs)	1,941	2,323	3,689	6,015	1,344	1,623
Employment	196,300	115,400	63,000	323,200	83,200	54,900
Value Added per Employee in dollars	5,364	9,775	21,698	7,426	7,680	15,064

Source: Compiled by author from North Carolina Input-Output Tables, 1972.
a Parentheses indicate imports by sector.
b Asterisks indicate less than $500,000—figures have been rounded to nearest million.

Purchasing (Input)

Metals -Machinery -Equipment	Transportation -Communications -Utilities	Wholesale -Retail Trade	Services	Final Demand	Unallocated	Exports		Total Value (Outputs)
						Industry	Final Demand	
* (*)	* (*)	3 (*)	12 (38)	66 (68)	15	884	135	1,941
3 (20)	40 (38)	4 (4)	98 (77)	1,178 (691)	41	253	613	2,323
* (*)	* (*)	* (*)	4 (9)	886 (980)	22	188	1,863	3,689
* (9)	* (*)	* (*)	1 (4)	148 (286)	31	3,580	1,487	6,015
19 (8)	* (*)	* (*)	* (*)	75 (65)	20	273	713	1,344
9 (81)	* (22)	9 (68)	13 (72)	84 (832)	49	668	205	1,623
110 (503)	* (11)	* (6)	1 (71)	83 (1,998)	60	827	871	2,038
18 (33)	81 (76)	52 (58)	102 (156)	420 (590)	39	57	56	963
22 (34)	4 (6)	24 (29)	29 (29)	1,827 (925)	56	263	421	2,873
54 (52)	37 (41)	192 (278)	254 (347)	3,821 (3,643)	13	6	19	4,790
740	194	443	803	10,070				
1,023	579	2,117	3,437					
2,038	963	2,873	4,790	18,658	346	6,999	6,383	
81,000	77,000	280,500	523,800					
12,631	7,519	7,547	6,562					

puts; the mining-construction-stone sector, $65 million; the food and
tobacco sector, $153 million; the textiles-apparel sector, $379 million;
and so on (as shown by the total value of inputs in table 2.7). Also, since
some industrial sectors provide most of their products or services to local
inhabitants only, the new export demand raises their total required inputs
somewhat less: transportation-communications-utilities by $8 million,
wholesale-retail trade by $51 million, and services by only $2 million.
Each column in the new dollar-flow table gives the dollar value of additional inputs that are required for every sector, including the import
sector.

To project the new employment that each sector requires in order to
meet its export demand, the value-added-per-employee ratio for each

Table 2.6. Interindustry Transactions—Cents Worth of Input per Dollar of
Output (Constant Production Coefficients)

SECTOR Producing (Output)	Purchasing (Input)					
	Agriculture	Mining-Construction-Stone	Food-Tobacco	Textiles-Apparel	Wood Products	Paper-Chemicals-Leather
Agriculture	$0.127	$0.000	$0.133	$0.014	$0.004	$0.000
Mining-Construction -Stone	.006	.022	.001	.002	.003	.007
Food-Tobacco	.056	.000	.166	.000	.000	.002
Textiles-Apparel	.001	.000	.000	.123	.018	.001
Wood Products	.001	.024	.000	.000	.122	.015
Paper-Chemicals -Leather	.019	.000	.012	.062	.034	.051
Metals-Machinery -Equipment	.000	.030	.000	.000	.009	.000
Transportation-Communications -Utilities	.006	.012	.005	.008	.007	.014
Wholesale- Retail Trade	.014	.036	.005	.011	.010	.008
Services	.019	.029	.034	.015	.019	.029
Imports	.178	.336	.259	.359	.224	.338
Value Added	.543	.484	.371	.399	.516	.510
Total Inputs	1.000	1.000	1.000	1.000	1.000	1.000

sector can be used. For example, the agriculture sector's annual value added from the original flow table was $1,053 million and employment was 196,300 workers, which is $5,364.24 per worker ($1,053,000,000/ 196,300 = $5,364.24). In order for the agriculture sector to produce $76 million of new export products, it must pay $41.3 million for additional value-added inputs. In terms of value added per employee, this means that the agriculture sector will require 7,694 new workers to meet its export demand ($41,268,000/$5,364.24 = 7,694). Similar calculations project the additional basic employment required by the mining-construction-stone sector to be 3,218 workers, the food and tobacco sector to be 2,616 workers, the textiles-apparel sector to be 20,364 workers, and so on, until only 219 additional workers are required by the service sector.

Purchasing (Input)

Metals -Machinery -Equipment	Transportation -Communications -Utilities	Wholesale -Retail Trade	Services	Final Demand
$0.000	$0.000	$0.001	$0.003	$0.004
.001	.042	.001	.020	.063
.000	.000	.000	.001	.047
.000	.000	.000	.000	.008
.009	.000	.000	.000	.004
.004	.000	.003	.004	.005
.054	.000	.000	.000	.004
.009	.084	.018	.021	.023
.011	.004	.008	.006	.098
.026	.038	.067	.053	.205
.363	.201	.154	.168	.540
.502	.601	.737	.718	——
1.000	1.000	1.000	1.000	1.000

The estimates project that 51,565 new basic jobs will be directly generated by the increased export demand.

But what about the new nonbasic jobs indirectly generated by the increased export demand? How many new jobs are going to be created to provide the 51,565 new basic workers and their families with products and services? First, the table of constant production coefficients (table 2.6) shows that the final demand sector required 4 mills ($0.004) of products and services as inputs from the state's agriculture sector, 6.3 cents ($0.063) from the mining-construction-stone sector, and so on to include 20.5 cents ($0.205) from the local service sector. If the 51,565 new basic export workers received most of the total value-added inputs ($460 million from table 2.7) required to produce the $1 billion of new export demand as salaries, wages, and other income, then the agriculture sector (shown in table 2.8) needs to purchase an additional $1.84 million in total inputs to meet the new final-demand requirements of these workers ($460 million $\times$ .004 = $1.84 million). The mining-construction-stone sector would have to purchase an additional $28.96 million of total inputs ($460 million $\times$ .063 = $28.96). The greatest impact is made on the wholesale-retail trade and service sectors. The wholesale-retail trade sector would have to purchase total inputs of $45.04 million ($460 million $\times$ .098 = $45.04 million) and the service sector $94.22 million of total inputs ($460 million $\times$ .205 = $94.22 million) to meet the additional final-demand requirements of the 51,565 new basic workers.

The number of new nonbasic workers needed to produce these inputs can once again be determined from the first-round value-added inputs required by each sector, shown in table 2.8. For example, the agriculture sector's value-added-per-worker ratio was $5,364.24. Its first-round value-added is approximately $1 million, which generates an additional employment requirement of 186 workers ($.999 million/$5,364.24 = 186). In all, the total first-round nonbasic employment indirectly generated by the $1 billion of export demand is 18,006 workers, most of whom are employed by the wholesale-retail trade and service sectors (4,399 and 10,310 jobs, respectively).

However, just as the 51,565 additional new basic workers had to be supplied with local goods and services, so also do these 18,006 additional new (first-round) nonbasic workers. Hence, a second round of indirect effects has to be calculated, followed by a third round, and so on until the indirect effects reach zero. The method of calculating each subsequent round of indirect effects is the same as for the first round, and generates 5,278 workers for the second round, 1,548 for the third, 458 for the fourth, 135 for the fifth, and 38 for the sixth round (table 2.9). The indirect effects of the $1 billion in increased export demand result in a total of 25,463 new nonbasic workers.[9] Counting both direct and indirect effects, over 77,028 new jobs are created.

To specify the exact length of time required to achieve all the direct and indirect effects of the increased demand would be difficult. But once the employment and value added by each sector are calculated, estimates can be made of the skill categories of the workers and their wage and salary payments. If data on the average participation of the population in the labor force are available, the expected new total population can be projected. For example, since about 40 percent of the total population is in the labor force, the 77,028 new jobs created would generate a population increase of 192,570. With information on the skill categories of the new workers by sector and other population census data, the number of new families and the age-sex distribution of the population can be estimated. From this information the number and types of new houses and schools can be projected. Similarly, information from each sector that gives the land requirements per worker (or per dollar of value added) can be used to estimate new land use requirements for manufacturing plants and business establishments, information valuable for land use planning. Given the preceding data for each sector of the economy, planners can estimate tax revenues that can be expected by different levels of government and the expenditures that will be required for various services. It can then be determined whether sufficient revenues will be available to meet the projected costs, and plans can be made to increase the revenues, scale down the services, or provide alternative programs.

Other Applications

Input-output analysis does have limitations, among which is the assumption that worker productivity, product demand, industrial mix, and interindustry, input-output relations will remain the same over time. The technique is, however, useful in other aspects of the planning process.[10] Through this type of analysis, planners can investigate, by simulation, which industries have the greatest beneficial effect on alleviating specific economic problems in a community, such as reducing unemployment, providing jobs for unskilled workers, or reducing balance-of-trade deficits. Strategies can then be developed to attract those industries that will provide the desired benefits.

For example, input-output indicators of North Carolina's industrial linkages reveal both strengths and weaknesses in its economic structure. An examination of the amount of input that each local industry sector is

Table 2.7. Basic Input-Output Requirements for $1 Billion of New Export Demand (in thousands of dollars)

SECTOR Producing (Output)	Purchasing (Input)				
	Agriculture	Mining-Construction-Stone	Food-Tobacco	Textiles-Apparel	Wood Products
Agriculture	9,625	0	20,349	5,306	296
Mining-Construction-Stone	456	1,430	153	758	222
Food-Tobacco	4,256	0	25,398	0	0
Textiles-Apparel	76	0	0	46,617	1,332
Wood Products	76	1,560	0	0	9,028
Paper-Chem.-Leather	1,444	0	1,836	23,498	2,516
Metals-Mach.-Equipment	0	1,950	0	0	666
Trans.-Comm.-Utilities	456	780	765	3,032	518
Wholesale-Retail Trade	1,064	2,340	765	4,169	740
Service	1,444	1,885	5,202	5,685	1,406
Imports	13,452	21,905	39,627	136,440	16,576
Value Added	41,268	31,460	56,763	151,221	38,184
Total Inputs	76,000	65,000	153,000	379,000	74,000
New Basic Employment	7,694	3,218	2,616	20,364	4,585

able to provide to all industry sectors in the state indicates that only 8.5 percent of the required metals, electrical and nonelectrical machinery, and equipment inputs could be obtained from local producers (table 2.10). Also, only 22.7 percent of the required paper, chemicals, and leather inputs could be obtained locally. The attraction of industries in these sectors to the state would help to improve its trade balance. Industry sectors that export a high percentage of output are the metals-machinery-equipment, textiles-apparel, and wood products sectors (table 2.10). Only 14.2 percent, 15.3 percent, and 25.7 percent, respectively, of the value of their

Purchasing (Input)

Paper -Chemicals -Leather	Metals -Machinery -Equipment	Transportation -Communications -Utilities	Wholesale -Retail Trade	Services	
0	0	0	51	6	
455	127	336	51	40	
130	0	0	0	2	
65	0	0	0	0	
975	1,143	0	0	0	
3,315	508	0	153	8	
0	6,858	0	0	0	
910	1,143	672	918	42	
520	1,397	32	408	12	
1,885	3,302	304	3,417	106	
21,905	46,288	1,608	7,854	336	
33,150	63,754	4,808	37,587	1,436	
65,000	127,000	8,000	51,000	2,000	
					Total
2,201	5,048	640	4,980	219	51,565

products are sold locally. Other industry sectors, such as transportation-communications-utilities, wholesale-retail trade, and services, are more highly localized. Nonetheless, the state still has to import about 50 percent of its service inputs.

Input-output analysis can be used to examine these problems by simulating which new industries, if they were located within the state, could make the best use of the outputs of existing industries (backward linkages) and which products new industries could provide to already existing industries (forward linkages). Simulation can also help to examine which industry sectors respond most favorably to expansion induced by public investment and also have the most beneficial impact on the community and its economy.

Community Economic Development Strategies and Public Policy Instruments

Economic development strategies range from uncoordinated efforts to stimulate the growth of new business to comprehensive programs with substantial budgets, specialized personnel, and the support of a variety of

Table   2.8. First-Round Nonbasic Input-Output Requirements for $1 Billion of New Export Demand (in thousands of dollars)

SECTOR Producing (Output)	Purchasing (Input)					
	Agriculture	Mining -Construction -Stone	Food -Tobacco	Textiles -Apparel	Wood Products	Paper -Chemicals -Leather
Agriculture	234	0	2,873	51	7	0
Mining-Construction -Stone	11	637	22	7	6	16
Food-Tobacco	103	0	3,586	0	0	5
Textiles-Apparel	2	0	0	452	33	2
Wood Products	2	695	0	0	224	34
Paper-Chemicals -Leather	35	0	259	228	63	117
Metals-Machinery -Equipment	0	869	0	0	17	0
Trans.-Comm. -Utilities	11	347	108	29	13	32
Wholesale -Retail Trade	26	1,042	108	40	18	18
Services	35	840	735	55	35	67
Imports	327	9,730	5,595	1,320	412	777
Value Added	999	14,015	8,015	1,467	949	1,172
Total Inputs	1,839	28,957	21,603	3,677	1,839	2,298
New Nonbasic Employment	186	1,434	369	198	114	78

public policy instruments designed to influence the expansion or retention of business. Whatever the degree of effort behind a certain strategy, in principle it must improve the community's ability to influence investment in particular types of economic activities. In practice it must modify the economic, social, or other criteria by which entrepreneurs judge a community during the process of locational decision making (in this case, industrial location decision making).

An economic development strategy should include six steps: (1) identification of particular development objectives; (2) identification of candidate industries to help fulfill the objectives; (3) development and im-

Purchasing (Input)

Metals -Machinery -Equipment	Transportation -Communications -Utilities	Wholesale -Retail Trade	Services	
0	0	45	283	
2	444	45	1,384	
0	0	0	94	
0	0	0	0	
17	0	0	0	
7	0	135	377	
99	0	0	0	
17	888	811	1,979	
20	42	360	565	
48	402	3,018	4,994	
668	2,125	6,937	15,830	
923	6,354	33,197	67,653	
1,839	10,572	45,044	94,224	
				Total
73	845	4,399	10,310	18,006

Table 2.9. Summary of Nonbasic Input-Output Requirements for $1 Billion of New Export Demand (in thousands of dollars)

Purchasing (Input)

SECTOR Producing (Output)		Agriculture	Mining-Construction-Stone	Food-Tobacco	Textiles-Apparel	Wood Products	Paper-Chemicals-Leather
Agriculture		330	0	4,062	73	10	0
Mining-Construction-Stone		16	901	31	10	8	23
Food-Tobacco		146	0	5,070	0	0	7
Textiles-Apparel		3	0	0	639	47	3
Wood Products		3	983	0	0	317	49
Paper-Chemicals-Leather		49	0	367	322	88	166
Metals-Machinery-Equipment		0	1,228	0	0	23	0
Trans.-Comm.-Utilities		16	491	153	42	18	46
Wholesale-Retail Trade		36	1,474	153	57	26	26
Services		49	1,187	1,039	78	49	94
Imports		463	13,757	7,911	1,866	582	1,099
Value Added		1,412	19,816	11,332	2,074	1,342	1,658
Total Inputs		2,600	40,943	30,545	5,199	2,600	3,250
Nonbasic	1	186	1,434	369	198	114	78
Employment	2	55	420	108	58	33	23
by Round	3	16	123	32	17	10	7
	4	5	36	9	5	3	2
	5	1	11	3	1	1	1
	6	0	3	1	0	0	0
Total		263	2,027	522	279	161	111

Total basic and nonbasic employment 77,028

Purchasing (Input)

Metals -Machinery -Equipment	Transportation -Communications -Utilities	Wholesale -Retail Trade	Services	
0	0	64	400	
3	628	64	2,665	
0	0	0	133	
0	0	0	0	
23	0	0	0	
10	0	191	533	
140	0	0	0	
23	1,256	1,146	2,798	
29	60	510	800	
68	568	4,267	7,063	
944	3,005	9,808	22,388	
1,305	8,984	46,938	95,680	
2,600	14,948	63,688	133,259	
				Total
73	845	4,399	10,310	18,006
21	248	1,290	3,022	5,278
6	73	378	886	1,548
2	21	111	264	458
1	6	33	77	135
0	2	10	22	38
103	1,195	6,221	14,581	25,463

Table   2.10. Indicators of North Carolina Industrial Linkage

a. Percentage of North Carolina's Total Demand Supplied by North Carolina Industries (by value)

North Carolina Producing Industry	Percentage of Demand Supplied
Agriculture	51.96
Mining-Construction-Stone	57.49
Food-Tobacco	54.49
Textiles-Apparel	43.96
Wood Products	59.92
Paper-Chemicals-Leather	22.68
Metals-Machinery-Equipment	8.50
Transportation-Communications-Utilities	40.27
Wholesale-Retail Trade	61.81
Services	49.85

b. Percentage of Total Output Sold in North Carolina by North Carolina Industries (by value)

North Carolina Producing Industry	Percentage of Output Sold
Agriculture	47.09
Mining-Construction-Stone	62.08
Food-Tobacco	44.07
Textiles-Apparel	15.33
Wood Products	25.69
Paper-Chemicals-Leather	44.52
Metals-Machinery-Equipment	14.15
Transportation-Communications-Utilities	87.77
Wholesale-Retail Trade	75.71
Services	99.48

plementation of policy instruments designed to attract those industries; (4) promotional efforts; (5) evaluation of the instruments' effects in attracting the industries and the industries' potential for fulfilling the development objectives; and (6) modification of the objectives, candidate industries list, and/or policy instruments. Only the third step, that dealing with policy instruments designed to attract industry, will be discussed here.

Development strategies usually involve the community's willingness to make some changes in the criteria which industrialists judge when making locational choices, but the criteria that are changed in any individual situation depend on the particular development objective, the particular industries needed to fulfill the objective, the costs of the change, and the legality of the change. Whatever the planned objective, whether improving overall per capita income, promoting more balanced regional economic growth, reducing unemployment, improving the community's balance of trade, or providing a higher level of public services at lower per capita cost, the criteria to be changed and the policy instruments implemented to effect the changes need to be attuned to the community development process described earlier (fig. 2.2).

The cumulative causation effects built into the process suggest there are three main groups of policy instruments that can be implemented to influence the location of industry. These are policies that influence changes or improvements in the community's urbanization economies, pool of trained labor, and ability to reduce the amount of working or fixed capital needed for industrial operations.

In most cases the criteria to be changed involve public policies that improve the community's urbanization economies and its associated infrastructure, including changes such as investment in new roads, airstrips, and other means of transportation, in technical schools, public utilities, recreation areas, better police and fire protection, and in various other services. As a whole, such improvements can increase the attractiveness of the community for many types of industry, but particular industries may be interested in specific improvements only—a new road, water, or sewage service extension or treatment plant expansion, for example.

Policies designed to enhance the quantity and quality of the community's labor pool involve technical training programs—either those that train individuals as part of their formal education within the community or those that retrain workers, both on and off the job, to perform new tasks. Other policies can provide funds to pay the moving costs of migrants who have needed skills or to pay to send workers elsewhere to obtain new training before returning to work in the community. Another method of attracting migrants possessing needed skills is to provide public housing to them at low cost, thereby, in effect, providing a labor subsidy to industry.

Communities may adopt policies that reduce the amount of working or fixed capital required by industries to conduct their operations. The community can provide financial subsidies, low-interest loans, or high-risk loans for land, buildings, machinery, or pollution abatement equipment. Also, special tax arrangements, favorable depreciation allowances, and the provision of water and sewage service at reduced rates all directly affect the amount of needed capital. In addition the community can directly invest its own capital in factories, plant sites, or industrial parks at desired locations in order to fulfill some development objectives. The factories and sites can then be sold or leased to industry at reduced rates.

Most communities engaged in industrial promotion efforts use different types of policy instruments to promote economic development. The communities are bolstered by the belief that the instruments are unlikely to do any harm and may even be beneficial. However, it is doubtful that many of the individuals responsible for the enactment of policy instruments possess adequate knowledge of the community population and economic development process, of methods by which community economic development is planned, or of the need to make development strategies more industry-specific in order to fulfill the community's development objectives.

Notes

1. Many of the statements expressed in the first section have their foundation in propositions suggested by such researchers as Douglas C. North, "Location Theory and Regional Economic Growth"; Niles M. Hansen, ed., *Growth Centers in Regional Economic Development*; Eric E. Lampard, "The Evolving System of Cities in the United States"; J. R. Borchert, "American Metropolitan Evolution"; Allan R. Pred, *The Spatial Dynamics of U.S. Urban Industrial Growth, 1800–1914*; W. W. Rostow, *The Stages of Economic Growth*; A. O. Hirschman, *The Strategy of Economic Development*; and Gunnar M. Myrdal, *Economic Theory and Under-Developed Regions*.

2. If the export industry continues to grow either by its own expansion or by the location of similar types of firms in the area, the community is established as a growth point.

3. A common economic development tactic for an area is to attract industries that manufacture products required by already existing industries. The effect of the development of these early-stage-of-production industries is to reduce capital outflows from the area.

4. This pattern of outside financing occurs because capital in the community is apt to be in short supply, especially if the population growth rate is substantial. Substantial growth in a short period of time creates excessive demands for home mortgage and business loans.

5. As the community grows, employment in the nonbasic sector accounts for a greater and greater proportion of the total employment, since that sector is able to provide increasingly higher-ordered functions that the inhabitants need not travel elsewhere to obtain and to which people from outside the community will be attracted.

6. The larger the community becomes, the greater is the demand for merit services and the less is the relative amount expended on joint services. Hence, sufficient expenditures are not allocated to replace various portions of the infrastructure that have outlived their usefulness or to maintain needed levels of services. Instead, much is expended on maintaining minimal standards. This situation results in such external urbanization diseconomies as traffic congestion, air and

water pollution, high crime and fire incidence rates, and blighted buildings and structures. The diseconomies have the effect of slowing or even reversing employment and population growth trends.

7. *Community* multipliers can be lower than *county* multipliers because part of the worker's income will be spent in the county outside the community.

8. The data were aggregated from the North Carolina fifty-eight-sector interregional input-output model obtained from the Center for Development and Resource Planning, Research Triangle Institute, Research Triangle Park, North Carolina.

9. The indirect employment resulting from the growth of export-base employment is less than the average one nonbasic job for one basic job found in some studies. Part of this difference results from continually rounding numerical values to simplify calculations. Another reason for the difference is that North Carolina is an economy with a large segment of its employment in low-wage agriculture and labor-intensive industry, a considerable proportion of its population residing in small communities and rural areas, and per capita incomes 20 percent below the national average.

10. Input-output analysis can also be used to project additional energy requirements or environmental pollution associated with the growth of different sectors of the economy. As a supply-constrained model it can be used to examine such problems as the effect of reduced energy supplies (Cumberland and Korbach 1973).

Chapter 3
Land Use Planning for
Industry

The purpose of this chapter is to provide those in the industrial and economic development profession with a glimpse of the community planner's
perspective on planning for industrial development. With such knowledge, industrial and economic developers will be better prepared to assist
planners in the creation of appropriate industrial development planning
policies and guidelines. The views presented are intended to represent
those of the land use planning professional who is working in the public
realm, at the local level of government or possibly at the metropolitan
level.[1] In this discussion the term *industrial development* refers to manufacturing and wholesaling activity but not to the extraction of raw materials or the retail distribution of goods and services.[2]

**The Land Use Planner's Conceptual Model
of Industrial Development**

The community land use planner conceives the industrial development
planning problem as consisting of three related parts: the community
development guidance system (by which the planner hopes the community may influence the course of industrial development toward community welfare objectives), the industrial development system per se,
and the evaluation system that assesses the impact of industrial development on community welfare (fig. 3.1).

The Industrial Development System

It is the middle part of this conceptual model with which industrial
development organizations are most concerned and to which they devote

Figure 3.1 The Planner's Conceptual Model of Industrial Development (Simplified)

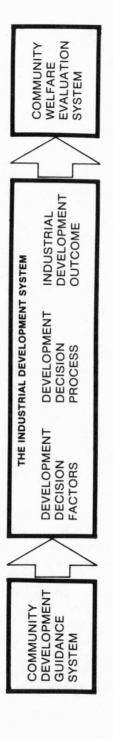

COMMUNITY
DEVELOPMENT
GUIDANCE
SYSTEM

THE INDUSTRIAL DEVELOPMENT SYSTEM

DEVELOPMENT
DECISION
FACTORS

DEVELOPMENT
DECISION
PROCESS

INDUSTRIAL
DEVELOPMENT
OUTCOME

COMMUNITY
WELFARE
EVALUATION
SYSTEM

the most time and effort—the industrial development system. This system itself consists of three parts: factors that influence the industrial development decision process, the actual decision process, and outcomes of the decision process.

Three types of decision factors are of interest to the land use planner: contextual factors, property characteristics, and decision-agent characteristics. Each influences the decision processes in a unique manner, and each is related to the guidance system in a unique manner (fig. 3.2).

Contextual factors include considerations that limit and determine the overall rate and type of change in the community, thus determining the community's relative attraction to industrial development compared to other communities, the relative impact of property characteristics (such as zoning) on development decisions, and the impact such development will have on the community's goals and solution of its problems. Tax rates, water and sewer capacities, power supply, availability of raw materials, economic structure, overall characteristics of the industrial land supply, labor market, access to regional markets, labor union attitudes, quality of schools, and general community livability are examples of contextual factors.

Property characteristics may be physical, locational, or institutional. Since physical characteristics, such as topography and soil conditions, cannot be changed except by direct modification of the site itself, such as by grading, they must generally be accepted as constraints that cannot be influenced much by the community. Locational characteristics, on the other hand, are not inherent in the land but are derived solely from the relative location of the site with respect to the geographical pattern of prospective employees and markets, transportation networks, and surrounding properties. Neighborhood quality and accessibility to the regional transportation system are examples of locational characteristics. Changes in locational characteristics thus depend on what occurs off-site, since the site itself is fixed. Locational characteristics therefore might be considered more susceptible to influence by a community's guidance system than physical characteristics. The third category represents attributes that apply directly to the site, but that are not inherent in the site. Imposed by institutions, including government, these characteristics include, for example, the site's zoning, minimum parcel size, cost, and its inclusion or exclusion from various service districts such as those for water, sewer, fire protection, police protection, trash collection, and taxation. Institutional characteristics are of course subject to change in relation to policies established by the local government's guidance system.

Decision-agent characteristics, including those of the predevelopment landowner, the development agency, industry type, and type of firm, are

Figure 3.2 The Urban Land Use Planner's Conceptual Model of Industrial Development

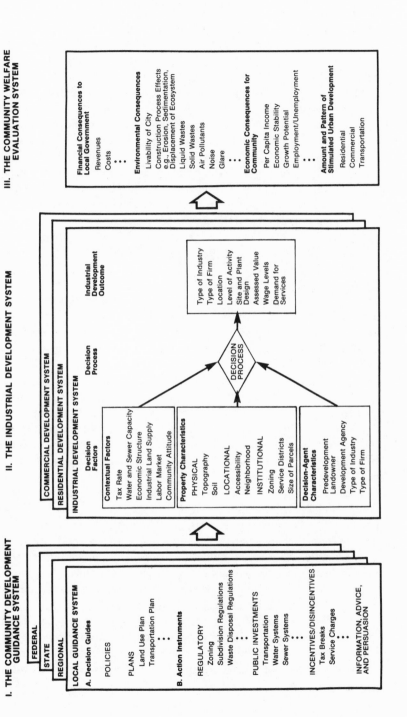

I. THE COMMUNITY DEVELOPMENT GUIDANCE SYSTEM

II. THE INDUSTRIAL DEVELOPMENT SYSTEM

III. THE COMMUNITY WELFARE EVALUATION SYSTEM

FEDERAL
STATE
REGIONAL

LOCAL GUIDANCE SYSTEM

A. Decision Guides

POLICIES

PLANS
Land Use Plan
Transportation Plan
...

B. Action Instruments

REGULATORY
Zoning
Subdivision Regulations
Waste Disposal Regulations
...

PUBLIC INVESTMENTS
Transportation
Water Systems
Sewer Systems
...

INCENTIVES/DISINCENTIVES
Tax Breaks
Service Charges
...

INFORMATION, ADVICE,
AND PERSUASION

COMMERCIAL DEVELOPMENT SYSTEM
RESIDENTIAL DEVELOPMENT SYSTEM
INDUSTRIAL DEVELOPMENT SYSTEM

Decision
Factors

Contextual Factors
Tax Rate
Water and Sewer Capacity
Economic Structure
Industrial Land Supply
Labor Market
Community Attitude

Property Characteristics
PHYSICAL
Topography
Soil
LOCATIONAL
Accessibility
Neighborhood
INSTITUTIONAL
Zoning
Service Districts
Size of Parcels

Decision-Agent
Characteristics
Predevelopment
Landowner
Development Agency
Type of Industry
Type of Firm

Decision
Process

DECISION
PROCESS

Industrial
Development
Outcome

Type of Industry
Type of Firm
Location
Level of Activity
Site and Plant
Design
Assessed Value
Wage Levels
Demand for
Services

Financial Consequences to
Local Government
Revenues
Costs
...

Environmental Consequences
Livability of City
Construction Process Effects
e.g., Erosion, Sedimentation,
Displacement of Ecosystem
Liquid Wastes
Solid Wastes
Air Pollutants
Noise
Glare
...

Economic Consequences for
Community
Per Capita Income
Economic Stability
Growth Potential
Employment/Unemployment
...

Amount and Pattern of
Stimulated Urban Development
Residential
Commercial
Transportation

the third important set of factors influencing the location of industries. Decision-agent characteristics are not usually influenced directly by public policy in the same way as contextual factors and locational or institutional property characteristics, unless perhaps the municipality itself forms an industrial development agency and becomes a direct participant in the industrial development process.

Outcomes of the industrial development decision process that are of interest to the land use planner are items such as the type of industry (whether it is heavy or light or whether it has a history of labor problems); its level of activity (the number of employees, its output capacity); its location, site and plant design, wage levels, assessed value of plant and equipment; and its demand for public services, including solid- and liquid-waste collection and treatment, fire protection, power, and water.

The Guidance and Evaluation Systems

While the industrial developer focuses directly on the development system by playing an activist role in trying to influence the participants involved in the decision process, the urban land use planner extends the model to include the guidance system and the evaluation system and then usually concentrates on these two extensions rather than becoming actively and intimately involved in specific industrial development decisions. His interest in the guidance system derives from the purpose of planning, which is to guide development so that the interests of the general public are served. The planner's concern for extending the model in the other direction, to include the evaluation system, is based on his need to project the impact of a potential industrial firm on the welfare of the community. In this role the planner has more contact with individual industrial prospects.

The community's urbanization guidance system includes decision guides and action instruments. The decision guides are the plans and policies of public decision makers, such as the county commissioners or the city council. The land use plan, which will be discussed in detail later, is an example of a decision guide. Decision guides intervene *indirectly* in the industrial development process through their influence on the action instruments created by local government decision makers and more subtly through their persuasive power on private decision makers.

The action instruments, on the other hand, intervene *directly* in the industrial development process. Action instruments include regulations (zoning regulations, building codes, health and sanitation codes, or pollution emission standards), public investments (highways, water and sewer systems, or land acquisitions for industrial parks), incentive/disincentive programs (tax practices and allowances and charges for water and sewer), and finally the planner's provision of information and advice, as well as the persuasion he may exercise in his role as a participant in the development decision process when the opportunity arises. It is through this guidance system that the land use planning process can influence industrial development to achieve community welfare.

To the urban land use planner, industrial development is not an end in itself. In addition to influencing the industrial development system through the guidance system, the planner is interested in evaluating the effects of new industry on community welfare. The evaluation of new industrial development is included in the model, so that the planner can review the new industry with regard to the local government's fiscal picture (that is, its implications for revenues and costs to local government), its impact on the local economy (on the community's economic stability, per capita income, growth potential, spin-off economic growth and unemployment), and the further stimulus to urbanization provided by increasing the number of jobs in the community (such as residential development, commercial development, and new highways).

The remainder of this chapter will examine more closely three of the model's components: the land use plan as an example of a decision guide, the various action instruments available to the guidance system, and cost/revenue analysis as an example of evaluating impact.

Designing the Long-Range Land Use Plan as a Policy Instrument

Stuart Parry Walsh, president of Development Planning Associates, has stated that a frequent initial mistake in industrial land development is the failure to obtain specific information about the future development of surrounding land. "The adjoining farms may be about to produce heavy crops of subdivisions whose residents will probably protest the nearby presence of an industrial tract. . . . Or the city may have one of the adjacent farms in view for a new sewage treatment plant. Or a new airport may be planned for a location that will be considerably more distant from the property than the present one" (Walsh 1963, p. 1). Attention to a long-range comprehensive land use plan and the planning process behind it by the community's legislative body, industrial development organizations, and prospective industrial firms can protect both public and private decision makers from this mistake.

The land use plan is essentially a design for the future physical form of the city. The plan usually features a large-scale, maplike drawing of the long-range physical design of the whole community, calibrated to a fixed point in the future (usually some twenty to twenty-five years) or to a fixed population level. This physical design is expressed in general rather than detailed terms and covers the geographical distribution and densities of land use activities, including industrial uses, public and private facilities, roads and utilities, and sometimes a civic design proposal. The land use plan is perhaps the most traditional and may still be the most common context from which an urban planner views his role in industrial development. The process of land use plan making includes three phases: "tooling-up" studies, estimating future location and space requirements, and formulating the land use design plan.

Tooling-up Studies

In preparing for land use plan making, the planner usually conducts a series of studies under the general heading of "tooling up" for land use planning. Studies of the urban economy, analyses and projections of employment and population, surveys of resident attitudes and behavior, studies of the natural physical setting and natural processes in the urban region, studies of the existing man-made urban physical plant (houses and utilities, for example), and vacant-land studies all provide the planner with useful data.

The structure and vitality of the urban economy are key considerations in gauging the amount and the rate of land development that is likely to occur in the city. Accordingly, considerable attention is given to methods of studying the makeup and general health of the urban economy. Employment and population prospects, projected as extensions of these foundation studies, supply the tools needed for estimating the amounts and rates of future land development.

These basic studies demonstrate the planner's recognition that the growth destiny of an urban area is determined largely by its productive activity. Production and distribution activities in the city or metropolitan area create jobs, and employment opportunities attract people. The land use planner assumes that the urban economy, especially the economic base industries, conditions the amount of future land development that needs to be accommodated. For industrial development, estimates of future land requirements for industrial uses are based on manufacturing employment prospects in various sectors. Studies of basic employment are also a key element in population forecasts, which are then used in scaling land requirements for the urban residential and service employment activities required by those residents.

In addition to estimating the demand for land space, the tooling-up studies are also concerned with the supply of land and facilities available for new development—for example, a study of the existing land use pattern and a survey of the condition of present public and private property improvements and their capacities (industrial plant capacity, water and sewer capacity, and available vacant land). The data collected from these studies describe the characteristics of the land supply and general environment for urban development, including industrial development.

During the tooling-up stage, planners may, as part of the vacant-land study and with the help of local, regional, and state industrial development professionals, assemble a list of sites that are available for industrial use. In developing the land use plan, available sites can be ranked according to the community's recommended priority, a ranking that should be based on the availability of utilities, the cost of their extension where necessary, transportation, and the size of the site. While some industry may locate on sites not on the priority lists, it is important that planning and development agencies cooperate in this phase of the process.

Estimation of Future Requirements for Base Economic Activity

After the economic analysis and other tooling-up studies, the second step in the traditional approach to land use plan making is the establishment of locational principles and standards and of space-using requirements.

The establishment of locational requirements begins with statements of general principles on the location of employment. Chapin (1965, pp. 372–73) suggests the following criteria for manufacturing areas:

1. reasonably level land, preferably with not more than 5 percent slope, capable of being graded without undue expense;
2. range of choice in close-in, fringe, and dispersed locations—
    a. extensive manufacturing: large, open sites for modern one-story buildings and accessory storage, loading and parking areas in fringe and dispersed locations, usually 5 acres as a minimum, with some sites 10, 25, 50, or 100 or more acres, depending on the size of urban areas and the economic outlook for industrial development of extensive lines of activity
    b. intensive manufacturing: variety of site sizes for modern one-story or multiple-story buildings and accessory storage, loading, and parking areas in close-in and fringe locations, usually under 5 acres;
3. direct access to commercial transportation facilities; in fringe and dispersed locations, access to railroad, major trucking routes, cargo air-

ports, and, in some urban areas, deep water channels; and in close-in locations, for a major proportion of sites, access to both railroad and trucking routes, with the balance adjoining trucking thoroughfares or, if appropriate, port areas;

4. accessibility to transit and major thoroughfare routes directly connected with housing areas;

5. availability of utilities at or near the site such as power, water, and waste-disposal facilities;

6. compatibility with surrounding uses, considering prevailing winds, possibilities of protective belts of open space, development of industrial parks, and other factors of amenity both within the manufacturing area and in relation to adjoining land uses.

These locational principles are then often refined into a set of *location standards*, which provide more specific criteria. For example, "easy commuting time" may be converted to a convenience standard of "twenty to thirty minutes maximum commuting time." Sometimes the locational principle can be converted to a performance standard, particularly for industrial uses. Deriving from health, safety, and amenity aspects of the public interest and neighborhood private property interests (as opposed to convenience aspects above), performance standards might provide criteria for evaluating the hazards or nuisance of smoke, dust, noise, glare, odor, waste, or traffic often created by industrial uses of land.

The locational principles and standards, together with the major assumptions and results of the tooling-up studies may be used to outline tentative locations of industry (and other uses) in schematic form. That is, the locational principles are applied to the specific urban site in map form to suggest a desirable land use pattern without regard to the amount of space needed.

Another question here is, How much space should be reserved for industrial uses? residential uses? commercial uses? public facilities? At this point the task is to scale the land area required to accommodate industrial growth as well as the concomitant residential and commercial growth over the next twenty to thirty years. The process of estimating space requirements for industrial land uses can be broken down into three steps:

1. Analyze the characteristics of existing manufacturing and wholesale uses in the planning area with particular attention to densities, conditions of plants, excess site capacities, and trends in space usage.

2. Develop local standards for future densities in number of employees per acre for each category of manufacturing and wholesale activity based on anticipated growth in each category, expected and desired changes in

intensity of use due to modern industrial technology, goals and objectives, and location in the metropolitan pattern (inner-city versus suburban location).

3. Apply the density standards to employment projections for each category of manufacturing and wholesale employment to obtain an estimate of future land requirements in acres by category of industrial activity, and by general location in the urban area. (For a more detailed explanation of these steps see Chapin 1965, pp. 386–400.)

The Land Use Design

The final step in the process of land use plan making is the creative integration of the information generated in the previous steps. This procedure includes determining how the supply of vacant and renewal land, as described by the tooling-up studies, matches the locational and space requirements. Trial distributions of projected industrial land demands are made by referring to the locational principles and standards, the schematic land use design, and the estimated space needs. The result of this process is a land use plan, which includes industrial uses as an integral part of a proposed design for the future urban activity pattern of the community.

In addition to the general land use plan, special, more thorough industrial development land use plans are sometimes undertaken. In general approach, none differ greatly from the rationale described above. All, however, devote more specific attention to particular local problems, to recommendations for their solution, and to the implementation of solutions.

Perhaps one of the more commonly used examples of such an industrial land development plan is Dorothy Muncy's plan for the Baltimore region. The purposes of this industrial land study were

(a) to determine the land area requirements of industries which have long been basic to the Region's economy, and of new industries growing from an expanding technology, which could advantageously locate in the Baltimore Region; (b) to recognize the diversity of location requirements of industries that are now or will be in the Baltimore Region, particularly noting new trends in industrial management's location criteria; and (c) to identify future locations for industry in the Baltimore Region that would be best served by the highways, deep water channels, and utility extensions to be built within the next twenty years. . . . The Baltimore Regional Planning

Council decided to look at the total land of its Region and to identi-fy general areas (but not specific sites) which could provide the most attractive and efficient sites for the factories, laboratories, warehouses, and terminals to be built in the next twenty to twenty-five years. [Muncy 1959, p. 8]

The report contains four elements: an analysis of industrial employment and a projection for 1980, an inventory of industrial land use and in-dustrial zoning, an estimate of industrial land requirements for 1980, and a map recommending for local consideration major areas with poten-tial for industrial development. The similarity between this special report on industrial land and the general approach in the comprehensive land use plan outlined above is obvious.

Strengths and Limitations of the Land Use Plan

The land use plan and the planning inquiry process that lies behind it provide some useful assistance in industrial development. First, it pro-vides

an overall general policy statement about the pattern of future de-velopment for the community. Such a plan is a useful step toward identifying the land needs and a potentially appropriate land sup-ply. Nature alone cannot create good industrial sites. And industry has special land and location requirements that cannot be met most efficiently from land left over after residential, commercial, and pub-lic uses have been designated. Advanced planning for industry, in the context of the full network of urban functions, is necessary. Zoning, advanced land acquisition, the location of airports, high-ways, water and sewer trunklines and treatment facilities, flood control projects all enhance or even largely create prime sites for in-dustry (when planned and coordinated). Conversely, planning with-out an awareness of industry's needs, or the implementation of local governmental regulations and public investments without either planning or an awareness of industry's needs, can destroy potentially excellent sites from what is almost always a limited supply. [Muncy 1959, p. 5].

Second, the process used in designing a land use plan accumulates a rich inventory of background information that is useful to both public and private decision makers, including industrial developers. This data takes the form of base maps and tables created from surveys of existing urban uses, densities, vacant-land characteristics, natural resources, natural features and processes, utilities and other services, and economic and population characteristics and projections.

The comprehensive planning context for industrial development also has definite limitations, however. The plan itself focuses on ends, not means. It describes where to go but not how to get there. Thus it does not ordinarily include schedules, priorities, cost estimates, zoning ordinances, capital improvement programs, or detailed project or small area development plans. The plan is also long range, usually looking ahead at least twenty years and focusing only on the end of the twenty-year time period. Little attention is given to the intervening years or to ongoing development after the period is over.

It is important to note that the planner's traditional attitude toward economic development in the planning process described above is largely passive. He is not planning the amount and type of economic development. He is primarily concerned with deriving the space requirements and most appropriate location requirements for an already given level and structure of economic production activity and then specifying the spatial solution to those requirements. The planner's concerns do not include actively influencing the level and structure of economic activity. Implementation instruments are viewed as a means of accommodating a given amount of industrial development with as little impact on the residential areas as possible and of designing transportation and utility systems to accommodate the activity levels at the least cost to the local government.

With the still-growing concern for environmental quality, however, studies of land use, population, and economic growth, including local industrial activity, are gaining a new position. Many planners are now part of the burgeoning group that challenges the pro-growth consciousness taken for granted in the past. At any rate, planners can be expected increasingly to question industrial development instead of, as in the past, merely accepting it as desirable, asking how much, finding the space for it, tracing out the related implications on a map, and proposing appropriate zoning and community improvement programs to accommodate the growth (Finkler 1972 and 1973; Kaiser et al. 1974).

Whether passive or active in considering the level of future economic activity, comprehensive planning may account for industrial growth and may allocate sufficient and appropriately located space for industry, but it does so only on paper, not in the real world. At best, comprehensive planning is a useful but indirect influence in the real-world evolution of the community. Therefore there is a need to look to the potentially more active roles of the land use planner in the local government's attempts to influence the level and type of industrial development, influence its location within the community, and control its consequences for the immediately adjacent properties, for the larger community environment, and for the municipal government.

The Action Instruments of the Guidance System as a Means to Reserve and Control Land for Industry

One of the more active roles of the land use planner is that of an adviser and participant in the formulation of the action-oriented or policy instruments of the land use guidance system. These instruments deal with zoning, land acquisition and development, provision of public facilities and services, taxation practices, and other local, state, and national policies.

Zoning

At first glance, zoning would appear to be an ideal means to reserve adequate space for industry, in suitable locations, as the real-world counterpart of the spatial allocation made on paper by the land use plan. Unfortunately, industrial zoning has been rooted historically in the concepts of health and safety and in nuisance control, instead of in concepts of reserving suitable land for industrial development. Furthermore, urban planners' own natural biases emphasize the city as a place to live and not as a production center. The political game of zoning further aggravates the problem.

Zoning began as a way to protect residential property environments and values and on balance even today largely retains that role in built-up areas. Furthermore, since most existing zoning ordinances were first written in the 1920s and 1930s, usually long before planning began in those cities, zoning is not necessarily even related to planning. As a result, the zoning recipe is mostly a reinforcement of the status quo, with considerable greed and politics mixed in, and with only a pinch (or less) of planning. Most current zoning practices are based on antiquated concepts and are in direct conflict with the objectives of both comprehensive land use planning and industrial development planning.

One particular zoning practice that adversely affects industrial development is making zoning districts progressively inclusive, with industrial districts being almost all-inclusive and in the least preferred position in the hierarchy of zones. For example, the typical zoning ordinance extends preferred protection to lower-density, single-family dwellings by excluding all other uses. Each succeeding district in the hierarchy of districts then allows most, if not all, land uses of the preceding district. Under this system, all but a few property uses permitted under the zoning ordinances are allowed in the final districts—the industrial districts. Thus single-family residential districts are given maximum protection in many of the more traditionally oriented zoning ordinances, and industrial districts receive the least protection.

Since World War II, many ordinances have been revised at least to exclude residences, except mobile homes, from industrial districts. But the fundamental principle of cumulative permissible uses as one proceeds down the hierarchy of zoning districts still operates in many places, and its consequences are still felt in many communities across the nation.

This progressive districting practice causes several problems (Shenkel 1964, p. 250). First, such zoning limits the supply of industrial land, thereby increasing its price. The market competition for industrial space is increased because nonindustrial land users may compete for industrially zoned space. At the same time, industry is limited to industrially zoned space and cannot compete for land in other zoning categories. This situation encourages a rise in industrial land prices to such a point that prices can become a detriment to industrial development by rising above the threshold levels of some firms and discouraging others.

Second, the same zoning practice that creates the scarcity of land for industry may provide little compensating protection for industry, since the industrial district often has few or no zoning restrictions. A mix of transitional uses (so-called cast-off uses, such as trailer parks and junkyards), poor site planning, and traffic congestion often characterize industrial zones. This catch-all situation often encourages that the poorest land be zoned industrial in the first place.

The net result of such progressive district zoning practice is a limited supply of low-quality industrial land. Encroachment by other uses, often upon the best sites in the industrially zoned district, seriously impairs the efficiency of the land use and circulation pattern within the district and spoils its appearance.

The thrust of suggested improvements to zoning is toward providing a sufficient range of districts based on industry needs as well as the needs of surrounding properties. Some firms require a zoning district that is less restrictive with respect to allowable uses, performance standards, or yard regulations. Other firms prefer a more restrictive industrial zoning district to protect their investment from encroachment by residential, commercial, and incompatible industrial land uses. However, the community needs to avoid excessive restriction of industrial districts, which can make sites practically unfeasible to all but a few firms (City of San Diego Planning Department 1970, p. 110).

Industrial zoning innovations over the past twenty years have included the use of performance standards, the industrial park zone, planned multiple-use zones, and protective covenants. The last is a private rather than public control (Industrial Council of the Urban Land Institute 1975, pp. 17–22). Performance standards provide for aesthetic requirements and measurable control standards for such potential industrial nuisances as noise, smoke, glare, odor, dust and dirt, heat, solid wastes, liquid and gaseous wastes, and traffic. The standards do not list allowable industrial activity in an industrial zone; rather, any industry would be permitted to locate there, provided it could meet the standards. This approach adds an important degree of flexibility, while retaining protection for the surrounding residents and the community as a whole. The standards are difficult to administer, however, requiring a highly qualified enforcement agency. The industrial park zone, actually a more widely adopted approach in practice, requires a planned subdivision of a large site (minimum twenty-five to a hundred acres), to be developed under fairly restrictive site design standards featuring low-density development, extensive landscaping, and attention to aesthetic and amenity considerations. Planned multiple-use zones are applied to even larger tracts (four hundred to several thousand acres) and allow industrial uses along with residential and commercial uses, but they require careful overall planning and site design. Examples of this approach include planned unit development provisions and new community zones. Protective covenants are legally enforceable standards, adopted by the developer-landowner and applied to land being sold for industrial development, which can supplement public regulations by imposing further standards to which development must adhere.

The best protection can probably be achieved through industrial zoning codes that allow a range of districts, each of which sets reasonable space standards, such as off-street loading and parking requirements, yards, and percentage of site covered by structures. Each would also include reasonable but adequate performance standards on noise, smoke, odor, water and air pollution, radiation, and electromagnetic interference to insure both environmental health and the general livability of the community.

While some urban planners are likely to need education on the purposes of zoning for industrial needs, they are not likely to forget or deemphasize the more traditional concerns of controlling consequences of industrial activity on surrounding properties, on the environment, and on the city's fiscal position. The planner's view is probably that industry and the community need assurance that future industrial plants will be compatible with the other land uses and environment. Although zoning is somewhat successful as a means of protecting industrial developments once in place, even a properly written and administered zoning ordinance is not a totally satisfactory way of preserving land for future industrial development. Although it obviously goes a step further than preserving land on a piece of paper or in a policy statement (perhaps an unfair characterization of the comprehensive land use plan), it is vulnerable to political pressure for rezonings over the long run.

Zoning does not seem to be a critical factor in the locational criteria of industries.[3] Enticed by the prospect of jobs for residents and the potential expansion of the local property tax base, local communities are often quick to grant rezonings. Whether such rezoning undermines the community's overall welfare or represents a safety valve permitting escape from an inappropriate ordinance varies from situation to situation.

In 1951, the National Industrial Zoning Committee drafted twelve principles of industrial zoning, endorsed by seven professional organizations, including the American Institute of Planners and the American Society of Planning Officials (see appendix to this chapter). Industrial development professionals should be aware of these principles and perhaps augment them with others that address environmental quality, energy conservation, and equity in employment opportunities.

Land Acquisition and Development Policies

Direct land acquisition for industrial development is usually accomplished in the private sphere when those who have a service to sell to industry, such as a railroad or utility, or when private organizations with capital seek an investment opportunity from the sale or development of land (banks, realtors, pension funds, and insurance companies). Sometimes, however, a nonprofit body, such as a port authority, an urban redevelopment authority, an industrial development authority, or a research park authority, is directly involved in industrial development activity. Even more directly involved are numerous communities that have purchased and developed land, including buildings, for industrial development. This places industrial development in a class of unusual land uses that have been accorded special treatment in the United States. Others in this class are public housing, urban renewal, new towns, and community facilities.

The public purchase and lease or sale of developed parcels does allow both fuller, more direct control over the type of industry that exists within a community and greater potential efficiency in the provision of utilities. This approach to industrial development can minimize potential land use conflicts by assuring a proper location for the industrial park and appropriate site design practices through deed restrictions. And it can provide better assurance that the land will be held for industrial use and not sold for housing or shopping center development. The possibilities for attracting an industrial occupant that will contribute to a broader range of public interests than the provision of jobs alone are also greater.

Within central cities, urban industrial renewal is able to take advantage of eminent domain and public borrowing to assemble parcels and make the necessary infrastructure investments. The sites are then sold or leased to firms, often at costs less than those of development. Through deed restrictions the community can achieve a high level of control over the types of industry locating in the renewal areas. Industrial renewal can be an effective development alternative for central cities because of the high cost of the land and the problems that the private sector encounters in the assembly of land. Also, because of both the long holding periods involved in industrial development or redevelopment and the difficulty in rearranging for transportation and other utilities, the needs of industry may be more easily met through the public sector than through the private market (Muncy 1959, pp. 5, 13–17; New York Division of Housing and Community Renewal 1963).

Unfortunately, it is unlikely that sufficient land can be reserved through purchase because of the shortage of venture capital and public funds and the alternative opportunities for the use of such funds. Thus, outright public purchase and development of land for industry will not do the whole job.

Public Facilities and Services

The provision of utilities is perhaps the strongest guidance instrument that local government can use to reserve and control land for industry— if government has the will to use this instrument. Early in its plant location analysis, an industrial firm checks the quantity, quality, and cost of public utilities and services. The firm or industrial development agency asks whether water, sanitary sewer, storm sewer, electric power, gas, fire protection, police protection, mail delivery, telephone service, truck and rail service are adequate or whether they can be made adequate. The definition of *adequate* will vary, of course, among industries and even among firms belonging to the same industry type.

Other chapters in this volume discuss utilities, including water and sewer, and railroad transportation. However, it is appropriate to add something here about the importance of public transportation investment from the planning point of view, since land use and transportation planning are regarded by many physical planners as going hand in hand. Comments here will be limited to highways.

Muncy and others have noted the shift from rail to truck for transportation of incoming raw materials as well as outgoing product shipments (Muncy 1970, p. 4; U.S. Department of Commerce 1967, pp. 18–19). Furthermore, industrial employees, who as late as the 1940s used the bus, elevated railway, streetcar, or subway for their journey to work (particularly in larger metropolitan areas), now rely on the private automobile for transportation to suburban plants, laboratories, and warehouses. Thus, freeways have become a significant factor for new plant sites. Prime industrial land, defined in the past by the availability of rail service and in the future perhaps by other transportation modes is at present defined primarily by frontage on or proximity to the freeway system. Of course, future energy limitations may change this perspective.

The effectiveness of transportation as a guidance instrument of local government is limited, however, because the investment decisions most important to the industrial firm are those concerning the regional transportation system, and these decisions have traditionally been made at the federal and state levels. Nevertheless, local government can coordinate industrial zoning with freeway capacity. The aim, however, is not continuous industrial zoning along both sides of the highway. Too great a concentration of industrial employment would overload freeway interchanges, thereby detracting from the major advantage of the freeway system to industry—fast, safe, and uninterrupted travel for employees and for trucks delivering raw materials and distributing the output products. At the smaller scale of the individual industrial district sites, transportation planning needs to consider the access or connecting roads from the site to the freeway system, and communities should have definite policies for the extension of access roads to industrial sites.

Taxation

Some state constitutions permit local governments to exercise home-rule options in assessing the value of property, and some permit localities to offer legal tax concessions in the form of reduced assessments specifically to industry (Bridges 1965a, p. 8). Even in communities where these exemptions are illegal, some local governments will offer low assessments as an incentive to firms.

While local tax exemptions may be appreciated and welcomed, or perhaps even negotiated by the firm, the evidence suggests that their impact is not large enough to affect significantly the firm's location. Chapter 11, "Taxation," shows that the differential in tax burdens among the various state and local governments is usually not an important cost factor for many firms. Furthermore, since industry ordinarily requires high service levels from local government, exemptions, if broad enough, could reduce both the community's financial ability to provide these services and its ability to attract new industrial development. Tax exemptions to industry can also shift the tax load to families, thereby lowering the quality of life in the community. Given the limited impact and the potential backlash, the merit of tax concessions in a local urban development guidance system is questionable.

Other Local Guidance Instruments

Some communities around the nation seek to attract industrial plants through policies that offer specific financial incentives. These include loan guarantees or direct loans financed through the issue of tax-free general obligation bonds, or bonds floated by a local or state development corporation. The Investment Banker's Association estimated the volume of state and local industrial-aid bonds at $200 million in 1960 and as high as $1.8 billion in 1968 (Thompson 1969, p. 189). Since all states in the country now offer low-interest loans through public financing of private industrial development, this amount has increased substantially. However, the evidence suggests that "inducements are certainly a secondary factor in the choice of a region and are probably also a secondary factor in the choice of location within a region" (Bridges 1965, p. 142; Wallace and Ruttan 1961, p. 142; Thompson 1969, p. 199).

A less direct, perhaps, but still important inducement for industrial development is the maintenance of a high-quality living environment. This point is stressed repeatedly in research featuring surveys with industrial locators. Actions that detract from the quality of the environment, even though perhaps offering a handsome short-run economic gain for the community, could be a serious detriment to the long-range economic health of the community. The numerous factors that contribute to or detract from the overall quality of life and of the physical setting include

> practices of massive grading in relation to land development; the proliferation of outdoor advertising signs and grotesque business identification signs; the rate at which overhead power distribution lines are being put under ground; the disappearance of valuable open and natural terrain features; the amount and quality of landscaping along the streets, in neighborhood parks, on school sites, and throughout the city's residential neighborhoods; the exercise of air and water pollution controls; the quality of design in public

buildings; the rate of renewal, conservation, and rehabilitation of deteriorating sections of the city; the quality of education. [City of San Diego Planning Department 1970, p. 142–43]

Thus a number of communities follow the practice exemplified by one industrial development study that recommended the local adoption of policies that would place as much emphasis as possible "on preserving and enhancing the natural and manmade attributes of [the city], including: the preservation of open space and natural beauty; preservation and enhancement of beach areas and marshes; control of air, water, odor, noise, and visual pollution; retention and expansion of recreational facilities; and the encouragement of high standards of design and beauty in all physical improvements undertaken within the City" (City of San Diego Planning Department 1970, p. 143).

It is the policy in some communities that the local industrial development organization, although not formally a part of local government, does have a role in the community's industrial development guidance system. In communities where working relationships and cooperation exist between these two sectors, including land use planners, the industrial development organization serves as a link between prospective industrial firms and the city's land and service resources. It provides important information to prospective firms and coordinates local programs and activities both to meet the needs of the prospective firms and to assess the potential impact of prospective firms on the public welfare of the community. In short, its main contribution is to implement a more comprehensive and systematic approach to industrial development at the local or metropolitan level. Such an approach aims to insure greater compatibility between industry and the community's existing and planned resources, employment needs, and environmental concerns.

Some State and Federal Guidance Instruments

This discussion of guidance instruments has been limited primarily to those associated with the local level of government. The local government is by no means the only level that exercises controls. Increasingly, the location, development, and operation of industrial and other employment centers have become subject to restrictive policies that are established by state and national legislation but that may be implemented by local administrative decisions. Air and water quality, the availability of public transportation, electric power, natural gas and other fuels have become major concerns, along with increasing environmental standards and scarce water resources, both of which affect public water supply and sewage treatment capacity. Land use controls, once strictly local, now are being applied by regional, state, and federal agencies.[4] Many of these controls will be discussed in greater detail in later chapters.

Planner as Evaluator: Cost/Revenue as an Example

In addition to his other roles, the urban land use planner is sometimes a resident government analyst along with personnel in the finance and budget department of a community. In that role, he may examine cost/revenue impact as well as the economic, social, environmental, and urban growth impacts of the industrial development proposals.

A review of available cost/revenue studies reveals that industrial investment produces a positive ratio of revenue to cost of from three to one to five to one for the local government (U.S. Department of Commerce 1967). This figure is based on comparison of revenues accruing directly from the new establishment with costs of the services directly chargeable to it. The outcome is much less clear when the cost/revenue evaluations also include an assessment of the less direct costs and revenues attributable to the additional industrial, residential, and commercial development spin-offs stimulated by the initial industrial development.

In evaluating the fiscal impact on the local government the following seven factors need to be taken into account:

1. *Assessed value of the industrial investment* (land, plant, equipment, and inventory). Assessed value appears to vary widely among industries and even among firms within industries. In general, of course, the higher the capital investment per employee, the more favorable will be the cost/revenue ratio and generally the higher the wages. The greater the tax incentive granted to attract industry, the poorer will be the ratio (U.S. Department of Commerce 1967; Isard and Coughlin 1957).

2. *Demands on public services, particularly water and sewerage,* especially if the demands will exceed present capacity and involve large new capital expenditures. "Some communities have undertaken heavy financial burdens to provide water supplies far in excess of normal needs in the expectation that such supplies would attract industry. Too often these water supplies have to be financed by general obligation debt which pushes the tax rate above a competitive level. To accommodate 22 percent of the firms interested in water they have reduced their capacity to attract 78 percent of the firms where this is not a prime consideration" (McMillan 1965, p. 245). This example signals caution in seeking industry in ways that raise local government tax rates.

Local government's policies regarding the distribution of capital improvement costs can have considerable effect on the net cost/revenue picture. In some areas, off-site and on-site improvements, for streets, sidewalks, water and sewer lines in the industrial subdivision or in housing developments stimulated by the new jobs, for example, must be met by the developer. These expenditures become a part of the assessed value of the developed properties, and local government, in effect, benefits twice, since capital expenditures are transferred to the private sector and property tax revenues are increased. In other areas government shares some of these costs. To the extent that local government shoulders costs of capital improvements implied by industrial development, the cost/revenue picture is worsened (Isard and Coughlin 1957; U.S. Department of Commerce 1967).

3. *Proportion of employees establishing residence in the area.* The largest item of government costs and revenues for local government in most states is education. The net revenues generated by a new industry decrease as the percentage of employees establishing new residence in the community increases (Isard and Coughlin 1957; U.S. Department of Commerce 1967).

4. *Average earnings per employee.* As household income increases, investment for housing tends to increase. Thus property tax revenue accruing from new residences should be higher for high-wage industries than for low-wage industries. Also, higher income implies high local consumer expenditure.

Unfortunately, exclusive zoning is sometimes used to assure limitation on the proportion of employees establishing residence in the area at the higher end of the new industry's salary and wage range, a practice that merely shifts the burden to another community and discriminates against lower-income families.

5. *Average income and level of services in the community.* The impact of a new or expanded industrial development project on revenue rates is greatest in low-income communities with a medium level of service or medium-income communities with a high level of service, since revenue obtainable from industry is of greater relative importance in such communities than in communities with an already higher tax base or with lower costs because of lower levels of public services, or both (Isard and Coughlin 1957).

6. *Size of industrial project.* Smaller industrial firms, regardless of type, have little effect on tax rates; the introduction of a large industrial district can have a significant effect (reducing the tax rate from four to ten mills in one study) (Isard and Coughlin 1957).

7. *Spatial distribution of industrial development.* A study of Greensboro, North Carolina, showed that a well-dispersed industrial land use pattern provides the most favorable cost/revenue ratio. The basic econo-

my underlying the desirability of a dispersed pattern assumes that by diffusing the work-trip traffic, the street system may be more fully utilized (Longabaugh 1960).

Physical planning for economic growth can help to create a generally favorable climate for industrial development and at the same time help the community control the nature and location of such development; hence, its impact on the community's fiscal condition, quality of life, and environment.

More specifically, the local planning agency can assist industrial and economic development in several ways. First, the agency can provide future-oriented policy in the form of a policy plan, a long-range land use plan, a shorter-term land development plan, and/or a comprehensive plan. Such planning provides guidelines for sound economic development by identifying land best suited for industrial use on the basis of general community welfare objectives. Second, the agency can build up a valuable information base for public and private decision makers, including industrial development agencies. Data on existing industrial plants, relatively unbiased and current data on vacant industrially zoned land, zoning and development regulation restrictions applicable to the land, data on the existing and projected population and labor force, economic studies, and data on schools and other public facilities—all these types of information may be assembled by the local planning agency.

Third, the planning agency can participate in the formulation of the action instruments—regulations, public investments, and incentives—that intervene more directly in the industrial development decision process. Zoning, for example, can help to reserve an appropriate land supply for future industrial development and help to control that impact on the community.

Finally, planners can participate in the analysis of the impact of proposed industrial development on the economic structure, government fiscal balance, urban activity, and physical environmental quality of the community.

The planner's "review of the stated objectives of existing industrial development agencies, whether at the regional, state, or community level, reveals a preoccupation with economic growth in terms of number of jobs. In its simplest form this objective involves the creation of manufacturing payrolls in an area as a means of providing employment and income for the population, and business for the service sector of the local economy" (U.S. Department of Commerce 1967, p. 87). At the risk of oversimplification, it may be said that most urban land use planners feel that in focusing on such a limited objective, the industrial development professional follows the credo, "bigger is better." This objective is sound as far as it goes. The land use planner recognizes that manufacturing and wholesaling provide not only jobs and income, but that they also tend to expand the size of the local markets, in turn providing the base for additional development, and so on. But land use planning is more fundamentally an attempt to coordinate economic development with the development of community welfare and the quality of life. That is, the planner wants increased per capita income, a healthy and livable physical environment, an efficient and livable spatial pattern of land use, and the efficient (least expensive) provision of public services—none of which is automatically achieved through industrial growth. The land use planner is increasingly more interested in "better" rather than "bigger." Perhaps by working together, the planning and industrial development professions can help to assure that economic development does in fact lead to a better community as well as a bigger one.

Notes

1. The views expressed here are not necessarily those of the economic development planner or the social policy planner concerned with providing compensatory social services. Neither are they necessarily those of the private consultant interested in industrial development strategies or site development. In this last situation, a land use planner is sometimes a consultant member of an industrial development team. His role in such a case, however, would include evaluating impacts, preparing alternate site designs and serving as an expert witness at zoning and other approval hearings.

2. Although this restricted definition of industrial development is consistent with the focus of this book, the reader should be aware that a more comprehensive concept of "planned employment centers" is catching hold and replacing the notions of industrial development and industrial parks in the economic development field. A planned employment center is a multi-use district designed to provide for a community's land use and transportation pattern and its land, water, air, energy, and utility resources (Industrial Council of the Urban Land Institute 1975).

3. In her study of plant location factors in North Carolina in the early 1960s, Ruth Mace noted that only 16.5 percent of the firms in the sample viewed planning and zoning protection as an essential service, while 43 percent viewed these measures as unimportant (Mace 1963).

4. For example, the National Environmental Policy Act of 1969, or its derivatives at the state or local level where they exist, may require filing an environmental impact statement (costing perhaps one thousand to twenty thousand dollars and requiring sixty to ninety days). The Clean Air Act of 1970 can impose controls on the location of industries that emit gaseous and particulate pollution. It also controls the location of industry that generates considerable automobile

traffic, because of the air pollution thereby generated. The Federal Water Pollution Control Act of 1972 requires the enforcement of a national permit system covering industries discharging any pollutant into navigable and some non-navigable waters. The National Flood Insurance Act of 1968 affects financing of industral development in flood-prone areas.

Appendix

Principles of Industrial Zoning

Although first published in 1951 by the National Industrial Zoning Committee, these principles are still relevant. They have been endorsed by a number of professional organizations in both the planning and the industrial development fields. Principles referring to environmental protection, energy conservation, and economic opportunity might be added to bring the set up to date.

The twelve principles of industrial zoning are:

Principle 1. Most communities require a certain amount of industrial development to produce a sound economy.

Principle 2. Zoning controls are basic tools in the reservation of space for industry, guidance of industrial location into a desirable pattern, and provision of related facilities and areas needed for a convenient and balanced economy.

Principle 3. Industrial use is a legitimate land use possessing integrity comparable to other classes of land use established under zoning and is entitled to protection against encroachment.

Principle 4. Through proper zoning, industrial and residential areas can be good neighbors.

Principle 5. Industry will continue to grow and most industries will require larger areas in the future.

Principle 6. There is need for a reclassification of industry based on modern manufacturing processes and the prevailing policy of plant construction in order to determine the desirability for inclusion in a given area.

Principle 7. Industrial potentialities of lands bearing a favorable relationship to transportation should be recognized in the zoning process.

Principle 8. Industrial zoning and highway planning should go hand in hand.

Principle 9. Special consideration should be given to the street layout in industrial areas.

Principle 10. Zoning ordinances should be permissive rather than prohibitive.

Principle 11. A good zoning ordinance should be sufficiently definite to convey to a landowner a clear concept of what he can do with his land.

Principle 12. Industrial zoning can be most effective when considered on a metropolitan basis.

Chapter 4
Government Programs for
Industry

Industrial development is a competitive activity involving many types of private, quasi-public, and public organizations. But whereas the private and quasi-public organizations are usually the promoters, government organizations contribute to industrial location in other ways. This chapter will examine these functions, the forces molding them, and the regulatory role of government participation in industrial development for nearly the past two decades.

The Role of Government in Industrial Development

The overall mission of government agencies involved in industrial development programs is to improve the economic well-being of the communities served. This goal is accomplished by stimulating private investment through a wide variety of activities, which are frequently categorized by referring to the government roles of catalyst and coordinator. These activities, which include the usual industrial attraction techniques as well as participation in research, planning, infrastructure, and community improvement often involve relationships between federal, state, and local government regardless of which level assumes responsibility for a specific project.

Intergovernment relationships are more complicated than a simple federal-state-local breakdown would demonstrate (Advisory Commission on Intergovernmental Relations 1964). In the federal arena, several agencies may be involved, each with its own mission that may support or conflict with the others. The same may be true at the state level. At the local level, few complications will develop if the task is limited to only a county or a town. However, there may be an intervening regional group with powers ranging from merely advisory to practically veto. It is also possible that the county and the town may be jointly involved. Or a subsidiary unit such as a township may be involved. To complicate matters even more, there may be different grades of townships (as in Pennsylvania) with varying levels of power. In addition, the industrial development agency may have to work with special taxing districts, school districts, sanitation districts, and others, each of which has decision-making power over one crucial segment of an industrial project.

The saving feature in all this potentially frustrating maze, however, is the coordinating ability of most state industrial development agencies, which usually have both the resources and the desire to smooth out potential rough spots. Since their position is midway in the hierarchy, these agencies are ideally situated to act as coordinators, and this service usually fits well into their mission. The coordinative role is one of the most important functions of a state industrial development agency.

To varying degrees, modern industry is dependent upon five factors of production. The first three are the primary factors of land, labor, and capital, which have been recognized by economists for centuries. Since these must be coordinated for production to take place, business enterprise (or entrepreneurship) has generally been considered the fourth factor.

In today's milieu there is a fifth factor of production without which modern industry could not function—infrastructure, the basic underlying framework of utilities and community facilities without which today's manufacturer would be stymied. Within the past century, a manufacturer could find raw land, build his own roads, dig his own wells, install a sewerage system, build housing for his workers, and establish a complete community, including the infamous company store. But today, if the infrastructure is not entirely in place, the industrialist must suffer through the bureaucracy to obtain it. Most industrial prospects would prefer to avoid the delays inherent in the tortuous process of obtaining roads, sewers, water, and other important components of the infrastructure. The infrastructure is usually the responsibility of government; but what level of government provides it is a complex issue that has varied noticeably since 1960, along with marked changes in the public approach to industrial development.

Over the years each level of government—federal, state, and local—became involved in industrial development through the creation of policies and programs that are intertwined with the five production factors (see tables 4.1, 4.2, and 4.3).[1] At the close of World War II, a trend toward federal and state participation was set in motion. The Full Employment Act of 1946 established relatively full employment as a national goal. At the same time, states began to concentrate on economic growth. The trend gained momentum until by 1960 almost all states had some type of economic development activity. The efforts of the states at that time were strongly oriented toward promotion, which included an aggressive posture in the form of financing incentives, tax exemptions, and concessions. By 1960 about half the states were using some kind of industrial financing device, and most permitted local government to offer tax exemptions or concessions. But a comparison of the government programs that existed in 1960 and the 1970s shows that the contributions of government to productive facilities have grown substantially in coverage and depth during the intervening period (tables 4.1 and 4.2). Until the 1960s, except for industrial financing, an industrial agent could offer a prospect very little from any governmental source.

In the early 1960s the field of industrial development was flooded with creativity at all government levels (U.S. Economic Opportunity Office 1965). In 1961 the Area Redevelopment Administration (ARA), now the Economic Development Administration (EDA), was started and in 1963 the Appalachian Regional Commission (ARC) was established. Both of these organizations required or encouraged state or local participation in government business loans as an indication of confidence in the prospect and as proof of seriousness of purpose (see table 4.2, the "Capital" column).[2]

Table   4.1. Government Contribution to Productive Facilities, 1960

	Land	Labor	Capital	Enterprise	Infrastructure
Federal	SBA (LDC)[a] HUD (Urban renewal)[a]	Apprenticeship USES	SBA REA	———	HUD Categorical grants
State	———	USES	Revenue bonds in South DCC (in statute, not in fact) PIDA	State university MBA	Planning
County	Zoning Urban renewal[b]	Agricultural Home economics	———	———	Implementation Planning
Town	Zoning Urban renewal[b]	Vocational schools	———	———	Implementation Housing authority Planning

Note: With special references to the state of Maryland.
[a] Alphabetical designations: DCC—Development Credit Corporation, HUD—Housing and Urban Development, LDC—Local Development Corporation, PIDA—Pennsylvania Industrial Development Authority, REA—Rural Electrification Administration, SBA—Small Business Administration, USES—U.S. Employment Service.
[b] Rarely used for industry.

Table 4.2. Government Contribution to Productive Facilities, 1978

	Land	Labor	Capital	Enterprise	Infrastructure
Federal	Rural Development Act EDA SBA (LDC)	ARC MDTA-CETA Apprenticeship USES services Jobs WIN	SBA EDA Rural Development Act–FmHA IRS (incentives) Flood insurance HUD (UDAG)[b]	SBA-SCORE MESBICS SBICS OMBE	ARC EDA HUD[b] Rural Development Act Revenue sharing Public Works Employment Act
State	Industrial Land Act Critical areas laws Power plant site acquisition Agricultural assessment Acts	Industrial train- ing program USES	MIDFA DCC EDA–5%	State university MBA International Trade Desk OMBE Professional train- ing	Housing program Codes Administration, Planning, Historical Trust, Arts Council, CDA MES
County	Industrial Land Act Zoning Urban renewal Interim growth control acts	Industrial train- ing program Vocational schools Community colleges	MIDFA Revenue bonds EDA–5% SBA Tax incentives	———	Housing authority Planning Implementation Regional group participation
Town	Industrial Land Act Zoning Urban renewal	Industrial train- ing program Vocational schools	MIDFA Revenue bonds EDA–5% SBA Tax incentives	Aid to existing industry (Baltimore City)	Housing authority Planning Implementation

Note: With special reference to the state of Maryland.
[a] Alphabetical designations: ARC—Appalachian Regional Commission, CDA—Community Development Administration, CETA—Comprehensive Employment Training Act, 1973 (phasing out MDTA), EDA—Economic Development Administration, FmHA—Farmers Home Administration, HUD—Housing and Urban Development, JOBS—Job Opportunities in the Business Sector (contracts to offset costs of making people productive), MES—Maryland Environmental service, MESBIC—Minority Enterprise Small Business Investment Corp., MIDFA—Maryland Industrial Development Financing Authority, OBL—Office of Business Liaison, OMBE—Office of Minority Business Enterprise, SBA—Small Business Administration, SCORE—Service Corps of Retired Executives, USES—U.S. Employment Service, WIN—Work Incentive Program (1971) trains welfare recipients.
[b] Housing and Community Development Act of 1974 (Public Law 98-383) includes provisions for Community Development Block grants. The 1977 act provides urban development action grants (UDAF), including industrial.

Forces Stimulating Government Participation

Although it is easy and convenient to date the dramatic increase in government participation in the construction of productive facilities, ten strong forces moved toward that end throughout the 1960s.

1. Whereas economic location factors appeared to be of overriding importance in the fifties, in the sixties they were at least being challenged by probing questions concerning *community awareness*: community attitudes, community weaknesses, and community plans to remedy the problems.[3] A typical approach by the industrial prospect became to recognize that every community has weaknesses, but that the attractive community is one with a solid plan to correct them—if the economic factors are favorable. This new approach apparently had not been much in evi-

dence before the 1960s. The prospect's interest in community development filtered through to local leaders and led to a substantial commitment
to community improvement at the local level.

2. It was widely recognized in the decade of the sixties that economic
development requires sound community development, but that the economic base so essential to sound community development may not be
adequate itself unless supplemented by greater participation at the state
level, participation that can mount a coordinated attack upon all infrastructure issues. This *functional integration at the state level* was achieved
in most states by attaching the industrial development staff administra-
tively to the governor's staff or by simply informally creating ease of entry
to the governor for the industrial development professional. The governor therefore became the instrument for the functional integration of
state programs as needed. In some states, interagency coordination was
accomplished more routinely by combining economic development and
planning in the same agency. It must be noted, however, that some of
these combinations were short-lived. New governors have shown a strong
tendency to reverse the administrative decisions of their predecessors in
many states. But regardless of the administrative vehicle, the need for
meshing infrastructural responsibilities at the state level was not often
overlooked.

3. Local community leaders during this era demonstrated *an increasing
recognition of the role of investment*, of the close relationships between
public investment and private investment, and of the relationship of both
to job development. This awareness resulted in a plethora of imaginative
financing devices and other incentives to attract industry, often with
government as a participatory lender or a subordinate lender, which in
effect would be tantamount to an equity position. In some cases, all three
levels of government would participate with the private investor. The
phenomenal growth of investment incentives in the 1960s was quite
competitive. Many states and local jurisdictions found that, with industry
becoming more footloose (less tied to particular locations) and economic
factors tending to draw closer to parity over wider areas, a company so
inclined could shift its interest a few miles and take advantage of the
investment hunger of a neighboring community. Thus many jurisdictions
reluctantly joined the game, reflecting the "green-stamp" syndrome, that
is, providing local taxation, financial, and infrastructure inducements to
industry.

4. By 1965 most states had organized their counties into *regional
groups or multicounty districts*. The advantage of such groups is obvious,
but they have been most effective in serving as a pipeline for transmitting
local wishes to state resource allocators. The mere unification of local

desires seems to make the state more responsive. Regional groups rarely cooperate in the area of industrial development promotion, but their effectiveness in community development planning has been salutary, notwithstanding their lack of power to implement plans in most cases.

5. The expanding use of the *systems approach* reinforced regionalism, giving new meaning to the term *comprehensiveness*. As all sectors of the economy became linked into a more meaningful gestalt, the old-fashioned tendency of the 1940s and 1950s toward fragmented incrementalism slowly gave way to at least a formal recognition of the total approach. This approach required technical skills that were usually not available at the local level, which encouraged local leaders to seek and obtain increasing state participation. But the states were not fully prepared for such an effort. In order to institute a systems approach, states found it necessary to overcome certain rigidities, such as the inertia inherent in the development objectives of local jurisdictions, the functional realities of limited resources, and the needs of such economic sore spots as high-unemployment areas in central cities, rural areas, and low-income areas. More conscious leadership was required at the state level than had been offered in the past, as well as more active participation in development planning at the local and regional levels. In 1960 planning was the sole prerogative of the United States Department of Housing and Urban Development and of state and local land use planners who often gave little deference to economic development and even less to industrial development. But today EDA shares the planning burden and provides planning assistance to multicounty districts, as well as to state and local governments (table 4.2 and the appendix to this chapter).

6. *Environmentalism* was the most visible force manifest throughout the country, putting public pressure on all bureaucrats. But this issue was felt most acutely by industrial developers, who suddenly realized that they no longer enjoyed the relative warmth and acceptance in the seventies that was theirs in the sixties. Along with this change, the new industrial development buzz words became *balance* and *selectivity*. New laws made sympathetic cooperation among government agencies with similar goals more urgent and led, in turn, to a broader approach to impact analysis requiring a threefold evaluation for every investment proposal—namely, environmental, economic, and social.[4] If a given proposal survives these three impact investigations, it may be a viable project. This compromise is satisfactory to the industrial developer, since for a short period at the beginning of the decade a "no-growth" attitude threatened to gain influence. The nature of the three impact analyses, however, does require more time for a project to wend its way through government

approvals (Andrews 1975; Schaenman and Mueller 1975; Gruen, Gruen, and Associates 1975).

7. The unusual combination of *economic changes* that originated in the 1960s but became more acute in the 1970s led to more government participation. Nine types of economic change or persistent economic forces had significant effects on the efforts of industrial developers:

 a. rising interest rates;

 b. accelerating inflation, especially when accompanied with high unemployment of the mid-1970s;

 c. rising land costs;

 d. increased use of tax structures to stimulate consumption and investment;

 e. decrease in labor cost differentials among regions;

 f. persistent increase in service industry employment and steady decrease in manufacturing employment;

 g. persistent maldistribution of prosperity, vividly manifest in hundreds of pockets of high unemployment and low income scattered through the country;

 h. increased competition from foreign manufacturing in both underdeveloped countries and fully industrialized countries; and

 i. a steadily worsening fiscal crunch in states and cities, stemming from a combination of increasing demands by the public for more and better services and pressure on legislators to hold down taxes.

Many government programs implemented during the period were direct results of some of the economic forces and changes cited above (table 4.2). For example, high interest rates were an important factor in the substantial increase in the number of programs designed (particularly at the state level) to improve community infrastructure. The infrastructure programs were, of course, simultaneously influenced by environmentalism. The economic changes affected all kinds of enterprises from the smallest to the largest. The Small Business Administration (SBA) provided a wide variety of aids to smaller firms, while revenue bonds tended to favor larger ones (see appendix to this chapter). Of course, special consideration was given to giants such as Lockheed and Penn Central. But it does not require that the imagination be unduly stretched to anticipate that economic conditions, if they continue to change in the future as they have in the past few decades, will produce a far larger number of state and federal programs.

8. Increased government participation itself generated the *new federalism*, a term coined in the early 1960s from the unique federal-state partnership that was legislatively built into the Appalachian program. In that

program, projects are typically generated at the local level and screened at the state level prior to final approval by the ARC. The commission is comprised of the governors of the thirteen member states, or their representatives, and the federal co-chairman, who is appointed by the president. ARC and similar types of regional programs have been most helpful to industrial development through the construction of infrastructure and the funding of development staffs at local government levels by both the regional commissions and the EDA (see appendix; United States Economic Opportunity Office 1965 and 1968; Office of Management and Budget 1975). Other manifestations of the new federal-state relationship are revenue sharing and the Comprehensive Employment Training Act (CETA).

9. Since 1960 there has been a widening *dichotomy between urban and rural development*. In the classic pattern, urban areas have received the migration caused by the steady decline in agricultural employment. Since 1970, however, nonmetropolitan counties have been growing at a faster rate than metropolitan counties (McCarthy and Morrison 1977). This reversal in population trends probably reflects the diminishing attractiveness of urban areas to people and industry. In the absence of a national policy on the direction of growth, the building of the interstate highway system and the extension of communication, electrical, and water service made outlying areas cost-competitive with the major metropolitan areas. Whereas too many people in urban areas caused the kinds of problems associated with congestion, including a polluted environment, the disadvantages of the rural areas resulting from the sparse distribution of development began to erode in the sixties and seventies. Simultaneously, the forces described above were making rural leadership more aggressive. As urban areas began to press for additional fiscal and social resources for renewal, rehabilitation, and revitalization, rural areas were also demanding development resources. Since the federal mood has favored decentralized decision making, this dichotomy has placed a special burden on state governments to develop the role of referee. The distinctions between metropolitan and nonmetropolitan and between rural and urban areas, while easy to determine, are often inadequate to cope with acute sub-area problems. The statistical problem of counting the unemployed in part of a county or part of a city, for example, has caused substantial delay in getting help where it has been needed.[5]

10. The last force to be mentioned is the long-overdue improvement in general awareness of the importance of an *occupation orientation in education*. Increased federal funding of vocational education in the mid-1960s, the simultaneous phenomenal growth of community colleges, and the widespread recognition of the link between economic growth and

adult job training has opened an important avenue of participation for all levels of government. Aside from financial incentives, a most noteworthy change since 1960 has been the growth of industrial training programs (see table 4.2, "Labor" column). These programs, pioneered in the Carolinas before the 1960s and quite common today, address the problem of training a community's inadequately trained labor force at state expense during the construction of the plant.

Changes in Government Intervention

All of the forces discussed above help to explain the increment in government participation and why the categories of assistance more than doubled between 1960 and the late 1970s. The greatest increase occurred at the state level, with federal program categories a close second. It must be recognized, however, that the federal expansion was qualitative as well as quantitative. Whereas in 1960 the programs provided assistance with the decisions as to the use of the funds made at the federal level, in several of the more recent programs (shown in table 4.2), the funds are provided by the federal government, but the decisions as to where they will be spent are made at the state and local levels. The most obvious example, of course, is federal revenue sharing, but a similar principle applies to such programs as CETA.

In terms of contribution to particular factors of production, the most dramatic increase in government programs has been associated with the enterprise factor; that is, programs dealing with the entrepreneur's ability successfully to combine the other factors of production. In 1960 state universities offering courses leading to a Master of Business Administration (MBA) degree were the only government-supported help available to management for any problems not directly related to the other factors. By the early 1970s, federal agencies such as the Office of Minority Business Enterprise (OMBE) and the Senior Corps of Retired Executives (SCORE) offered counseling on a variety of business problems. Also available is the Small Business Investment Corporation (SBIC), which can help in organizing ventures (albeit at a price). Many states have created ombudsmen agencies that help businessmen deal with problems involving government and other agencies that assist entrepreneurs in the intricacies of entering the export market. A most important addition to the enterprise factor is the aid provided to existing industry, available through municipal industrial development agencies. As practiced by a number of cities, this is an outreach program in which the city's economic and community development staff interview industrial, commercial, and other business executives, frequently accompanied by the mayor or other influential leaders, to ascertain what problems may be impeding their operations. The impact of this program may be weighed in terms of the fact that economic development professionals believe that most of any city's new industrial employment expansion is likely to come from existing industry. In fact, some estimate as much as 80 percent of the expansion from this source. But a significant feature of the outreach program is that it provides help to all employers, not only to manufacturers.

The next largest program increase has been associated with the capital factor, in particular, industrial financing devices. At the same time that the number of jurisdictions using these devices was doubling, the clients using them more than doubled. Part of the increase is due to revenue bonds implemented in response to pollution problems. Even conservative jurisdictions that have never felt the need to use any industrial financing device have begun to issue revenue bonds because local industrial firms have discovered that they can thereby save money in interest costs and be able to finance new environmental pollution-abatement equipment.

One of the most significant increases during the period was the number of programs created by state governments to improve community infrastructure (table 4.2). Here the economic forces cited above led to the development of programs to fill the gaps left by federal agencies. Programs such as those that provide direct loans and mortgage insurance for both low- and middle-income housing; that establish building standards (formerly the province of local government); or that create trusts, art councils, and community development administrations are guided by the philosophy that the total community must be improved through both public and private investment.

The number of government programs existing in the late 1970s that are directed toward industrial location is even more impressive when one realizes that many of them have greater scope and flexibility than those of 1960. The Rural Development Act carried out under the Farmers Home Administration (FmHA), for example, makes available two grant programs (one to refinance industrial parks and one for water and waste facilities) and two loan programs (one for sewer and water and one covering practically all needs of a public body). Thus, within the limitations of funding (which were also present in 1960), a community can obtain assistance for almost any type of project. Similar flexibility is possible with revenue sharing, EDA, and CETA programs. Thus the resources available for assistance to local leaders interested in making their communities more attractive to industries or in offering incentives to industrialists to ease the burdens of gathering the factors of production are considerably closer at hand than ever before. These resources have become so complex by their very numbers and flexibility, however, that local leaders are becoming more dependent upon state staffs to guide them through the government resource maze. To assist communities in such matters many states have opened liaison assistance offices in Washington, D.C. Virtually all states, though, have at least one staff member in each state agency with substantial federal activity (such as transportation, planning, and economic and community development) who is referred to in the professional vernacular as a grantsman. Often when a state or local program director thinks that no federal money is available for his program, the grantsman can show him how to obtain funding. Sometimes when the program director thinks he cannot participate because he cannot find matching funds, the grantsman shows him how to have the requirement waived or how to package "in-kind" matching contributions. The grantsman, in short, is expert in the art of adapting federal programs to state and local needs, or vice versa.

The complexity of government programs is only one aspect of the problems involved in intergovernment relationships. Other difficulties are so well known as to be axiomatic. For example, long delays in obtaining a definitive response have become notorious. A less well-known difficulty is that of conflicting strategies; the strategies of one agency sometimes blur or tend to reverse the action of another. For example, the Appalachian Regional Development Act, the Public Works and Economic Development Act, and the Economic Opportunity Act all dealt with problems of poverty. But the programs authorized under these acts were implemented according to different strategies. Some assisted poor people where they lived; others stimulated job development in favorable locations, thereby encouraging poor people to migrate.[6] Of course, even worse than these examples are the efforts of EDA and SBA to encourage employment, while environmental agencies tend to discourage it. Nor is all of this conflict apparent at only the federal level; quite a bit exists at the state level and in some cases the conflicting programs are not easily discernible, nor do they stem from opposing objectives that are not properly balanced. Employment growth vis-à-vis environmental improvement is a case in point. Another example is the long-term goal of the United States to encourage international trade, which led to concessions for certain products, which led in turn to certain undesirable employment impacts. The Trade Act of 1974 represents an effort to address this problem, providing assistance to individuals, companies, or communities adversely affected by imports (see table 4.2, "federal" row).

Thus the tremendous expansion of available government resources has not always been matched by a similar expansion in the use of those resources because of the inadequacies of a delivery system that has been plagued by the difficulties noted above. One approach to this problem employs the grantsman at the state level and, in some cases, at the local level as well. Another, more positive, approach is the use of a development coordinator attached to the office of the governor or local chief executive. The coordinator's major duty is the careful assembly of development resources essential to the comprehensive implementation of comprehensive plans. The development coordinator is an executive expediter whose responsibility is to integrate public and private investment while programming the pace of development to keep the various functions marching in step. The concept is at least twenty years old, but it is more necessary now than ever if the large numbers of government programs at all levels are to be used effectively.

Regulatory Intervention by Government

Up to this point the positive contributions of various levels of government to the entrepreneur in his effort to make productive facilities operational and profitable have been discussed. The other side of the coin is the effort made by government to regulate productive facilities in order to protect the community from potential negative effects of their operation (table 4.3).

Since federal regulations have a nationwide effect, most of them create few, if any, ripples in the industrial development pond. But some federal regulations, such as those dealing with environmental pollution, can affect individual communities differently.[7] Industrial development agents should be aware of these regulations and should also be aware that in some regulatory areas the states have the option of adopting controls more stringent than federal regulations require. If a state does choose the more stringent controls, however, loss of manufacturing jobs may result.

Land use control bills have been introduced in Congress over the years but have not gained support from industrial developers, and none have been enacted to date. On the other hand, numerous states have passed legislation in recent years to control land use, some with very strong regulations. Most regulatory controls placed on land use, however, are enacted at the local level of government through zoning ordinances.

While no federal regulatory land controls have been enacted, antipollution laws promulgated by the Environmental Protection Agency (EPA) have some effect on where industrial plants can locate, depending upon the effluent they discharge into the air or water and the extent to which they are willing or able to meet environmental performance standards (see chapter 10). As a case in point, many states have regions in which traffic conditions have led to the air's being declared so dirty that further development, which would increase traffic, has been ruled out. But now there is an air quality maintenance principle promulgated by the Supreme Court that restricts many of the other regions in these states from developing because the air is too clean. Two questions are raised by this inconsistency. First, if industries cannot build in one location because the air is too dirty and they cannot build in another location because the air is too clean, where will industrial development be permitted? The second question obviously is, since the people who will need jobs (tens of millions of them) will be entering the labor force in a steady stream over the next generation, what level of unemployment is the country willing to accept as the price of clean air?

Government ordinances regulating labor and capital, for the most part, are well known and well entrenched. The newest federal ordinance affecting labor is the Occupational Safety and Health Administration (OSHA) Act, which provides environmental protection inside the plant for workers.

The regulatory ordinances lack a clear-cut delineation between enterprise and infrastructure. Those regulating the enterprise factor are all restrictions on management's ability to operate, but in many cases they are limitations in the use of infrastructure as well. For example, in the case of sanitation, management is told exactly how to handle effluents and any deviation spells trouble; but the handling process often requires the use of infrastructure facilities—roads, sewage lines, sewage treatment plants, solid-waste landfills, incinerators, and the like. Other regulatory controls related to the enterprise factor are those associated with environmental protection. As already discussed, federal and state agencies are exerting a strong force in this area. At the local level of government the regulatory controls are all related to performance standards enacted through zoning ordinances.

In some instances all three government levels work closely on the same problems, such as solid-waste disposal. However, neither is it unusual for all three levels to be in conflict on an issue of great importance to industry. For example, the number of highways approved by federal and state agencies that have been delayed or canceled by local government protests are legion. Within the country many major highways presently under construction have been delayed by one study after another, even though the highway plans have existed for a decade or two or even longer.

These problems point out the need for a more stable, realistic approach to government regulation, the need for better coordination among the three levels of government where regulating functions overlap, and the need for more efficient government management procedures (Widner 1974; Parker 1975). Since the bureaucracy is necessary and regulation is essential to the use of public facilities for economic activity, the industrial developer must be alert to this bureaucratic deficiency and learn to cope with it through sheer persistence. In response, some states have created the business ombudsman's office or business liaison office already discussed; regardless of the name, the function is very important and is becoming more frequently available.

In all fairness it must be recognized that governments, particularly the federal government, realize that their intervention does cause problems for business and try to provide programs to ease these problems. For example, tax-exempt revenue bonds, discussed earlier, are available to any firm that must make capital expenditures to meet federal or state anti-pollution regulations. Another example is the low-interest loans that small businessmen can obtain from SBA for many kinds of economic injury, including some resulting from such government actions as OSHA, military-base closings, treaties, trade agreements, air and water quality regulations, coal mine safety laws, meat and poultry inspection, and products taken off the shelves because of toxicity findings.

A comparison of the government benefit programs in 1960 (table 4.1) and those of the late 1970s (table 4.2) and an examination of the regulatory ordinances (table 4.3) reveal a steady broadening and deepening of government intervention in the field of industrial location. Industrial developers, accustomed to a role as a friend of the private investor, have deplored the kind of intervention represented by the regulatory ordinances, but have been major proponents of that shown by the benefit programs that had been enacted. As do most other advocacy groups, industrial developers recognize the need for and are quick to develop rationales for new government intervention that contributes to their objectives. And, as do most other advocacy groups, industrial developers never develop rationales for dropping older intervention tools when new ones are adopted. Thus the notorious creeping incrementalism that has become so damaging to the effectiveness of federal government has already substantially affected state government, particularly in the densely populated northeastern states, and even local government. Since most states employ a strict constitutional barrier against deficit spending, several states and cities have undergone urgent fiscal crises in recent years. The long-run effect of these crises is likely to be a tougher attitude toward the kind of expanded government intervention that has occurred during the past few decades. But a new foundation must be laid, regardless of which attitude prevails. The most prevalent basis in the past has been the "squeaky wheel" syndrome; that is, the loudest or most powerful pressure groups got the most prompt response, even though such groups do not necessarily represent the most urgent needs of the community.

Table   4.3. Regulatory Relationships Affecting Industrial Development

	Land	Labor	Capital	Enterprise	Infrastructure
Federal	FPA[a,c]	OSHA FLSA LMRA Bacon-Davis Act Equal Employment Opportunity Commission	SEC Anti-trust Flood insurance	Air quality (EPA)[i] Water quality[i] OSHA Energy consumption (FPC, NRC) Solid waste[g]	ICC DOT Corps of Engineers
State	Building code[h] Land use Wetlands Land fill Boiler inspection Elevator inspection	Working hours[e] Safety[d] Minimum wage Wage payment law[c] Human Relations Commission[h]	Interest rates Blue-sky law	Air quality, noise Water quality Solid waste[g] Safety Glazing Act Oil storage[f] Fire	PUC DOT Port Authority Soil Conservation District Access for handicapped
County	Building codes Zoning Performance standards Soil erosion	Human Relations Commission[h]		Radiation-heat Noise pollution Sanitation Vibration Fire Solid waste[g]	County health officer Sanitary commission
Town	Zoning Building codes	Minimum wage (Baltimore $2.10) Human Relations Commission[h]		Radiation Sanitation Noise controls	Odor controls Vibration Fire

[a] Federal agency designations: DOT—Department of Transportation, FPA—Environmental Protection Agency, FLSA—Fair Labor Standards Act (minimum wage and overtime), ICC—Interstate Commerce Commission, LMRA—Labor Management Relations Act (collective bargaining), NRC—Nuclear Regulatory Commission, OSHA—Occupational Safety and Health Administration, PUC—Public Utility Commission.
[b] Assistance to counties in setting up codes and training inspectors.
[c] Governs terms of salary payment.
[d] Boiler inspection, elevator inspection.
[e] Child labor, overtime.
[f] Bulk storage of petroleum products beyond 126,000 gallons requires permit.
[g] Monitored by the state, regulated by County Soil Conservation District (federal funding).
[h] Subject to memoranda of understanding. Issues settled at lowest level and cover housing and employment.
[i] As related to the Clean Air Act of 1970 and the Water Pollution Control Act of 1972.

Therefore, it seems inevitable that eventually government intervention in the private investment process will be based on a development rationale more productive and practical than the noise of pressure groups. Since increased taxes have become anathema to political leaders, a new awareness has apparently developed of the harsh reality that each new program at the state or city level requires either added revenue or the curtailment of an existing program.

Government is doing more today than ever before to create incentives and tools through which the factors of production that are required for private investment can be coordinated. In so doing, it can and does guide the location of economic activity more positively than ever before and even may increase the pace somewhat (Polenske 1969; Friedlander 1976; Sulvetta and Thompson 1975; Vaughan 1977; Barro 1978).

But a decision-making process that will allocate dollars more effectively is urgently needed. The process must include a method for evaluating the extent to which each government program is achieving the objectives delineated when the allocation was made. Furthermore, the problem of pacing private investment so that it is in step with public development requires much closer attention. Simultaneously, both government and private industry must begin to wrestle with the issue of how to allocate investment in order to balance several pressing needs, including profits to feed the investment process, the elimination of geographical sore spots in the economy (areas of high unemployment and low income), public investment in infrastructure, and a complex combination of public services, including regulatory intervention in enterprise.

Notes

1. The sources of government responsibility for industrial development begin with the United States Constitution, which gives to Congress power to regulate commerce among the states and gives to the states all powers not delegated to the federal government. This arrangement would seem to rule out any exercise of industrial development powers by counties, towns, or other local jurisdictions. But by tradition local government has enjoyed the power of land use decisions and the privilege of pursuing job development. In many cases, local governments have been content to leave the task to local civic groups such as chambers of commerce and committees of "100."

2. For example, many states participated in ARA loans to the extent of 5 percent, which cut in half the federal requirement that the community participate to the extent of 10 percent in all business loans.

3. Location research in the mid-1950s, for example, showed land and building suitability and costs, transportation costs, and labor availability to be the most important locational factors for manufacturers in the Philadelphia metropolitan area.

4. The economic impact analysis has two main facets: job and income generation and the fiscal analysis. The fiscal analysis may create problems if opponents to a project can demonstrate negative economic impact as a result of tax exemptions or low-cost government services provided to the new industry. One of the most important facets of the social impact analysis is the effect of the project on identifiable historical landmarks; no project shall have a detrimental effect on an officially designated historic area or building. Another component of the social impact analysis is the objection to low-wage industry, which is usually reflected as a concern that the industry may attract workers who may change the character of the community.

5. At one time, for example, Maryland officials were aware of a relatively sparsely populated low-unemployment county in Delaware obtaining EDA assistance based on the section of the act that provided for designation of at least one county in every state, while a sizable part of the city of Baltimore with three times the population of the Delaware county and four times the percentage of unemployment (seven times the unemployment in absolute numbers) could not be designated. This disparity was corrected in later years, but sub-areas remain more difficult to handle statistically. The Rural Development Act approaches this problem with a flexible definition of the term *rural*.

6. See the report on National Growth and Development transmitted to the Congress in December 1974.

7. For a more detailed discussion of federal and state ordinances regulating environmental pollution and their effect on industrial location see chapter 10, "Environmental Quality."

Appendix

Selected Federal Government Programs for Industrial and Economic Development

I. United States Department of Agriculture
   A. Programs administered by the community programs division of the Farmers Home Administration
      1. Loans for business and industry
      2. Grants and loans for community facilities
II. United States Department of Commerce Programs
   A. Programs administered by the Economic Development Administration
      1. Grants and loans for public works and development facilities
      2. Business development assistance loans
      3. Grant support for planning organizations
      4. Technical assistance grants
      5. Public works impact project grants
      6. State and local economic development grants
      7. District operational assistance grants
      8. Special economic development and adjustment assistance program grants
   B. Programs administered by the Small Business Administration
      1. Displaced business loans—displacement by a federally aided project
      2. Economic injury disaster loans—to pay current liabilities that could not be paid due to disaster
      3. Economic opportunity loans—to economically disadvantaged persons
      4. Lease guarantees
      5. Management assistance—advisory services, counseling, training
      6. Minority business development—procurement assistance
      7. Management and technical assistance for disadvantaged businessmen —grants for planning and research

8. Physical disaster loans—to repair or replace damaged realty, machinery and equipment, or personal property
9. Procurement assistance to small businesses
10. Product disaster loans—to pay current liabilities due to inability to market a product because of discovery of toxicity
11. Small business investment companies
12. Small business loans—regular business loans
13. State and local development company loans (501 and 502 loans)
14. Coal mine—health and safety loans
15. Bond guarantees for surety companies
16. Meat and poultry inspection loans—to meet requirements imposed by federal or state law
17. Occupational safety and health loans—to help with problems traceable to OSHA
18. Minority vendors program
19. Base closing economic injury loans
20. Handicapped assistance loans
21. Emergency energy shortage economic injury loans
22. Strategic arms economic injury loans—injury as a result of arms limitation treaties
23. Water pollution control loans
24. Air pollution control loans

III. United States Department of Labor Programs
  A. Programs administered by the Office of Trade Adjustment Assistance
    1. Trade Act of 1974—technical and financial assistance to businesses adversely affected by foreign imports

Part 2
Industrial Location
Practices

Chapter 5
Locational Trends in Manufacturing

Industrial location decisions not only influence where people work and live but also play a major role in determining the prosperity and life-style of a community. This chapter first discusses some of the factors that influence the industrial location search process and then examines the changing geographical pattern of manufacturing activity within the United States.

The Industrial Location Search Process

The selection of a manufacturing site is a continuous process of elimination as a firm narrows the scope of its search from the broadest geographic scale down to a specific site.[1] In simplest terms, the process may be described on only two levels. The initial decision leads to the selection of a region within the country or perhaps a specific market area for the location of the industrial plant. This decision is usually based on particular location factors, such as transportation and labor costs, that affect the cost structure of the firm. The secondary decision involves selecting the most appropriate community within the chosen region and a suitable site within the chosen community from among those that are available. This decision may require consideration of a large number of communities and sites based on numerous factors, or it may be a relatively simple choice among a small number of existing plant facilities. It is at this secondary level that the industrial developer assumes a key role because the information he provides the industrial prospect may determine the eventual site decision.

For a large number of manufacturing firms many factors may stimulate the decision to search for a plant location. In fact, at least ten types of stress may prompt a firm to make a locational change: (1) planned growth of existing product lines; (2) development of new regional markets; (3) unplanned growth of existing product lines; (4) diversification of product lines; (5) vertical integration; (6) horizontal integration; (7) externally generated stresses; (8) stress exerted by pattern of market distribution; (9) a decision imposed by the parent company; and (10) rationalization of operations (North 1974). Different kinds of locational adjustments may come out of the above stresses. When possible, firms attempt to minimize the energy required for the decision by remaining at existing locations. This response is especially typical of older firms and larger firms in capital-intensive industries. Only when severe locational stress, such as that caused by fire, labor problems, or obsolescence of plant and equipment, impairs an existing site are such firms likely to relocate. This inertia factor is reflected in considerably stable manufacturing locational patterns even when the original advantages of a site have substantially diminished. When growth at an existing site is impossible or undesirable the firm must make a decision to relocate entirely or to establish additional capacity elsewhere. The decision for total relocation can tremendously affect a community and its labor force; therefore, most firms try to avoid such a change. Massive relocations by firms in an industry, such as the migration of the labor-intensive textile industry out of New England, can be devastating, particularly in the short run (Estall 1966).

The addition of greater capacity at new sites to meet either new product lines or expansion of old ones can be accomplished through construction of branch plants or the acquisition of existing firms. If new product lines are being added, strong ties to original production sites help to facilitate communication and other intra-firm linkages. Expansion of existing product lines is usually a response to increased demand, which often dictates the focus of the regional search process. This type of locational adjustment is quite common in the established corporate structure of the United States. Large corporations are more likely to be in a position to absorb the expense of new capital expenditures and lengthy start-up times than are new firms (North 1974).

Before the search process is formalized, then, a number of decisions pertaining to corporate structure, product type, scale, and type of production and geographic extent of the market must be made by the firm. Once these factors are determined, the search process can begin with some criteria already established. The traditional assumption has been that most industrial location decisions are made toward a specific goal, such as profit maximization or satisfaction. However, the goals of market penetration or minimization of uncertainty are also recognized as legitimate decision-making criteria.

Greater material substitution, standardization of production methods, and increased specialization of manufacturing production have allowed more industries to become footloose, with a large number of economically feasible locations from which to choose. Thus, given the expanded range of site opportunities, the final locational choice can reflect personal preferences.

The manufacturing process involves (1) procurement of raw or already processed materials from supply areas, (2) processing or assembling of these materials into a final product or component at some location, and (3) distribution of the product or component to a specified market or set of markets. Associated with each step is a set of costs. Traditionally, a good location has been judged as one that allows the minimization of these costs. Determination of a least-cost location requires knowledge of the cost structure of the firm and its peculiar requirements for energy, utilities, capital equipment, labor, and materials inputs. For example, the importance of labor as a location factor can be determined only in relationship to its importance in the total cost picture. Estimates of the total payroll expended by industry in recent years varied from 5.7 percent to more than 32.6 percent of the total value of shipments for different industry groups (table 5.1). However, the cost and availability of specific types of labor is an even more important factor. For example, a firm in the cotton weaving industry, in which hourly wages for production workers represent 87.9 percent of the total payroll, would place a different emphasis on the availability and cost of production workers than the pharmaceutical manufacturer, who allocates only 41.3 percent of the payroll to such workers.

The Regional Search Process

After the necessary background information is gathered, the regional search process, whether conducted by the company itself or by professional consultants, becomes an exercise in comparative shopping. Ideally, the search process encompasses a large number of possibilities; more realistically, its scope includes comparatively few areas and is constrained by both predetermined biases on the part of management and the promotional efforts of certain areas. The following discussion identifies some of the significant location factors involved in the regional search process.

Transportation Factors. Before the current energy shortages and in-

Table   5.1. Total Payroll as a Percentage of Value of Shipments, 1972

Industry	Total payroll as percentage of value of shipments	Value of shipments (millions of dollars)	Wages as percentage of payroll
Industry group			
Food	11.2	115,060	61.9
Tobacco	8.4	5,920	79.9
Textiles	21.6	28,072	79.4
Apparel	25.9	27,809	75.7
Lumber	20.9	23,816	78.9
Furniture	28.3	11,309	72.5
Paper	17.7	28,262	72.1
Printing	32.6	30,132	55.5
Chemicals	15.2	57,350	54.4
Petroleum and coal	5.7	28,695	65.0
Rubbers and plastics	24.7	20,924	69.8
Leather	27.5	5,770	77.5
Stone, clay, and glass	25.8	21,538	72.8
Primary metals	20.8	58,430	75.6
Fabricated metals	26.7	51,739	69.1
Non-electrical machinery	28.1	65,821	61.3
Electrical machinery	28.4	53,433	58.0
Transportation equipment	21.0	94,705	64.6
Scientific instruments	27.6	15,566	52.1
Miscellaneous	26.1	12,186	65.5
Specific industries			
Cotton weaving	28.0	2,661	87.9
Drugs	17.6	8,091	41.3
Reclaimed rubber	30.0	1,020	64.7
Aircraft	34.2	15,451	49.5
Optical instruments	35.9	538	44.0

Source: Compiled from U.S. Department of Commerce, *Statistical Abstract of the United States, 1975*, pp. 742–47.

creased costs of petroleum, transportation costs were of declining importance as a factor in location decisions. While reduced mobility now affects everyone to some extent, the cost of transporting materials and products is particularly important for firms that move a considerable amount of perishable, bulky, or fragile raw materials or finished goods. If raw materials are classified as either ubiquitous or localized and either pure or gross, certain locational tendencies result. *Ubiquitous raw materials* (materials that are found everywhere) and *pure localized raw materials* (materials not needing further processing, but found at only a few locations) require that the industrial plant be located close to its market. For example, soft-drink bottling companies, which essentially convert ubiquitous water into an inexpensive product, are found in every community of moderate size. *Gross localized raw materials* (those found at specific locations but that contain large amounts of impurities that must be disposed of) require that plants be located close to the material site in order to avoid transporting waste material. For example, the copper refiner who processes a highly localized ore that is less than 5 percent pure is strongly attracted to a location near the copper deposit. With the passage of time more and more industries have shifted from using basic raw materials as major inputs to using finished component parts. Such components are actually localized pure raw materials, which are more easily transported than the fully assembled final product. Firms manufacturing such products have a great deal of flexibility in the locational decision.

A major factor in the cost structure and profit margin of a manufacturing firm is the geographic location of its markets. Firms in many industries, such as the automobile industry, have close linkages to related industries, which constitute the sole market for their product. The market may actually consist of a single location, making geographic proximity vital. Often extensive interindustry linkages have evolved that are closely related to a complex system of firms that serve as markets for one another's production. Cities such as Detroit have emerged as centers of specialized production because of the need for geographic proximity among suppliers.

If the manufacturer may be supplying consumer products for a set of warehouses, retail outlets, or households, the market is better viewed as an area. At the regional search level, consideration of the geographic extent of this area can be a crucial location factor, a factor that has too often been neglected; consequently, the costs of distributing products have been underestimated. Such miscalculations can result in overlooking some customers who may be within the economical market range of the industrial plant.

Historically, manufacturing has been greatly affected by transportation linkages and access. Since the beginning of the Industrial Revolution man's ability to overcome the friction of distance has continually improved. Initially, bulky products could be moved only by water and so, ports necessarily developed as important break-in-bulk industrial locations. The advent of the railroad greatly influenced the number of potential sites for manufacturing. The combination of rail and water spurred the development of extensive manufacturing complexes along the East Coast and the Great Lakes. However, as the country switched from railroad to interstate highway freight, new manufacturing cities emerged (table 5.2). For firms that specialize in high-value products, time of delivery is more important than low transportation costs, and many of their transportation needs are met by fast, scheduled air freight. Such firms are likely to be attracted to locations near airports. Also, innovations in containerization and piggybacking, which combine the advantages of different modes of transport and reduce terminal costs, have affected industrial development (Hunker 1974).

Physical proximity to raw materials or markets has become less vital as a factor in the regional search process because a wide variety of intermediate locations may now be considered, allowing savings in production costs and thus balancing the higher transportation costs. At the regional search level the factors that affect production costs are principally geographic differences in the cost of labor; but costs of utilities, energy, taxes, and land can also vary. As with transportation costs, any evaluation of the relative importance of these factors is dependent upon the individual characteristics of the firm.

Labor Factors. Since the payroll of a manufacturing firm may represent more than 30 percent of the value of its shipments, labor factors assume a major position in locational decisions. Labor difficulties are frequently cited as reasons for plant relocation, and the availability of labor is often mentioned as a determining factor in the selection of a new site (Mandell 1975). Nevertheless, the idea that "industry moves to cheap labor" appears to be a gross oversimplification. In addition to cost, labor markets must be evaluated on the basis of their size, quality, mobility, and trainability.

Table 5.2. Volume of Domestic Intercity Freight Traffic by Mode of Transport, 1940–1976 (percentage of total ton-miles)

Year	Railroads	Motor vehicles	Inland waterways	Oil pipelines	Airways
1940	63.2	9.5	18.1	9.1	0.002
1950	57.4	15.8	14.9	11.8	0.029
1960	44.7	21.5	16.6	17.2	0.058
1970	39.8	21.3	16.5	22.3	0.170
1976	36.52	23.31	16.1	23.90	0.182

Source: U.S. Department of Commerce, *Statistical Abstract of the United States,* 1978, p. 639.

Some researchers have maintained that labor costs are probably the most difficult location factor to measure accurately (Smith 1971). Although data are available on the geographic variation in average hourly wage rates for production workers, these figures in isolation are rather meaningless (Hunker 1974). Labor costs in an area are affected by a variety of factors, including the cost of living, level of unionization, skill levels, industry mix, population size, and the location of the manufacturing plant within the area. For example, it is difficult to explain specifically why a production worker in Michigan earns nearly 60 percent more per hour than a blue-collar worker in North Carolina. Michigan is unique in that more than 30 percent of its production workers are in the high-wage transportation equipment industry, nearly 40 percent of its production workers are unionized, and most of its manufacturing is located in metropolitan areas. In North Carolina close to 40 percent of the production workers are employed in the low-pay textile industry. Union membership is the lowest in the nation (less than 8 percent), and much of the industry is located outside metropolitan areas. Research indicates that the settlement-size location of industry within a region may be one of the most significant factors accounting for differences in wages and union membership among states (Moriarty 1977 and 1978). While unionization is increasing in the South to some extent, strong resistance to union involvement still springs from several sources: from industries that have fled areas with labor problems, from communities that wish to preserve their attractiveness to industry, and from the worker himself, who is happy to be working regularly and realizing a better standard of living than he has ever known.

The cost of labor obviously depends also upon supply and demand. Southern labor-draw areas were once the source of abundant supplies of unemployed or underemployed workers who were quickly attracted to steady work even at low wages. However, in some areas of the South, such as the Piedmont Crescent, the work force composition has changed and competition from new industry has decreased the labor pool. To compensate for this scarcity manufacturing has begun to locate in nonmetropolitan areas, which are growing at an even faster rate than the region's urban areas (Till 1973).

An accurate measure of the cost of labor must also include a measure of productivity. For an increasing number of manufacturers the ability to attract highly educated technicians, engineers, and managerial personnel is of paramount importance in their locational decisions. Such labor pools remain concentrated in the major cities of the Northeast. Those industries with large research and development components must either gravitate toward these centers or select regions that are associated with high levels of "residential desirability," which can lure this highly mobile segment of the labor market. If the role of transportation in the regional search process has been superseded by the more complicated role of labor factors for some industries, the task of the industrial developer will become even more important in the future and he will need to be aware of an ever-increasing variety of plant location factors.

Relative Importance of Regional Factors. The relative importance of various location factors at the regional level is often estimated through direct surveys of industrial location decision makers. Although many such studies suffer from poor design, biased formats, or inappropriate respondents, they do provide some indication of the overall importance of the different factors. An evaluation of twenty-three of these studies, including over 17,000 responses from all parts of the country, confirms the growing importance of market access as the most important factor in the search for a region (Ziehr 1975). In twenty of the twenty-three studies, market access was considered to be a primary factor in the decision. Labor was judged to be of primary importance by respondents in sixteen of the studies; materials, in twelve; and transportation, which denotes accessibility to both markets and materials, in seven. Regional differences in taxes were significant in only two studies, while financial inducements were generally considered to be of little or no importance.

A study of 247 new or expanded manufacturers in South Carolina sheds some light on the factors that were deemed important by firms establishing plants in the rapidly growing Southeast (Ziehr 1975). The survey indicated the importance of transportation, labor, and markets (table 5.3). The responses also suggest that other factors, such as water and natural gas supplies, are of increasing importance.

Local Search Process

Once a firm has determined the regional location of its plant, whether it is relocating, expanding, or newly opening, it then embarks on a more localized community and site search. The scale of this search varies considerably. Some companies with specific requirements may evaluate every qualified community in a region covering several states. The search process of other firms may be limited to communities and sites in only a particular part of a state or to sites in a specific community. Since most major cost decisions are made at the regional search level, the promotional efforts of various public and private development organizations can assume a critical role in these local search decisions. Competition among states and among communities within the same state can become fierce. Communities with their own development organizations try to attract

Table   5.3.   Importance of Regional Factors to New or Expanded Manufacturing Firms, 1965–1974

Location factors judged essential by more than 10 percent of respondents	Percentage of responses essential	Percentage of responses important
Highway facilities	48.7	29.6
Room for expansion	37.1	40.8
Extent of unionization	36.7	35.8
Access to regional market	32.5	18.3
Productivity of labor	31.3	40.8
State industrial climate	28.7	34.6
Water supply	28.3	27.9
Railroad	25.0	15.0
Labor costs	22.9	51.2
Skilled labor supply	18.8	34.2
Unskilled labor supply	18.8	34.2
Proximity to materials	15.4	25.0
Local taxes	14.2	44.2
State taxes	14.2	42.9
Construction costs	13.7	42.9
Natural gas supply	13.3	19.6
Public training assistance	13.3	22.9
Residence of owner	11.7	9.2
Tax exemptions	11.2	28.3

Source: Ziehr 1975, p. 50.

the prospective industry to their locality, state agencies try to direct it to depressed areas, and numerous private organizations such as railroads and real estate development firms try to attract it to specific sites that they own. The industrial developer must be aware of the strengths and weaknesses of all the sites that are available in his area when he meets with the industrial prospect.

Critical and Trade-Off Factors. The local search process also involves two decision levels. On the broader level different communities are evaluated on the basis of relative costs and accessibility to markets, material suppliers, services, labor, utilities, transportation facilities, and their general attractiveness as a place to live. Sometimes only one critical factor may determine the selection of a particular community. Critical factors are defined as necessary criteria or conditions that must exist in a community before it can even be considered for the location of a plant facility. Critical factors differ from one industry to another but may include such criteria as the availability of a certain size work force possessing required skills within the site's labor-draw area, or easy access to the interstate highway system or a well-linked airport facility. Other critical factors may be a guaranteed and uninterruptable supply of natural gas, electricity, or pure water to meet present and future needs or proximity to specific vendors, consumers, or intermediate markets. When one factor dominates the community or site selection process, the choice may be greatly constrained by a stringent elimination process. For other firms different factors can be substituted one for another in the site selection decision. Examples of these trade-off factors are the substitution of lower-cost labor, land, utilities, and/or taxes to compensate for higher transportation costs or the added costs of internalizing necessary external economies as firms locate in less accessible areas.

Agglomeration and Deglomeration Factors. Manufacturing has historically been an urban activity. In fact, it is generally assumed that urbanization was the logical outgrowth of the development of the factory system. Many modern cities in the Western world originated as mill towns, which were often little more than industrial slums. Urban areas provided the labor, the transportation system, and the markets for the development of modern industrial complexes. This attraction of manufacturers to urban sites is also related to a collection of external economies that are often labeled "urbanization economies." In one way or another, these economies suggest that it is cheaper to manufacture a product at an urban site. The savings resulted from the provision of urban public services including police and fire protection, utilities (water, sewer, natural gas, and electricity), and educational and recreational facilities. From an economic point of view, a move from a city to a rural location would be feasible only if the increase in costs were more than offset by the reduced costs of labor and land, as well as those that accrue to the firm from internal scale economies.

In addition to the set of urbanization economies that are commonly associated with a metropolitan area, another group of savings accrues to interrelated business firms locating in the same area. These localization economies are associated with the specialized services and interindustry linkages that develop in the area to support a particular industry. The proximity of specialized services and related industries helps not only to reduce transportation and communication costs but also to increase the speed of supply, availability, dependability, and quality of materials and services.

Perhaps the major decision to be made at the local level is whether to internalize a significant proportion of the firm's cost structure. If a firm is large enough to take full advantage of internal scale economies, it may be able to locate without concern for services provided by other firms. Therefore, metropolitan sites would be unnecessary, and the firm could operate at rural sites that offer extensive tracts of inexpensive land within commuting distance of a sufficient labor pool. While it is obvious that rural sites would reduce some costs, such as the cost of property and taxes, selection of a rural site offers other advantages that are not so readily apparent. For example, a survey of rural manufacturers in Nebraska suggests that nonmetropolitan sites also provide access to a quality labor force that is of "better value" than that available in more populous communities. Measures relating to the quality of life and general accessibility were also judged favorable (Lonsdale, Kinworthy, and Doering 1976). It has been suggested that part of industry's positive attitude toward labor in outlying sites springs from the recognition that the wider dispersion of workers tends to thwart discontentment and sympathetic views toward labor organizers.

In addition to differences in the accessibility of sites because of their relative location within a community, other factors also vary among sites. Perhaps the most crucial are those of site size and site cost. Initially, products were manufactured in crowded, multiple-story plants. Now manufacturing is a major space consumer, often occupying large tracts of land. In many metropolitan areas, sites of sufficient size can be found only in suburban areas. Unfortunately, the complex patterns of property ownership that dominate central cities make industrial rehabilitation there particularly difficult.

A basic assumption has been that property values in an urban area declined as distances from the city's center increased. However, the intraurban expressway systems of the 1960s and 1970s have negated this pattern of land value. Now suburban sites, especially at key expressway interchanges, are so highly prized that property cost curves appear to be reversing themselves. For example, a firm in Boston paid $4.75 per square foot for a prestigious suburban site when it could have purchased similar central city space for about a quarter of that amount (Muller 1976). Planned industrial parks further emphasize the shift of manufacturing to the suburbs. Such parks not only provide sites that are equipped with the necessary utilities and transportation linkages, but they also help to insure some degree of land use compatibility. The suitability of these parks for even the small manufacturer accentuates the challenge to central cities to provide adequate sites for manufacturing.

This situation is also complicated by taxation and zoning policies. It is typically assumed that taxes are higher in the city than outside. This assumption may be one of the most incorrect beliefs that industrial location decision makers have. All other things being equal, a firm may reduce its costs slightly by locating at a suburban site, but this saving may be more than offset by hidden costs such as users fees for garbage collection, sewage treatment, security personnel, and the like. Thus, although taxes may often be mentioned in the choice between a central city and suburban site, they rarely constitute a significant cost factor (Hunker 1974). The effect of zoning, on the other hand, may have considerable impact. Although the use of land in many rural and suburban locations is still unregulated, most central cities have established zoning ordinances that exclude the industry that they so desperately need. Finally, noneconomic or personal factors such as the quality of life, psychic income, and area-image perception can enter into the site selection process if there is little economic difference among alternative communities and their sites.

The tension between urbanization and localization forces pulling for agglomeration and nonmetropolitan forces vying for deglomeration has caused the local search process to become extremely confusing. Since World War II deglomeration forces have been winning the struggle. In fact, it could be argued that many urban areas have reached a stage at which their diseconomies have offset some of their formerly important economies.

Relative Importance of Local Factors. The survey of South Carolina manufacturers mentioned earlier reveals the local search factors most important to their location decisions (table 5.4). Although the factors are somewhat similar to those in the regional search process, a few important differences should be noted. Four of the first five factors listed are specific site features—highway and rail facilities, water supply, and room for expansion. The list suggests that while close to 40 percent of the respondents considered local tax differences to be important, only 11.5 percent believed that they were essential. Interestingly, the same percentage judged a noneconomic factor, residence of the owner, to be just as essential. The survey tends to confirm the relative importance of the factors discussed above and suggests that space for industrial growth is a crucial factor for future development. A community that expects to attract new industry must make a serious effort to prepare adequate tracts of land with good access to highways and rail facilities, as well as to water. In the highly competitive business of industrial development the economic well-being of a community may be entwined with the availability of accessible sites for manufacturing.

Industrial Location Patterns and Trends

The previous discussion outlined the influence of certain location factors and to some extent has shown the variation in the relative importance of

Table 5.4. Importance of Local Factors to New or Expanded Manufacturing Firms, 1965–1974

Site factors judged essential by more than 10 percent of respondents	Percentage of responses essential	Percentage of responses important
Highway facilities	50.6	31.3
Room for expansion	35.8	44.0
Extent of unionization	32.9	33.7
Water supply	30.5	23.5
Railroad facilities	27.2	14.0
Productivity of labor	26.3	44.0
Access to regional market	23.9	20.6
Labor costs	22.2	45.7
Community industrial climate	20.6	41.6
Unskilled labor supply	19.8	34.2
Skilled labor supply	19.3	29.2
Access to local market	17.7	14.8
Proximity to materials	16.0	25.1
Public training assistance	13.6	20.2
Natural gas supply	13.2	19.8
Construction costs	12.3	35.4
Local taxes	11.5	39.9
Residence of owner	11.5	10.3
State taxes	10.3	35.0

Source: Ziehr 1975, p. 53.

these factors over time. The shifts in importance of the location factors are, however, difficult to measure because industry's response to the changing factors is slow to materialize. A time lag frequently occurs between the recognized need for a change in location and the actual change. Often the desired changes never take place because of the powerful stabilizing influence of industrial inertia, especially in capital-intensive industries. An examination of the locational shifts in the distribution of manufacturing offers an indirect method of appraising these changing location factors, although any causal relationships between the altered patterns and the changing factors can only be implied.

Interregional Location Trends

The present distribution of manufacturing employment in the United States continues to reflect the tremendous advantages that have made the

Northeastern Manufacturing Belt one of the great manufacturing regions of the world. However, an examination of long-term trends reveals that the dominance of this region is on the wane (fig. 5.1 and table 5.5). Although 54 percent of the nation's manufacturing employment was still located in the Manufacturing Belt in 1972 (the Middle Atlantic, East North Central, and New England census divisions), this figure represents a tremendous decline since the turn of the century when the same region accommodated 79 percent of the manufacturing labor force.

In order to put this decline into its proper perspective the manufacturing employment changes should be compared with population changes (fig. 5.2). Several trends are readily apparent when the data are analyzed in this manner. The relative decline of manufacturing employment in New England and the Middle Atlantic states has been considerably greater than the relative decline in their population, a reflection of the fact that the oldest manufacturing regions of the nation have advanced to a higher level of economic development in which their economic bases are more diversified and greater emphasis is placed on tertiary employment. The relative growth of manufacturing in the South and West reflects a shift from primary to secondary employment as these areas move into the economic mainstream of the country (Naylor and Clotfelter 1975). Per-

Table 5.5. Percentage of United States Manufacturing Employment by Census Divisions, 1899, 1967, and 1972

Census division[a]	1899	1967	1972
Middle Atlantic (MA)	35.7	22.6	20.7
East North Central (ENC)	24.3	26.7	25.9
New England (NE)	18.5	8.1	7.2
South Atlantic (SA)	10.0	13.0	14.4
West North Central (WNC)	6.1	6.2	6.3
East South Central (ESC)	3.9	5.7	6.6
West South Central (WSC)	2.5	5.6	6.5
Mountain (MT)	1.0	1.6	2.0
Pacific (PAC)	2.8	10.6	10.4

Source: U.S. Bureau of the Census, *1972 Census of Manufactures, General and Comparative Statistics*, vol. 1, pp. 47–57, table 7.
[a] Middle Atlantic includes N.Y., N.J., Pa.; East North Central includes Ohio, Ind., Ill., Mich., Wis.; New England includes Maine, N.H., Vt., Mass., R.I., Conn.; South Atlantic includes Del., Md., D.C., Va., W.Va., N.C., S.C., Ga., Fla.; West North Central includes Minn., Iowa, Mo., N.Dak., S.Dak., Nebr., Kans.; East South Central includes Ky., Tenn., Ala., Miss.; West South Central includes Ark., La., Okla., Tex.; Mountain includes Mont., Idaho, Wyo., Colo., N.M., Ariz., Utah, Nev.; Pacific includes Wash., Oreg., Calif., Alaska, Hawaii.

Figure   5.1 United States Manufacturing Labor Force per Square Mile, 1870, 1920, and 1970

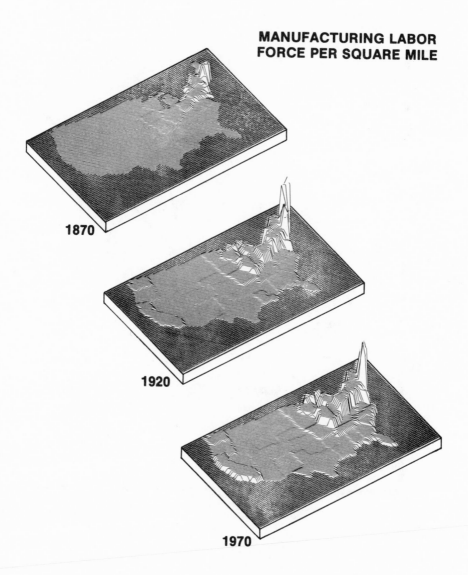

**MANUFACTURING LABOR
FORCE PER SQUARE MILE**

1870

1920

1970

Figure 5.2 Percentage Change in Population and Manufacturing Employment by Region, 1900–1970

Source: U.S. Bureau of the Census, *Census of Population: Characteristics*, 1900, 1910, 1920, 1930, 1940, 1950, 1960, and 1970.

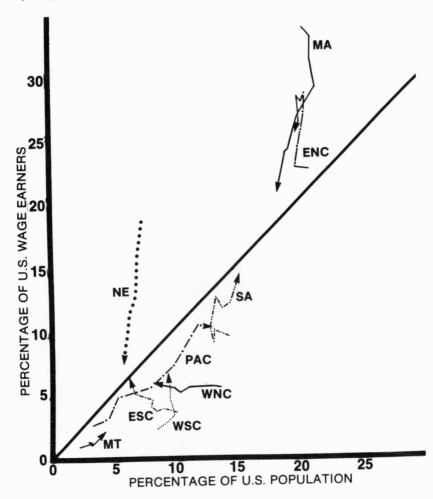

Figure 5.3 Change in Manufacturing Employment by State, 1967–1972

Source: U.S. Bureau of the Census, *Census of Manufactures, 1972*, vol. I, pp. 26–29.

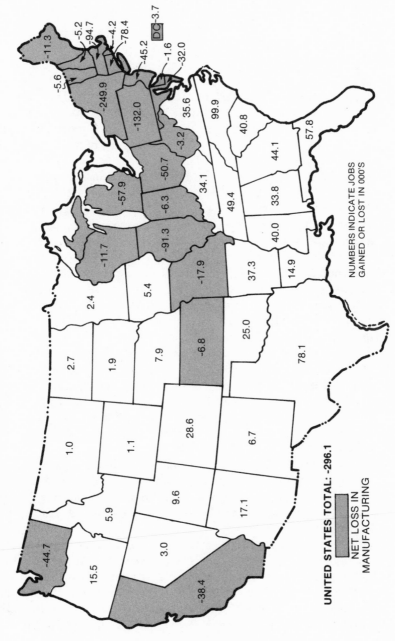

UNITED STATES TOTAL: -296.1

NET LOSS IN
MANUFACTURING

NUMBERS INDICATE JOBS
GAINED OR LOST IN 000'S

haps the most significant trend revealed by this analysis is the movement toward equalization of manufacturing employment and population within every region of the country, which demonstrates that manufacturing employment is becoming increasingly market-oriented. Since substantial markets now exist throughout the country, regional dominance may disappear in the future (Moriarty 1975 and 1976).

A more detailed analysis of employment changes on a state-by-state basis for 1967 to 1972 further dramatizes the nature of the shifts (fig. 5.3). First of all, manufacturing employment in the United States declined by close to 300,000 workers during the period and represented only about 25 percent of the total labor force. The geographic variations in the employment shifts are also interesting. Every state in a continuous belt stretching from Maine to Maryland on the East Coast west to Kansas witnessed an absolute decline in the number of manufacturing workers. While the decline in some of these northern states amounted to only a few thousand workers, New York alone lost almost 250,000 manufacturing jobs. The losses in several other states exceeded 50,000. Washington and California were the only states outside this northern belt to experience similar declines in manufacturing workers. The consistent increase in manufacturing employment throughout the South, however, is almost as evident as the declines in the North.

The preceding information should not be viewed as evidence that manufacturing plants are moving from the North to the South. More than half the manufacturing employment losses in the Northeast between 1970 and 1972 occurred because existing firms went out of business. Almost another half resulted when existing firms reduced the sizes of their work forces. Only 2 percent of the lost jobs could be attributed to the out-migration of firms from the region (Allaman and Birch 1975). In the South (South Atlantic, East South Central, and West South Central regions) 64 percent of the new manufacturing jobs resulted from the expansion of existing plants, one-third from completely new firms or branch plants starting up in the region, and only 1.2 percent from the in-migration of firms that had shut down plants elsewhere. It is clear that the industrial relocation process is very complex; to describe it merely as firms closing plants in one place and opening new ones in other areas is inadequate.

A more detailed analysis of each region's manufacturing employment location-quotient changes from 1958 to 1972 reveals some of the main factors contributing to the geographic redistribution of industry.[2] The location quotients were calculated for each of the twenty major industries in relation to each region's total manufacturing labor force (U.S. Bureau of the Census 1958 and 1972). Based upon the similarity of the location-quotient changes, the industries can be classified into four groups, and each group can be associated with different location criteria.

The first group consists of those industries with fairly stable location quotients (near 1.0 in each region) (fig. 5.4). These industries are present within each region in nearly the same proportion as total manufacturing employment and consequently are neither concentrated nor underrepresented. Included here are the paper products industry; printing; stone, clay, and glass products; and fabricated metal products. The nearly equal distribution of these industries throughout the nine regions reveals that market orientation is their most important locational criterion. New and existing industries in this group as a whole can be expected to grow in regions where population and business are expanding, while stagnating regions cannot expect much in the way of additional new employment from them. The North, for the most part, exhibits fairly small location-quotient shifts that registered industry declines. Most of the other regions are more stable, with increases that offset declines.

The second group of industries encompasses those that had been fairly concentrated in some regions and underrepresented in others, but that in recent years have become more equally distributed in proportion to the region's total manufacturing labor force (fig. 5.5). Most regions exhibit location-quotient shifts toward 1.0 for these industries, which can be interpreted as a trend toward greater market orientation on the part of some industries in the group or a more footloose position on the part of others. Included in this group are food products, chemicals, rubber and plastic products, machinery, electrical machinery, and transportation equipment, all of which (with the exception of food products) have above-average growth rates when cyclically adjusted (Bureau of Economic Analysis 1977). Regions that are deficient in these industries can expect some additional expansion in the future, and those in which the industries are presently concentrated can expect contraction in their proportion of total manufacturing employment. All regions in the country exhibit this kind of give-and-take. New England, for example, was deficient in all except electrical machinery and rubber and plastic products, yet grew in all deficient industries and declined in the one most concentrated there.

The third group of industries includes those that, because of comparative advantages, traditionally have concentrated in certain regions of the country and continue to do so (fig. 5.6). Each of these industries—tobacco products, textiles, lumber, petroleum and coal products, and leather goods—has a close orientation to a specific location factor and is concentrated in one region where the location quotient is greater than 3.0. Consequently, most other regions are deficient in their share of these indus-

Figure   5.4 Location Quotients for Stable Market-Oriented Industries by Region, 1958–1972

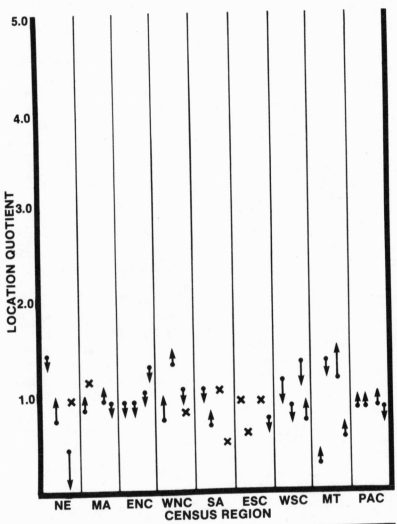

paper and allied products, printing and publishing, stone, clay and glass products, and fabricated metals products (from left to right in each region)

Figure   5.5   Location   Quotients   for   New   Market-Oriented   and   Footloose   Industries by Region, 1958–1972

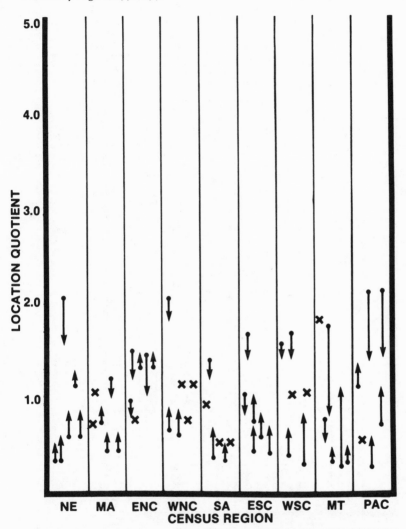

food and kindred products, chemicals and allied products, rubber and plastic products, nonelectrical machinery, electrical machinery, and transportation equipment (from left to right in each region)

Figure 5.6 Location Quotients for Material-Oriented Industries by Region, 1958–1972

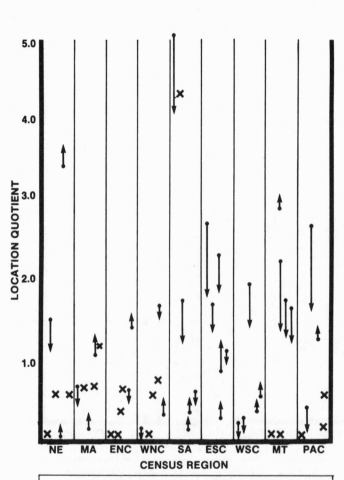

tobacco products, textile mill products, lumber and wood products, petroleum and coal products, leather and leather products, and primary metals products (from left to right in each region)

tries and can be expected to remain so in the future. Important factors influencing the location of the industries are raw materials sources (lumber, petroleum, and coal), low-cost experienced labor (leather), or both (tobacco and textiles). Employment growth in many of the group's industries is small or declining because of either increased automation (tobacco and petroleum) or increased competition from imports (textiles, leather products, and primary metals). The North is deficient in all the industries except for leather products in New England, but import competition (49 percent of all shoes in 1977, for example) has caused absolute employment declines in this industry throughout the country. Three of the industries exhibit major concentrations in the South. Some of these have declined in relative importance as manufacturing employment has expanded and diversified within the region. In the North where many of the industries are underrepresented, with the exception of the leather industry, employment trends have remained fairly stable throughout the period. The primary metals industry is also included in this group because of its orientation to raw materials and fuel or energy resources. With the exception of a decline in the Mountain region, other regions have experienced small locational shifts because of the availability of an assortment of metal ores in some regions but not others and the likelihood that metal-ore processing will remain close to the sources. It is unlikely that any region will undergo substantial shifts in employment in this industry in the near future, especially the North, unless competition from imports changes.

The industries in the fourth group—apparel, furniture, instruments, and miscellaneous products including ordinance—are those that were more concentrated in certain regions in the past but recently have begun to concentrate in other regions (fig. 5.7). Location quotients decline from about 2.0 in one region and increase to 2.0 in another. Labor-intensive apparel and furniture manufacturing exhibit substantial declines in the high-wage North, with equivalent increases in the low-wage South. Instruments and miscellaneous products are more concentrated overall in the North than other regions, but the formerly deficient South is also increasing its share of employment in these industries. The Pacific and Mountain regions experienced substantial gains in instrument manufacturing but fell from their prominent positions in miscellaneous and ordinance manufacturing. The stagnating North has increased its share of employment in the industries requiring an assortment of different types of highly skilled labor and accessible interindustry linkages, and the developing South has increased its share in industries whose production methods or products have become standardized enough to employ unskilled or semiskilled workers.

Figure   5.7 Location Quotients for Labor-Oriented Industries by Region, 1958–
1972

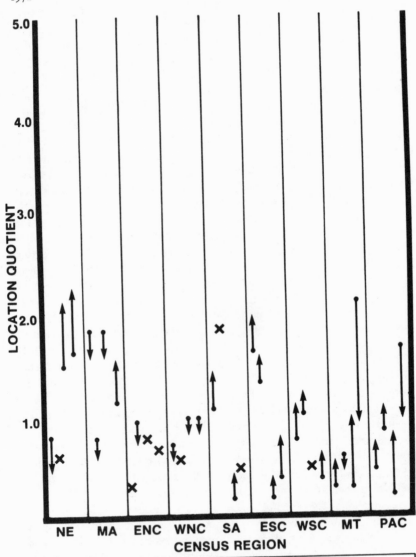

Apparel and related products, furniture and fixtures, instruments and related products, and miscellaneous products (from left to right in each region)

A projection of these shifts into the future shows that the gains in manufacturing employment in the stagnating northern regions will be more than balanced by the losses, so that manufacturing's share of the total work force there will continue to decline. In the developing southern and Pacific regions industry gains will more than compensate for losses, so that manufacturing's share of total employment will continue to grow.

The present interregional locational patterns reflect the response of industrial site selectors to geographic variations in location factors. Although the Southeast is growing and diversifying, it is still dominated by low-wage, nondurable-goods, labor-intensive industries. Conversely, the industry remaining in the manufacturing belt relies on higher-wage, durable-goods, capital-intensive manufacturing. As the nation has matured the industrial mix of the country as a whole has shifted. Recently, foreign competition has been affecting the growth of many labor-intensive industries, and this competition will become more significant as worldwide economic development progresses. Each region of the country evidences its own development cycle. As New England, the original manufacturing region, has matured it has lost much of its former importance in the realm of manufacturing. With a poor physical resource base, New England has had to rely on its human resources. As a result, highly skilled research-and-development-oriented industries have been able to replace other industries. Other parts of the manufacturing belt have been forced to make adjustments to their declining raw materials base, transport advantages, and markets. Parts of the Southeast have been able to advance beyond a reliance on low-wage, labor-intensive industries, illustrated by the decline of some of their lowest-paying industry. The textile industry has been struggling to save its labor from the threat of unionization, at the same time facing competition from new, higher-wage industries such as electronics, machinery, and rubber products. The Gulf Coast states have witnessed a boom based on their energy supplies, and the West continues to mature and diversify by attracting high-growth, footloose industries that can recruit a mobile labor force.

Intraregional Location Trends

Not only has manufacturing dispersed among regions of the country, but it has done so within most regions as well. In 1929, 78 percent of the nation's industry, as measured by value added by manufacturing, was located in metropolitan areas, primarily in the North's manufacturing belt (Zelinski 1962). Of the total, 54 percent was located in the central cities of these areas. At that time manufacturing was regarded as a metropolitan central-city phenomenon. By 1954, twenty-five years later, metropolitan areas accounted for nearly the same proportion (76 percent) of manufacturing's value added, but only 42 percent was located in central cities. Metropolitan areas surrounding central cities had increased their share of manufacturing from 24 percent of the total to 34 percent, while nonmetropolitan areas increased their share slightly by 2 percent to account for 24 percent of the total value added. This trend toward decentralization has been going on ever since (Nelson and Patrick 1975).

The average percentage of the total labor force residing in nonmetropolitan areas and employed in manufacturing has also been increasing for some time—from an average of 13.7 percent in 1950 to 20.6 percent in 1970 (table 5.6, Heaton and Fuguitt 1978). This growth has taken place at the same time that employment has been rising faster in the tertiary sector of the economy and declining in the primary sector. In 1970, nonmetropolitan urban and rural counties adjacent to metropolitan areas had higher proportions of their working residents employed in manufacturing (25.1 percent and 21.4 percent, respectively) than did nonadjacent urban and rural counties (19.8 percent and 14.8 percent). Many of the workers residing in nonmetropolitan counties, of course, commuted to jobs in metropolitan areas, since the majority of those who recently migrated from urban to rural areas relocated in counties adjacent to or within a thirty-mile radius of a Standard Metropolitan Statistical Area (SMSA) (Regional Economic Analysis Division 1976). The proportion of the labor force residing in nonmetropolitan areas employed in higher-wage industry nearly doubled between 1950 and 1970 (from 5.9 percent to 11.5 percent), while the proportion of low-wage manufacturing workers increased only slightly (from 7.9 percent to 9.1 percent). Also during the period, the number of high-wage manufacturing workers residing in nonmetropolitan areas surpassed the number of low-wage manufacturing workers. This growth, in part, reflects the fact that higher-wage earners are better able to pay commuting expenses between their residences in nonmetropolitan areas and jobs in metropolitan ones. Nonetheless, average total employment increased 13 percent in rural areas, compared to only 7 percent in metropolitan areas between 1970 and 1975 (Ledebur 1977). Much of the rural increase in the seventies, however, has been attributed to the growth of retirement and recreation activities (McCarthy and Morrison 1977).

Nonmetropolitan areas in the sunbelt had a larger proportion of their labor force employed in manufacturing (24.8 percent) by 1970 than did similar areas in the frostbelt (17 percent). The proportion of low-wage manufacturing workers residing in nonmetropolitan areas of the frostbelt throughout the fifties and sixties was relatively small and remained

Table 5.6. Average Percentage of Labor Force in Nonmetropolitan Areas Employed in Manufacturing, 1950–1970

	Total United States	Adjacent to SMSA		Nonadjacent to SMSA		Region	
		Urban	Rural	Urban	Rural	Frostbelt	Sunbelt
Total mfg. employment							
1950	13.7	20.1	13.4	14.2	9.1	13.1	14.6
1960	17.3	22.8	17.4	17.1	12.5	15.4	19.5
1970	20.6	25.1	21.4	19.8	14.8	17.0	24.8
Low-wage mfg. employment[a]							
1950	7.9	8.9	8.6	8.0	6.7	5.5	10.6
1960	9.1	9.4	10.1	9.1	8.3	5.9	12.7
1970	9.1	9.5	10.4	9.0	8.1	5.3	13.7
High-wage mfg. employment							
1950	5.9	11.2	4.8	6.2	2.4	7.6	4.0
1960	8.2	13.4	7.3	8.0	4.2	9.5	6.8
1970	11.5	15.6	11.0	10.8	6.7	11.7	11.1
Net population migration							
1950–1960	—1.4	—0.4	—1.2	—1.3	—2.1	—1.1	—1.7
1960–1970	—0.7	—0.2	—0.4	—0.8	—1.1	—0.7	—0.7
1970–1975	0.5	0.6	1.0	0.3	0.5	0.6	0.5
Number of counties							
1950	2792	563	213	1129	887	1495	1297
1960	2656	684	257	982	733	1416	1240
1970	2440	806	283	771	580	1337	1103

Source: Compiled from Heaton and Fuguitt 1978.

[a] Low-wage industries are food processing, textiles, apparel, lumber, and furniture.

almost stable at about 5.5 percent. The low-wage proportion in the sunbelt was twice as large and increased slightly from 10.6 to 13.7 percent. More interesting was the sizable increment in the proportion of high-wage manufacturing workers residing in southern nonmetropolitan areas; the proportion nearly tripled, from 4.0 to 11.1 percent of the labor force.

Even within the metropolitan area the geographic distribution of manufacturing activity reflects an attraction to different location factors. An investigation of the relationship between the distance that firms in an industry group located from the city center and four characteristics of industrial plants (employment size, wage rate, size of female labor force, and employee work space) offers some evidence of this difference (table 5.7; Cowen 1971). Industries located close to the city center (leather, apparel, and printing) frequently employ high percentages of female labor in multiple-story, crowded facilities and pay low wages. Industries located in suburban areas (electrical and non electrical machinery, transportation equipment, and furniture) tend to employ high percentages of male labor in single-story, spacious facilities and pay high wages. Within the metropolitan area, wages increase as distance from the city center increases, but the percentage of females in the manufacturing work force and the number of employees per work area decrease (table 5.8). No relationship existed between the size of the firm and its distance from the city center. Large plants were just as likely to be located close to the city center as in the suburbs, for many plants were established years ago at a time when access to rail facilities and the labor market close to the city's center were important location factors. Although the reliance on rail transportation has declined and labor has become more mobile, these older firms have too much capital invested in existing facilities to abandon them. Small plants were just as likely to be found in the central city as in the suburbs. However, many small plants near the city center were relatively new, supporting the idea that the city acts as an incubator for firms just beginning operation because it provides high accessibility to a supply

Table 5.8. Correlation Analysis of Metropolitan Industrial Plant Characteristics, Columbus, Ohio, 1968

	Median Distance of Firm from City Center	Median Number of Employees per Firm	Average Hourly Wage Rate	Percentage of Female Labor
Median number of employees per firm	.095			
Average hourly wage rate	.536*	.016		
Percentage of female labor	—.752*	.052	—.627*	
Average number of employees per acre per firm	—.679*	—.118	—.564	.773*

Source: Cowen 1971, p. 37.
* Significant at the 95% level of confidence.

Table 5.7. Characteristics of Metropolitan Industrial Plants, Columbus, Ohio, 1968

Industrial group	Median distance from city center (in miles)	Median number of employees per firm	Average hourly wage rate	Percentage of female labor	Average number of employees per acre
Food	2.35	16.0	$3.04	23	44
Apparel	1.50	8.0	2.04	61	182
Lumber	2.55	19.0	2.31	12	20
Furniture	2.75	7.0	2.82	22	28
Paper	2.48	50.0	2.93	37	33
Printing	1.68	7.0	3.40	35	51
Chemicals	2.15	9.0	3.37	18	13
Petroleum, rubber, and plastics	2.53	19.0	3.48	28	21
Leather	1.02	20.0	2.13	61	94
Stone, clay, and glass	2.37	14.0	3.01	28	15
Primary metals	2.38	27.5	3.56	6	37
Fabricated metal products	2.44	15.0	3.33	20	31
Non-electrical machinery	2.73	10.0	3.38	11	34
Electrical machinery	3.02	15.0	3.21	29	27
Transportation equipment	2.70	15.0	3.70	14	24
Scientific instruments	2.14	18.0	2.64	29	30
Miscellaneous products	2.34	9.0	2.64	19	9

Source: Cowen 1971, p. 36.

of labor having a variety of skills, to inexpensive small sites (essentially loft space), to a large number of business and public services, and to transportation linkages (Struyk and James 1975).

Although the present industrial makeup of the central city may to some extent be a legacy of the past, suburban industrial development is a different matter. One method of evaluating the changing character of manufacturing firms within an urban area is to examine the locational patterns of industrial "births" and "deaths." The distribution of manufacturing deaths implies that the central city is an unhealthy location. The concentration of plants that went out of business in the central city is related to both the seedbed function of the core area and the common ills often attributed to the nation's large metropolitan centers. Although the predominant pattern of births is one of dispersal, the central city showed a greater number than might be expected. Despite this finding, the net result of this demographic process was the greater suburbanization of industry, which has important implications for public policy. The increasing differences between the nation's cities and suburbs have created real discrepancies between the location of jobs and low-income residences. As one authority warns, "A population policy that does not seek to eliminate the growing spatial mismatch between residences and work places will prevent millions of low-income and minority-group workers in central cities from entering the mainstream of American economic and social life" (Gold 1972, p. 482).

The purpose of this chapter has been to introduce some basic features of the industrial location search process. The information presented has attempted to convey the impression that the selection of a site for manufacturing is a complex process interwoven with conflicting goals, biases, compromises, and uncertainty. The patterns that emerge from these decisions reflect a conscious effort on the part of the entrepreneurs to make rational choices. Although the relative importance of some factors may have changed, firms still attempt to make decisions that will enable them to realize satisfactory profits or minimize their costs.

The arguments presented in the chapter suggest that the traditional importance of raw materials and transportation costs is waning, while factors of labor and quality of life are becoming more significant. The net effect of these changes has been a distinct shift of manufacturing activity out of the Northeast and outward from the central cities. In a number of instances the long-term effects of these trends may be devastating. If present trends continue, the country's economic landscape may undergo an extensive reshaping.

Two changing factors may profoundly affect the future distribution of manufacturing activities. The first is the availability of energy supplies. If the typical American factory worker cannot depend on the automobile for his journey to work and if the American manufacturer is forced to revert to the use of the railroad to move his products, locational factors favoring industrial concentration could emerge once again. The second factor concerns the development of organized labor. Much of the industrial growth in the sunbelt has been spurred by labor disputes in the North. Thus, the abolition of right-to-work laws in the South and West could have considerable impact on future industrial decisions.

The industrial developer must be aware that many communities are adopting no-growth policies and are beginning to question the "bigger is better" philosophy. The role of the industrial developer in a region of declining manufacturing employment and confusing goals will involve the careful analysis of community advantages and barriers to specific types of industry, the elimination of real and imagined barriers to local industrial and economic development, the preparation of the community and its leaders to promote the local area to potential industrial prospects, and the development of programs and policies to assist existing industries.

Notes

1. For many small-scale enterprises the locational decision process is a relatively simple one. In most instances, the decision is necessary when the entrepreneur decides to go into business or when external forces such as traffic congestion, high crime rates, overcrowding, condemnation, or rezoning cause an extreme level of stress at an existing industrial site. The manufacturer is often closely attached to an area because of knowledge of local demands, family ties, or simply a desire to minimize uncertainty, while maintaining the present labor force; also, it may be that only local capital may be available. Usually, the industrialist makes his own locational decision, thereby greatly limiting the number of factors evaluated. Because of the financial restrictions associated with a small-scale operation, this search is probably restricted to existing structures that are available at the time of the decision.

2. Location quotients are used to measure the concentration of employment in a particular industry in a region compared to its concentration in the nation as a whole. A location quotient of 1.0 indicates that the individual industry is neither concentrated nor underrepresented in a region. Values close to 1.0 are characteristic of market-oriented industries, although for areas with a large proportion of the country's total manufacturing activity such a value could represent a relative concentration. While values greater than 1.0 suggest a definite concentration of the

industry in a particular region, values approaching zero indicate an underrepresentation within a region. If location quotients were calculated for each state, several would be considerably higher than for all states combined within a region, as shown in the figures. Also, several states would have lower location quotients than shown for the region because as the geographic area becomes larger concentrations and deficiencies are more likely to equalize.

Chapter 6
The Industrial Site Selection Process

Theoretical models of the industrial location decision-making process have often been criticized as being unrealistic in describing the method by which industrial location seekers select a particular plant site from among alternative opportunities (Yaseen 1956; Smith 1971; Harris and Hopkins 1972; Wheat 1973). Much of the criticism is valid if plant location decisions are made by private industrialists whose main objective is to operate as efficiently as possible in a known or convenient location rather than in an unknown or undesired location, even though the profit margin may be higher at the latter. The criticism is also valid if industrialists are induced to locate in specific areas by national or regional governments interested in spreading social benefits more equitably to backward, underprivileged, or problem areas, or for purposes of national security. The criticism is not as valid for private and corporate industrialists whose motive is to operate as efficiently as possible in a competitive market so as to obtain a satisfactory profit return on investments.

This chapter describes the site selection process by such a corporate industrialist, the Kelly Springfield Tire Company, a wholly owned subsidiary of the Goodyear Tire Corporation.[1] The plant location team began its site search in November 1968 (fig. 6.1).[2] Four months later, in February 1969, the team made its decision, which was announced in March. Ground was broken the following month (April), and the first tire was produced before the end of the calendar year (December). In March 1970, a plant expansion that tripled the size of the original plant was announced, and by June 1971, the building was erected. All equipment was installed by June 1972. In November 1972, another expansion was announced and the program completed by December 1973.

Figure 6.1 Site Selection, Construction, and Expansion Time Schedule

Source: Site selection team.

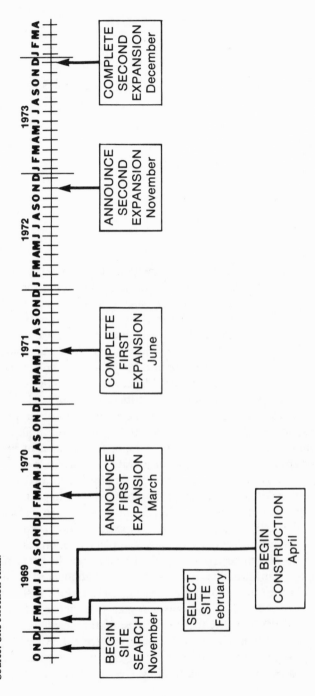

The site selection process typically includes other factors besides the search for a plant location. For the new Kelly plant an analysis was first made of the geographic distribution of the firm's markets and present production capacity in order to establish its regional location. On the basis of the market analysis the potential plant size was established, including requirements for machinery, materials, floor space, utilities, and personnel. With information on the regional location of the new plant and its labor requirements, an analysis of several labor supply areas that would be able to meet the specific requirements was made to determine a number of alternative qualifying communities. Next, preliminary and comprehensive analyses of each community's localization economies (transportation facilities, industrial mix, and labor productivity), urbanization economies (utilities and industrial training facilities), and living conditions (housing, education, medical, recreation, and shopping facilities) narrowed down the number of competing communities. Finally, the ability of available sites to meet the physical plant requirements in each remaining community was evaluated before choosing the plant location.

Geographic Distribution of Markets and Production

At the beginning of the site search Kelly Springfield had nine tire distribution centers located throughout the United States. The selection team anticipated that the new plant would supply tires to the distribution centers in the same proportion as the respective share that each center contributed to the firm's total sales. The West Coast and central United States market demand, however, could be economically supplied from the low-cost Tyler, Texas, plant, leaving the demand in the eastern portion of the country to be supplied by the new plant. The market analysis revealed that 72 percent of the firm's automobile tires were sold through the five eastern centers (fig. 6.2), as were 70 percent of its truck tires (fig. 6.3). Since the locational distribution of truck tire sales was similar to that of automobile tires, the future production of truck tires at the new plant would be geographically compatible with a location selected on the basis of the location of the automobile tire market alone.

At the same time, the firm had three production plants located in Freeport, Illinois, Cumberland, Maryland, and Tyler, Texas (fig. 6.4). The Illinois and Maryland plants produced 58 percent of the total automobile tires manufactured by the firm, as compared to its eastern United States market demand of 72 percent. The 14 percent shortage was made up by the Texas plant. Given the production capacity of the existing three plants and the projected 1973 market demand, the new plant would have to supply 30 percent of the projected demand. The Illinois and Maryland

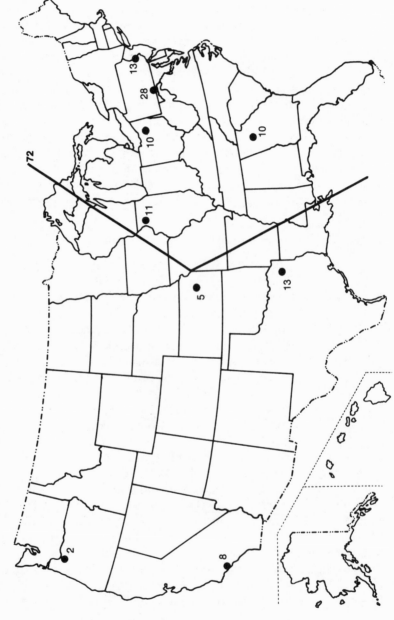

Figure 6.2 Locations and Percentage of Automobile Tire Production Marketed from Distribution Centers

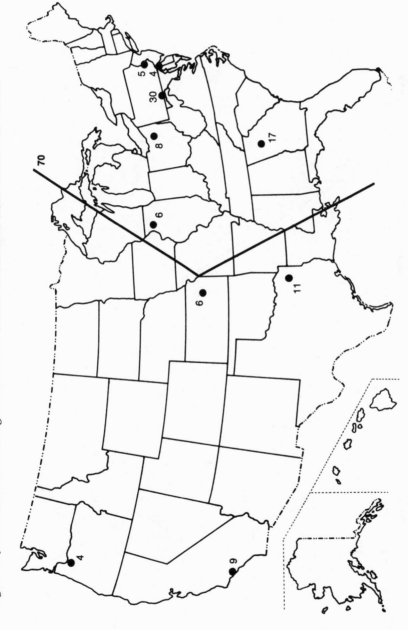

Figure 6.3 Locations and Percentage of Truck Tire Production Marketed from Distribution Centers

Figure 6.4 Percentage of Existing and Expected Tire Production Capacity from Manufacturing Plants

$\frac{58}{71}$

$\frac{25}{18}$

$\frac{0}{30}$

$\frac{33}{23}$

$\frac{42}{29}$

1968 CAPACITY
1970 CAPACITY

plants could supply 41 percent of this demand, so that the three together would supply 71 percent—almost matching the eastern market demand of 72 percent. Hence, the geographic analysis of market demand and production capacity demonstrated that the new plant should be located in the eastern part of the country.

Using the 1973 projected market demand of the five eastern distribution centers that needed to be supplied by the new plant, a preliminary freight cost study was made for over twenty communities. The study revealed that Memphis, Tennessee, was the least-cost transportation location, with a total annual cost of $1,877,000—$643,000 to assemble raw materials and $1,234,000 to distribute the finished product (table 6.1). Of the twenty other communities, Fayetteville, North Carolina, had the greatest disadvantage, with a total annual cost of $2,243,000, which included a large expense for raw material freight ($875,000). At the outset of production carbon black, which comprises approximately 75 percent of the weight of the finished tire, had to be shipped to the new plant from the Texas-Louisiana area. The total freight cost of $3,975,000 for Los Angeles, California, illustrates how uneconomical it would be for a West Coast plant to supply the eastern market.

Plant Size Requirements

In designing a tire plant, the optimum size that efficiently uses the minimum basic machinery that has to be installed needs to accommodate the production of 12,500 tires per day. The projected 1973 eastern market-demand shortage to be supplied by the new plant was estimated at 26,000 automobile tires per day in addition to the demand shortage for truck tires. The experience of the parent company (Goodyear) indicated that an ultimate production of up to 50,000 tires per day would make the best use of internal scale economies. These figures made it clear that the new plant would be required to expand rapidly and that its projected growth had to be a factor in the search for both a community and a site location (table 6.2).

Table   6.1. Preliminary Freight Costs (dollars per year)

City	Raw material	Finished product	Total	Excess over Memphis
Memphis, Tenn.	643,000	1,234,000	1,877,000	0
Fayetteville, N.C.	875,000	1,368,000	2,243,000	366,000
Los Angeles, Calif.	1,445,000	2,530,000	3,975,000	2,098,000

Source: Site selection team.

Table 6.2. Potential Plant Size

Requirements	1970	1973	Ultimate
Production potential			
Passenger tires/day	12,500	26,000	50,000
Truck tires/day		Plant capacity potential	
Physical plant			
Floor space area			
(in square feet)	476,000	800,000	2,000,000
Investment (in dollars)	27,000,000	50,000,000	100,000,000+
Utilities			
Water (gallons per month)	32,000,000	57,000,000	105,000,000
Electricity (kilowatt hours per month)	4,500,000	9,000,000	18,000,000
Gas (cubic feet per month)	36,000,000	72,000,000	144,000,000
Sewage		Sanitary use only	
Personnel			
Total	575	1,075	1,900
Transfers	40–50[a]	0	0

Source: Site selection team.

[a] Actually 75 employees were transferred.

Given the projected growth figures, the new plant would require a floor area of 576,000 square feet at the beginning, increasing to over 800,000 by 1973, with an ultimate design of 2 million square feet. The completed plant could conceivably involve an investment as high as $100 million.

In addition to the building space needed, the availability of sufficient water, gas, and electric power utility service was a major concern. Monthly water requirements would increase from an initial 32 million gallons to 57 million in 1973, up to a total of 105 million. Both the electric power and the gas loads were sizable and involved considerable investments on the part of utility firms. The ability to meet such levels in the past had presented no problems to utility firms, as they have been able to justify such investments. Also to be considered because of the emphasis on pollution control was the connection of the plant to a city sewer service for sanitary needs, although this was not a mandatory requirement.[3]

The need for plant personnel was the single most important aspect of the search for a community within the region. Increasing economies of scale would result in an increase in employees from 575 to only 1,075 as the plant doubled in size and to just 1,900 as it doubled again to reach its final production capacity of 50,000 tires per day. Included in the initial plant staffing would be 40 to 50 supervisors and specialized personnel transferred from other plants. Since these key people were vital to the start-up phase, the selected community must offer good living conditions.[4]

The Community Search

Basic Location Criteria

Decisions as to the regional location of the new plant, its projected growth rate, and experience with competing labor supply areas established two criteria to be used in the preliminary search for a community location. First, the plant should not be located in proximity to existing tire plants; second, it should be located in an area having a population size range geared to its ultimate production requirements. To avoid intruding on the labor supply areas of existing plants, a map of the fifty-nine tire manufacturing plants in the United States was prepared (fig. 6.5). An analysis of the map revealed the proximity criterion to be a severe constraint, but geographic voids appeared in central Kentucky, the South Atlantic Coastal Plains, Missouri, and central Mississippi. Another map of corporation tire plants revealed a possibility for geographic balance among Kelly's Illinois, Maryland, and Texas production facilities by locating a new plant in the southeastern United States (fig. 6.6). The site selection team agreed that the minimum population range necessary to provide reasonable living conditions for the firm's transferees and to man the completed plant (even without population growth) was an urban community of 25,000 persons having a labor supply area of 150,-000 inhabitants within a radius of thirty miles. In the opinion of the team, the maximum urban community should not be more than 150,000 people, since experience showed that urban areas larger than this were unlikely to provide the best labor climate for a tire plant.

Constrained by these criteria, as well as by the fact that the cost of labor, utilities, and taxes must offset freight cost disadvantages as the potential plant was moved away from Memphis, a list of twenty-six cities was prepared from a search of documents containing population and other information. For various reasons, such as inadequate water availability or site problems, established by communications with local or state

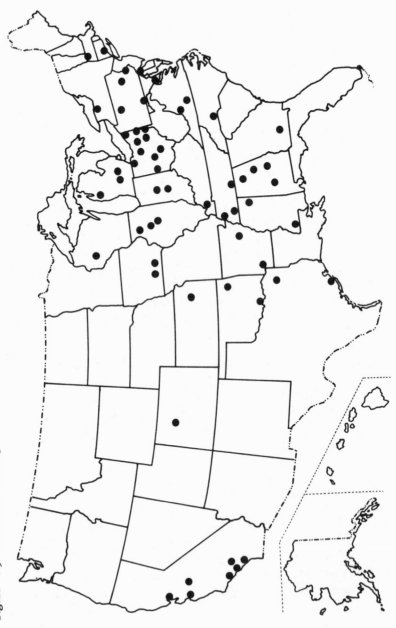

Figure 6.5 Locations of Existing Tire Manufacturing Plants, 1968

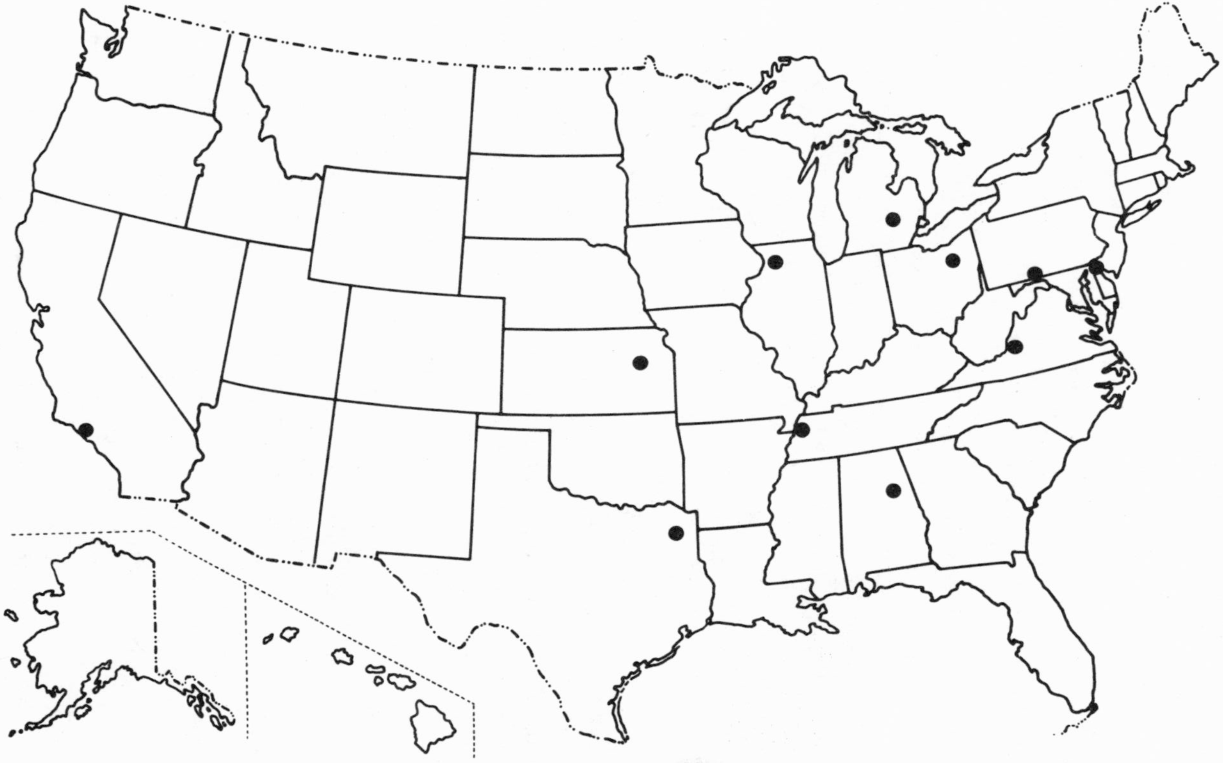

Figure 6.6 Locations of Corporation Plants—Goodyear, Lee, and Kelly Springfield Tire Companies

industrial development representatives, the list was reduced to sixteen cities for a preliminary field analysis.

The Preliminary Field Analysis

The preliminary field analysis was conducted by a team of three individuals: a production specialist, a personnel representative, and a plant planning engineer. Community evaluation trips involved contacting industrial developers and local industrial managers during brief, one-day visits, collecting readily available printed information, and visiting potential sites. Of the sixteen cities visited, eleven were eliminated by the team on the basis of one or two problems such as present industry mix, labor rates, or living conditions. The remaining five became the subject of a preliminary economic analysis (table 6.3).

The analysis covered the variable operating costs required to manufacture 12,500 tires per day. For each of the five communities the total labor costs, in dollar amounts, exceeded the combined freight, utility, and tax costs. Freight costs were the second greatest expense, followed by the cost of utilities and taxes. The labor cost variation of $312,000 per year between the most expensive and least expensive community was based on estimated hourly rates of $2.75 and $3.00. The freight cost studies resulted in a spread of $261,000 between Fayetteville, North Carolina, and Greenville, Mississippi—the latter being the closest to the source of raw materials. Utility costs were a factor, but less so than labor and freight. The Johnson City area in Tennessee was supplied by low-cost TVA power, while city X had low-cost gas. The maximum cost difference for utilities was between Fayetteville, the most expensive at $677,000, and city X, with a cost of only $497,000, a spread of

Table 6.3. Preliminary Economic Analysis (dollars per year variable operating costs, 12,500 tires per day)

Cost factor	Greenville, Mississippi	Fayetteville, No. Carolina	Johnson City, Tennessee	City X	City Y
Labor	3,438,000	3,438,000	3,625,000	3,750,000	3,750,000
	($2.75/hr.)	($2.75/hr.)	($2.90/hr.)	($3.00/hr.)	(3.00/hr.)
Freight	1,982,000	2,243,000	2,019,000	2,131,000	2,046,000
Utilities	650,000	677,000	516,000	497,000	676,000
Taxes	367,000[a]	212,000	276,000	239,000	284,000
Total	6,437,000	6,570,000	6,436,000	6,617,000	6,756,000

Source: Site selection team.
[a] Ten-year tax moratorium not utilized in calculations.

$180,000. Tax costs, the most difficult figures to obtain on a preliminary field investigation, were determined by examining the property-tax records of local industrial firms at the tax office and estimating taxes for the new plant. Other corporate taxes, a large part of the total tax costs, were calculated by each state's corporate tax department. Total taxes ranged from a low of $212,000 in Fayetteville to a high of $367,000 in Greenville, a difference of $155,000. The difference between communities in total variable costs amounted to $320,000 per year between city Y and Johnson City, with Johnson City the total least-cost location at $6,436,-000. The variable cost difference among Greenville, Fayetteville, and Johnson City, however, was not sufficient to allow a final locational decision among them; but it was a factor in eliminating cities X and Y from further consideration.

The Comprehensive Field Analysis

Greenville, Fayetteville, and Johnson City were put through a comprehensive comparative field analysis (fig. 6.7). The site selection team, augmented by a member of the corporation's central engineering staff, extended their contacts beyond industrial developers and managers to include local government officials and representatives from utility firms. Two or three days were spent in each community to supplement and confirm the previously collected information, which would then be used in a detailed community analysis. For each city, the industrial climate, labor climate, transportation facilities, economic costs, and living conditions were evaluated. Before the trip, local industrial developers were contacted to secure options on adequate sites so that the firm would be in a position to break ground soon after the final community choice was made.

The most authoritative source of information about a community's *industrial climate* is existing local industry—in this case, the larger manufacturing firms. Of interest are size, product lines, wages, union and labor experience, and opinions about the local industrial climate.[5] On the basis of this information all three communities were evaluated as having a diversified industrial base that could provide an atmosphere not conditioned to any single industry, type of service, or category of employment (see table 6.4, for example).

The comparative analysis of the *labor climate* revealed an adequate level of labor availability in each community, along with a substantial population within a thirty-mile radius (table 6.5). The Fayetteville area had the largest potential labor supply with a population of 379,000. None of the communities, however, possessed a sufficient supply of skilled labor in the required categories.[6] Employers in Greenville described local labor

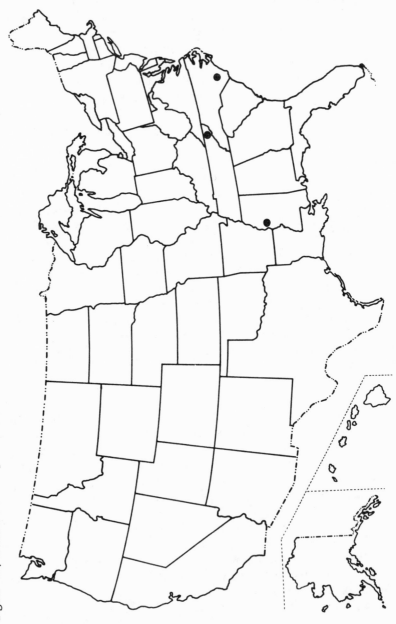

Figure 6.7 Locations of Competitive-Cost Communities

Table   6.4. Fayetteville, North Carolina, Industrial Climate

Industry	Product	Employees	Wages per hour	Union
Black and Decker	power tools	600	2.37	No
Rohn and Haas	Nylon 6	600	2.40	No
Burlington Mills	men's wear	425	2.25	No
Purolator[a]	filters	300	2.10 (hire rate)	—
Dupont[b]	Butacite	200	—	—
Fort Bragg	—	4,500	2.65	AFGE

Source: Site selection team.
[a] Operation to start May 1969.
[b] Construction to start March 1969.

as unchanged in quantity but decreasing in quality over the past few years. Two new industrial plants had opened in Fayetteville during 1967, but the state's employment security division estimated that the local labor reserve had increased from 8,200 in 1967 to 9,300 in 1969. Also, a large number of people were discharged each year from the army at Fort Bragg, adjacent to Fayetteville. They could provide a supply of skilled labor, and the base itself appeared to be a local labor-stabilizing factor. A decline in employment at one of Johnson City's larger firms was an important plus factor in evaluating its local labor supply.

The productivity level of each community's labor force was more difficult to evaluate. The management of a multi-plant firm in Greenville felt that the labor there was not up to par when compared to their other plants. In both Fayetteville and Johnson City, plant managers felt it unnecessary to qualify the productivity of their workers.

Labor in the three communities differed considerably in attitudes toward unions, as reflected by the existing level of unionization. Greenville workers were extensively organized, whereas Fayetteville showed little unionization. Johnson City's workers were moderately unionized, but the fact that no recent prolonged strikes had occurred indicated a moderate attitude toward unions.

The availability of programs and facilities for improving the skill levels of local workers was also evaluated. A federal training program was just getting under way in Greenville, and a state-operated industrial crafts technical school was located thirty miles away. The oldest of fifty state-operated technical institutes for industrial training was located in Fayetteville. In addition, a $1 million expansion program was under way at the institute. A similar state-operated training school was located in Johnson City. The overall evaluation of each community's labor climate

Table   6.5. Comprehensive Comparative Analysis

Characteristic	Greenville	Fayetteville	Johnson City
Industrial climate			
Industry compatibility	good	good	good
Labor climate			
Availability	good	good	good
Population	231,000	379,000	296,000
Productivity	fair	good	good
Unionization	extensive	little	moderate
Training	federal	state	state
Transportation facilities			
Highways	U.S. 81, U.S. 61	I 95, U.S. 401	Interstate 81
Truck terminals	8	11	6
Railroads	IC	Seaboard Coastline Norfolk & Southern	Southern Norfolk & Western
Economic costs **(12,500 tires/day)** **(dollars per year** **except labor)**			
Labor	3,310,000	3,310,000	3,625,000
Labor ($ per hr.)	2.65	2.65	2.90
Freight	1,982,000	2,243,000	2,019,000
Utilities	650,000	677,000	516,000
Taxes	376,000[a]	212,000	276,000
Total	6,309,000	6,442,000	6,436,000
Living conditions			
Urban population	51,000	60,000	38,000
Housing	reasonable	very good	very good
Public education	fair	good	good
Colleges	none	two	four
Hospitals	good	good	good
Recreation	fair	good	good
Site adequacy			
Size (acres)	235	405	210
Topography	excellent	good	very poor
Cost ($ per acre)	1,000	1,500	1,000–2,000
Option status	in hand	in hand	available

Source: Site selection team.

[a] Ten-year tax moratorium of $100,000 not utilized in the analysis.

rated Fayetteville the highest, Johnson City second, and Greenville a poor third, primarily because of its poorer worker productivity and labor training facilities.

The comparative evaluation of each community's *transportation facilities* revealed that all had excellent highway connections. Fayetteville, with eleven truck terminals, could provide superior service. Greenville with eight and Johnson City with six were also well qualified. Rail service within each community presented no problems. In all, each community possessed good transportation facilities.

The comparative analysis of *economic costs* associated with locating in each community revealed minor changes from the costs found in the preliminary investigation. The freight costs remained the same, and despite negotiations with utility firms on alternative service designs, important cost adjustments were not necessary. Meetings were held with county tax officials, but after gathering information on other taxpayers, the original tax costs, including federal, state, and local ones, were believed to be conservative and remained unchanged. The Greenville location, though, provided a $100,000 moratorium for ten years. The tax concession, while an incentive, was not used at this stage of the comparative analysis. It would be taken into account if Greenville and one of the other communities were equally ranked in the final evaluation. The only factor to change was associated with labor costs, for Greenville and Fayetteville. The average hourly pay rate in both cities was reduced from $2.75 to $2.65. Johnson City's rate of $2.90 remained the same. The adjustments were based upon information supplied by a few industries in each community on local job standards and rates. Kelly's skill requirements were then compared job by job, and an average pay scale was determined for the firm's particular skill mix. A more exhaustive analysis would be made for hiring purposes to be certain that each individual skill rate would be consistent with existing local rates. The economic analysis revealed that the three communities were almost equally competitive, with Greenville favored by a slight margin and Fayetteville the least attractive because of higher freight and utility costs. But, because of the lowering of the labor cost, Greenville replaced Johnson City as the total least-cost location.

The *living conditions* in each city were also examined. Although a relationship does exist between the size of an urban population and the number and type of public and private services provided, Greenville, with a population of 51,000, was not as well endowed as Johnson City, with only 38,000. Fayetteville at 60,000 provided better services—recently built shopping centers and a new downtown area, air terminal, and civic auditorium. Hospital and recreation facilities were adequate in all three communities, although Greenville did not fare as well as the others in recreation opportunities. Each of the communities contained sufficient housing, but Fayetteville had many more attractive subdivisions. Fayetteville was, therefore, ranked ahead of Johnson City on living conditions, followed by Greenville.

An evaluation of the educational opportunities in each community showed that Greenville had no higher education institutions, but a junior college was located only thirty miles away. Also, some local adjustments would have to be made if the state's "freedom-of-choice" school policy erupted as a civil rights integration issue. Fayetteville had handled its school integration problems to date, and Fayetteville State College, a predominantly black school, contributed much in the way of community leadership. A new Methodist college was also located in the community. In Johnson City both the pupil-teacher ratios and the public school buildings were considered good. Higher education facilities were also excellent, with two schools for women and a four-year college in addition to the technical school. In education, Greenville had to be ranked behind the other communities.

The Final Site Selection Analysis

Concurrent with the gathering of information for the comparative analysis, local industrial development organizations obtained site options in their own names for the new plant. The cost of the land exhibited some degree of inflated speculative value, even though the precaution was taken to have the local development people start to work on options about ten days before the comprehensive analysis trip was made. Still, all met the minimum size requirement of two hundred acres. The Greenville and Fayetteville development organizations had specific site options in hand, but the Johnson City option had not been completely negotiated. The Greenville site possessed excellent topography, and the terrain of the Fayetteville site was also good. But the Johnson City site had miserable topography. Calculations based on aerial photographs showed that nearly 2 million cubic yards of earth grading would have to be completed in preparation for the plant, which would cause a sixty- to ninety-day delay in the construction schedule. Since production at the new plant was to "start up" as quickly as possible, this delay, as well as the lack of a site option in hand in the first place, gave Greenville and Fayetteville an added advantage over Johnson City.

With all of the communities being so nearly equal, each entered the competition by offering some local cost-reducing inducements. Johnson City came up with site alternatives and agreed to pay for some of the site grading. Greenville withdrew its first land price and submitted a lower price in addition to its ten-year tax moratorium offer of $100,000. Fayetteville revised the site options to include adjacent land parcels and also agreed to extend water and sewage mains 4.5 miles beyond its corporate limits to service the plant. The state agreed to upgrade 2.4 miles of highway to provide a five-lane access road, as well as to upgrade and extend two other roads bordering two sides of the site.

For the final evaluation the communities were ranked first, second, or third in each of the categories investigated (table 6.6). In categories where they were equal, as in industrial climate, a first-place rank was assigned to all three. Each of the communites exhibited distinct advantages and disadvantages. Greenville provided slightly lower total economic costs. Fayetteville offered more favorable living conditions. Johnson City possessed low-cost TVA power. The more critical requirements in the evaluation, though, were labor availability and site readiness. In the final analysis the presence of labor unions was not decisive, nor was the cost of the land. Of considerable significance was the fact that Greenville had labor quality and labor training problems that would delay production in building up to capacity. Similarly, problems at the Johnson City site would delay construction for two to three months. Problems that might delay production did not exist at Fayetteville, and its location was more geographically balanced with the firm's existing plants. In the final analysis, Fayetteville, which had the most first-place rankings, was chosen as the location for the new plant. It was the city most attractive to the key staff people who would be transferred from other plants, and it also met

Table 6.6. Summary of Comparative Rankings

Locational Factor	Greenville, Mississippi	Fayetteville, North Carolina	Johnson City, Tennessee
Industrial climate	1	1	1
Labor climate	3	1	2
Transportation facilities	1	1	1
Economic costs			
Labor	1	1	3
Freight	1	3	2
Utilities	2	2	1
Taxes	3	1	2
Living conditions	3	1	2
Site conditions	1	1	3
Total rank	16	12	17

Source: Site selection team.

the near-term need for production at the earliest possible date. In addition, it met the long-range requirements for economical, large-scale production (in part by reduced freight costs to the plant when a new carbon-black facility began operation in Alabama before the Kelly plant reached its ultimate size).

A Summary of Site Selection Guidelines

While the industrial location decision-making process may vary for different types of location seekers, the procedures used by corporate site selectors such as Kelly Springfield usually follow some generally accepted guidelines (fig. 6.8). First, a market analysis is made to establish geographic areas of growing demand and the ability of existing plants to supply economically the projected levels in each area. The market analysis may be conducted to estimate the demand for a competing product line in which substitute materials replace more traditional materials: plastic for metal, glass, wood, or rubber, for example; or aluminum for steel, zinc, or copper. Such material substitutions can involve different plant production processes and geographically different locational orientations. The market analysis should also determine the type of pricing system (f.o.b. —freight-on-board, c.i.f.—cost-insurance-freight, or zoned) to be used in distributing the finishing product, since different pricing systems entail different transportation costs, fix the extent of the market area, and set the level of market demand. Market projections should be estimated for a five-year period. Projections for longer periods are likely to be inaccurate, since new plant start-ups, expansions, and market penetrations by competing firms—all of which are unpredictable—can distort long-term estimates.

On the basis of the projected market demand, the plant and material engineers determine the production process to be followed, substituting new technologies for older manufacturing methods. Involved in determining the particular production process to be used are the scale economies that can be achieved by substituting alternative technologies, capital equipment, materials, and skill-level combinations. With the scale of production and manufacturing process established, the material, equipment, utility, and labor force requirements by type and amount can be determined. The next step is to design the actual plant layout, including the building(s), parking, loading, and storage facilities; landscaping and area sufficient for expansion if the eventuality is either planned or foreseen.

The site selection process itself proceeds at successive levels, with the scale of production an important factor in evaluating the accessibility of alternative locations to materials, utilities, labor supply areas, and markets. First, the regional location of the new plant is identified by a comparative economic analysis of specific communities in different regions. This is accomplished by evaluating the freight costs required to distribute the finished product to previously identified markets and to assemble production materials from known vendor locations.

Once the least-cost transportation region is ascertained, specific communities within the region able to furnish the minimum requirements for labor and utilities are identified, with some attention to the firm's preference for small communities or metropolitan centers. Census documents, supplemented by information from industrial specialists with railroads, chambers of commerce, utilities, financial institutions, and state or local government agencies, can all aid in selecting the half dozen to two dozen qualifying communities. Since different communities are subject to variation in utility, tax, and labor costs for the same level of service or productivity, lower-cost communities are able to offset the additional transportation costs involved in shipping goods to or from them. A comparative analysis of each community's transportation, utility, labor, and tax costs can eliminate those with the higher total locational costs. Generally, if the firm's market distribution costs are greater than the sum of the assembly and labor costs, the plant is located close to its market. If the material assembly costs are greater than the combined distribution and labor costs, the firm probably locates close to the high-cost material. On the other hand, if labor costs are greater than the combined assembly and distribution costs, the plant's location is oriented toward low-cost labor areas, as was the case for Kelly Springfield. If no cost is sufficiently greater than the other combined costs, the plant's location depends more on non-economic factors.

The next step in the process is to choose the most preferred community. At this point the remaining qualifying communities undergo a comprehensive comparative analysis with more specific information obtained on a confidential basis from community officials and local industrial managers. The economic costs, previously considered, are examined again in greater detail. Each community is also evaluated with respect to its localization economies and diseconomies: [7] transportation facilities and frequency of service; availability of working capital or capital for plant, land, and equipment, if needed; and the adequacy of business services associated with the firm's maintenance, repair, legal, engineering, and banking needs. In addition, the communities' urbanization economies and diseconomies are evaluated: the local tax burden, communication services, the level of police and fire protection and their impact on insurance costs, and the adequacy of labor training or education programs and their im-

Figure 6.8 The Industrial Location Decision-making Process

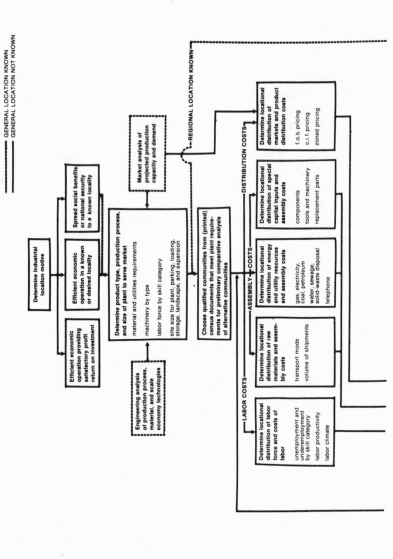

GENERAL LOCATION KNOWN
GENERAL LOCATION NOT KNOWN

Determine industrial location motive

Efficient economic operation providing satisfactory profit return on investment

Efficient economic operation in a known or desired locality

Spread social benefits or national security to a known locality

Determine product type, production process, and size of plant to serve market

material and utilities requirements

machinery by type

labor force by skill category

site size for plant, parking, loading, storage, landscape, and expansion

Engineering analysis of production process, material, and scale economy technologies

Market analysis of projected production capacity and demand

Choose qualified communities from (printed) census documents that meet plant requirements for preliminary comparative analysis of alternative communities

REGIONAL LOCATION KNOWN

LABOR COSTS

Determine locational distribution of labor force and costs of labor

unemployment and underemployment by skill category

labor productivity

labor climate

Determine locational distribution of raw materials and assembly costs

transport mode

volume of shipments

ASSEMBLY COSTS

Determine locational distribution of energy and utility resources and assembly costs

gas, electricity, coal, petroleum

water, sewage, solid-waste disposal

telephone

Determine locational distribution of special capital inputs and assembly costs

components

tools and machinery

replacement parts

DISTRIBUTION COSTS

Determine locational distribution of markets and product distribution costs

f.o.b. pricing

c.i.f. pricing

zoned pricing

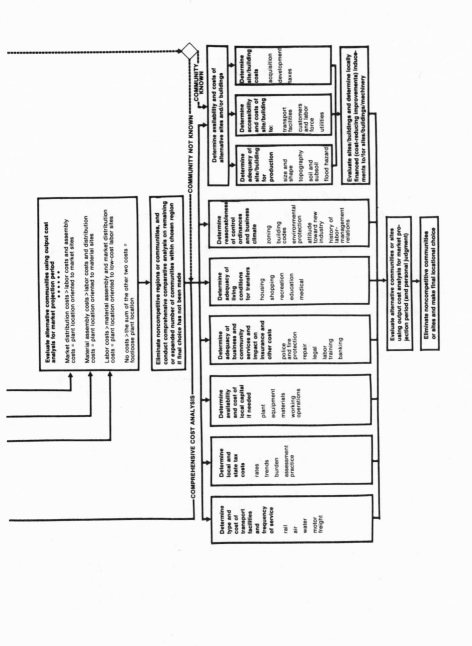

pact on labor costs. Also evaluated are the adequacy of housing and general living conditions for technical and management personnel, the reasonableness of building, environmental protection, and zoning codes compared with other areas, the community attitude toward new industry, and its history of labor-management relations. If the localization and urbanization economies prove to be diseconomies, this means higher costs to the firm and these communities are eliminated from further consideration.

At the same time that the communities are being evaluated, individual sites associated with each are investigated. The site must have a size and shape that will meet the plant's design requirements and be accessible to its personnel and customer representatives. Cost items pertaining to each plot include topographic, soil, subsoil, and flood-hazard conditions that could result in added construction expense. Other characteristics that account for cost variations from site to site are extension of utilities; transportation of goods to and from rail, air, truck, or water-carrier terminals; site acquisition; site preparation, including environmental quality control; and local property taxes.

After reviewing prospective sites in the qualifying communities and estimating the acquisition, and operating costs of each location, taking into account any local cost-reducing inducements (tax concessions, provision of land or plant buildings at lower cost, public utility service at reduced rates, or access-road improvements), a comparative cost ranking is assigned to each. The other economic and non-economic factors are similarly ranked for each community and a final selection made. And, to be sure, the non-economic factors become the controlling consideration for locations where the economic factors are nearly equal.

Notes

1. The case study presented in this chapter is based upon a report to the board of directors of the Goodyear Tire Corporation by William R. Schultz, who has had over twenty years' experience in plant planning and has participated in well over a dozen site selection programs. While none of the pertinent factors has been left out of the chapter, a few figures have been altered and some information deleted to preserve confidentiality.

2. Site selection teams for large corporations are usually composed of four individuals: a plant manager, plant engineer, chief accountant, and personnel manager.

3. The firm obtained a commitment for gas before severe shortages occurred. The water-system design turned out to be more economical than expected, and the sewer treatment service provided by the city in which the firm decided to locate made the plant's water pollution nil.

4. Actually, 75 transferees were moved.

5. The pertinent data cannot be disclosed without violating confidence.

6. The new plant experienced a significant level of labor absenteeism and turnover, attributed partly to the lack of previous industrial experience on the part of the labor force and partly to changing attitudes toward work in the country as a whole.

7. The term *localization economies* as used here refers specifically to all services provided by the private sector of the local economy that can reduce the industrial firm's overall operating cost. *Urbanization economies* refers to services provided or regulated by the public sector. The level of provision determines the firm's overall cost of operating in the area.

Part 3
Industrial
Development
Factors

Chapter 7
Transportation and Industrial Location

The effects of transportation upon the location of industry may be observed in four different ways: freight costs, accessibility to market, accessibility to labor, and accessibility to information. This chapter will examine each in turn, making some attempt to assess its relative importance.

Freight Rates and the Location of Industry

The emphasis in a discussion of the effects of transportation upon the location of industry is usually upon freight rates and the choice of a location where the total costs of transportation would be minimized. Although this factor has recently declined in importance, it still deserves attention as an initial step in the locational decision-making process.[1]

Tapering Freight Rates

Consideration of transport costs in the industrial site selection decision would be a simple matter if transport rates were well behaved and followed a clear and consistent distance principle, so that a given increase in distance would result in a proportionate increase in transport rates. The resulting flat per-mile rates are characteristic only of passenger transport rates, for almost all rates for commodity transport depart markedly from the distance principle. The most common deviation is the tapering freight rate, whereby the per-mile rate for a long haul is less than that for a short haul. The basic rationale for a tapering freight rate structure is based on two components of freight costs: line-haul costs, which may vary proportionately with distance, and terminal costs, which are fixed and do not vary with distance (table 7.1). If the terminal cost is 30 cents and the line-haul cost is 1 cent per mile, the total transport cost for a one-mile haul is 31 cents; for a ten-mile haul it is 40 cents; for a twenty-mile haul it is 50 cents. On a per-mile basis, however, the total transport cost declines from 31 cents for a one-mile haul, to 4 cents for a ten-mile haul, to 2.5 cents for a twenty-mile haul. As the length of haul increases, the per-mile transport costs continue to diminish, since the 30-cent terminal cost is spread over increasing mileage.

Tapering Rates and Intermodal Competition

Different modes of transportation have different ratios of terminal to line-haul costs (fig. 7.1). For example, truck transport has lower terminal costs relative to line-haul costs than does rail transportation. Consequently, the per-mile transport costs for trucks decline *less* rapidly with distance. Water transport, on the other hand, has a relatively high ratio of terminal to line-haul costs and the per-mile transport costs decline *more* rapidly with distance than do rail costs. Low terminal costs make the truck the lowest-cost carrier over the short haul (from O to B in figure 7.1), and high terminal costs make water the lowest-cost transport mode over the long haul (beyond C on the figure). For intermediate distances (from B to C), rail transport is the lowest-cost form of transportation. The actual distance at which one mode has a cost advantage over another in terms of mileage differs according to the commodity being shipped, as well as a number of other factors. As a rough rule of thumb, the average distance over which rail will have a cost advantage over highway is ap-

Table 7.1. Hypothetical Tapering Fare Structure

Distance (miles)	Terminal costs	Line-haul costs	Total costs	Per-mile costs
0	$0.30	$0.00	$0.30	—
1	.30	.01	.31	$0.31
5	.30	.05	.35	.07
10	.30	.10	.40	.04
20	.30	.20	.50	.025
30	.30	.30	.60	.02
40	.30	.40	.70	.017
50	.30	.50	.80	.016
100	.30	1.00	1.30	.013
1,000	.30	10.00	10.30	.010

Source: Taaffe and Gauthier 1973, p. 39.

Figure   7.1 Rate Structure of Major Transportation Modes
Source: Hoover 1948, p. 20.

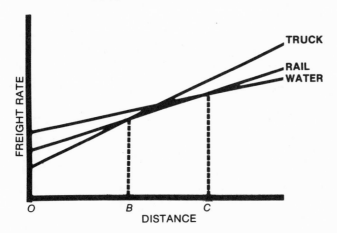

proximately 500 miles. The average distance for motor carriers is approximately 250 miles, and for water carriers it is 850 miles.

Piggyback or TOFC (trailer-on-flatcar) services represent an attempt to combine the short-haul advantages of truck transport with the long-haul advantages of rail transport. The net result, however, is a mode of transportation that is intermediate between truck and rail in its cost structure. Additional handling results in terminal costs for TOFC that are higher than truck costs, although still lower than rail terminal costs. Thus TOFC has cost advantages over truck transportation only on hauls that are greater than 250 or 300 miles.

Two characteristics of rail freight costs and rail freight rates have had a significant impact on the pattern of competition between trucks and railroads (fig. 7.2). First, line-haul *rates* tend to increase less rapidly than line-haul *costs* (thus flattening the rate curve). Second, rates have been adjusted so that the short-haul rates are set above short-haul costs and the long-haul rates are set below long-haul costs. This pricing pattern is essentially the same as that followed by the railroads in their early efforts to open up new production areas in remote parts of the country.[2] The losses on long-haul services could be balanced out by higher rates on the short-haul services. The resulting rail freight rate structure provided a protective "umbrella" for truck competition, allowing truckers to price their short-haul services well above costs and still stay safely below rail rates.

Figure   7.2 Freight Rates and Freight Costs

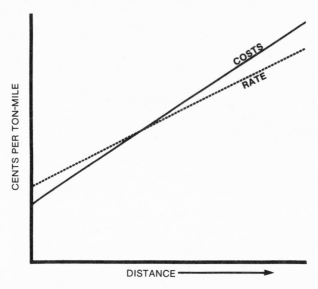

Tapering Rates and the Location of Industry

The effects of tapered rates upon the location of industry can be illustrated by the simplest kind of locational problem. Consider an industry
with only one raw material source, no weight loss, and only one market.
The locational effects of a flat per-mile structure in this simple case with
the raw material source at location *A*, the market sixty miles distant at
location *B*, and the rate set at 10 cents for each ten-mile block (not 10
cents per mile) for both raw material and processed goods would be neg-
ligible (table 7.2). That is, the firm could locate at the material site or
the market or at any intermediate location and incur the same transport
cost. If the firm located ten miles from the material source *A*, it would
incur 10 cents in transport costs to assemble the raw material and 50 cents
in transport costs to distribute the finished product to the market *B*. If it
located twenty miles from *A* it would incur 20 cents in assembly costs
and 40 cents in distribution costs. If it located at the market *B*, sixty miles
from *A*, it would incur 60 cents in raw material transport costs but no
distribution costs. The firm located at the raw material source *A* would
incur market distribution costs of 60 cents but no raw material assembly
costs. Thus, the total transport costs associated with a firm located at the
material source, at the market, or at any intermediate location would be
60 cents in the flat per-mile rate case.

Table   7.2.   Locational Effects of Flat per-Mile Fare Structure

Distance from A (raw material)	Rate per Ten-Mile Block	Total Raw Material Transport Cost from A	Distance from B (market)	Rate per Ten-Mile Block	Total Distribution Transport Cost to B	Total Transport Cost
0	$0.00	$0.00	60	$0.10	$0.60	$0.60
10	.10	.10	50	.10	.50	.60
20	.10	.20	40	.10	.40	.60
30	.10	.30	30	.10	.30	.60
40	.10	.40	20	.10	.20	.60
50	.10	.50	10	.10	.10	.60
60	.10	.60	0	.10	.00	.60

Now take a case that includes a moderate taper in the transportation rates (table 7.3). The transport rate for the first ten-mile block is 10 cents, for the second ten-mile block 9 cents, and a total of 45 cents rather than 60 cents for sixty miles. Thus, a firm located at the material source A will pay a total of 45 cents rather than 60 cents for sixty miles, with the total amount paid out for distribution costs. Similarly, a firm located at the market B will pay 45 cents in raw material transport costs. Intermediate points in this case, however, all have total transport costs of more than 45 cents. If a firm originally located at the material source A were to move ten miles closer to the market B, it would incur an additional 10 cents in transporting raw material from A and save only 5 cents in distribution costs by shipping fifty miles rather than sixty miles to the market at B. The resulting total transport cost would be 50 cents, or 5 cents more than if the firm remained at the material source A.

Thus, a tapering freight rate structure benefits the end point for any given shipment. Cities that serve as terminals for a large number of shipments therefore usually have relatively low freight rates. More specifically, large market centers tend to be advantaged by a tapering freight rate structure, since raw material centers are usually more dispersed.

One important exception to the generalization that freight rate structures tend to benefit terminal rather than intermediate centers should be mentioned (table 7.4). If there is a commodity transfer or break of bulk involving terminal costs at an intermediate location, that location does not suffer the disadvantages of the general type of intermediate location, even though it is neither a raw material source nor a market. For example, if there is a break of bulk with terminal costs of 10 cents at a location thirty miles from both the material source A and the market B, the net result is to establish a minimum transport cost location since a manufacturer locating there would not have to pay any of the terminal costs. At this location the total transport cost would be 54 cents, whereas it would be 55 cents at the material source and the market, and even higher at other intermediate locations. Break-of-bulk points have been of considerable importance in

Table   7.3. Locational Effects of Tapering Fare Structure

Distance from A (raw material)	Rate per Ten-Mile Block	Total Raw Material Transport Cost from A	Distance from B (market)	Rate per Ten-Mile Block	Total Distribution Transport Cost to B	Total Transport Cost
0	$0.00	$0.00	60	$0.05	$0.45	$0.45
10	.10	.10	50	.06	.40	.50
20	.09	.19	40	.07	.34	.53
30	.08	.27	30	.04	.27	.54
40	.07	.34	20	.09	.19	.53
50	.06	.40	10	.10	.10	.50
60	.05	.45	0	.00	.00	.45

Source: Taaffe and Gauthier 1973, p. 42.

Table   7.4. Locational Effects of Break of Bulk

Distance from A (raw material)	Rate per Ten-Mile Block	Total Raw Material Transport Cost from A	Break-of-Bulk Costs	Distance from B (market)	Rate per Ten-Mile Block	Total Distribution Transport Cost to B	Total Transport Costs
0	$0.00	$0.00		60	$0.05	$0.55	$0.55
10	.10	.10		50	.06	.50	.60
20	.09	.19		40	.07	.44	.63
30	.08	.27	$0.10	30	.08	.27	.54
40	.07	.44		20	.09	.19	.63
50	.06	.50		10	.10	.10	.60
60	.05	.55		0	.00	.00	.55

Source: Taaffe and Gauthier 1973, p. 45.

the past. The many cities where there is a shift from water to land transportation are examples, as are cities where railroads of different gauges used to meet. Most United States cities that were important break-of-bulk points, however, have become major terminal cities. In addition, the United States transportation system has become progressively integrated so that break of bulk now plays a considerably smaller role in freight movements.

Other Departures from the Distance Principle

In addition to the taper, some other forces also cause freight rates to vary from the distance principle. Rail freight rates are divided into two major types—class rates and commodity rates. Class rates, which consist of a limited number of classes into which commodities may be grouped, form a more regular pattern with relatively few departures from the distance principles as modified by a taper. Commodity rates, on the other hand, are established for many commodities. Commodity rates are lower than class rates and may be made up for specific commodities shipped between specific origins and destinations. For the most part, commodity rate structures are made up by railroads to encourage rail shipments by industries located along their rights-of-way.

Departures from the distance principle are also related to the grouping of origins and destinations. Unless rates are established on a consistent per-mile basis, it is clearly necessary to group cities as origins and destinations. Otherwise, it would be necessary to publish rates, in the case of commodity rates, for each commodity for each possible pair of cities in the United States. Location of a city within a rate group can be advantageous or disadvantageous. A city located at the end of the same rate group that is farthest from the origin has an advantage (e.g., location B in fig. 7.3). It costs the shipper no more to ship goods to the farthest city in the same group (B) than to the nearest city (A). To ship to a city just a short distance farther (C), however, will cause the rates to jump into the next highest rate group. Cities such as Chicago and a number of Missouri River and Ohio River crossing points such as St. Louis and Cincinnati have benefited from their location at the far end of a number of rate groups. To some extent, these groups have residual elements of the old basing point system. The impact of grouping locations is related to the size of the groups. Only in the case of large groups will strong effects be noted.

Closely related to rate groupings are the effects of interregional competition in bringing about departures from the distance principle. The

Figure   7.3 Class C Rate Profile: San Francisco to New York
Source: Daggett and Carter 1947, p. 89.

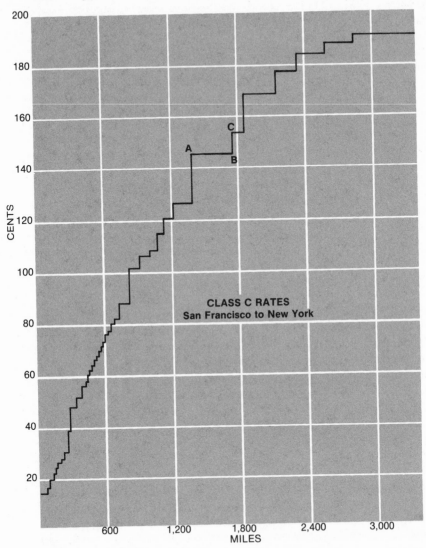

effects of these departures, as well as of rate groupings, can best be observed by examining some specific rate structures. The old transcontinental rate structure offers some of the best examples (Daggett and Carter 1947).

An example of a class rate is provided in figure 7.3, a rate profile drawn for all Class C goods originating in San Francisco and shipped to New York or any destination lying on a traverse between the two cities. Several freight rate characteristics may be noted from this figure. First, the Class C rates show a taper. If they did not, the rates could be represented by a straight line rising considerably more rapidly with distance than is actually the case. An example of a profile for a commodity rate, citrus fruit, again between California (Los Angeles) and New York, is shown in figure 7.4. The commodity rates for citrus show a greater taper with distance than the class rates, and the destination groupings are larger. In order to observe the effects of interregional competition, however, it is necessary to look at the geographical pattern of commodity rates rather than at a profile or traverse between two different locations (fig. 7.5). The geographic irregularity of the citrus rate groups shows marked departures from the distance principle. Competition from Florida citrus led to large rate blankets advantaging most of the eastern United States. Nearly all of the American Manufacturing Belt was covered by the same rate. It cost no more to ship California citrus to Portland, Maine, than to South Bend, Indiana. An even more striking rate group extended from the northern Great Plains through the Southeast to the Florida border, thus including Atlanta in the same rate zone as Minneapolis. Competition from citrus production in the lower Rio Grande Valley accounted for the large rate group extending from the central Rockies down through Texas.[3]

Raw Material Versus Processed-Goods Rates

In addition to departures from the distance principle, the rate differences that exist between raw material and processed goods affect the location of manufacturing. The rate on the processed good is higher relative to the raw material rate. Other things being equal, if the difference is substantial a firm would be more likely to locate in or near a market area so as to minimize the transport costs entailed by the high processed-goods rate. The greater the difference, the greater the pull of the market.

To complicate further the entire subject of freight rates, the railroads in certain cases will offer in-transit privileges that have the effect of eliminating rate differentials between processed goods and raw materials. Milling-in-transit privileges, for example, permit intermediate locations

Figure   7.4 Citrus Rate Profile: Los Angeles to New York
Source: Daggett and Carter 1947, p. 97.

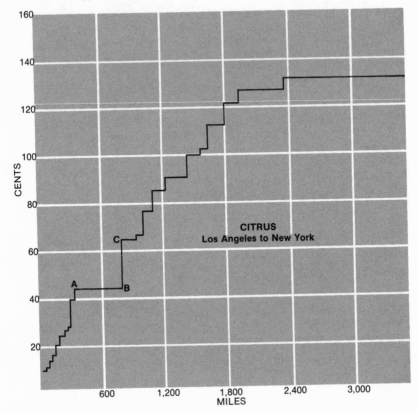

Figure 7.5 Citrus Rates from Los Angeles
Source: Daggett and Carter 1947, p. 64.

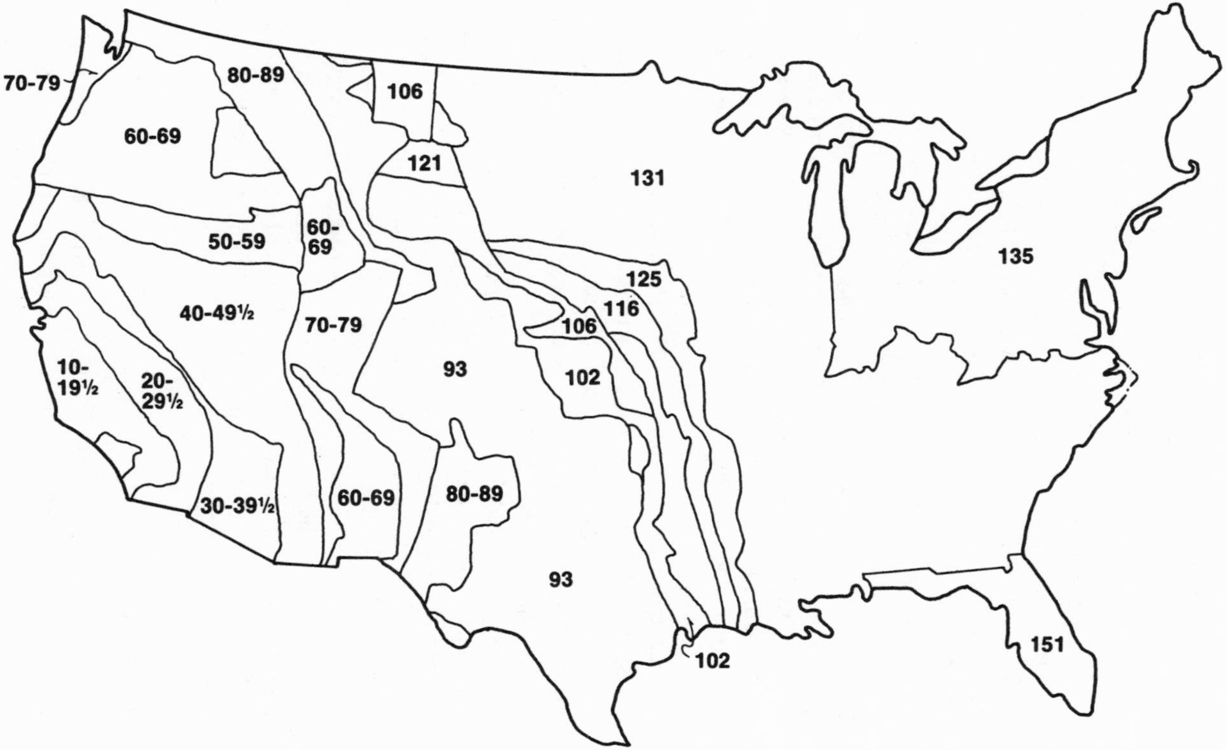

to bring wheat in at low raw material rates, process it, and ship the flour to the ultimate destination—still at the through-wheat rates. Such privileges are similar to commodity rates, however, in that they are arrived at by negotiation between the railroads and firms regarded as potentially large shippers.

Declining Importance of Transport Rates in Industrial Location

Thus far this chapter has considered the classic effects of freight cost upon location. For some time it has been assumed that freight costs have played an important role in locational decisions. More recently, however, some evidence has suggested that freight costs are diminishing in importance as locational factors.

One reason for this decline has been the recent tendency toward greater market orientation. The rate differences between materials and finished products have increased, thereby strengthening the pull of the market. Even more important has been the increased stress on services. Most shippers are more concerned with obtaining the best possible transport services than they are with minimizing transport cost. Easy shipments of small lots, door-to-door service, low risk of damage, and predictable arrival times are all significant transport service characteristics, which also happen to be service characteristics more typical of truck than of rail transport. Changing product characteristics such as higher value per unit of weight, changing design, and minimum inventory further enhance the importance of fast, reliable services as opposed to costs. Technological improvements in transport have also had the effect of reducing the importance of cost. Particularly in rail transport some major technological improvements have taken place, with the general effect of reducing costs rather than improving services, as in the case of classification-yard automation. Most of the technological improvements have affected pipelines, waterways, and those aspects of rail transportation that emphasize bulk haulage. As far as industrial location is concerned, however, these cost reductions have had greatest impact on industries such as oil refineries, power plants, and others that depend upon bulk shipments—large-scale, well-established industries that are less likely to move than to expand at their existing location.

Accessibility to Market

In most cases of industrial location, the firm's desire to maximize sales is a more significant factor than is its desire to minimize costs, even though the two should really be considered simultaneously if a maximum-profit location is to be chosen. In order to maximize sales, the location closest to a firm's total anticipated market would seem to be most desirable.

Potential Maps

One way in which geographers have measured accessibility to an aggregate market is by using the potential map. In a potential map made up by Chauncy Harris (fig. 7.6), he first assumed that the expected sales of a city to any United States county could be computed by assuming that the sales would be directly proportional to the retail sales of that county (M) and inversely proportional to the distance (D) between city and county (or a generalized average freight rate). For the given city he then calculated the M/D figure to all counties in the United States. This total was recorded for the city and the same process continued until each major city had a total market potential figure $(\Sigma \frac{M}{D})$ recorded for it. The city with the largest market potential was then identified, and a series of contour lines were drawn to represent the percentages below the leading city. In the retail market potential map the leading city is New York and the cities within the shaded contour zone are those that recorded market potential totals within 20 percent of the New York total. The map shows most of the Southeast to be within the contour line indicating market potential totals between 30 and 40 percent below that of New York. Potential maps may be constructed for other types of markets as well, such as on value added by manufacture for specific industries located in each county of the country. Maps could also be constructed for regional markets. Once a regional market area was delimited it would be an easy matter to determine which city was closest to the total market. An interesting variation on this theme, using input-output tables, can be used to determine possible markets for specific industries. The input-output coefficients are used as weights so that proximity to those types of manufacturing that use inputs from electrical equipment (for example) is given greater weight than proximity to industries that do not use electrical equipment inputs (see chapter 15).

Isochrone Maps

It is also useful simply to consider accessibility in terms of driving times to and from a specific location (fig. 7.7). Places having the same driving time from a location can be shown on a map by use of driving time contours or isochrones. It would then be an easy matter to tabulate the number of

Figure 7.6 Market Potential Map
Source: Harris 1954, p. 324.

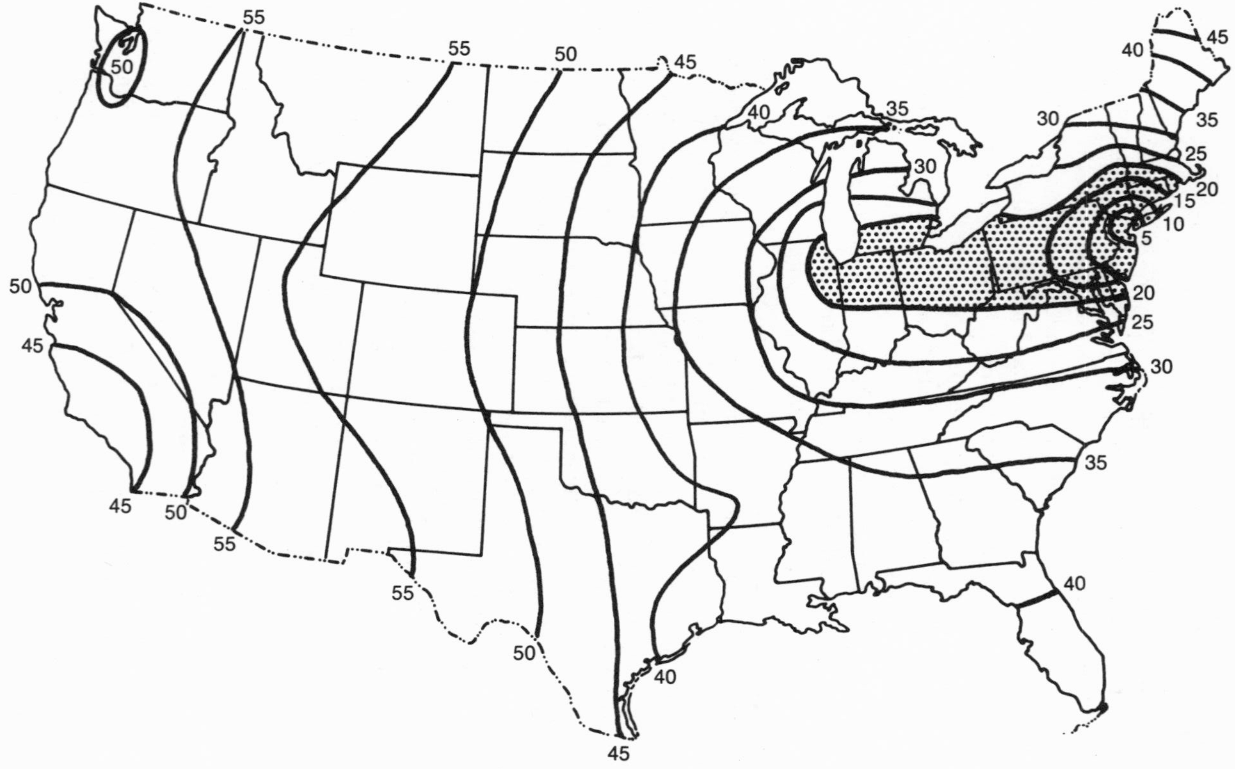

industries of appropriate types located within certain critical driving time zones. The same could be done with railroad, truck, airline, or truck-on-flatcar (TOFC) time schedules. Schedule isochrones differ from driving time isochrones, not only in timing but in their geographic pattern. For example, TOFC services from any terminal are available only along specified routes that form a more restricted radial network than does the highway system.

Total Accessibility Maps

Total accessibility maps provide a means of comparing the aggregate accessibility of different places, such as the shortest-path driving time between major cities in the United States (fig. 7.8). If the one hundred largest United States cities were used, it would take 1,741 hours to drive from Louisville to each of the other ninety-nine cities, starting from Louisville each time and assuming an average speed of fifty miles per hour on the completed interstate system. As on isochrone maps, contour lines could be drawn to connect cities with similar total driving time. For the one hundred major cities in the United States the accessibility center (Louisville) on such a map would be located east of the country's geometric center, both because of the greater number of major cities in the Manufacturing Belt and because of the more interconnected network characteristic of the interstate highway system in the Manufacturing Belt. If each city were weighted by its population size, a measure much like the potential accessibility index would be produced. The shortest-path accessibility measures for railroad show a generally similar pattern to driving time accessibility at the national scale (fig. 7.9). Chicago and Cincinnati, for example, are more central to the rail network than to the highway network. Accessibility maps such as these can also be drafted for specific regions of the country.

Air accessibility presents a more complex pattern. The relation with distance is, in fact, not strong enough to warrant drawing a contour map. The existence or non-existence of nonstop jet connections between centers is the most important single factor in air accessibility. In terms of air travel, large cities such as New York, Chicago, Los Angeles, and San Francisco are more accessible to the other cities of the country than are smaller cities. The central location of cities such as Louisville, Nashville, and Columbus, while quite important to highway accessibility, is only slightly significant in considering air accessibility. Intermediate-sized and small metropolitan areas are generally well connected to the very largest metropolitan areas but poorly connected to each other.

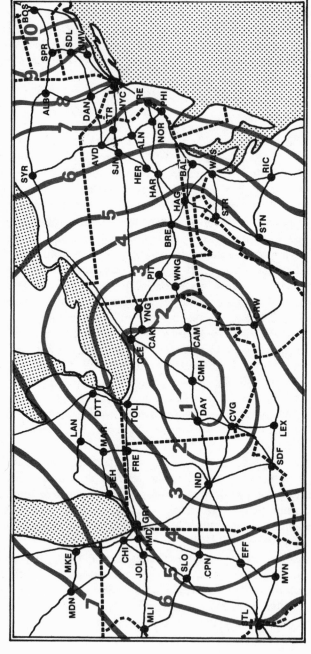

Figure 7.7 Driving Time Isochrones from Columbus, Ohio
Source: Taaffe and King 1966, p. 128.

Figure 7.8 Interstate Highway Accessibility Rankings
Source: Taaffe and Gauthier, p. 150.

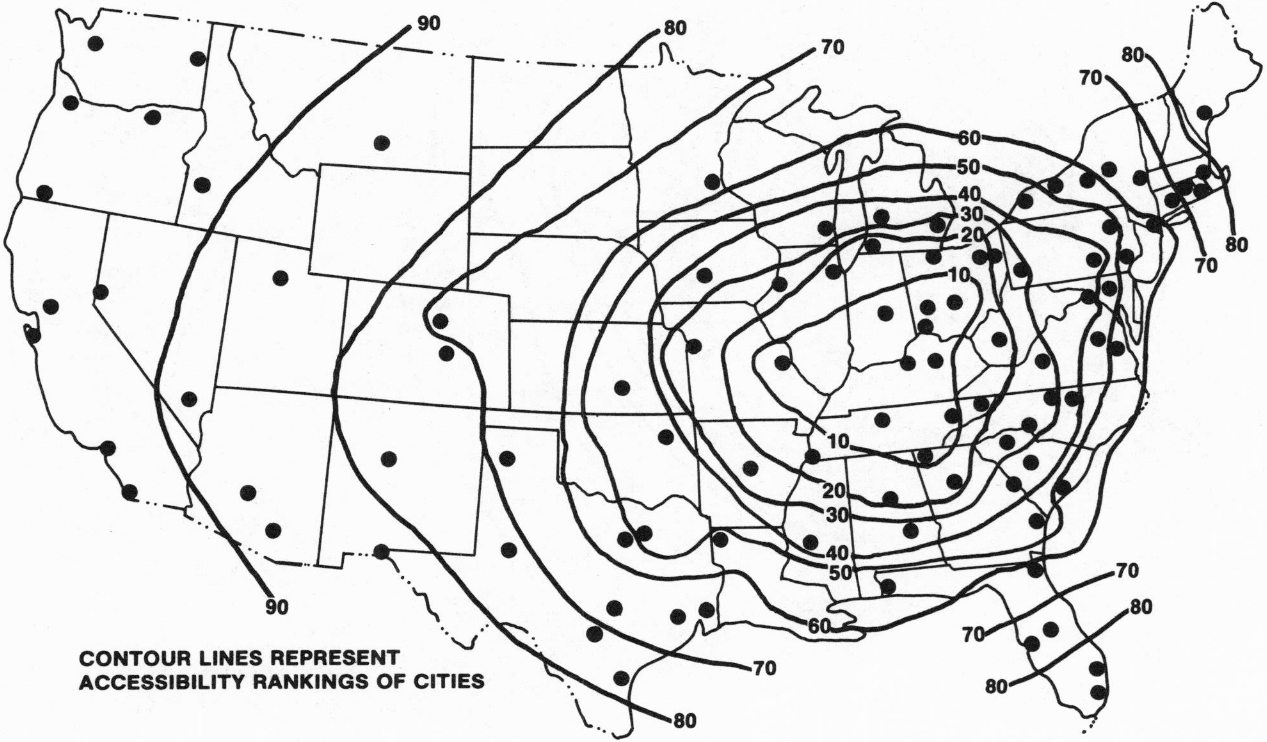

CONTOUR LINES REPRESENT
ACCESSIBILITY RANKINGS OF CITIES

Figure 7.9 Interstate Rail Accessibility Rankings
Source: Taaffe and Gauthier, p. 151.

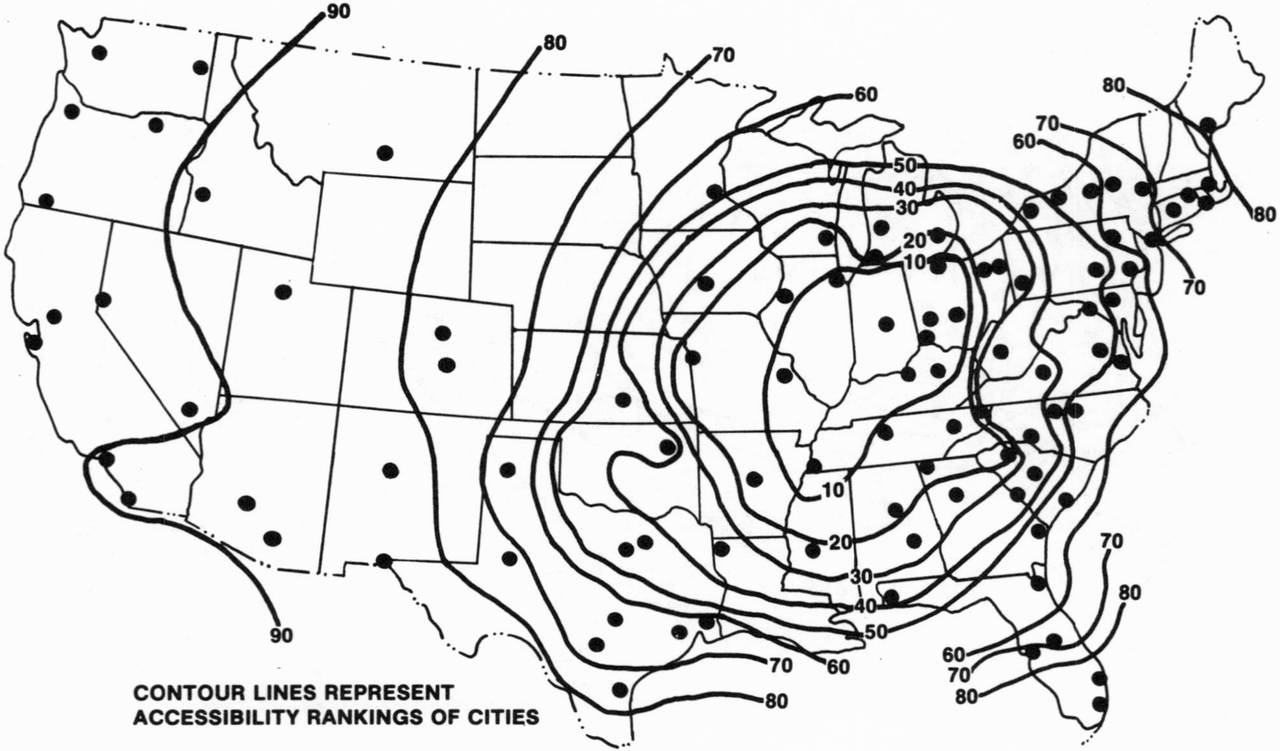

CONTOUR LINES REPRESENT
ACCESSIBILITY RANKINGS OF CITIES

Accessibility to Labor

An examination of accessibility to labor requires a different geographic scale; that of transportation within and around the metropolitan area itself. The location of a firm within the city is of considerable importance. A firm located in or near the central business district (CBD) has a different set of transport needs than does a firm located at the periphery of the city.

CBD Access

Most discussions of commuting problems associated with industrial locations have been focused on the CBD. Improvements in mass transit are of particular importance to CBD commuters. Current problems of congestion are related, at least in part, to the marked decrease, both relative and absolute, in mass transit commuters since well before World War II. Owen (1972) notes the significant decline of mass transit during the 1950s and 1960s. With an index of 100 in 1950 used as the point of departure for both motor vehicle commuters and transit commuters, the motor vehicle index in 1970 was 221 and the transit rider index was 43. Recent years have not demonstrated a significant upturn in mass transit traffic, but there is evidence that the decline has leveled off. Owen notes, however, that there has been a revival of building plans for mass transit facilities.[4] Many researchers doubt the efficacy of new mass transit facilities as solutions to urban transport problems, however. Owen points to the example of European cities, where congestion has actually become worse and financial losses have continued despite considerably greater investments in rail mass transit. In the United States experimentation is continuing with new technology and with more modest, but nonetheless promising, solutions such as preferential bus lanes, and peak-hour pricing.

The Periphery

Commuting to the periphery of the city differs in many important respects from commuting to the CBD and now merits closer examination, since so many new firms are locating in peripheral areas of the city. In a study of commuting to a suburban manufacturing district in the Chicago area, differences in mode of transport, distance and locational relationships, and characteristics of the labor force were examined for both the CBD and the west suburban manufacturing district (table 7.5). Private automobile commuting by drivers and passengers was overwhelmingly dominant among commuters whose jobs were located in the suburban district, accounting for approximately 84 percent of the total as opposed to 30 percent for commuters whose jobs were in the CBD. The commuting distance difference is equally striking (table 7.6). Nearly half of the suburban commuters traveled less than three miles, as compared to less than 15 percent of the CBD commuters.

Commuters to the CBD came from a wide area of origins dispersed both within the city and along each of the suburban radial routes. The west suburban commuters were considerably less dispersed throughout the city. Most of their residences were concentrated along the adjacent suburban radial route, as well as in the adjacent city sector within a three- or four-mile zone around the west suburban district. Further comparisons of the two commuting patterns revealed a number of other differences, including a relative shortage of female workers and a greater concentration of manufacturing workers among the suburban commuters.

External Commuting

Associated with the growth of industry at the periphery of the city has been an increase in longer commuting trips from areas surrounding metropolitan areas. These extended commuter zones demonstrate that the reach and influence of larger metropolitan areas has been underestimated (Berry 1973, pp. 12–13 and fig. 7.10). The measure of the distance some commuters are willing to travel shows that a sizable portion of the United States is included within the metropolitan area commuting zones.

Some studies have revealed the impact of a large city on the commuting patterns of smaller cities and rural areas in the same region (fig. 7.11). In an investigation of such patterns for Ohio, the commuting zones of the large metropolitan areas covered much of the state, and the commuting zones of a few large metropolitan areas covered a large portion of the twenty-eight counties in Appalachian Ohio. Only the south

Table 7.5. Mode of Transport among CBD and Suburban Commuters

Mode	CBD (percentage)	West Suburban (percentage)
Automobile driver	24.4	65.4
Automobile passenger	5.7	18.3
Railroad	16.6	0.7
Elevated or subway	24.4	1.3
Bus	28.4	7.4
Walk to work	—	6.2

Source: Taaffe, Garner, and Yeates 1963, p. 9.

Table   7.6. Commuting Distance among CBD and Suburban Commuters

Distance traveled (miles)	CBD (percentage of commuters)	West Suburban (percentage of commuters)
0– 0.9	1.94	18.89
1.0– 1.9	5.13	16.10
2.0– 2.9	6.71	10.97
3.0– 3.9	8.54	7.57
4.0– 4.9	9.45	6.70
5.0– 5.9	9.24	6.35
6.0– 6.9	9.51	6.35
7.0– 7.9	10.42	4.70
8.0– 8.9	9.99	4.96
9.0– 9.9	6.37	3.92
10.0–10.9	4.54	4.09
11.0–11.9	3.03	3.57
12.0–12.9	2.00	1.13
13.0–13.9	3.03	1.57
over 14.0	10.10	3.13

Source: Taaffe, Garner, and Yeates 1963, p. 16.

central part of Ohio's Appalachian counties lay beyond the commuting zones of the major centers. For each metropolitan center in the state 50 percent of the commuters resided within a distance of approximately ten miles. Forty percent of the commuters lived between ten and twenty-five miles away, and 10 percent lived approximately twenty-five to forty-five miles distant. Commuters were able to live farther away if their residential zone was connected to a center by a major access highway, but not as far away if the road accessibility was poor.

A still closer look at Columbus's commuting extension into Appalachian Ohio was provided by Smolin (1974), who also examined the relation between the Columbus commuting area and those of two small cities east of Columbus, Newark and Zanesville (fig. 7.12). The Columbus commuting field extended well into Appalachia, particularly to the southeast, where fewer alternative employment opportunities were available. The commuting zone divide between Columbus's and Newark's 10 percent contour lines is considerably closer to Newark than to Columbus; and Newark's 50 percent commuting zone is pushed almost entirely to the east of Newark by the competition of Columbus. Zanesville, on the other hand, is insulated from Columbus's competition by somewhat greater distance and by the intervening position of Newark and therefore has a more symmetric commuter-shed. The commuting profile shows a

Figure 7.10 Commuting Areas of Cities over 50,000 Population, 1960

Source: Berry 1973.

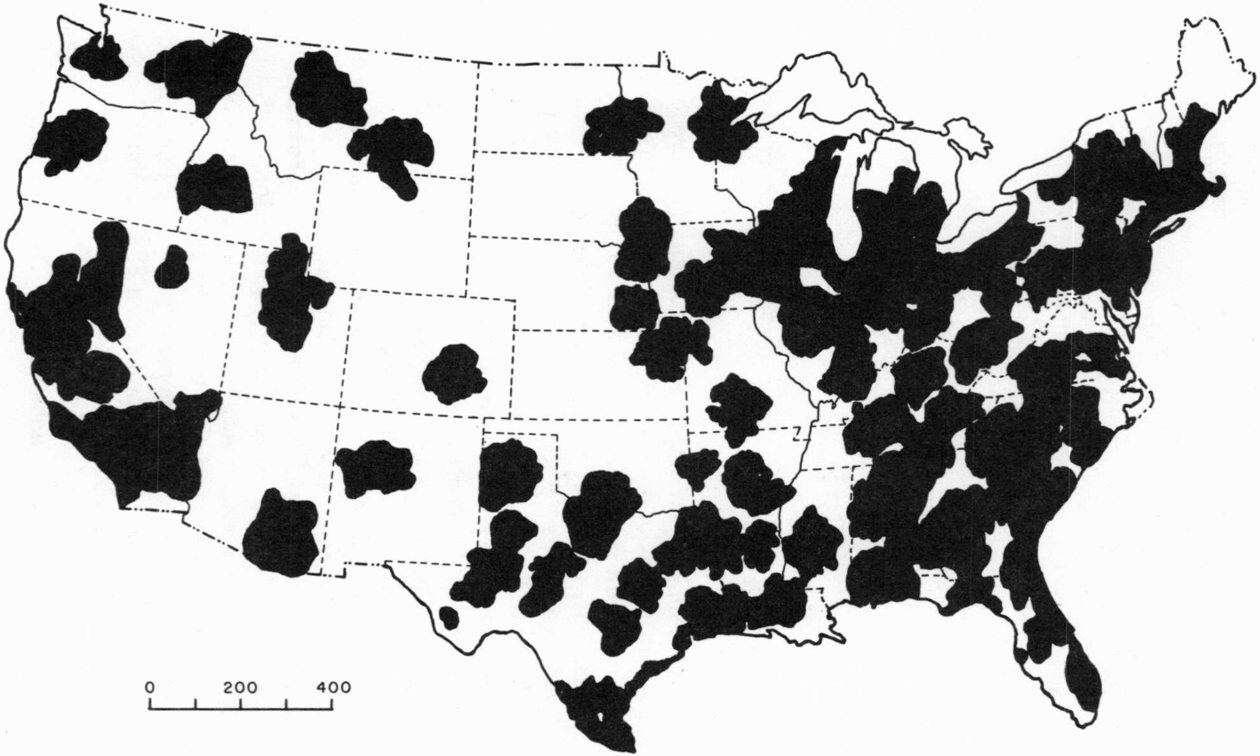

0   200   400

Figure   7.11 Commuting Fields of Principal Metropolitan Areas
Source: Compiled from Berry 1973.

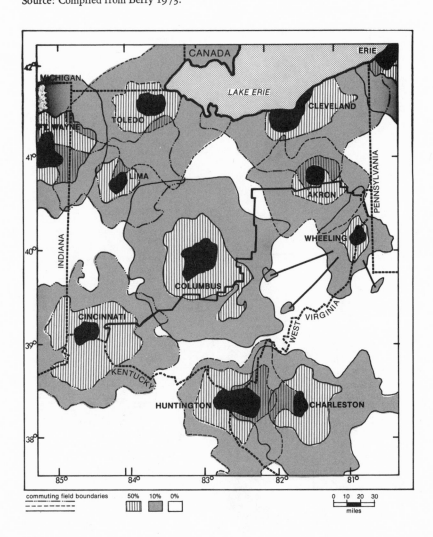

Figure 7.12 Commuting Fields of Columbus, Newark, and Zanesville, Ohio, 1970
Source: Compiled from Smolin 1974.

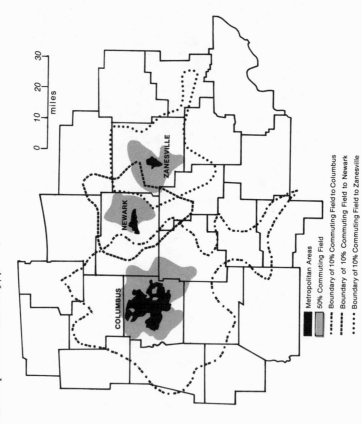

Figure 7.13 Commuting Profiles of Columbus, Newark, and Zanesville, Ohio, 1970

Source: Smolin 1974.

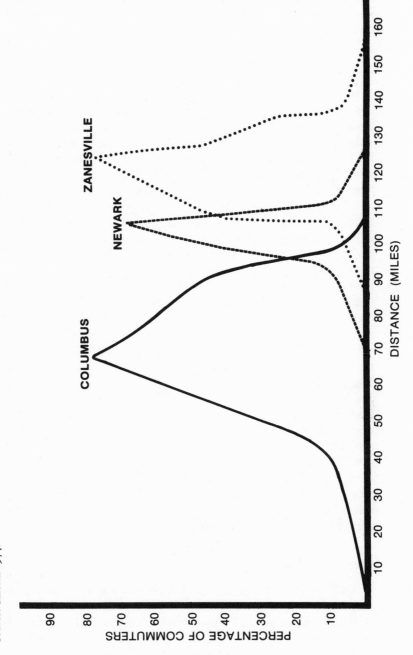

typical pattern for large-center, small-center competition (fig. 7.13). Columbus has a gradual decline with distance in its commuting percentages, and Newark has a sharp decline, particularly on the west side that faces Columbus.

Peripheral Highways

In the course of examining peripheral and external commuting, it became apparent that a key feature of the highway pattern within metropolitan areas is the peripheral highway, also called the outerbelt, the ring highway, or the circumferential highway. The best-known highway of these is Route 128 around Boston. Others include the Tri-State Expressway around Chicago, Interstate 465 around Indianapolis, and Interstate 270 around Columbus. The peripheral highway acts as a locus for industry and therefore for employment, as initially demonstrated by Boston's Route 128 and more recently by other cities. Nodes of particularly high accessibility are established at points where major radials intersect these peripheral highways. In addition to access to points around the ring, the nodes are readily accessible to the CBD by way of the major radial. Also pulled toward these nodes are other key transport facilities such as airports, consolidated truck terminals, and TOFC terminals. External commuting is also facilitated by the development of peripheral highways. The radials that intersect the ring are usually interstate highways that offer easy, relatively fast access to metropolitan area employment for nearby rural areas and small cities located outside the metropolitan area itself. Long-distance commuting to the CBD, which involves rush-hour traffic and increasingly difficult parking problems would seem much less attractive than commuting over an uncrowded expressway, usually through an open countryside, to a destination with a comparatively modest parking problem. If one were to take a one-hour journey to work as a maximum, the commuting zones from the peripheral nodes would probably extend farther than Berry's commuting zones. In addition, this arrangement seems to encourage a corridor development of industry out along the interstates from the peripheral highway, a trend that should have the effect of further extending commuting ranges.

Access to Information

A final aspect of transportation that is relevant to industrial location might be called, for want of a better term, *access to information*. One evidence of a city's access to information is its position within the intermetropolitan hierarchy. As this hierarchy has developed, the largest metropolitan centers have increased their influence, particularly on each other. Many of the metropolitan areas originally functioned predominantly as regional centers with their own hinterlands. Now they function as nodes in an increasingly interconnected national network.

Air connections and air traffic trace out the intermetropolitan hierarchy reasonably well, and an examination of the changes over the past twenty years in the pattern of air passenger flows among the large cities can provide information about this hierarchy (figs. 7.14 and 7.15). In a study of air passenger linkages between one hundred United States metropolitan areas, Filani (1972) linked each city to the city that accounted for the greatest number of air passengers from that city. A city was classified as a *dominant center* if its largest flow of passengers was to a smaller center. The four dominant centers in 1950 included New York, whose largest flow was to Boston; Los Angeles, to San Francisco; Seattle, to Portland; and Dallas, to Houston (fig. 7.14). A city was classified as a *satellite center* if its greatest flow of passengers was to a larger city but it had smaller cities linked to it. Atlanta, for example, dominated the air traffic of eleven smaller centers, but it, in turn, was dominated by New York. Closer examination of the traffic of the fourteen satellite centers in 1950 revealed in several cases a hierarchical structure with second- and third-level satellite centers. In addition to the sixteen smaller cities that had their largest linkages directly to Chicago, two other centers were linked to Kansas City, which, in turn, was dominated by Chicago. One center was linked to Memphis, which was linked to Louisville, which, in turn, was linked to Chicago. Since Chicago's largest traffic flow was to New York, Kansas City and Louisville should be considered second-level satellite centers and Memphis a third-level satellite center. With the advent of the jet, the structure became more simplified in 1970 (fig. 7.15). Seattle linked to San Francisco, bringing the Pacific Northwest into the Los Angeles system and reducing the number of dominant centers to three. The number of satellite centers was reduced to six, and the focus on New York and Los Angeles increased markedly. The number of cities with their greatest air passenger flows to New York increased from twenty-four in 1950 to fifty of the one hundred cities in 1970. Approximately thirty-eight cities shifted linkages from smaller to larger cities. In the American Manufacturing Belt, direct linkages to New York replaced linkages to satellite centers such as Detroit, Pittsburgh, and Washington. In the South, many smaller cities formerly linked to Atlanta shifted to direct New York linkages.

Fuel restrictions placed on airlines have forestalled network changes

Figure 7.14 United States Air Traffic Linkages, 1950
Source: Compiled from Filani 1972.

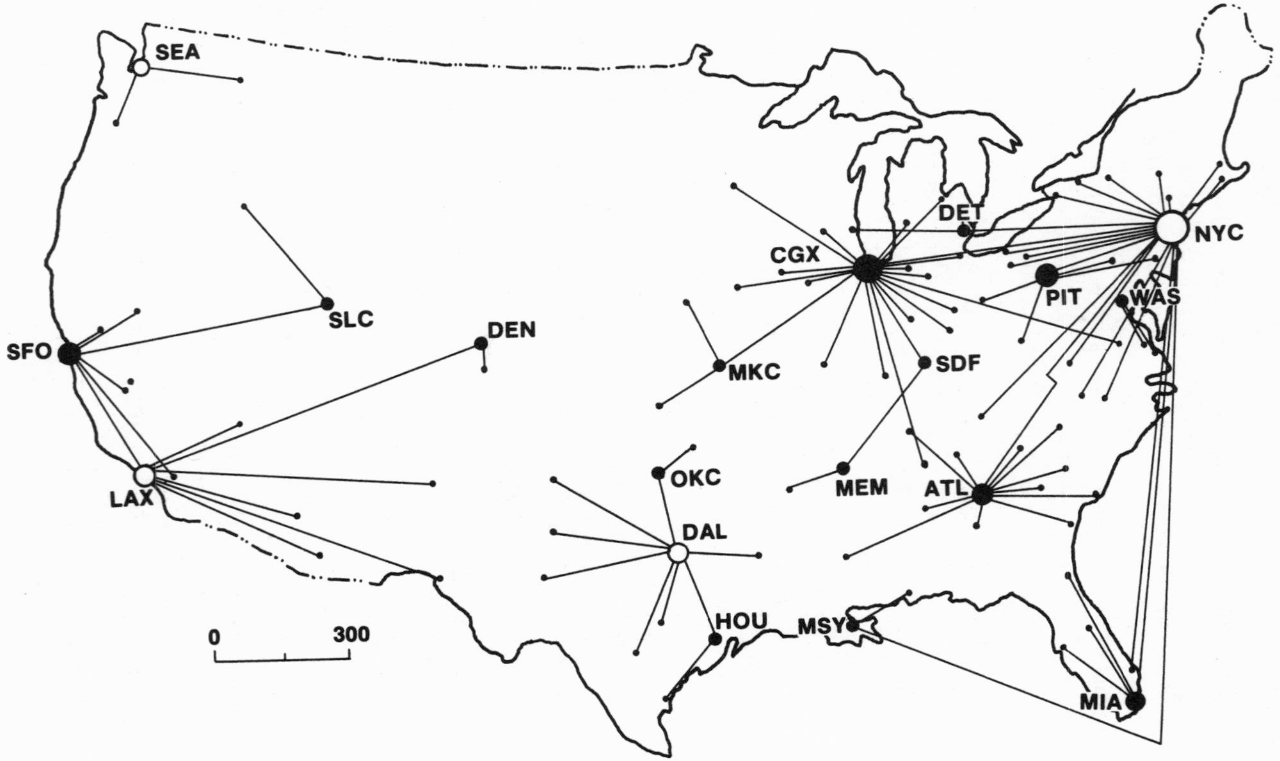

Figure 7.15 United States Air Traffic Linkages, 1970
Source: Compiled from Filani 1972.

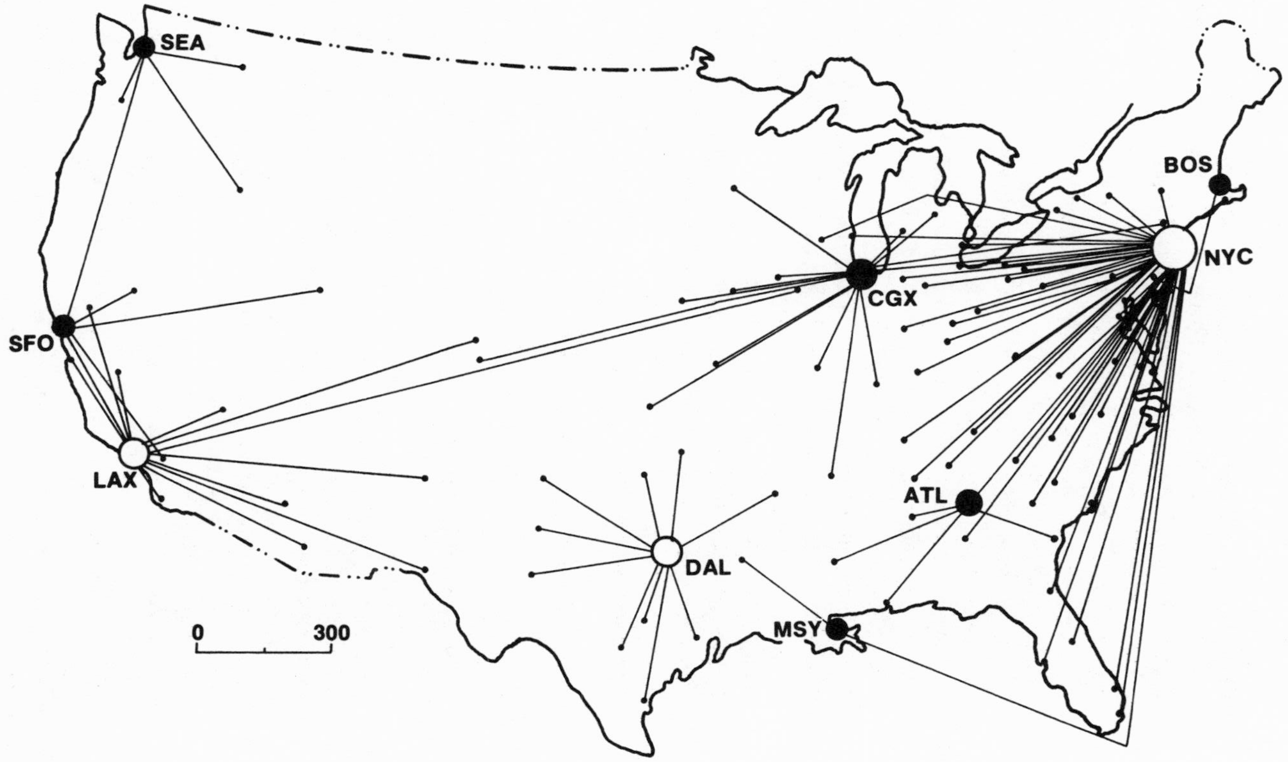

in recent years, and if this trend continues, by 1980 an integrated inter-metropolitan network may exist, with New York as the only dominant center. The four first-level satellite centers will be Chicago, Atlanta, Dallas, and Los Angeles. Only Los Angeles will have second-level centers—Seattle and San Francisco. This sort of linkage will make it imperative for a firm to take into account available connections to its personnel for the major centers of this intermetropolitan network. Single-plane service that operates at convenient hours will be a prime consideration.

This chapter has surveyed four different ways in which transportation affects the location of industry, which may be summarized as follows:

1. The structure of freight rates usually favors larger centers, but their importance in industrial location is diminishing.

2. Accessibility to market seems to be the most important aspect of transport costs. The locating firm is more concerned with maximizing revenues than with minimizing costs.

3. An increasingly relevant part of the transportation problem is the sort of access that is provided to labor. Firms located in the CBD are more dependent upon mass transit; firms located in the suburbs are dependent on commuting over highways, as well as on reverse commuting from the city. For suburban firms, extended commuting from outside the metropolitan area also may become an important factor.

4. A city's degree of involvement in a national air network of inter-metropolitan linkages is significant to many locating firms.

Notes

1. The appendix to this chapter provides a brief annotated list of transportation data sources.

2. For example, railroads serving California offered low promotional rates on citrus so that the developing California citrus industry could compete with Florida citrus; railroads serving the Pacific Northwest offered low rates on lumber so as to make western lumber competitive in midwestern and eastern markets.

3. Perhaps the most extreme example of rate grouping was the wine rate structure as it existed in the old transcontinental rate patterns. An enormous rate blanket covered most of the United States. Competitors in this case are the importers bringing in wine from Europe. The railroads serving California wine districts charged New York buyers no more than Denver buyers in order to improve the prospects of California wine sales on the East Coast.

4. From 1945 to 1970, only sixteen miles of new subway were built in United States cities. From 1970 to 1975, however, more than sixty miles of new subway were planned and from 1975 to 1990, ninety-one additional miles of subway are planned (Owen 1972).

Appendix

Annotated Bibliography of Selected Sources of Transportation Data

1. A. Reuben H. Donnelley, (pub.). *Official Airline Guide.*
Information on all scheduled airlines, i.e., departure, arrival, flight number, type of aircraft, stops, etc. There are four major issues: (1) North American Timetable Edition, (2) Quick Reference: North American Edition, (3) Quick Reference: International Edition, and (4) Worldwide Timetable Edition.

2. Civil Aeronautics Board. *Domestic Origin-Destination Survey of Airline Passenger Traffic* (Air Transport Association of America, 1000 Connecticut Ave. N.W., Washington, D.C. 20036).
These data are sampled by a 10 percent continuous sampling method. Two major sections are published for each year: the first reports passenger flows between all scheduled cities in the United States, and the second illustrates the routing between city pairs with detailed traffic flows.

3. Department of the Army. Corps of Engineers. *Waterborne Commerce of the United States.*
This set of data is geographically divided into four regions: (1) Atlantic Coast, (2) Gulf Coast, Mississippi River System, and Antilles, (3) Great Lakes, and (4) Pacific Coast, Alaska, and Hawaii. Data focus on movements of commodities and vessels at ports, harbors, waterways, and canals. Both foreign and domestic commerce of United States by water are included. A summary section is also included.

4. Porter, John S., and St. Clair, Frank J. *Moody's Manual of Investments; American & Foreign: Transportation.*
Information on railroad, air, water, pipe, and road. General operating, traffic, and financial statistics are available for the various companies, as well as route maps.

5. U.S. Department of Commerce. Bureau of the Census. *Census of Transportation.*
Consists of the following surveys:
Travel survey. Person-trips, person-miles, trips classified by modes of travel, trip frequency, income, occupation, census region of origin and destination, length, duration, and purpose of trip.
Truck inventory and use survey. Trucks and truck-miles classified from states and census geographic divisions (nine divisions) by size class, body type, fuel, major use. Major products (twelve categories) carried by geographic divisions.
Commodity Transportation Survey.
SHIPPER GROUPS. These data are from a sample of shipping records drawn from the files of manufacturing establishments. Commodities are classified into twenty-four shipper groups and eighty-six shipper classes. Tons and ton-miles by shipper group and class by mode, by geographic division of origin and destination.
PRODUCTION AREAS AND SELECTED STATES. Origin-destination data for production areas for groups and classes of commodities. For selected states, com-

modity groups and classes by mode, by distance and by geographic division of destination.

COMMODITY GROUPS. Detailed commodity breakdown using TCC (transport commodity code) categories at three-, four-, five-, and six-digit levels. Commodities by length of brand and weight of shipments. Selected commodities (major three-digit TCC classes) by geographic division of origin-destination by mode.

6. U.S. Interstate Commerce Commission. Bureau of Economics. *Carload Waybill Statistics.*

Consists of three sections as follows:

a. *State-to-State Distribution*: Data have been collected for state-to-state rail carload movements for five major commodity groups: agriculture, animal, mining, forest, and manufacture.

b. *Mileage Block Distribution*: This illustrates the distribution of rail carload traffic by specified mileage blocks for the commodity groups. The purpose of this section is to show differences in the selected characteristics for short line hauls.

c. *Territorial Distribution*: Selected characteristics have been tabulated for rail carload movements by commodity groups among the five railroad territories (Mountain Pacific, Western Trunk Line, Southwestern, Southern, and Official).

7. U.S. Interstate Commerce Commission. Bureau of Economics. *Transport Economics: Monthly Comment.*

This is a monthly publication that deals with selected facets of railroad transportation. Data are included for each item studied. Includes such general data as growth of various sectors of railroad, comments on *Carload Waybill Statistics*, etc.

8. U.S. Interstate Commerce Commission. Bureau of Economics. *Tons of Revenue Freight Originated and Tons Terminated in Carloads by Classes of Commodities and by Geographic Areas.*

Essentially a summary of the rail waybill statistics by broad state groupings.

Chapter 8
Labor and Industrial
Location

It may not be far-fetched to state that labor is the most important single factor influencing plant location (and plant relocation) decisions. Without a supply of competent workers no plant can operate efficiently and competitively in a market economy. For this reason proof of the availability of a qualified labor force that can be hired at a reasonable cost is often required by an industrial firm before it will locate in an area—especially if the area has a low unemployment rate or questionable labor productivity, or both. Despite labor's importance, however, few reliable standards have been developed for evaluating the labor resources of an area.

An area's overall unemployment rate is frequently viewed as the key index in evaluating the labor market. Partly because of past experience, many industrialists intuitively believe that where unemployment rates are high, many people are in the job market and they will have little difficulty in attracting workers. Conversely, where unemployment rates are low, the reverse is true: they anticipate greater difficulty in filling labor requirements. As a result, industrialists often reject areas with low unemployment rates as locations for their plants. Those who use the local unemployment rate as the only criterion in evaluating the labor market will, in all probability, dismiss some profitable locations. Industrialists and economic developers alike need to understand that the unemployed may be only a portion of the recruitable labor available in an area. Likewise, industrialists that reject areas because their workers have a poor labor image would be well advised to evaluate the labor markets for themselves, paying particular attention to the requirements of their own plants. This chapter presents some techniques for evaluating labor availability and costs. First, some general characteristics of the labor force and the labor requirements of industry are discussed. This is followed by a description of useful methods for evaluating an area's labor force and determining local wage and fringe benefit data.

Labor Forces and Labor Requirements

Industries vary in their labor requirements just as labor forces vary in a number of ways in different areas. From an economic development point of view, the more successful industrial development projects are those in which the labor force characteristics can easily be made to match industry requirements, particularly if some upgrading of the labor force occurs. This section discusses the relationships between workers and jobs and the labor requirements of industry.

Relationships between Workers and Jobs

A general relationship exists between a person's educational attainment, occupation or skill category, and income level. The relationship also extends to the person's propensity to migrate from one area to another and the distance he or she is willing to commute daily to a job. An understanding of these relationships is important to evaluate an area's labor market successfully.

Education, occupation, and income. The best-known relationship about the characteristics of labor is the one among education, occupation, and income. One's level of educational attainment helps to determine his occupation category, which in turn is associated with a particular income level. Only when considering income levels within similar occupation categories does some allowance need to be made because of differences in the age and sex of its workers and the income convergence that has occurred between some of the occupations in different categories over the past few decades.

Occupation data reveal that nearly half the workers (46 percent) with less than eight years of school are employed as unskilled laborers and service workers (table 8.1). The other half (45 percent) are primarily employed as semiskilled operatives or skilled craftsmen and foremen. Very few workers with less than an eighth-grade education are employed in other occupations. Virtually the same occupation distribution is apparent for persons completing eight to eleven years of school. Three-fourths (77 percent) are employed in the unskilled, semiskilled, and skilled categories. A smaller percentage are laborers (32 percent), and a slightly larger percentage are clerical and sales workers (14 percent).

These figures demonstrate that the vast majority of workers with less than twelve years of education are employed in blue-collar jobs. Income data show that the unskilled laborers and service workers are among the lowest-paid occupations (table 8.2). The semiskilled operatives are paid somewhat higher rates, and skilled craftsmen and foremen receive up to 50 percent more than the unskilled worker.

Those with a high school education only are employed primarily as clerical and sales workers (33 percent) or as semiskilled operatives or skilled craftsmen and foremen (31 percent). Half of the high school graduates are employed as white-collar workers and the other half as

Table 8.1. Percentage of Employed Persons in Occupation Group by Years of School Completed, 1971

Occupation	Education (in years)				
	<8	8–11	12	13–15	≥16
Professional and technical	0.7	1.7	6.7	19.8	63.4
Managers and administrators	5.2	7.6	10.8	16.2	19.2
Clerical and sales workers	4.2	13.7	33.0	34.5	12.0
Craftsmen, foremen, and operatives	44.5	45.3	30.8	15.4	2.7
Laborers, farm, and service workers	45.5	31.7	18.8	14.1	2.8
Percentage of 1975 population over 25 years old	11.6	25.9	36.2	12.4	13.9

Source: The Conference Board 1972, supplemented by U.S. Department of Commerce, *Statistical Abstract of the United States, 1977*, p. 123, table 199.

Table 8.2. Median Income in the United States by Occupation and Sex, 1974

Occupation	Male Income	Female Income
Professional and technical	$14,873	$9,570
Managers and administrators	15,425	8,603
Sales workers	12,523	5,168
Clerical workers	11,514	6,827
Craftsmen and foremen	12,028	6,492
Operatives	10,176	5,766
Service workers	8,638	5,046
Laborers	8,145	5,891
Farmers and farm managers	5,459	—
Farm laborers	5,097	—
Private household workers	—	2,676

Source: U.S. Department of Commerce, *Statistical Abstract of the United States, 1977*, p. 383, table 617.

blue-collar workers. Members of the labor force with some college education (one to three years) are primarily employed in white-collar occupations (70 percent). Over a third (36 percent) are employed in professional, technical, managerial, or administrative positions. A similar number (35 percent) work in clerical and sales positions. Four-fifths (83 percent) of those having a college degree are employed in upper-level positions, most notably in professional and technical occupations. Again income levels correspond with occupation and education levels, with professional and technical workers averaging nearly twice as much as unskilled workers.

Female workers in every occupation category receive considerably less income than their male counterparts. In part this disparity results from discrimination within any particular industry. Another reason for it is that many low-wage, labor-intensive industries employ a substantial number of female workers, while higher-wage, capital-intensive firms tend to favor employing males in the same occupation categories. The difference also results partly from different types of careers within the same occupation category selected by males and females.[1]

Not only do income or wage levels vary among different occupation categories and between male and female workers in the same category, but they differ across regions of the country for identical jobs and even within the same region (Fuchs 1967; Goodstein 1970; Hoch 1972; table 8.3). The South has been and still is the region having the lowest wage levels. From the time of the Civil War up to the present, the South's average hourly manufacturing wage rate has remained nearly 20 percent below the national average (Scully 1971). The Northeast, North Central, and West tend to pay successively higher rates. It should also be noted that regional wage differences tend to be wider for unskilled, blue-collar workers than for those in white-collar positions. One major reason for regional wage level differences is the type of manufacturing activities that make up their industrial structures. Southern manufacturing is dominated by labor-intensive industry whereas manufacturing in the Northeast, North Central, and West is characterized by a diversified mix of both labor- and capital-intensive types. The greater the proportion of capital-intensive firms in a region's industrial structure, the higher is its average manufacturing wage, because the potential for improvement in labor productivity, and thus the wage level, is greater for capital-intensive types (Moriarty 1977 and 1978).

Another important index, which helps to explain not only regional wage rate differences but also wage rate differences within the same region for identical jobs, is the size of the city in which the manufacturing firm is located (table 8.3). An industrial plant located in a small town

Table 8.3. Relative Pay Levels for Selected Occupation Groups by Region and Size of Metropolitan Area, 1969–1970 (percentage of average United States pay level for each occupation group)

Region and population size of metropolitan area	Office clerical workers	Skilled maintenance workers	Unskilled plant workers
Northeast			
1,000,000 or more	100	99	104
250,000–1,000,000	96	90	93
Less than 250,000	90	85	90
North Central			
1,000,000 or more	100	105	107
250,000–1,000,000	98	100	105
Less than 250,000	99 [a]	98 [a]	112 [a]
South			
1,000,000 or more	97	96	82
250,000–1,000,000	90	91	80
Less than 250,000	92	98 [a]	77 [a]
West			
1,000,000 or more	106	107	111
250,000–1,000,000	94	100 [a]	96
Less than 250,000	90	n.a.	93 [a]

Source: U.S. Bureau of Labor Statistics 1972, pp. 195–96, table 92.
[a] Pay level based on fewer than five SMSAS; n.a. = no data available.

or rural area would pay lower wage rates for identical jobs than one located in a large city within the same region. This fact also helps to explain the South's manufacturing wage level. Unlike those in other regions in the country, a large proportion of southern industrial plants, notably those that are labor-intensive, tend to locate in small towns and rural areas (Lonsdale 1969; Lonsdale and Browning 1971; table 8.4). Industrial plants in the Northeast and elsewhere, on the other hand, exhibit a preference to locate in or adjacent to larger cities and metropolitan areas.

Migration and commuting patterns. It is commonly accepted that workers tend to migrate from areas where they receive low pay to areas where higher wages are paid for the same skills, provided that the cost of living in both places is approximately equal. Workers also migrate from stagnant areas of high unemployment to places where employment is expanding. Recent studies of migration, however, reveal that depressed areas in general are not characterized by high rates of out-migration, as

Table 8.4. Percentage of Manufacturing Wage Earners by Type of Location, 1920–1961

	Major industrial area	Dispersed counties with cities of 100,000 or more	All other counties
United States			
1929	58.8	8.1	33.2
1939	56.3	8.3	35.3
1947	60.0	6.6	33.4
1954	60.5	6.3	33.2
1958	59.2	8.0	32.8
1961	58.2	8.3	33.5
Southeast			
1929	4.4	19.6	76.0
1939	3.7	19.3	77.1
1947	10.4	15.1	74.5
1954	11.4	15.1	73.5
1958	10.8	22.0	67.2
1961	9.9	21.9	68.2

Source: Cramer 1963, n. 6 and tables 4, 7, and 23.

commonly believed. On the contrary, such areas have low out-migration rates. More important are their very low in-migration rates. Prosperous areas, on the other hand, have high rates of in-migration and high rates of out-migration as well because there is a great deal of counterstream or cross-migration between prosperous areas, particularly by well-educated young adults. These mobility patterns show that the labor force, and especially certain members of the labor force, are not as mobile as commonly accepted. The fact is that migration rates differ substantially for workers among occupation categories and among stages of the life cycle (table 8.5). Female migration rates follow the same general pattern as that found for males.

Probably the most important characteristic of migration is that the dominant migrating group is young adults in their twenties and thirties, the most sought-after work-age group. People over the age of forty are less likely to move often. Within any age group, workers that have gone to college are more mobile than those with successively less education.[2] Because a worker's occupation category is related to his or her level of educational attainment, it is also related to migration rates (table 8.5). White-collar workers, regardless of age, migrate more than blue-collar workers. Salaried professional and technical workers are most likely to change location and unskilled laborers, least likely. This fact helps to explain why regional wage rate disparities are greater for unskilled workers. Highly trained people are quick to respond to better job opportunities in other regions. Consequently, employers throughout the country tend to pay them competitive salaries. The relative immobility of unskilled workers makes them subject to accepting the prevailing rate in the region in which they are located.

Because of regional wage differences and differences in the propensity for workers in different occupation categories to migrate, industries that employ a substantial number of unskilled and semiskilled workers are more sensitive to locational differences in the availability, cost, and quality of labor than those that employ skilled and technical workers. These latter industries are likely to be more concerned with other locational factors, including local amenities or other special attributes that make a place attractive for the types of workers they need to recruit from other areas. This means that industries that employ primarily minimally skilled workers have a poor chance of attracting them to areas where they are in short supply, either because their numbers in the labor force are

Table 8.5. Intercounty Migration Rates per 100 Males by Age, Education, and Occupation Group, 1965–1970

	Age		
	25–34	35–44	45–64
Years of school completed			
College (4 or more years)	51.7	28.3	15.8
College (1 to 3 years)	33.8	21.5	13.0
High school (4 years)	24.5	15.5	9.4
High school (1 to 3 years)	21.0	12.9	7.9
Elementary (8 grades or less)	17.6	11.9	7.2
Occupation group (employed males only)			
Professional and technical workers (salaried)	46.2	26.0	15.0
Professional and technical workers (self-employed)	41.3	17.6	7.8
Managers and administrators (except farm, salaried)	37.8	24.4	13.2
Managers and administrators (except farm, self-employed)	26.7	13.0	7.0
Sales workers	34.8	19.8	10.3
Clerical workers	26.4	13.9	7.5
Craftsmen and foremen	23.2	13.1	7.6
Operatives, including transport	20.5	11.6	6.3
Laborers (except farm)	19.1	11.1	6.4
Service workers (including private household)	21.2	12.1	7.8

Source: U.S. Bureau of the Census, *Census of Population Subject Reports: Mobility for States and the Nation, 1973*, pp. 23–25 and 52–60, tables 5 and 9.

small or their unemployment rate is low. On the other hand, industries that employ more highly skilled workers are better able to locate in labor-deficient areas because of the greater mobility of this labor force segment.

This leads to the problem of determining the size of a labor supply or labor-draw area. Too often labor force statistics are provided by political or statistical districts such as counties, cities, or metropolitan areas only. For an industrial plant located at a specific site within some district, such data are misleading. The data are likely to be out of date and not sufficiently detailed to be useful for a thorough labor analysis. In addition to those deficiencies, the same data cannot be used for a plant located at the periphery of a district and for one located at its center because the plants are in two different labor-draw areas by virtue of the feasible commuting ranges of their employees. That is, people are willing to commute a certain distance daily to their jobs. If they must travel beyond this distance, they will change either their residence location, their place of work, or, in some cases, both (see chapter 7).

Research on commuting patterns reveals that a majority of workers reside close to their jobs and that fewer and fewer reside further away as the commuting distance increases (Lonsdale 1966). For practical purposes, the maximum labor-draw area extends thirty miles from the plant location—or more important, within one hour of commuting time. The prime labor-draw area, from which about 60 percent of the labor force is drawn, is fifteen miles, or approximately a half hour of commuting time. Time-distance calculation is viewed as the more accurate method of determining the extent of labor-draw areas. For example, the geographic extent of a labor-draw area is likely to be greater in a rural area than in a metropolitan district because traffic congestion is less of a problem. On the other hand, rural areas with poor roads or poor road networks can have more limited labor-draw areas than metropolitan districts that have extensive networks of limited access highways and commuter rail service. Despite the geographic setting, about 85 percent of the labor force live within a distance of twenty miles or forty-five minutes of commuting time. An industrial plant that anticipates recruiting a large percentage of its necessary labor force from beyond this twenty-mile radius may find that new places of employment may locate in the area at a later time, closer to these long-distance commuters and thus they may transfer to the new places. Conversely, if a large number of workers in the labor-draw area out-commute daily over a distance of twenty miles, the chances of recruiting them for local employment are relatively high.

While the sixty-, forty-five-, and thirty-minute travel zones are useful in delimiting the maximum, general, and prime labor-draw areas overall, commuting distances traveled by workers vary with their occupations. Professional and technical workers travel greater distances than unskilled and semiskilled workers. This difference can be explained partly by differences in incomes. Skilled white-collar workers receive higher incomes and thus can afford to spend more on commuting than lower-skilled, blue-collar workers. In fact, many industrial plants located in the suburban areas of large metropolitan districts have considerable difficulty attracting and retaining low-skilled, blue-collar workers because the cost of commuting from their homes in the central core area is too high. In order to retain these workers, manufacturing firms have found it necessary to pay them a commuting subsidy—in essence, a higher wage rate. This fact again points out an important locational consideration for many types of manufacturing establishments: it is far easier to locate an industrial plant in an area that already fulfills the requirements of the industry than to locate in an area where the labor force either needs extensive training or has to be attracted from other areas in order to fulfill the requirements.[3]

Unemployment and labor force participation rates. When investigating the availability of labor in an area, manufacturers and developers need to analyze which workers are unemployed, which are underemployed, and which are underutilized. It must also be ascertained at the outset that the supply of potential workers is not the result of seasonal conditions in other places of employment having overlapping labor-draw areas.

It has become a well-known fact that unemployment rates differ by age, sex, occupation, race, marital status, and the worker's interest in full- or part-time employment only. Married, full-time, white-collar, caucasian, male workers between the ages of twenty and fifty-four have the lowest unemployment rates. High unemployment rates are generally found among unmarried, part-time, blue-collar, noncaucasian, female, teenage workers. If a substantial number of the unemployed in a labor-draw area have the required skills and are married full-time workers between twenty and fifty-four years old, the chances are excellent that a qualified labor force is available. However, if the unemployed are unskilled, unmarried, part-time, female, teenage workers that tend to change jobs or move in and out of the labor force frequently, fulfilling labor requirements can be difficult. Because these workers have high turnover rates in addition to high rates of absenteeism, industries that employ many persons from this segment of the labor force need a far larger number of available workers than those that employ people from categories having lower turnover rates.

Underemployed workers fall into two groups: those that are working in part-time jobs but would like full-time employment and those whose skills are underutilized in their present jobs. Workers in both groups are interested in seeking better employment if it becomes available. As a result of the close association between occupation and education, a comparison of these data for the labor-draw area can reveal whether its labor force is underemployed or working to its full potential. If a considerable number of workers in the area have relatively high educational attainment but are primarily employed in unskilled and semiskilled positions, they probably have the potential to be employed in more highly skilled jobs. Such workers can easily be trained for better positions. On the other hand, if a large number of workers in an area have relatively low educational attainment in comparison to the skill levels of the jobs they hold, the labor force is employed at its maximum skill potential and extensive training programs would be required to upgrade skill levels even moderately. Labor-draw areas with a large number of part-time workers in labor force categories that usually exhibit high, full-time job participation rates also indicate that underemployment exists in an area. Another clue to underemployment is a large number of household domestic workers, whether employed on a part-time or full-time basis. A large number of domestics generally indicates the availability of a good female labor supply for firms employing unskilled or semiskilled women, since wherever the demand for female labor is high, domestic help is unavailable. Low family incomes and poor female labor participation rates in an area also indicate that females can be easily drawn into the labor market.

The unemployed and underemployed are only a portion of the recruitable workers available in a labor-draw area. A significant number of underutilized workers may also be available. Comparison of labor force participation rates in a labor-draw area with those of the nation as a whole is one logical method of determining worker utilization. For the United States the proportion of working-age people participating in the labor force has remained at 58 to 59 percent for some time. But for a more accurate determination of the number of underutilized workers, the participation rates by age and sex are more important (table 8.6). While over three-fourths of the males and nearly one-half the females over the age of sixteen are full-time workers, the greatest participation rates are between the ages of twenty and fifty-four for both sexes. Over 90 percent of the males and 54 percent of the females in this age group are employed in full-time jobs. It should also be remembered that for any age group the rate of labor force participation is higher for married males and single females and lower for single males and married females. Any age or sex group that has an actual percentage of employed persons in the labor-draw area lower than that of the nation as a whole is probably an underutilized group. The percentage difference can be used to calculate the potential number of recruitable workers within each group. On the

Table   8.6. United States Labor Force Participation Rates by Age and Sex (percentage of age group)

Age group	Male		Female	
	1975	1980[a]	1975	1980[a]
16–19	60.2	62.0	49.0	51.3
20–24	84.5	84.5	64.0	67.5
25–34	94.1	94.3	54.4	58.4
35–44	94.9	94.7	55.7	58.1
45–54	91.9	90.5	54.3	56.3
55–64	74.7	73.8	40.7	41.6
65 and over	20.8	19.4	7.8	7.7
Total	77.2	77.4	45.8	47.9

Source: U.S. Department of Commerce, *Statistical Abstract of the United States, 1977*, p. 355, table 570.
Note: Add 5 percent to the participation rate for married males and 10 percent for single females. Subtract 10 percent for married females and 5 percent for single males.
[a] Projected participation rate.

other hand, the participation rates for each group can also indicate which groups are being overutilized.

Unionization. Perhaps no single labor force characteristic is analyzed more carefully in plant location decisions than the degree to which the area's workers are involved in trade union activities. Nearly 50 percent of all manufacturing workers are members of unions. However, the degree of union involvement should not be measured simply by the proportion of the manufacturing labor force that belongs to trade unions; the area's history of labor negotiations and contract agreements is more important. Some areas of the country and some types of manufacturing industries are notorious for labor disputes and work stoppages. Other areas and industries either are not heavily unionized or are able to reach accord in contract agreements with less difficulty.

Two factors influence the degree to which a particular type of industry is unionized: the number and size of the manufacturing firms in the industry and the size of the settlement in which the industry's manufacturing plants are located. Industries that have relatively few manufacturing firms operating a small number of large plants (metal, transport, machinery, tobacco, and some chemical industries, for example) are likely to be more highly unionized than industries having a large number of firms operating a large number of small plants (such as lumber, furniture, textile, apparel, and leather industries). It is easily seen that less effort is required to organize a small number of large firms than a large number of small firms. Industries that locate plants in large metropolitan areas are more likely to be unionized than those that locate plants in small towns and rural areas, regardless of the region of the country because fewer job opportunities are available to workers in small settlements. The history of the labor movement has demonstrated that severe personal disruptions may result from involvement in union activities; workers in small towns have fewer possibilities for other employment, should union activity result in the loss of their jobs. In large cities, with numerous job opportunities, this is less likely to be true. In large cities, also, numerous small firms are apt to be unionized, especially when workers in small firms have skills similar to workers employed by large-scale, unionized plants in the same area. The small firms have to provide the same wages and benefits as the unionized firms or lose their workers to the organized plants. As time goes by, though, unionization tends to filter down to plants located in successively smaller cities and towns further and further from the large metropolitan centers.

Regional differences in unionization are a consequence of the manufacturing structure of their economies and the propensity for manufacturing plants within the region to locate either in small settlements or in metropolitan areas. Manufacturing in the South is dominated by numerous, small-scale, labor-intensive, nonunion plants that tend to locate in small towns and rural areas (table 8.4). In other regions of the country, particularly in the traditional Manufacturing Belt of the Northeast, manufacturing is highly diversified, highly unionized, and a metropolitan area phenomenon. These characteristics are partly explained by the nature of industry in the Northeast—capital-intensive, and requiring specialized labor, business, financial, legal, repair, transportation, communication, public, and other services that are not easily provided in small settlements. Urban services are not as important to many of the South's traditional industries, so they are attracted to small settlements that offer lower-cost land and labor.

Unions view areas having lower wages as a threat to employment in areas of high unionization and high wages, since manufacturers are tempted to locate new plants in the low-wage areas to save on labor costs. Within certain industries unions have reduced the regional differences in labor costs by gaining sufficient strength to conduct industrywide labor bargaining. For these industries the importance of labor cost as a plant location factor is reduced.

Labor Requirements of Industry

In some ways one industry does not differ from another in its labor requirements. All want a day's work for a day's pay, and all prefer that their work force is not too old or too young. In other ways they differ substantially. Depending on the products manufactured, industries employ work forces with considerably different occupation mixes, as well as different sex mixes.

Age requirements. While the labor force is usually made up of people over age sixteen, industry prefers to employ those between the ages of twenty and fifty-four. The most desirable work-force age structure resembles a bell-shaped normal curve in which approximately 68 percent of the workers are between the ages of thirty and forty-five; 14 percent, between twenty and thirty; another 14 percent, between forty-five and fifty-five; and 4 percent, under age twenty and over fifty-five. This age structure insures an industry the stability provided by older workers and a continuing supply of younger workers who can be trained in the skills required to replace the retiring workers.[4] Consequently, it is important that the supply of recruitable labor within any skill category be neither too old nor too young, but with an age spread that will allow an industry to employ a work force having a normally distributed age structure. The percentage and number of high school graduates who enter the labor force each year, as well as those who go on to college are also important indices in estimating future labor supplies.

Sex requirements. Almost every industry employs different sex mixes (for example, see table 8.7). Some employ nearly all males; others, nearly all females; and still others, an almost equal number of both sexes. In the past the physical strength needed by workers was important in determining an industry's sex mix, but that is not so important today. The important factor now is tradition, along with labor laws and some amount of discrimination. The tendency persists, however, for labor-intensive, heavy industry to employ more males and for labor-intensive, light industry to employ a large number of females. The same holds true for capital-intensive industry, although a more evenly distributed sex mix is sometimes likely. It is nevertheless important to point out that many jobs traditionally in the domain of male workers are held by women in areas of low unemployment where male workers are in short supply. In areas of high unemployment women are likely to have low labor force participation rates, and a high percentage of men are employed in manufacturing

Table 8.7. Average Labor Requirements for Selected Industries (percentage of total employed)

Occupation	Sawmill wood products			Optical and health service equipment			Leather footwear		
	Males	Females	Total	Males	Females	Total	Males	Females	Total
Professional	2.0	0.0	2.0	11.5	2.0	13.5	1.0	0.5	1.5
Managerial	5.0	0.0	5.0	7.0	0.0	7.0	2.5	0.5	3.0
Sales	1.0	0.0	1.0	3.0	0.0	3.0	1.5	0.0	1.5
Clerical	2.0	4.5	6.5	4.0	12.0	16.0	3.0	6.5	9.5
Craftsmen	17.0	1.0	18.0	15.0	4.0	19.0	10.0	5.0	15.0
Operatives	36.5	3.0	39.5	14.0	24.0	38.0	19.0	47.0	66.0
Transport operatives	7.0	0.0	7.0	0.5	0.0	0.5	0.5	0.0	0.5
Laborers	18.0	1.0	19.0	1.0	1.0	2.0	1.0	0.0	1.0
Service workers	2.0	0.0	2.0	1.0	0.0	1.0	1.5	0.5	2.0
Total	90.5	9.5	100.0	57.0	43.0	100.0	40.0	60.0	100.0

Source: Compiled from U.S. Bureau of the Census, Census of Population Subject Reports: Occupation by Industry, 1973, pp. 241–504, table 8.

jobs usually assigned to women. In evaluating an area's labor force participation rates for each sex group, the analyst needs to keep two things in mind. First, labor force participation rates for females are increasing throughout the country, and more and more women are being employed in skills and industries that have traditionally been dominated by men. Consequently, industry can expect to employ a higher percentage of women in the future. Second, an area with low female labor force participation rates may be an attractive location for industrial firms that employ a number of unskilled and semiskilled women.

Occupation skill requirements. The mix of occupation skills employed in manufacturing varies from one industry to another (table 8.7). Most employ a substantial percentage of semiskilled operatives and a fair proportion of skilled craftsmen and foremen. Some employ a high percentage of white-collar workers and few unskilled blue-collar job holders. Others are the opposite; a high percentage of the laborers are unskilled blue-collar workers, along with a low percentage of white-collar workers.

An industry's average wage scale is closely tied to its occupation and sex distribution. Industries that employ a high percentage of women or unskilled blue-collar workers, or have a low percentage of white-collar workers frequently pay a low average wage. Industries dominated by male workers or skilled craftsmen pay a higher average wage, and those that employ a high percentage of white-collar professional and technical workers and relatively few unskilled workers pay an even higher average wage.

Evaluating Work Forces in Labor-Draw Areas

Almost every industry that is considering an area as a possible location needs to conduct a specific study of labor availability plus wage rates and of the number of men and women within a desired age group who are available for work in each skill level (Dunshee 1970; Howard 1974). Additionally, growth trends of the labor force need to be examined to verify whether a continuing supply of workers will be available. To determine the availability and quality of a recruitable work force in a labor-draw area with any degree of reliability involves a great deal of work. The area's available census data are out of date and not detailed enough to be useful in constructing a current assessment. Also much cooperation is required from people not directly involved with economic development activities. The freedom with which this cooperation is extended can greatly affect the reliability of the survey results. Three different survey techniques can be used to identify potential recruitable workers in an area: (1) the industry labor registration survey, (2) the employment service office applicant survey, and (3) the geographical allocation manpower survey. Whatever method is used, manufacturers planning to locate in an area need to supplement the survey results with information obtained from interviews with management personnel in already existing industries.

The Industry Labor Registration Survey

For an industry conducting a comprehensive site search in a smaller community, a labor registration survey can be a practical means of evaluating labor availability when current statistical data are unavailable. Local developers should resist any such registration unless the firm provides a clear assurance that it will locate a plant in the community if sufficient labor is available. Experience has taught economic developers that once a labor registration survey has been conducted by a manufacturing firm that decides not to locate in their area, other manufacturers tend to shy away from the community for some time in the future. Therefore, if local developers are not reasonably sure that the availability of labor in their area meets the needs of the industry, they would be wise to discourage a labor registration. Labor registration surveys are not as effective a tool in large metropolitan areas as in smaller settlements.

A labor registration survey may be conducted in two ways: by personal interview held at a central location chosen by the manufacturing firm or by telephone interview. The personal interview is the method most commonly used because it draws more registrants who are actually interested in new employment; many of the telephone registrants only want to satisfy their curiosity about the new firm. If the personal interview method is used, the number of qualified registrants should exceed the actual number of required workers by a ratio of three to one in order to assure the availability of a recruitable work force. With the telephone interview method, the ratio should be at least five to one or higher.

In order to solicit registrants, the industry publicizes its intention of locating in the area (usually without revealing its name), along with the type of product(s) it manufactures, the major kinds of job skills it wants to employ, and the time and place (or telephone number) where job applicants can register for employment. The job registration may be publicized throughout the labor-draw area by newspaper, radio, television, and billboards, direct mail and circulars, and sometimes by sound truck. The registration period usually lasts three days (one of which should be a Saturday) and includes hours at night as well as during the day.

To obtain the type of information necessary for an accurate evaluation of the available workers in the area, specific, well-phrased questions reflecting the plant's requirements must be asked. Among them may be questions about the applicant's present occupation, place of employment, home address, age, marital status, sex, height, weight, and educational background. The applicant may also be asked whether he or she is willing to work rotating shifts or night shifts, work for a specific wage rate, work full time or seasonally, undergo a training program at reduced pay, and whether any physical handicap might interfere with job performance. Applicants that are too old or too young, do not have the ability to meet required skills, are not willing to work at the stated wage rate or shift time, live beyond the plant's labor-draw area, or for other reasons cannot meet employment requirements are dropped from the list. For public relations reasons applicants who work for already existing industrial firms in the community should also be disqualified except in cases where he or she is underemployed. Depending on the requirements of the plant and the characteristics of the area's labor force, it is not unusual for as many as one-half to three-fourths of the total number of applicants to be disqualified. Still, the remaining number of qualified applicants should be three to five times the number of workers required. For example, a plant requiring one hundred workers should have about three hundred qualified registrants out of as many as six to twelve hundred total registrants.

The Employment Service Office Applicant Survey

The most commonly used method of evaluating labor availability, particularly in and around larger towns and metropolitan areas, is through a survey of the job applicants currently registered by sex and occupation title at public and private employment service offices located throughout the labor-draw area. The applicants are workers who are either new to the labor force, unemployed, or employed but looking for different jobs. Care should be taken not to count applicants twice who are registered at more than one job placement office. Employment service offices vary in the type of labor force information they will supply. Most state employment offices will provide information on the aggregate number of job applicants residing in each county in their service area by occupation title and sex. They can also give the general wage rates in the area by job type and skill level. At times, some are willing to conduct local labor registration surveys. However, data from most employment offices can be misleading and often are useful only for a preliminary work force availability analysis. One reason for its unreliability is that the information is not detailed enough to determine accurately the number of applicants qualified to meet a particular industry's work force requirements. Another reason is that the number of applicants is larger than the actual number of workers searching for jobs. Many of those registered have already found new employment but continue to be listed for sixty days or longer after their last visit to the employment office. Others have left the labor force and are registered only as long as they are able to collect unemployment benefits. For these reasons, when using applicant data from employment service offices, the number of qualified registrants should exceed the actual number of required workers by a ratio of, at least, ten to one.

The purpose of the preliminary analysis is to determine roughly whether a sufficiently large recruitable work force possessing the required occupation skills and sex distribution is potentially available in the area. In the preliminary analysis it is important to determine the number of registered applicants by sex and occupation title for each month of the past year to see if any major fluctuations occur. The number of applicants tends to increase during the summer months when schools are closed, but other seasonal trends can influence the numbers as well. By discounting months that have seasonally high numbers of applicants, a net number of available workers in each occupation category can be determined. To estimate more accurately the number of available qualified workers, this net number of applicants in each occupation category should be compared against the monthly job openings in the area for the same period of time. A record of jobs not readily filled indicates the lack of qualified, available labor in the associated skills, and a record of easily filled jobs reveals an abundance of suitably skilled workers. Unfortunately, many employment offices fail to maintain the data required for this type of longitudinal analysis. Sometimes a sample examination of Sunday newspaper want ads over the past year can reveal the job skills most in demand, the general wage rates paid, and the urgency of the skill needs.

State employment service office restrictions on the type of information that they can provide about available workers limit the degree to which a comprehensive labor force analysis can be made in most areas. In a few circumstances, some state and most private employment offices will provide more detailed information to industrial developers or plant personnel managers. It may be possible to obtain information on the age, sex, former job position, primary and secondary skills, previous wage, and residence location of each individual registrant who is tentatively qualified to fulfill the industry's work force requirements. This data can help the analyst determine more accurately the number of well-qualified registrants, after eliminating the overaged, the seasonally unemployed, the drifters, females receiving aid to dependent children, those with unsuitable skills, those interested only in nonmanufacturing jobs, and those who live beyond the labor-draw area of the plant site. However, the analyst compiling the profile must take care that age, sex, and other forms of illegal discrimination are not practiced.

Whether or not detailed registrant information is provided by the area's job placement offices, the comprehensive analysis should investigate labor force growth and employment trends for the near future. The employment service offices are often able to furnish reasonable forecasts, but other sources are available. Estimates of the number of school dropouts and graduates who enter the local labor market should be obtained from school administrators for three or four years hence, along with the numbers that have been trained in specific skills. The number of new rival jobs likely to be created in the area from the planned expansion of new or existing retail and service establishments or other manufacturing plants can be obtained from local planning departments or chambers of commerce.

The Geographic Allocation Manpower Survey

The geographic allocation manpower survey technique also requires a good bit of preliminary work before it can be used effectively as a method of evaluating· an area's labor force availability. Once the initial work is completed, however, this survey can provide highly accurate and current statistics for a labor-draw area without a great deal of additional effort, especially in nonmetropolitan areas where it is more difficult to acquire current labor force statistics. The technique cannot be used unless the electric utility firms (or at least the telephone companies) servicing the area are willing to provide certain information. To secure the cooperation of the area's electric utility firms is not usually a problem, since the required information is not confidential, and the firms have a long history of being actively involved in the economic development of their service areas.

The technique is called a *geographic allocation survey* because it allocates or, more correctly, reallocates population and labor force statistics collected for census areas (tracts, townships, counties, etc.) to utility company substation distribution districts. The technique relies heavily on the use of maps that accurately portray census area and distribution district boundaries so that the number of people per acre in each labor force category being surveyed can be calculated (fig. 8.1). The number of people per acre in a particular labor force category residing in each census area is allocated to each electric company distribution district in the same proportion that the land area (in acres) of the census area contributes to the land area (also in acres) of the distribution district. In this way the outdated census data can be readily updated on the basis of the total number

Figure   8.1 Geographic Allocation Manpower Survey Methodology

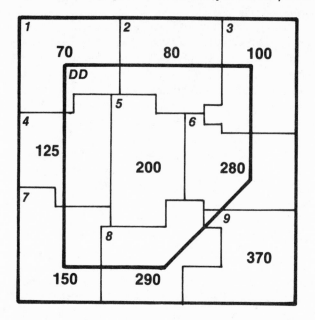

of residential services in each distribution district and the number of new and discontinued residential services since the census was taken. A 2 to 5 percent random sample of the names and addresses of the new service users, provided by the utility companies, is then used in a telephone survey to obtain current information necessary to update each district's labor force statistics (see the appendix to this chapter for a more detailed description of the allocation methodology). The increase (or decline) in the number of electrical services in the distribution districts can be used to estimate the size of the population and labor force fairly accurately, along with their geographic distribution. The telephone sample survey of new service subscribers is necessary to estimate the number of new workers that have moved into each district both by occupation, sex, and age, and by the categories of unemployed, underemployed, underutilized or interested in manufacturing employment. For example, if 10 percent of all the women of prime working age in the families sampled in a district were unemployed and interested in working full time, it is likely that 10 percent of the prime working age women estimated for the total number of new electrical services are unemployed and interested in working. Naturally, if only a 1 percent sample of new service subscribers is surveyed, the estimates are not as likely to be as accurate as those estimated from a 3 percent or 5 percent sample. The number of discontinued services allows similar estimates to be made for the remainder of the area's labor force who have not moved from their residences.

An important feature of the geographic manpower survey is that the work force statistics can be easily related to the labor-draw areas of specific industrial plants through the use of maps. After the important labor force statistics have been updated for each distribution district in an indusrial plant's labor-draw area, the information can be allocated to the prime, general, and maximum labor-draw zones in the same manner that the census area information was allocated to the distribution districts in the first place. The maps—showing the geographic distribution of (1) population, (2) population growth or decline, (3) occupation distribution by sex, (4) prime working age groups, (5) unemployed, underemployed, and underutilized workers, and (6) commuting patterns—are useful tools for analyzing the local labor market and assessing the availability of workers in an industry's labor-draw area.

The Personnel Manager Interview Survey

No matter what type of survey is used to evaluate work force availability in an area, it should be supplemented by interviews with personnel managers of the principal manufacturing firms in the same vicinity to determine their experience with workers. Personnel managers are reluctant to disclose unfavorable information to industrialists interested in locating in the area if local people are present during the interview. For this reason local economic developers should identify personnel managers who are favorably disposed to local workers and those who are not. By knowing the attitudes of personnel managers, developers can guide prospective industrialists to the more complimentary ones and steer them away from those likely to give poor evaluations. Industrialists, on the other hand, should interview personnel managers without local people present to obtain a more accurate assessment of the work force. Of course, personnel managers are not likely to present a favorable picture if they feel that the new industry's location in the area will make it more difficult for them to recruit labor or cause their labor costs to rise. To compensate for this possibility and obtain the best overall assessment of the area's workers, the industrialist should interview several different personnel managers. In some cases it may be wise for local developers to present the results of their labor force availability surveys to area personnel managers for their examination. A survey that demonstrates a sufficient supply of recruitable workers in the labor-draw area can encourage personnel managers to be less wary of new industry.

In an interview with a plant personnel manager a number of questions are important. The representative of a prospective industry wants to know whether existing industries have difficulty in attracting the labor skills it needs, whether it can be selective in its hiring, and how willing the work force is to give an honest day's work. He also wants to know how productive the local workers are compared to workers in similar jobs in other places about which the personnel managers may know. If any differences in the productivity is evident, it is important to find out whether the inconsistency between places results from differences in (1) the efficiency of equipment, (2) management techniques, (3) wage incentives, (4) employee-management relations, or (5) other business or environmental conditions—all of which affect labor productivity.

Other pertinent inquiries include questions about tardiness, absenteeism, and turnover rates. Plant workers who are satisfied with their jobs generally arrive for work on time; satisfaction is also reflected by daily absentee rates of not more than 3 or 4 percent of the total work force. High absentee rates (over 6 percent) indicate worker dissatisfaction with jobs. High labor turnover likewise indicates dissatisfaction, but it can also be caused by cyclical or seasonal employment fluctuations or changing conditions in the tightness of the labor market. For the average manufacturing plant a monthly net turnover rate of over 5 percent indicates job dissatisfaction. But in some kinds of industries that have particularly demanding or stressful working conditions, separation rates of 10 to 12 percent are not uncommon. Naturally, turnover rates are lower during periods of economic recession. Other interview questions deal with whether workers are constantly bickering over petty grievances, whether they respect work rules, and whether they engage in work slowdowns, stoppages, or strikes. Further information bearing on the area's labor problems can be gleaned from selected issues of local newspapers, from consulting publications of the Bureau of Labor Statistics, which annually lists strikes for selected places, and from interviewing local labor leaders to examine their attitudes, long-term demands, and prevailing union contracts.

Finally, the new industry wants information about local wage rates and fringe benefits so that it can be sure that its wages and benefits will not be out of line if it chooses the area as the location for its plant. The most important factor influencing wage rates is the buying habits of the area's inhabitants. In small towns and rural areas living costs tend to be lower because the entertainment opportunities and luxuries offered are simpler, and people partake of them less frequently than do people in larger towns and metropolitan areas. In the larger cities workers demand more money because they spend more. Fringe benefits also vary from one area to another and, in some places, account for over one-third of the total labor costs. Questions asked of personnel managers seek to determine what benefits the new industry will have to provide if it locates in the area: pensions, retirement programs, insurance, vacations, health and dental care, anniversary bonuses, recreation programs, education programs, workingman's compensation, workday and workweek lengths, and flextime schedules. In the final analysis, the cost of labor is affected by the wage level together with the cost of the fringe benefits adjusted by the productivity of the labor-draw area's work force.

Notes

1. A substantial number of female professional and technical workers are likely to hold lower-paying teaching and nursing jobs while male professional and technical workers are likely to have higher-paying jobs as engineers, doctors, and lawyers.

2. During a five-year period over half (51.7 percent) the male college graduates in the country between the ages of twenty-five and thirty-four migrated across a county boundary. Only one-sixth (17.6 percent) of the males in the same age group with an elementary school education did so. Comparing the two relationships in another way, older college graduates between forty-five and sixty-four years of age are just as likely to migrate as are young adults between twenty-five and thirty-four who have only an elementary education. The least likely to migrate are workers over forty-five that are school dropouts without a high school diploma.

3. Job tardiness rates for long-distance commuters (over 14 miles) are less than those for commuters residing close to their work places but their absenteeism rates are the same. Medium-distance commuters have lower tardiness and lower absenteeism rates than both long- and short-distance commuters (Kocher and Bell 1977, p. 276).

4. Without a substantial percentage of older employees in the work force younger workers are not as likely to learn better trade skills or such work habits as punctuality, low absenteeism, respect for work rules, and attention to the quality and quantity of output. In some areas of the country, notably those in which a high percentage of high school graduates go on to college, few younger workers are being attracted to learn trade skills; therefore, industry has difficulty in replacing retiring workers, and the average age of skilled trade workers is getting older and older.

Appendix
Geographic Allocation Manpower Survey Guidelines

The following is a guideline of the steps to be followed in conducting the geographic allocation manpower survey:

1. Draft a map of the census divisions that comprise the labor-draw area and calculate the number of acres in each census division (fig. 8.1).

2. Upon the map of the census divisions draft the boundaries of the electrical (or telephone) distribution districts and calculate the number of acres in each distribution district.

3. Calculate the percentage of the distribution district's total area made up by each census division's area that lies within its boundary (see following table):

4. Calculate for each census division the number of *workers* in an occupation category (for each sex, if necessary) *per acre* for the last census year.

5. Multiply the number of workers per acre in each census division by the percentage of the distribution district's area made up by the census division.

6. Sum the values for each census division making up the distribution district to determine the total density of workers per acre in the distribution district.

7. Multiply the worker density by the total number of acres in the distribution district to determine the total number of workers in the occupation category residing in the district. (For example, in the above table: 3,800 acres $\times$ 0.18157 workers per acre = 690 skilled workers in the distribution district.)

8. Find out the total number of residential electrical services in the distribution district for the census year, as well as the total number of new residential services in the distribution district at the time of the labor survey and the number of discontinued services that have occurred since the census year.

9. Calculate the percentage of total residential services associated with the occupation category for the census year. (For example, if there were 3,450 total residential services in the district at the time of the census, then the 690 skilled workers can be associated with 20 percent of the services.)

10. Multiply the percentage of the total residential services associated with the occupation category by the total number of new residential services to determine the present number of workers in the category. (For example, if at the time of the labor survey there were 4,000 residential services in the distribution district, then 20 percent of this number would imply 800 skilled workers at the time of the survey, or 110 more than during the census year.)

11. For a more accurate survey, obtain a 5 percent random sample of the names and addresses of the new residential services from the electric utility and conduct a telephone survey to check the employment and occupation status of the new subscribers. In this way the labor force data for the distribution district can be modified. (For example, if at the time of the labor survey 2,000 of the 4,000 total residential services were new subscribers since the time of the census, and the telephone survey revealed that 30 percent of the new subscribers were skilled workers, then 600 of the new residential services and 400 of the old residential services could be associated with skilled workers. By this method it is found that 1,000 skilled workers reside in the distribution district rather than the 900 calculated without the use of the telephone survey to check on the changing composition of the work force.)

Geographic Allocation Manpower Survey Methodology

Area ID	Tract Area (acres)	Tract Area in District	Tract as Percentage of District	Skilled Workers in Tract	Density of Workers in Tract	Density × Tract Percentage
1	1,000	200	.0526	70	.0700	.00368
2	1,000	450	.1184	80	.0800	.00947
3	1,000	250	.0658	100	.1000	.00658
4	1,000	580	.1526	125	.1250	.01908
5	1,000	1,000	.2632	200	.2000	.05264
6	1,000	560	.1474	280	.2800	.04127
7	1,000	260	.0684	150	.1500	.01026
8	1,000	480	.1263	290	.2900	.03663
9	1,000	20	.0053	370	.3700	.00196
Total	9,000	3,800	100.00	1,665		.18157

Note: Distribution district worker density (.18157) × distribution district area (3,800 acres) = number of skilled workers in distribution district (690).

Chapter 9
Utilities, Energy, and
Industrial Location

The individual utility and energy requirements of most industries account for a small portion of the total cost of the finished product. But every manufacturing plant requires water, sewage and solid-waste disposal, telephone communications, electricity, and fuel of some type. Even though the ranking of these requirements as a factor in the locational decision varies from one industry to another, all industrial location seekers evaluate the cost of making each available in sufficient quantity and quality at the plant site.

The unit cost of a utility or energy resource is not apt to vary substantially between similar types of sites within the same region of the country for an industrial plant, but differences may appear between regions and between different types of sites within the same region—urban versus rural locations, for example. Even more important than the unit cost in most site selection decisions is whether the required utilities and energy resources are available at the plant site and, if not, whether they can be made available without prolonged delay and at a reasonable cost. Even if the utility and energy requirements can be made available at a site, environmental quality standards and energy conservation measures may limit or prohibit the site's use for some manufacturing purposes, although it may be zoned for industry.

This chapter will examine the utility and energy requirements of industry and discuss the influence of these requirements and energy conservation measures on the location of manufacturing. The influence of environmental quality standards on the location of manufacturing are discussed in the next chapter.

Utility Requirements

Water

Ninety-seven percent of all manufacturing plants are classified as (dry) small water users, withdrawing less than 20 million gallons per year, primarily from public water systems. The remaining 3 percent are (wet) large water users, withdrawing more than 20 million gallons per year directly from surface or groundwater sources. The small percentage of large water users accounts for approximately 97 percent of all water withdrawn by manufacturing.[1] Most water withdrawn by industry is used for cooling purposes only, and 95 percent is returned to rivers and streams. Nevertheless, approximately one-third of the public water supply goes to commercial and industrial establishments.

For several industries (steel, aluminum, paper pulp, paper board, wool scouring, food, synthetic rubber, rayon, and chemical processing, for example) the problem of securing usable water at a reasonable cost is a prerequisite in the site selection decision (table 9.1). All industrial plants do require water for one or more of the following purposes: (1) sanitary

Table 9.1. Water Supply Minerals and Their Potential Effects on Industrial Products and Equipment

Mineral	Effect
Bicarbonate (HCO_3)	Affects taste.
Calcium (Ca)	Forms an insoluble curd in pipes and boiler tubes and consumes soap.
Chloride (Cl)	Affects taste and increases corrosiveness.
Fluoride (F)	Amounts greater than 1.5 parts per million will mottle enamelware.
Iron (Fe)	Amounts of about 0.3 parts per million or more will stain cloth, porcelain fixtures, and other materials.
Magnesium (Mg)	Forms an insoluble curd in pipes and boiler tubes and consumes soap.
Manganese (Mn)	Amounts of about 0.3 parts per million or more will stain cloth, porcelain fixtures, and other materials.
Nitrate (NO_3)	Large amounts indicate pollution.
Potassium (K)	Large amounts will cause foaming in boilers.
Silica (SiO_2)	Results in boiler scale and destructive hard deposits on equipment.
Sulfate (SO_4)	Can form permanent hardness and scale.

Source: Yaseen 1956, p. 105.

uses, (2) fire protection, (3) process uses, (4) cooling and air conditioning, and (5) boiler feed.

Regardless of whether the industry is classified as wet or dry, water must be available for sanitary purposes, including toilet use, floor cleaning, washdown, food service, drinking, and grounds maintenance. This water, called potable water, must meet standards of purity that make it suitable for human consumption, and Congress, under the Safe Drinking Water Act of 1974 (P.L. 93-523) has made EPA responsible for verifying that potable water meets federal purity standards. If the industry's water supply is to be drawn from a public utility, it is presumed to be of adequate quality for potable use. If the industry chooses to produce its own water, the source of supply should be given special consideration. Well water is usually suitable for potable purposes but, like water drawn from a surface supply, it must meet the standards of the regulatory agency on a year-round basis. Potable water use varies from 20 to 40 gallons per employee each day with 30 gallons a good average for estimates. Unless the plant employs a great number of workers, the effect of this relatively small amount of water use on a utility system is minimal. For a large industry, the use of water could be significant, particularly during shift changes when peak use amounts to about 2.5 times the average use calculated over a twenty-four-hour period. Therefore it is important to determine whether the industry will require potable water for one, two, or three shifts and whether it will operate on a five-, six-, or seven-day basis. Obviously, if the industry's total water requirement is concentrated in one shift, the supply problem is intensified.

Almost without exception, industries need to be equipped with a fire protection system. Such a system usually includes a loop around the outside of the plant with strategically located fire hydrants and a sprinkler system within the plant itself. The industry's insurance carrier will designate the flow of water in gallons per minute and the residual pressure that is required for the particular plant. These needs can vary widely and are based on the nature of the product manufactured, the design of the plant, the materials used in its construction, and other factors. One should not attempt to predict the fire protection water requirements for any particular industry without first obtaining a statement of needs from the insurance carrier.

The water volume and residual pressure that a water system can supply is determined by the characteristics of the system as a whole. The pressure available in a utility system is dependent on the elevation of its overhead storage, usually between 120 and 150 feet above ground level. An elevation of 150 feet will produce a static pressure of sixty-five pounds per square inch at ground level. As the water is distributed throughout the system, it loses pressure because of friction. An industrial plant located some distance from the source of supply could have a residual pressure too low to fulfill its fire protection flow requirements, even though the static pressure was relatively high. An even lower pressure results when water required for processing is added to the fire protection requirement. The system characteristics at any given location can be calculated accurately if the elevation, line size, and condition of the system are known. Sometimes the industry may be required to install its own water supply system or overhead storage tower as a standby measure.

Certain industries have practically no process water needs, while others are users of large quantities of process water. The same can be said for water used in cooling, air conditioning, and boiler feed. The industrial developer should become familiar with the industrial prospect's needs by determining the purposes for which the water will be used, the amount needed for each purpose, whether it is to be used on a one-, two-, or three-shift basis, and whether it is to be withdrawn for short periods of time with rest periods between.

Regardless of the source of the water (a public water supply, lake, reservoir, river, or well), the industrial developer will need a detailed analysis of the water characteristics, including tap-in distance from the plant site, pressure and volume of flow, the available amount, temperature, chemical content, hardness, and cost. For public utilities this information is usually available. If it is not, a private laboratory should be commissioned to assemble the data. Sometimes an industry cannot tolerate certain elements in its water supply. For example, hard water can cause scale and corrosion in engines, pumps, steam boilers, water pipes, circulation systems, and bleaching tanks, these leading to increased costs for replacements and disruptions in the plant's operation (table 9.1). Water that is too hot because of normal climatic or geologic conditions may require the construction of costly cooling towers, especially if the water is to be used for cooling.[2] In some cases an industry may need to have a special analysis made to determine whether certain elements are present that are incompatible with its requirements. If the water supply does not meet the industry's standards, in-plant treatment processes such as the removal or reduction of hardness, iron, manganese, or other minerals would add to the utility costs.

The selection of an industry's water supply source is based on economic consideration as well as on the reliability of the supply. As with most commodities, the cost of producing water is rising depending somewhat on the source and degree of treatment required. However, an industry using large quantities of water may frequently negotiate a special rate with public supply sources. The industry may sometimes find it more feasible to purchase potable water from a utility and to produce its own process or cooling water from streams, lakes, reservoirs, or wells, particularly if the process or cooling water can be of lower quality than the potable water. Industries that use water in their manufacturing process are wise to avoid total dependence upon public supply systems because whenever a water shortage occurs industry is the first sector that is forced to curtail its use.

In some cases the public utility system may have to expand in order to supply water to an industry. In the event of such a problem, the industry has to allow sufficient lead time for engineering, financing, construction, and start-up. Since many a prospect has been lost because of insufficient water supply, industrial developers should be aware that (as a rule of thumb) when a utility's demand reaches 75 percent of its capacity it is time to increase the system's supply capability. Also, industrial developers should make every effort to have local public officials adopt fixed policies outlining the conditions governing the expansion and extension of water facilities (as well as other public services) to industry. In many communities, if the cost of expanding or extending water service to an industry can be recovered by the community within a fixed period (say five years) through local taxes levied on the industry, the water is provided.

Wastewater Disposal

Many industries produce as waste nothing more than ordinary sanitary sewage that can be disposed of satisfactorily by the local community sewage system. For other industries the problem of obtaining a suitable supply of water is surpassed only by the problem of disposing of the effluent-loaded water after its use in production processes (table 9.2). The disposal of all industrial wastewater, whether discharged to a municipal system or directly to a stream, is governed by the 1972 amendments to the Federal Water Pollution Control Act (P.L. 92-500). The act governs such matters as (1) establishment of effluent standards for all industry in various wastewater pollution categories; (2) pretreatment of industrial wastewater before discharge to a municipal system; (3) requirements for obtaining a permit to discharge wastewater to a receiving stream; (4) payment of uniform charges for all users of a community sewage system; and (5) the pay-back required of an industrial firm for its proportional share of the federal grants received by the community for the construction of treatment facilities into which the industry's wastewater is discharged.[3]

The EPA has established effluent standards for all industries that discharge waste to the nation's waters. The industries are grouped into cate-

Table 9.2. Estimated Volume of Industrial Wastes before Treatment, 1964

Industry	Waste-water volume (in billions of gallons)	Process water intake (in billions of gallons)	Biochemical oxygen demand (in millions of pounds)	Suspended solids (in millions of pounds)
Food and kindred products	690	260	4,300	6,600
Meat products	99	52	640	640
Dairy products	58	13	400	230
Canned and frozen food	87	51	1,200	600
Sugar refining	220	110	1,400	5,000
All other	220	43	670	110
Textile mill products	140	110	890	N.E.[d]
Paper and allied products	1,900	1,300	5,900	3,000
Chemicals and allied products	3,700	560	9,700	1,900
Petroleum and coal	1,300	88	500	460
Rubber and plastics	160	19	40	50
Primary metals	4,300	1,000	480	4,700
Blast furnaces and steel mills	3,600	870	160	4,300
All other	740	130	320	430
Machinery	150	23	60	50
Electrical machinery	91	28	70	20
Transportation equipment	240	58	120	N.E.[d]
All other manufacturing	450	190	390	930
All manufacturing	13,100	3,700	22,000	18,000
For comparison: Sewered population of United States	5,300[a]		7,300[b]	8,800[c]

Source: Berry and Horton 1974, p. 198.
Note: Columns may not add, because of rounding.
[a] 120,000,000 persons × 120 gallons × 365 days.
[b] 120,000,000 persons × 0.167 pounds × 365 days.
[c] 120,000,000 persons × 0.2 pounds × 365 days.
[d] Not estimated.

gories based upon the products they produce, and all industries in the same category must meet minimum treatment requirements for the effluent they discharge. A higher degree of treatment is necessary if the use classification of the receiving stream is not met by the minimum effluent standards. When it is necessary to remove or render harmless all pollutants, the reuse of the treated wastewater by the industry might be most practical and economical.

The Federal Water Pollution Control Act requires that the best practicable control technology be applied to industrial wastes discharged directly to a stream. It also requires pretreatment for discharges of industrial wastewater to publicly owned treatment works if the industrial wastewater is not compatible with the treatment process employed in the publicly owned works. Community treatment works almost without exception utilize biological processes in the treatment process, and certain elements found in some industrial wastewaters either are harmful to the biological processes or pass through the works untreated or the strength of the wastewater might be higher than the treatment facility can accommodate. In these and other cases, pretreatment is required. Sometimes the pretreatment can render the industrial plant's effluent of a quality that can be discharged directly to a stream, thus eliminating the expense of having the wastewater treated by a public utility.

The act prohibits any industry from discharging pollutants to a waterway from a point source (such as a wastewater outfall pipe) unless so authorized by a permit issued by either EPA or a state agency whose procedure has been approved by EPA. When a new industry proposes to discharge wastewater to a stream, it must apply for a National Pollutant Discharge Elimination System (NPDES) permit at least 180 days in advance of the date on which the discharge will begin.[4] Developers should take particular note of this lead-time requirement, since the 180-day period must be considered in establishing plant start-up dates and other schedules. It is important that an industry proposing to build a new plant gather for the permit application complete and accurate information on product(s) produced, raw material(s) consumed, process(es) used for production, volume of wastewater flow, exact location of the discharge, and any information that might apply to toxic materials. The permit may specify conditions that the industry must implement in order to make the permit valid; any variation from the information recorded in the application will be considered a permit violation. When a permit is in force and a plant expansion is planned that will change the volume or other characteristics of the discharged wastewater, a new application must be submitted. Neither can a permit be transferred to another party without the prior approval of the regional administrator of EPA.

A publicly owned wastewater treatment facility that is enlarged, modified, or newly constructed with federal grant assistance must establish a system of charges for wastewater treatment. These charges are usually defined in a sewer-use ordinance and scaled to the cost of operating and maintaining the system, the additional cost of excess biochemical oxygen demand (BOD) and suspended solids resulting from an industry's wastewater, and the pay-back by industry of its proportional share of the federal grant received by the utility.[5] For example, if a new treatment plant (or extension) with a capacity of four million gallons per day was constructed at a cost of $4 million, a federal grant of up to 75 percent of the cost of the plant (or $3 million) could be obtained, leaving $1 million to be financed by the local utility. The utility determines that it costs 20 cents per thousand gallons to operate and maintain the system, including the debt service on its share of the construction cost. In addition, the utility establishes a sewer-use ordinance that includes a provision for any industry discharging wastewater to the treatment plant with BOD and suspended solids in excess of 250 parts per million per day to pay a surcharge of $40 per thousand pounds of such excess. The annual cost to an industrial plant having a BOD of 450 parts per million and suspended solids of 350 parts per million contained in a wastewater discharge of one million gallons per day (25 percent of the new work's capacity) for five days a week would then be nearly $103,000 (table 9.3).

The above example makes it clear that an industry's wastewater disposal can be an important factor in an industrial development undertaking. If a public utility cannot serve the site for wastewater disposal, it is recommended that before offering the site for industrial purposes, the industrial developer meet with the state environmental management agency to determine whether adjacent streams can accept effluent discharges.

Solid-Waste Disposal

As with disposal of wastewater, the disposal of solid waste has become an ever-increasing problem, one that is producing nearly one hundred pounds of waste each day for every person living in the United States (table 9.4). All solid-waste disposal is regulated by the provisions estab-

Table   9.3. Example of Annual Wastewater Treatment Cost

Sewer-use charge	(260 days × 1.0 mgd × $0.20/1,000 gals.) ...$52,000
Industrial surcharge	(200 ppm BOD × 8.33 upd × 260 days × $40/1,000 lbs.) 17,326
	(100 ppm ss × 8.33 upd × 260 days × $40/1,000 lbs.) 8,663
Grant pay-back	(.25 × $3,000,000/30 years) 25,000
	Total cost $102,989

Note: Cost = 39.6 cents per 1,000 gallons, 8.33 upd = weight in pounds of a gallon of water.

Table   9.4. Generation of Solid Wastes from Five Major Sources, 1967

	Solid wastes generated	
Pollution source	Pounds per capita per day	Million tons per year
Urban		
Domestic	3.5	128
Municipal	1.2	44
Commercial	2.3	84
Subtotal	7.0	256
Industrial	3.0	110
Agricultural		
Vegetation	15.0	552
Animal	43.0	1,563
Subtotal	58.0	2,115
Mineral	30.8	1,126
Federal	1.2	43
United States totals	100.0	3,650

Source: Berry and Horton 1974, p. 259.

lished under Title II of the Federal Resource Conservation and Recovery Act of 1976 (P.L. 94-580), known as the Solid Waste Disposal Act. Provisions regulating the disposal of industrial wastes are in sections dealing with state or regional solid-waste plans and hazardous waste management. Like other anti-pollution acts, the provisions are administered by EPA.

The Solid Waste Disposal Act requires the industrial developer to give more attention to the existing methods in his area for the disposal of refuse from industrial plants, particularly from plants that propose to locate in the area. The industry has two possibilities for handling its solid-waste problem—either by disposing of the refuse itself or by using the facilities provided by a waste-disposal service or utility. Of the two, the use of a public utility is by far the more advantageous, since the bulk of industrial waste is very similar in nature to refuse produced by other business activities and residents of the community. The most common methods for the disposal of this nonhazardous waste are sanitary landfill, incineration, or ocean dumping. Open dumps and incinerators that pollute the atmosphere are prohibited by law.

The cost to an industry for the disposal of its nonhazardous solid waste may be handled in a variety of ways. If the amount of waste is not excessive, the entire operation—collection, processing, and disposal—may be paid for by the community out of ad valorem taxes. In other cases the community levies a charge for the service and bills the industry on a monthly basis. When an industry is not located within the tax jurisdiction of the public utility providing the service or the volume of refuse is not amenable to a monthly charge, then a charge per load is made. In such cases, the industrial firm itself must either transport the waste to the dump site or contract with a private company to provide the waste pickup and disposal service. Private waste-disposal firms generally provide compactors and containers for removal of refuse from the industrial site. The industry can purchase or lease compactors and containers; this choice may affect the cost of the service, depending upon which equipment is selected. A survey of industry indicates that the most prevalent means of disposal is by contracting a private service to provide containers and compactors and haul the waste to either a public or a private landfill. The charge per load levied may vary widely from one (private service or public) utility to another.

Industrial developers should have information available for industrial prospects about the public and private solid-waste-disposal services in their areas and the costs of each. Moreover, the developer should obtain detailed knowledge about the nature of the waste before committing a disposal service to accept it, since some industrial wastes are classified as hazardous materials and must be handled by special methods, depending upon their specific characteristics.

It is estimated that approximately thirty thousand different hazardous substances presently exist in the country that are highly toxic, flammable, corrosive, explosive, radioactive, malodorous, or in other ways harmful to the public welfare. Under the provisions of the Solid Waste Disposal Act, standards have been established for the disposal of hazardous wastes by those that create them. Any industry that produces hazardous wastes must keep accurate records of the chemical composition and the amount of waste produced, use appropriate containers (properly labeled) for the particular type of waste, and employ a system to assure that the waste is correctly treated, stored, transported, and disposed of. Any firm transporting, treating, storing, or disposing of the waste must do so in accordance with established standards and must have a permit issued under the supervision of EPA.

Few public-waste utilities in the past have provided hazardous-waste-disposal service, and not many are likely to do so in the future. However, some private disposal firms do handle hazardous materials and thus relieve the industry from that task. Such firms should not be confused with general refuse-disposal firms that may or may not have a permit to handle hazardous waste. Industrial developers should compile a list of names and locations of hazardous-waste transportation and disposal firms serving their areas, including the types of wastes that each firm is permitted to handle and an estimate of the costs involved.

Sometimes the industrial firm may choose to dispose of its own solid waste, either in its own sanitary landfill or incinerator or by some process devised for storage of hazardous materials or treatment that renders them nonhazardous, all of which require approval permits. The Solid Waste Disposal Act has outlawed the use of open dumps for refuse, so that industry has to use either a sanitary landfill or an incinerator. The landfill must be operated and maintained in a manner that will protect the groundwater and surface water from contamination. The geologic, hydrologic, climatic, and other characteristics of a dump site must meet certain standards before a jurisdiction will permit refuse disposal, and the supply of land available in most communities for private solid-waste-disposal purposes is rapidly dwindling. More and more industry in the future will have to use on-site thermal methods of disposal (possibly in conjunction with electric power generation), as well as reduce the amount of waste by recovering useful materials, as mandated by the Resource Conservation and Recovery Act of 1976.

Communications: Telephone and Mail Service

An important factor underlying the concentration of industry in and around metropolitan areas has been the superior reliability of the different communication modes. New communication technologies such as non-wire relay modes, direct automated station-to-station access, conference transmission, computer-controlled information transmission, and wide area telephone service (WATS), have reduced the need for some industry to locate in metropolitan centers. However, many firms have made the decision to locate in a small town or rural area, have obtained all the necessary commitments for the operation of their plants and have begun construction, only to discover that the closest telephone transmission line that could handle their communication requirements was several miles away and that months would be required for the installation of an adequate feeder line, the cost of which would have to be borne entirely by the firm.

Other firms locating in small, outlying communities have found the mail service inadequate, forcing them to obtain post office boxes some distance from the plant location in a larger community that could provide more reliable service.

Industrial developers should contact their local telephone manager and postmaster to determine the availability and adequacy of their services for potential industrial firms. Telephone rate schedules should be obtained, including the cost to industry for installing (over and underground) lines and other equipment such as computer tie-in equipment.

Power and Energy Requirements

Electricity

For most of the factory system's history the location of power sources has been of primary importance in the choice of an industrial site. First stream-oriented water power sites controlled the location of factories, and then coal-oriented steam power sites, or those to which coal could be easily transported to power steam engines, dominated the location of manufacturing. Many cities that are important today grew and prospered through the years because of their proximity to power sources. Other formerly important industrial cities are only historical remembrances because their raison d'être was an energy resource that is now outmoded. The advent of electric power and continual improvement in long distance transmission technology has made most of today's industry less dependent upon the location of power sources.

Only a few industries have transmission requirements or electrical costs per dollar of product value sufficient to make them still dependent upon power source locations. These industries are primarily electrometallurgical firms that produce aluminum, magnesium, and other nonferrous metals and electrochemical firms engaged in manufacturing products like liquefied gas, calcium carbide, and silicon carbide, to mention a few. The electrical costs incurred by most industries are very low in comparison to the total value of their finished products (table 9.5). While this relative cost is increasing and is expected to continue doing so in the coming years, it is less than one cent per dollar of product value for manufacturing as a whole or only 0.79 percent—making it hardly a decisive locational factor for most industry.[6] Nonetheless, electric power is a commodity that is required by all industry and its cost can be a substantial constant expense for some.

The constant expense for electricity is reason enough for industrialists to examine the availability, adequacy, and reliability of service at different locations in their site selection search. In addition to transmission line voltage and the reserve capacity of the utility, the industrialists want to know the history of stoppages (blackouts and brownouts) and whether their plants will be subject to any seasonal restrictions.[7] The rate schedule, in-

Table 9.5. Energy Expenditure as a Percentage of Value of Shipments by Manufacturing Industry Group, 1971

Industry	Percentage
Food processing	0.44
Textiles	0.66
Apparel	0.13
Lumber and wood products	0.66
Furniture and fixtures	0.30
Paper and allied products	0.22
Printing and publishing	0.17
Chemicals	1.72
Petroleum and coal products	1.66
Rubber and plastics	0.42
Leather	0.31
Stone, clay, and glass	3.08
Primary metals	1.97
Fabricated metals	0.34
Nonelectrical machinery	0.31
Electrical machinery	0.21
Transportation equipment	0.18
Instruments	0.22
Miscellaneous	0.20
All manufacturing	0.79

Source: Compiled from U.S. Bureau of the Census, *Census of Manufacturers, 1972*, vol. 1, pp. 23–25, table 5.

cluding availability of off-peak rates, fuel adjustment clauses, lighting allowances, and any special discounts or penalties that may apply to their usage is also pertinent information needed by industrialists.

Small manufacturing plants with an electric requirement up to approximately 4,000 kilowatts (KVA), which are not susceptible to production problems created by momentary power interruptions or voltage dips, can locate at almost any site on a utility's system.[8] For interim electric loads, between 4,000 and 7,500 KVA, the plant would have to locate within a reasonable distance of transmission lines of 46 KV or more. Plants using over 7,500 KVA would have to be located close to primary transmission lines in at least the 115 KV range. If the plant site was not adequately serviced, a problem in many rural areas, the industrialist would have to negotiate with the utility for service.

For some manufacturing processes, momentary electrical interruptions or voltage dips create major problems. For instance, in the synthetic fiber industry (where the fiber filaments are made somewhat like cotton candy) a momentary interruption can cause a direct loss of the manufactured product worth thousands of dollars, not to mention the loss in production time required to clean up the mess. Some chemical and metalworking operations are examples of other manufacturing processes that are highly sensitive to power interruptions. A manufacturing operation sensitive to power interruptions needs, therefore, to locate on a site accessible to the most reliable service. The plant might locate on a site relatively close to a major substation where transmission lines from several different generating plants merge to provide an uninterrupted supply of power, even when one or more of the lines are out of service. The site must also be close enough to the substation so that the length of the transmission line serving the manufacturing plant is short enough (at least within three miles) to reduce the possibility of lightning interference. On sites further away from existing substations, manufacturers sensitive to power interruptions must negotiate with the utility for extra facilities to insure, as nearly as possible, against power failure. These extras may include the entire duplication of all facilities, along with interlocking and sensing devices to maintain continual service if trouble develops in one of the duplicate generating networks.[9] The standard facilities provided by the utility to an industrial plant include the primary feeder line, metering equipment, and the substation consisting of a transformer, devices to protect the substation (and unwary individuals that may accidentally come in contact with the high-voltage equipment), and support structures. Most utilities provide an option whereby the manufacturer can own the substation and pay a reduced rate for electrical service. Ownership, however, is not especially appealing to the average industrial firm, for the firm would then have to employ a specialist in high-voltage electricity and have spare transformers and other equipment available in the event of failure. Most utilities have mobile transformer units on hand for emergencies and, of course, have experienced help in handling high-voltage transmission.

More and more industries have begun to generate some of their own electric power to combat blackouts and brownouts and assure adequate service. Some arrangements allow industrial plants to have cogeneration tie-in arrangements with local utilities where they either sell or buy power to or from the utility as the need occurs.

Once an industry has narrowed its choice of a manufacturing site or an existing industry has decided on an expansion program, it is essential that the plant's electrical requirements be made known to the local utility as completely as possible, since the production time on substation equipment, particularly the 5,000 KVA and above models, requires twelve to fifteen months. This procurement time usually matches the plant construction schedule; if it does not, temporary use of equipment that the utility has on hand may be arranged.

The industrial developer should have at hand basic information on the local electric utility for industrial prospects: availability, adequacy, reliability, and cost of providing service at potential plant sites. The developer should also become familiar with the industrial prospect's electrical needs, including the main purposes for which the electricity will be used, the estimated amount to be used for each purpose, the hours during the day it will be used, and whether the demand will be relatively steady or fluctuate widely during the day, week, or year.

Fossil Fuel

Fossil fuel as a locational criterion varies in importance among industries. For most manufacturing operations it is a minor consideration. However, those using substantial amounts of coal, petroleum, or natural gas, either as a major raw material or for heat treatment, are likely to be greatly influenced in their site selection by the fuel's location, especially if it is difficult or impossible to substitute one fuel for another, as in the manufacture of coke, coke by-products, carbon black, and pig iron. Energy shortages, higher fuel costs, government-regulated pricing practices, environmental regulations, and mandatory fuel conservation measures will affect the locational patterns of high-fuel-consuming industries in the future. Industries that can work with substitute fuels, notably coal for petroleum or natural gas, will be less affected than those that must rely heavily on petroleum or natural gas. Natural gas users may face plant shutdowns from time to time unless they relocate near gas fields or are able to substitute manufactured gas in their production processes. Since industry is the major user of energy resources in the country (table 9.6), it may need to lead the way in conserving those resources.

Even before energy conservation measures stipulated the use of coal as a substitute for other fuels when possible, coal was one of the most important raw materials in use by industry. Not only is it a major fuel for space heating, power generation, and heat treatment, but its by-products are used in the manufacture of hundreds of other products such as tars, oils, ammonia, medicines, explosives, insecticides, fertilizers, plastics, and dyes. Fortunately, the nation has a large coal reserve located in several different regions, and it can be used as industry's major energy resource. The importance of coal as a source of energy in the future will be even greater than today, as once again it becomes the primary source for thermal heating, power generation, and coal-converted natural gas.

Table   9.6. Energy Use in the United States, 1974

Sector	Net consumption		Gross consumption	
	QBTU	Percentage	QBTU	Percentage
Residential	10.0	13.7	14.2	19.3
Commercial	7.5	10.3	10.0	13.6
Industrial	23.9	32.7	30.6	41.7
Transportation	18.3	25.0	18.4	25.1
Utilities (waste heat)	13.3	18.2	—	—
Other	0.2	0.3	0.2	0.3

Source: Moss 1976.
Note: QBTU = Quadrillion British Thermal Units.

Because of the mushrooming demand for coal, it would be wise for an industry planning to locate in a community to negotiate a firm commitment with a coal supplier for on-site delivery to serve its requirements. The agreement should stipulate the amount to be delivered, the delivery schedule, and the delivered cost per ton. Since wide variations in the heat value (BTU) and sulfur content of coal can occur, the agreement should also stipulate the delivered cost based upon this content. By stockpiling, delivery schedules can be spread evenly throughout the year, and delivery delays will be less critical. Industrial developers should compile a list of coal suppliers for major industry in their areas and be aware of their capability to supply new demands. They should also obtain some estimates of the average bulk-delivered cost of coal to local industry; the greater the volume delivered on a fixed schedule, the lower will be the cost.

Natural gas and, to a lesser extent, petroleum have been limited in quantity for several decades and supplies are now insufficient for the demand. Still, these are the major source of the country's energy (table 9.7). For years the federal government has urged industry to shift from the use of petroleum and natural gas as a fuel, but without much success. Henceforth, industry's use of these resources will be severely curtailed by the government, with coal as the primary substitute. The government's main reason for taking these measures is to reduce the country's dependence on imports of these strategic resources and to reduce its foreign trade payments. Any industrialist planning to use petroleum or natural gas for purposes that could be accomplished by coal is better advised to make the shift; if not, he must prepare to sustain the economic consequences that can result from the higher cost of these fuels, plant shutdowns, and the installation of conversion equipment. Even though a community may now have an adequate supply, local shortages are likely to occur in the future, especially in nonproducing states. The Depart-

Table   9.7. United States Energy Consumption by Type of Fuel, 1970

Type of fuel	Percentage of total
Coal	20.0
Steam power	11.7
Other	8.3
Natural Gas	33.4
Steam power	6.3
Other	27.1
Oil	42.1
Steam power	3.3
Other	38.8
Nuclear and hydroelectric	4.5

Source: Damstadter 1975.

ment of Energy priorities for the use of petroleum and natural gas (which rank domestic use over industrial use) will continually shrink industry's allocation in the years to come.

The supply of petroleum is not as limited as that of natural gas. For manufacturing purposes other than those that cannot be fulfilled by using coal, most industries will be able to obtain enough petroleum to meet their requirements, but at ever-rising prices. Delivery delays at certain times, particularly during the winter, may become common. This problem can be alleviated by the construction of sufficiently large oil storage facilities on or close to the plant site. Major petroleum users—those for whom petroleum is the principal raw material required for their product —will find it increasingly difficult to obtain long-term supply guarantees. In the future, such firms will have to construct major storage facilities near their plants or relocate their operations in petroleum-producing states or countries to increase their chances of obtaining adequate supplies.

The energy resource in shortest supply is natural gas, even though, at times, it is more available than at other times. Nearly every supplier in the country, outside major producing states, can provide natural gas only on an interruptible basis. That is, the gas utility has the right to interrupt the plant's supply for a specified period (hours, days, or weeks) by giving as little as an hour's notice. For some industries, natural gas is virtually irreplaceable in the manufacturing process: as a reducing agent in steel production or for dye processing in textile finishing and the production of glass, for example. Several gas-using industries will be attracted to plant sites near producing gas fields because of their dependence on this resource. Other industries will be able to offset the lack of natural gas or supplement its limited supply by constructing liquid petroleum gas, liquid natural gas, or synthetic natural gas storage facilities near their plants. The cost of these supplemental gas supplies, however, is substantially higher than the cost of regulated domestic natural gas, and the storage facilities themselves are an added construction cost. In most areas local gas utilities augment their natural gas supplies with other types of gas and calculate the average cost of all the gases used in the system to determine the rate. If an industrial plant is a small gas user that can withstand interruptions in service, dependence on the local utility may be sufficient. In the immediate future, gas manufactured from coal will be the most practical replacement for natural gas because of the size of the nation's coal reserves and the pipelines that exist for its transport. But, even though natural gas and petroleum are in short supply and will never again be the inexpensive forms of energy that they have been, industrial developers should prepare a list of the industrial suppliers serving their areas and obtain from them periodic data on the availability and cost of different grades of fuel oil and different types of natural and manufactured gas.

Energy Conservation

Federal, state, and local government can impose energy conservation measures on industry in three major ways: (1) through building codes that require energy conservation standards incorporated into the plant's architectural design, (2) through subdivision and other regulations that control off-street and on-street employee parking, and (3) through zoning ordinances that strictly control the use of land by industry. While these regulatory instruments have traditionally been the province of local government, federal legislation, such as the Energy Policy and Conservation Act of 1976 (P.L. 94-163), requires state government to develop and implement energy conservation programs under the direction of the DOE. It is evident that industrial energy conservation will become more and more a concern of the federal government in the future.

Cheaply constructed industrial plants require more maintenance and more energy for heating and cooling than do well-constructed plants. Energy efficiency is also related to the ratio between the plant's volume and exposed outside surface area. Thus, a single-story plant may be more efficient for production purposes, but a multiple-story structure is more efficient for energy conservation, provided that the construction quality is the same. For these and other reasons energy conservation standards can be incorporated into building codes. Energy use in industrial buildings can be curtailed somewhat by adjusting space heating and cooling temperatures and by capital investments in insulation, storm windows, and weatherstripping. The greatest energy efficiency, however, results from the incorporation of energy-saving features in the design of the building from the ground up. New construction designs that emphasize energy conservation have been drafted by the American Society of Heating, Refrigeration, and Air-Conditioning Engineers. The designs can reduce operating costs for lighting, heating and air conditioning by as much as 50 percent, with little change in the construction cost of the building. Federal law requires that minimum energy conservation standards (mandatory lighting and thermal efficiency standards) be incorporated into local building codes for new and renovated industrial plants. The law is enforced by prohibiting mortgage lenders from making loans to industrial firms locating in communities that have not adopted the standards. In addition, federal financing will not be made available to industries failing to incorporate the standards into their building designs.

The main purpose of imposing regulations to control off-street and on-street employee parking is to limit the use of private automobiles for commuting. If fewer cars are driven to work, less energy will be used. Many employees would have to shift their commuting pattern from the single-occupant automobile mode to either a carpool, vanpool, or mass transit mode. Vehicle pooling has proved successful in situations where at least one origin or destination location is fixed. Carpool arrangements involve either four or five employees, each of whom uses his own car on a rotating basis or one employee who provides all the transportation and is paid by the others. In vanpool programs the industry supplies a van for eight to ten employees. Mass transit is provided by the community over fixed routes at specific times. A bus with twenty passengers achieves about eighty passenger-miles per gallon, compared to fifteen passenger-miles per gallon for a car with a single occupant. In localities where plants are too small or dispersed, as in rural areas, to permit intracompany carpooling, carpool matching can be arranged between people working and living in different places relatively close together. Shifts in commuting modes can more easily be achieved by policies designed to discourage automobile use, particularly through parking restrictions. Parking can be discouraged in several ways: (1) by higher charges for the use of community-owned parking spaces, (2) by surcharges or taxes levied on parking in privately owned lots, including the plant's parking lot, and (3) a major change in subdivision regulations to allow only a small number of available parking spaces, forcing employees to carpool, vanpool, use public transit, or search elsewhere for parking. By reducing the number of vehicles used in commuting, not only will energy be conserved, but the area's air quality will be improved—a concern of environmental legislation.

Built-up areas with higher population and employment densities require less passenger and truck transportation than sparsely settled areas. Consequently, high-density development results in a substantial reduction in the per capita consumption of energy because accessibility is increased (table 9.8). This compact development can lead to poorer air quality unless coupled with restrictive parking measures, of course. Communities, though, can adopt zoning provisions to promote higher-density development by (1) reducing the number of employee parking spaces and outside yard space or (2) prohibiting industry from locating in areas at a considerable distance from residential land uses.

These energy measures vary from one community to another, depending on the conservation stance of local government. Many may be reluctant to impose strong measures, since they have little to gain except possibly increased parking revenues, mass transit passenger fares, and the savings that can occur in providing public services to a more densely settled community. Unless community energy conservation measures are mandated by state or federal government, industrial developers should take an active part in their drafting to verify that they are not unreasonably hard on existing and potential industry.

Table 9.8. Per Capita Energy Consumption in the United States by Land Use Activity

Sector	Millions of BTUS	Percentage
Residential	46.9	18.4
Commercial/public	30.1	11.8
Industrial	96.1	37.7
Transportation	81.9	32.1
Total	255.0	100.0

Source: Damstadter 1975.

Notes

1. Water Resources Council, *The Water Use Data Book* (Washington, D.C., 1969), p. 123.

2. As a general condition well water temperature increases above annual average surface temperature by 1 degree Fahrenheit (0.5 degrees Celsius) for every sixty-four feet of well depth, while surface water temperature tends to approximate the area's seasonal temperature changes.

3. These requirements will be discussed only briefly here because they are covered in greater depth in chapter 10.

4. A fee of one hundred dollars is charged for processing the application. If more than one discharge point is involved, an additional fifty dollars is charged for each additional point.

5. The Clean Water Act of 1977 (P.L. 95-217) exempted any industrial user with a discharge equivalent of less than 25,000 gallons per day of sanitary waste from the industrial cost recovery provision, provided that the industry does not discharge any pollutant that reduces the effectiveness of the treatment facilities.

6. This low average cost results partly from declining rate schedules favorable to large electric users such as industry, a practice that is likely to be modified in the future in some areas in favor of flatter rates or even inverted rates. Most utilities, though, have redesigned their rates to encourage off-peak usage and night shifts in plants.

7. Generally, fast-growing areas are apt to have less electrical reserve capacity than slow-growing areas, and shortages, induced primarily by weather conditions, are more likely to occur in the growing communities. Food processing and resort communities can strain power availability at certain periods of the year because of their seasonal nature. Also hydroelectric power generators may be subject to drought conditions at times. If such conditions exist in an area, the backup agreements between different power generation companies should be examined.

8. A kilowatt (KVA or KW) is a measure of the electric power required to operate a light bulb, appliance, machine, etc. For example, it would take one kilowatt of power to light ten 100-watt bulbs. If all ten burned for one hour, they would consume 1 kilowatt hour of energy (KWHRX). If all ten burned continuously for a thirty-day month they would use 720 kilowatt hours of energy. The user of the electric power would be charged on the basis of the monthly kilowatt-hour usage.

9. Another arrangement would be for the utility to install automatic circuit breakers in the transmission line to the plant in such a way that continual service could be maintained if trouble developed on either side of the feeder line.

Chapter 10
The Environment and
Industrial Location

The success or failure of the industrial developer in the past has been determined primarily by his ability to promote the traditional locational factors of access to markets, materials, labor, land, and so on in his state, region, or community. While many industrial developers believe that these traditional factors remain of paramount importance, it is increasingly evident that corporate concerns are being subjugated by the national environmental welfare. Henry Hunker, previewing the future of industrial development in the United States, has stated, "Increasing pressure brought upon society—and industrial development—by environmentalists . . . *may result* in a new set of societal goals and standards relative to development and in a new approach to resource management" (Hunker 1974, p. 259, emphasis added). In reality, the foundation for this new set of goals and standards has already been constructed by the United States Congress and built upon by EPA. This chapter will discuss the provisions of the major environmental legislation passed by Congress that affect industrial development. These provisions are included in the National Environmental Policy Act of 1969, the Water Pollution Control Act Amendment of 1972, and the Clean Air Act of 1970. The chapter is not intended to serve as an environmental handbook or guide for industrial developers, but rather is meant to point out potential effects of the legislation on the practice of industrial development.[1]

Environmental Policy Acts

A decade of unsuccessful attempts by Congress to define and implement a nationwide environmental policy culminated in the passage of the National Environmental Policy Act (NEPA) of 1969 (P.L. 91-90). The act states that it will be the continuing policy of the federal government to employ all practical means and measures to create and maintain conditions under which man and nature can exist in productive harmony (Berry and Horton 1974). While private citizens, municipalities, and states are not obligators under NEPA, the act contains an operational provision, which has become apparent to these parties because of its impact on community and economic development, that requires all federal departments and agencies to prepare an environmental impact statement in connection with any major federal action significantly affecting the quality of the human environment (Section 102). Not only does the provision require an impact statement in connection with any major federal project, but it also requires one for local and state government projects and private projects partly financed with federal money. In addition, the environmental impact statement has become the model for many state environmental policy acts.

Since the passage of NEPA, many states have approved legislation requiring that major projects directly undertaken by state agencies using public funds include an environmental impact statement. Projects financed entirely through private money are not necessarily bound by this provision. However, in instances where privately financed projects require federal environmental permits, the private firm has to prepare an environmental impact statement. A few states have passed environmental acts that require an environmental impact statement for any private project calling for a state permit.

Some state environmental policy acts require that the state industrial promotion agency be responsible for the preparation of an environmental impact statement when the agency's efforts culminate in the establishment of a new industrial plant. In other states where the state development agency has been designated a promotional/advisory agency and staff salaries are not considered to be an expenditure of public money for projects, the agency is not required to submit environmental impact statements for new industrial plants.

Specific content guidelines for comprehensive environmental impact statements also vary from state to state. At minimum, an environmental impact statement should include (1) the environmental impact of the proposed project, (2) significant adverse environmental effects that cannot be avoided if the project is implemented, (3) proposed mitigation measures to minimize the impact of the project, (4) alternatives to the proposed project, (5) the relationship between short-term environmental impacts and the maintenance and enhancement of long-term productivity, and (6) any irreversible and irretrievable environmental changes that would be involved in the implementation of the project (Leopold et al., n.d.).

While NEPA remains the cornerstone of the nation's environmental law, its applicability to local and regional industrial development agencies is not well defined. Industrial developers should be familiar with the basic guidelines of this federal law, but they should take care to be very well informed on the specific provisions of their own state's environmental policy act. Developers should know under exactly what circumstances the industrial prospect may be required to submit some type of environmental assessment or impact statement to the state's environmental management agency. Also, the developer should be able to provide the prospect with the specific requirements of the environmental statement, the agency to which it should be submitted, when it should be submitted, and any adverse circumstances not readily apparent to the prospect (Tremaine 1975; Andrews 1975). Most important, the developer should identify and foster a cordial relationship with "contact" people within his state's environmental management agency.

Anti-Pollution Acts

The anti-pollution laws established by Congress are far more important than NEPA for the industrial developer to be aware of because they may have an effect on the types of industry that can locate in the local community. To some degree the growth and development policies of all states have been influenced by the anti-pollution laws (Kirk 1975). This section of the chapter will focus on the provisions of the key acts and examine their potential impact on industrial location and economic development decisions.[2]

Federal Water Pollution Control Act Amendments of 1972

The Federal Water Pollution Control Act Amendments of 1972 (P.L. 92-500) establish a national framework for the administration of water pollution control programs. This act changed the philosophy of water pollution control from one based on the waste treatment necessary to protect the quality of surface waters to meet certain essential uses, to one based on treatment necessary to meet effluent limits unless a higher degree of treatment is required to meet water quality standards. The act established water quality goals to be achieved by dates designated therein. It is the national goal that by 1983 all the surface waters of the nation be of a quality that is fishable and swimmable and that by 1985 no pollutants be discharged. An interim goal of providing the equivalent of secondary waste treatment by 1977 was also included in the act. Amendments to the act in 1977 (P.L. 95-217) gave authority to federal officials to grant waivers from the 1985 cleanup requirement in some circumstances. Industrial plants whose pollution was not serious enough to harm public water supplies, fish or wildlife, or interfere with recreation could be granted an extension until 1987 to comply with the clean up requirement.

To achieve these goals, the act provided for the establishment of effluent limitations to be included in permits and established the National Pollutant Discharge Elimination System (NPDES) permit as the primary tool to assure achievement of the goals with respect to the control of point-source discharges. The act also contained provisions relating to the control of non-point sources such as urban storm water runoff; sedimentation and erosion control; and agricultural, silvicultural, and mining activities. To achieve these goals the act further provided for a construction grants program and made eligibility for these funds contingent upon the applicant's conforming to certain planning requirements.

Effluent Limits and Water Quality Standards. Before the Federal Water Pollution Control Act Amendments of 1972, most state water pollution control programs had been developed and were administered on the basis of requiring treatment necessary to protect the "best use" classification of a receiving stream. The states classified their waters according to usage—drinking, swimming, fishing, for example—and concurrently developed water quality standards to protect those identified uses. The systems applicable to fresh waters generally designated at least three classifications: waters to be used as a source of public water supply, waters to be used for recreation, and waters to be used for fishing and fish propagation. Salt waters were generally classified to protect shellfish or for recreational use. The water quality standards applicable to each use classification spelled out the maximum permissible concentration of a wide range of pollutants (such as organic and inorganic chemicals) and pollutant-causing conditions (such as water temperature and BOD) that a stream could have. Under this water quality classification, streams classified for the same use but having a greater volume of flow could accept higher effluent discharges than low-flow streams. In applying the classifications and water quality standards, the states generally made investigations and conducted studies designed to determine the present and potential uses to be made of the waters as well as their existing quality. Classifications were then assigned to all the streams in each drainage basin, which defined the minimum water quality standards that had to be achieved and maintained for the stream. The assignment also defined the minimum wastewater treatment requirements applicable to each type of effluent and the type of treatment necessary to maintain the standards of the receiving stream. The main point is that the stream use classification and the volume of water flow in the stream were the variables that determined the type and amount of effluent that could be discharged into it.

The Federal Water Pollution Control Act, on the other hand, provides for the establishment of maximum effluent limits for pollutants that can be discharged into any stream by a community or an industry, regardless of its flow capacity. Moreover, the act requires additional treatment for effluents in order to maintain the water quality standards established by the stream's use classification. A stream is considered *effluent limited* if the water flow is sufficiently high to require only treatment necessary to achieve the established maximum effluent limits of a particular industry or community. A stream is considered *water quality limited* if additional treatment is necessary to achieve and maintain the standards assigned to the receiving stream. For example, if town X or industry Y provides treatment necessary to meet effluent limits and none of the water quality standards applicable to the receiving stream are violated, then the stream is referred to as effluent limited. If town X or industry Y, on the other hand, discharges a large volume of waste to a small stream and if the industry provides only the treatment necessary to meet effluent limits for its industrial category, the stream's water quality standards may still need improvement, and additional treatment by the industry will be necessary to meet the standards. Such streams are referred to as water quality limited.

It is obvious that the pollution abatement costs would be lower for an industry that located adjacent to watercourses classified as effluent limited (fig. 10.1). This fact, however, must be considered within the context of some special requirements that can also be applied in addition to nationwide effluent-limit standards. For example, an industry may easily comply with the effluent-discharge standards of a site as determined by applying the federal or state guidelines but may still be required to provide a higher level of reliability, including duality of pollution abatement equipment, in order to assure continual effective treatment under all potential operating circumstances. Therefore, pollution abatement would be less costly for industry located along effluent-limited watercourses that are classified for fishing than for those along effluent-limited streams classified for recreation or water supply because locations on effluent-limited watercourses that carry a water supply, shellfishing, or recreation classification require greater pollution abatement expense. A much higher level of reliability is required, and dual treatment units or multiple units may be necessary. Additionally, for the recreation and shellfish categories, two-point chlorination would be necessary, and for all three classifications,

Figure   10.1 Pollution Abatement Cost Relationship to Stream Quality and Flow

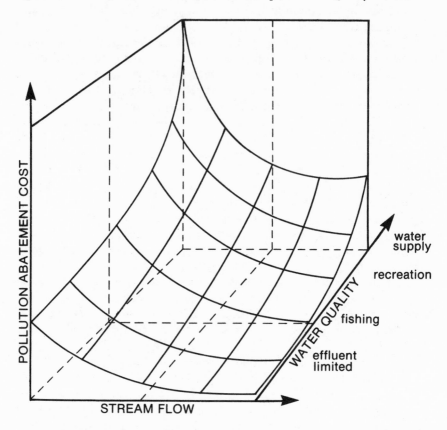

full standby power would be a requirement. Somewhat higher in cost would be the pollution abatement required of industry located on water-quality-limited fishing streams because of the additional treatment required over and above state and federal effluent limits. More costly yet would be those sites located near waterways where extreme treatment measures are required to assure maintenance of water supply and recreation quality limits. And for locations near shellfish waters, which require extreme measures to prevent effluent discharges, the cost of pollution abatement would be even higher. Of course, when the date is reached after which no pollutant discharge will be allowed into the nation's waters, the abatement cost advantages gained by locating on various kinds of streams will be nullified.

While these statements are general in nature, the actual cost to an industrial plant is site specific for a particular type of manufacturing operation. For example, in effluent-limited watercourses, an industrial discharge may require such a rigorous degree of treatment that the stream is classified as water quality limited for that particular industry. Since no applicable table or list of treatment requirements based upon the classification or characteristics of the receiving stream is available to the industry in such a case, specific requirements would have to be developed. Initially, then, the industrial developer must request from his prospect information about the type of effluent to be discharged from the plant, the volume of that effluent, and the level of in-plant treatment before discharge. This information, passed on to the state environmental management agency, will expedite the permit-granting process.

201 Facility Planning Areas. A more complex problem arises if none of the community's wastewater treatment works is adequate to meet effluent limits and water quality standards. Under the Federal Water Pollution Control Act Amendments of 1972 a municipality in this predicament can be designated a 201 Facility Planning Area. Section 201 of the act stipulates that an area can receive construction grant funds from the federal government up to 75 percent of the total cost of the project to upgrade any publicly owned waste treatment plant, provided that the local authority complies with the planning requirements of Section 201. The type of project planned must be environmentally sound and the most cost-effective facility.

Once a facility plan has been completed, it is subjected to three levels of review: first, by a clearinghouse of interested agencies at the local level (U.S. Office of Management and Budget 1969); second, by the state for compliance with its requirements and federal regulatory and statutory requirements; and third, by EPA. The industrial developer who is working with the community should be aware of the projected design capacity of the new treatment plant and the charges that will be levied on the various users. All treatment facilities constructed under Section 201 are required to have a capacity projected to serve municipal growth for a ten-year period. OBERS Series E Population Estimates (Bureau of Economic Analysis, U.S. Department of Commerce) are to be used to project population growth. The projected capacity of the treatment plant for industrial use must be based on binding contract commitments from each industrial user.

Expansions of publicly owned wastewater treatment works financed as part of P.L. 92-500 are based upon providing capacity for reasonable population increase, reasonable industrial growth, and the assurance of pollution abatement in the surface waters. Unless a new or expanding industry is committed during the planning period, those industries simply *will not* be included in public wastewater treatment plant expansion programs. The treatment plant capacity for future industrial growth is permitted at the rate of up to 10 percent of the total waste flow of the public facility. In the event that the 201 project also includes the upgrading of an existing treatment facility, all existing industries and future industries will be required to repay their share of the federal grant. Repayment of the federal grant (industrial cost recovery) is based on a period not to exceed thirty years and at no interest. A new or expanding industry is required to make a firm commitment to use a portion of the facility by agreeing to an enforceable contract document, and the industry must repay the federal grant portion of the cost whether it locates in the area or the planned expansion actually takes place.

The community or local agency responsible for construction and operation of the treatment facility must establish a system of user charges and industrial cost recovery. The user charges must be adequate to pay for the operation and maintenance of the facility, and the industrial cost recovery is levied so that each industry (except those discharging less than 25,000 gallons per day of sanitary waste) repays the federal share of the capital cost of constructing the capacity required to serve its particular needs, including interceptors. These industrial repayment charges are in addition to the charges for the operation and maintenance of the facility.

The purpose of the act is, of course, to clean up pollution, not to promote or encourage population expansion and industrial growth. Therefore, existing industry must pay its share of the cost of cleaning up existing pollution, and new and expanding industry must pay its own way to curtail any new pollution. Obviously, large municipalities will have reasonable excess treatment capacity for new and expanding industry under present guidelines and regulations. However, the 10 percent growth allowance will greatly limit the excess capacity of treatment facilities in smaller communities, where the excess capacity may be sufficient for industrial requirements ranging from a few thousand gallons to a few hundred thousand gallons of water per day; for most water-intensive industries, however, there will be little, if any, excess capacity. Consequently, the act serves to restrict the type and number of industries that can locate in smaller communities and increase the attractiveness of larger metropolitan areas for certain manufacturers.

An alternative approach is for the small municipality to construct additional wastewater treatment capacity on an "as needed" basis. Since the industry must pay its share, local financing might be arranged that would allow the municipality to construct a treatment facility capable of accepting the wastewater from moderately sized or even large wet industries. One difficulty inherent in this approach is that the treatment facility would have to be built concurrently with the construction of the industrial plant. The timing might well prove to be a hardship, particularly if the industrial plant were built on schedule and equipment delays or other difficulties caused the treatment facility not to be completed on schedule. Unless the municipality had sufficient excess capacity to handle the industry for an interim period, the industry would be unable to operate until the new facility was completed.

Another problem that has not been addressed is community attitude. While community attitude has been a locational factor for some time, its measurement is an exercise in subjectivity. Quantitative instruments for this task simply do not exist. As a rule of thumb, however, whenever public financing of facilities is required, no matter how favorable the cost-to-benefit ratio may be, a certain amount of opposition invariably results. For this reason small communities may need to consider limiting their industrial promotion activities to dry or semi-dry industrial prospects. Larger municipalities, on the other hand, may more easily promote their locations as sites for moderately sized wet industries. Since P.L. 92-500 is applicable throughout the nation, it is anticipated that communities will be capable of servicing future industry growth in direct proportion to the amount of waste treatment flow projected by their present population and industrial development trends. The purpose of Section 201 is to plan for the abatement of pollution by existing population and existing industry and to allow for "reasonable" population and industrial growth. Again, it is not intended to encourage industrial growth or population growth. No matter what kind of waste treatment problem exists between an industry and a community, the industrial developer can fulfill a key function by helping to integrate and coordinate the diverse concerns of the local community leaders and the industrial managers. While this task in itself is formidable, it becomes doubly difficult when political consequences are examined and when special interest groups apply pressure.

208 Area Wastewater Treatment. P.L. 92-500 also requires control of non-point pollution sources in addition to controlling point-source discharges. A *point source* is defined as effluent discharge from a pipe or other conveyance. A *non-point source* is defined as effluent discharge from an areawide surface and includes urban storm water runoff and runoff from agricultural land, as well as erosion and sedimentation resulting from construction activities. These requirements will be met through the areawide waste treatment planning provisions in Section 208 of P.L. 92-500. The purpose of the 208 program is to identify those areas that have substantial water quality control problems requiring an areawide approach to planning and the implementation of corrective action. Section 208 provides for the designation of the SMSAs within a state as areawide waste treatment management areas and the designation of an agency to develop the required plan. In nondesignated areas, the state water pollution control agency is required to develop the plan. These plans, regardless of the agency preparing them, must identify the non-point-source problems and set forth processes and procedures for their control.

Specifically, 208 plans are prepared for a twenty-year period and identify the anticipated municipal and industrial treatment works necessary to meet the requirements of Public Law 92-500. In addition, they identify control systems to prevent pollution from storm water runoff and establish construction priorities for waste treatment plants. They also establish effective regulatory control plans. During preparation of the plans, land use controls and practices must be analyzed to determine those that would be most cost-efficient in reducing pollutant loadings, based on the specific water quality problems of the area. For example, if sediment is a primary problem, special consideration would have to be given to grading regulations, construction ordinances, and sediment and soil erosion control ordinances. Since erosion and sedimentation must be controlled during the clearing and grading of a site, such characteristics as topography, soil stability, and compaction must be considered when selecting a plant site. In addition to the control of erosion and sedimentation during construction, plans must be made for the management of storm water runoff from roofs and parking lots. The site drainage system should, if possible, be designed to convey storm water runoff to a single point for any necessary treatment, thus preventing the need for duplicate retention ponds or other facilities.

It is impossible to calculate the impact of the 208 program on industrial development. However, there is some indication that the larger the SMSA, the more intense is its non-point-source pollution problem, so as to make it more costly for an industry selecting a site within its planning area to prevent non-point pollution. On the other hand, industrial runoff from one manufacturing plant in a large metropolitan area might be less environmentally damaging than runoff from that same plant at a smaller municipal location. In every case, the 208 program mandates stricter zoning ordinances and more stringent design and engineering standards. Grants of up to 75 percent of cost are available to communities from EPA to implement the plans. However, no EPA funds are available to industries for controlling non-point pollution attributable to their operations.

404 Dredge and Fill Operations. Section 404 of P.L. 92-500 requires an approval permit from the Army Corps of Engineers to conduct dredge or fill activities *in or adjacent* to all waters with any of the following characteristics: (1) streams having an average flow of five cubic feet per second, (2) lakes having a surface area greater than five acres, and (3) wetlands, marshes, and swamps subject to periodic inundation. Projects have been delayed for months by court orders stopping the construction of minor facilities, such as a water intake pipe or a wastewater outfall, connected to a small stream, lake, or marsh *some distance away* from the main plant facility. The permit procedure requires a minimum of four months, and consideration is given not only to the adverse environmental effects of the minor facility but also to those caused by the construction and *operation* of the major facility. In many cases the industrial prospect can be required to prepare an environmental impact statement to support the permit application. Controversial projects may require public hearings and over a year to complete the permit procedure. To determine the applicability of Section 404 to their projects, prospects planning to locate facilities near bodies of water should consult the District Office of the Corps of Engineers.

Clean Air Act of 1970

Air pollution control programs are administered by the states to carry out the requirements of the Federal Clean Air Act of 1970 (P.L. 91-604). This act directed EPA to establish national ambient air quality standards and directed the states to prepare and submit to EPA a plan to achieve and maintain these standards. EPA established national primary and secondary air concentration standards for six pollutants: sulfur dioxide (SO_2), photochemical oxidants, particulates, carbon monoxide (CO), hydrocarbons, and nitrogen dioxide (NO_2). The primary standards established for each pollutant were based upon the level of air quality necessary to protect public health, while the secondary standards were based upon the level necessary to protect the public welfare from any known or anticipated adverse effect. The secondary standards thus require cleaner air than the primary ones. The act required that the states achieve the primary standards by 1975 and the secondary standards within a reasonable time thereafter.

In keeping with the requirements of the act, the states prepared and submitted the required implementation plans and EPA acted on their approval. Following EPA's approval, however, a coalition of environmental groups brought suit against EPA, charging that the approved plans did not prevent deterioration of air quality in areas where existing air quality was already better than that required by the secondary standard. In late 1974 EPA responded to a court order by promulgating a set of significant deterioration regulations, which were challenged by both environmental and industrial groups. The environmentalists claimed that the regulations were too lax and should be strengthened, while business and industry representatives felt that they would lead to severe economic adjustments detrimental to the entire nation. The regulations provided for the establishment of an area designation system and allowed small increases in pollutant concentrations over baseline air quality levels of particulate matter and sulfur dioxide (table 10.1). The area designation system includes three classes. Each state is required to classify areas that are cleaner than the national ambient air quality standards as Class I, Class II, or Class III. Class I areas are those in which any change in air quality would

Table 10.1. National Ambient Standards and Maximum Allowable Increases in Concentrations of Sulfur Dioxide and Particulate Matter over the Baseline Concentration

Pollutants	Class I area Increment	Class II area Increment	Class III area Increment	National Ambient Standard
Particulate matter				
Annual geometric mean	5	20	37	75
24-hour maximum[a]	10	37	75	260
Sulfur Dioxide				
Annual arithmetic mean	2	20	40	80
24-hour maximum[a]	8	91	182	365
3-hour maximum[a]	25	512	700	1,300

(ug/m^3)

Source: Clean Air Act Amendments of 1977.

[a] May be exceeded once per year.

be considered significant, and so only a very small increase in pollutant concentrations is allowed over the baseline level.[3] Class II areas are those in which any air deterioration accompanying moderate, well-controlled growth would be considered insignificant. Class II areas can have air of less purity than Class I areas but still are above the national standard. In these areas the permissible increment for pollutants is greater than for Class I areas, so that growth can be more easily accommodated .Class III areas are those in which deterioration up to the national standard would be considered insignificant. In Class III areas where the baseline pollutant levels were low, the pollutant increments can be substantial, so that a considerable amount of growth can be permitted. Additional growth would be difficult in Class III areas close to the national standard and in Class I and Class II areas that have already achieved their maximum permissible pollution increments. The regulations initially designated all areas of the country as Class II and included provisions for allowing the states to reclassify any area to accommodate the social, economic, and environmental needs and desires of the public. The regulations became effective in 1975 and were applicable to all new construction, including industrial construction, which had to meet specific emission limits depending upon its industrial classification just as for water pollution abatement. EPA, however, had been slow in implementing the provisions of the regulation because of continuing congressional activity to amend the act's provisions. In 1977 the Clean Air Act Amendments were passed, which provided for the following area designation and redesignation:

1. On the date of enactment, the following are Class I areas and may not be redesignated:
All existing
a. international parks
b. national wilderness areas and national memorial parks exceeding 5,000 acres
c. national parks greater than 6,000 acres.
2. The following can be designated Class I or Class II:
national monuments
national primitive areas
national preserves
national recreation areas
national wild and scenic rivers
national wildlife refuges
national lakeshores or seashores exceeding 10,000 acres
national parks or wilderness areas established after the date of enactment and exceeding 10,000 acres.

3. All other areas with air quality better than the national ambient standards shall be Class II.

4. Any area may be redesignated Class III by a State, if

a. redesignation is specifically approved by the Governor after consultation with the legislature,

b. redesignation will not contribute to exceeding the increments or maximum allowable concentrations in any other classified area,

c. all other requirements are met.

These "other requirements" include a description and analysis of how the redesignation will affect health, environmental, economic, social, and energy factors. Also, the redesignating authority must hold public hearings and submit to a review by EPA. At least 120 days or longer would be required to redesignate an area. Obviously, a prospective industry could not be expected to postpone its plant site search while awaiting the resolution of a redesignation action.

The concept of significant air quality deterioration has been embroiled in a heated controversy since its inception. The United States Chamber of Commerce, and other industry-oriented groups, have opposed the significant deterioration provisions because of EPA's contention that pollutant sources can affect the air quality in areas many miles from the polluting source. The chamber has argued that large areas of many states will be closed to further industrial development if the amendments are enforced because climatic conditions and local air circulation can cause pollutant intrusion into Class I areas. The chamber maintains that extensive buffer zones would be required to prevent deterioration of the designated Class I areas. However, it should be pointed out that neither the act itself nor the proposed amendments require a buffer zone to surround Class I areas. Regardless of whether an air pollution source, such as an industrial plant, can be initially designed or subsequently modified to meet applicable Class I area increment requirements, it would be more feasible (for cost and time reasons) for the source to locate in a Class II or Class III area. In these areas the maximum permissible pollutant increments are usually greater, so that the industrial firm may encounter fewer problems in locating there. Problems, however, are likely to arise for industry and for industrial developers in any area, regardless of its classification, where the air pollutant levels are presently near the maximum permissible concentrations. Industries will either have to design more effective (and costly) pollution control equipment into their production process or find a location in an area with pollution significantly below the tolerance level.[4]

A more difficult situation arises in *nonattainment areas*, which are those (Class IV) areas where concentrations of any air pollutant, as verified by air quality monitoring or modeling, exceed any national ambient air quality standard. However, new air pollution sources can locate in nonattainment areas if EPA's "offset policy" is applied. The major requirement of the offset policy is that emissions from the new source must be more than offset by a reduction in existing source emissions. This means that an industrial firm with an emission problem planning to locate or expand in a nonattainment area must find another local firm or source with an air pollution problem and correct it enough to permit construction of the new facility. This policy was first applied in Pennsylvania in 1977. The new source in question was the Volkswagen assembly plant in New Stanton, Pennsylvania. The new plant would emit significant amounts of hydrocarbons, but at stake were a potential five thousand jobs. The Commonwealth of Pennsylvania, in order to offset the new hydrocarbon levels, agreed to substitute low-polluting water-based asphalt in all its road maintenance operations in the area to achieve the required reductions.[5] As a practical matter, however, the offset policy cannot be construed as a viable, easily implementable tool. Obviously, any new source (industrial plant) wishing to locate in a nonattainment area must have the cooperation and assistance of federal, state, and local governments as well as of the existing industrial community.

Industries with any new air pollution source, regardless of proposed location, must obtain a permit before construction and operation can begin. In certain cases industries will have to submit evidence of one year of ambient air monitoring with their permit application. EPA will then decide whether the proposed new construction can take place. The permit may be issued if the following requirements are met:

1. Total emissions from *all* sources in the area will be sufficiently reduced as to represent "reasonable further progress" toward attainment of the standard.

2. All of the applicant's major stationary sources in the state are in compliance, or scheduled to comply, with all emission limitations.

3. The proposed source will achieve the lowest achievable emission rate.

The new Clean Air Act Amendments of 1977 instructed EPA to conduct a study and promulgate regulations to prevent significant deterioration from hydrocarbons, carbon monoxide, photochemical oxidant, and nitrogen oxides within two years of enactment. These new nondeterioration regulations must be at least as effective as the increments established for sulfur dioxide and particulate matter.

Legally, the Clean Air Act and Clean Air Act Amendments of 1977 do not legislate against the location of industry in any region of the country.

In reality, however, the degree of difficulty and cost required to meet the stringent limitations and standards mandated for certain areas brunts industrial shifts to these areas and, other cost variables being essentially equal, will preclude many relocation decisions.

Federal (and state) environmental legislation influences industrial location decisions. Not only have specific environmental regulations been invoked to stop or modify the siting and construction of industrial plants, but the "spirit" of the acts themselves has stirred considerable controversy among regulatory administrators, environmental groups, entrepreneurs, and politicians. However, the economic recession of the 1970s, combined with a greater understanding by all parties of the need for both economic development and environmental quality, has produced a more conciliatory attitude. The affected parties are more willing to compromise and accept trade-off solutions. Consequently, court litigations have resulted (and will continue to result) in modifications of the acts' provisions. And as time goes on regional differences in administering the acts' provisions will cease to exist.

This is not to say that industrial location decisions of some types of industrial firms will not continue to be affected by environmental legislation. Whereas in the past industry has concentrated in certain areas to gain internal and external agglomeration advantages, the agglomeration economies from which some industries have benefited will be outweighed by the high cost of the pollution abatement procedures required of them should they locate in these same areas in the future. The environmental legislation is therefore likely to have a deglomeration effect on some types of industry because such industry can locate more cost-effectively along effluent-limited streams designated solely for fishing, in large urban areas with surplus sewage treatment capacities, or in Class II or Class III air quality regions.

The individual industrial developer can do little about changing local or regional plans and regulations mandated by EPA. Similarly, the task of knowing specific provisions and regulations of the acts is time consuming and not very productive. There may be some justification for state development agencies to hire a staff environmental specialist to apprise industrialists and industrial developers of new or changing regulations and their potential impact. State industrial development agencies operate within a geographic area large enough to warrant a staff position for environment. Conceptually, the smaller the area handled by the industrial developer, the fewer will be the number of potential environmental problems. This concept may apply to most rural areas, but it will not usually apply to most SMSAs. The level of economic activity in the nation's larger urban centers and the consequent high pollutant levels demand constant attention by the local industrial developer to insure that problems are forestalled.

Since it has been established that the range of knowledge and information needed by an industrial developer is dictated by the size of the area under his purview as well as by the physical infrastructure of that area, specific recommendations for action will not apply universally. However, the following steps, if taken by individual developers, may help to prevent costly mistakes:

1. Initiate and maintain close and constant contact with the state's environmental protection/management agency. These contacts can provide updates on federal and state regulations and laws, and assess their implications for different regions.

2. Find out if your state has adopted some type of environmental policy act. If so, study the scope of the environmental impact statement provision, if required by the act. Some states may require environmental impact statements for private developments.

3. Prepare, in cooperation with the state's environmental protection agency, a comprehensive environmental questionnaire. This questionnaire should be forwarded to all industrial prospects and should require precise information under the following topics: type of industry, process and housekeeping wastewater, cooling water, proposed treatment, air pollutants from process, and project site requirements.

4. Compile a list of towns in the area that have applied for or received federal funds to undertake wastewater treatment improvements or construct new wastewater treatment facilities under Section 201 of the Federal Water Pollution Control Act Amendments. Remember that agreements between the municipality and the federal government are very stringent with respect to excess capacity and pay-back arrangements.

5. Have your state industrial development agency prepare a handbook that can be used to familiarize potential industrial investors with the environmental permits required by local, state, and federal government agencies and with how these permits may be acquired; including the permit-letting procedure, timing of the permits, and the agencies responsible for their administration and enforcement.

Notes

1. Several additional environmental laws that can affect industrial development have been passed (Mack 1975), including:

a. The Noise Pollution and Control Act of 1972. Under the Noise Pollution and Control Act, for example, industry that is a major noise source cannot be located close to residential areas or other areas disturbed by noise unless effective sound buffers are provided or the plant has acoustically adequate construction.

b. The Coastal Zone Management Act of 1972. Although in itself not a regulatory act, the Coastal Zone Management Act has encouraged and fiscally supported the development of state regulatory laws in those states bordering the oceans, the Gulf of Mexico, and the Great Lakes. The state acts vary in scope but generally impose restrictions on the types of construction that may take place in counties bordering the coast and require that some form of zoning be implemented in these counties. Questions should be addressed to the state coastal management commission.

c. The Rivers and Harbors Act of 1899. This old act governing any construction in or *over* the navigable waterways of the United States was environmentally modernized following the passage of NEPA to require that decisions to issue a permit for construction should be based on the "public interest" (e.g., environmental balance) rather than on obstructions to navigable waterways. Questions should be addressed to local Army Corps of Engineer officers.

d. When any federal funds are part of the development package (HUD, EDA, SBA, FmHA, etc.): i. the Conservation, Protection, and Propagation of Endangered Species Act (P.L. 93-205), administered by the United States Fish and Wildlife Service, can stop construction on projects that may be harmful to the existence of endangered plant and animal life; ii. the Preservation of Historical and Archaeological Data Act (P.L. 93-291), can be used to insure that no federally supported projects destroy historical or archaeological landmarks *before* consideration can be given to relocating these landmarks or taking full measure of their importance (e.g., an archaeological survey). Failure to consider landmarks can cause the project to be delayed for months or years while the needed actions take place. Developers should be especially alert for the presence of Indian ruins or old (nineteenth-century) homes in the area of their proposed development. The State Historian can usually provide sound advice to the developer with regard to his specific project.

2. As a rule of thumb, heavy industry (including most fabrication and processing plants) has the greatest technical problem in meeting air and water pollution standards. Such manufacturing plants can entail substantial costs for pollution abatement. Medium industry (many assembly and lighter processing types) has fewer technical problems and spends less on abatement. Light industry (distribution and light assembly establishments) has no problem or only minor problems in meeting pollution standards. All three manufacturing types, however, have secondary environmental impact as a consequence of the vehicular traffic they generate.

3. A variance above the Class I increment can be granted by a state governor. The variance can range from 8 percent above the allowable increment for low-terrain areas to 15 percent for high-terrain areas.

4. "The primary way in which the Clean Air Act provides relief from unattainable standards is the extension of time in which compliance is required." "For a plant that is technically incapable of complying and thereby preventing attain-

ment of an ambient air quality standard . . . a total of eight years from approval of the state's implementation may be allowed" (Private communication from Michael A. James, Associate General Council, United States Environmental Protection Agency, 28 August 1978).

5. The amended Clean Air Act provides for waivers of offset requirements where a state has an adequate program for incremental reductions in emissions that will assure attainment of the standard by the 1982 deadline for pollutants other than automobile-related pollutants, and 1987 for automobile-related pollutants. To reduce emission levels in some nonattainment areas, communities will have to institute vehicle control on private car use. Strategies may include carpooling, commute-a-vans, staggered work hours, or providing fringe parking areas.

Chapter 11
Taxation and
Industrial Location

The widely held belief that tax differences among states and localities are an important factor in industrial location decisions has had a major influence on taxation and economic development policies for decades. This belief underlies the concern that industrial firms will migrate from communities and states that have high tax rates. It also underlies the attempts of state legislatures to keep business tax rates low and to make state tax structures favorable to business. It has led some states and many communities to offer special tax concessions or to provide other types of inducements to attract industrial firms.

Despite its prevalence and persistence, the belief is not supported by the considerable study devoted to assessing its validity. Research on the effect of state and local taxes on location decisions reveals that although tax differences may play a role in certain decisions and may sometimes be influential in the final stages of the decision process when the choice has been narrowed to a few locations that meet more basic criteria, their effect is not a significant factor in most industrial location decisions.

Although this conclusion has been confirmed again and again, the traditional belief is probably held as strongly today as ever. The continued decline of industry in central cities and industrial centers, the fiscal crisis of several northeastern United States cities, the persistence of ghetto and rural poverty, and the general aspirations for better jobs and higher incomes still provide strong motivation to make tax structures favorable to industry or to provide special tax inducements. But no matter how serious the problem to be confronted or how justifiable the goal, sound public policy requires that the essential question be asked, Do state and local tax differences have a significant effect on industrial location decisions?

This chapter reviews the two research approaches that bear on this question: (1) the theoretical inquiry into the nature of location decisions or patterns of industrial location and (2) the empirical study of the factors that may affect location decisions. Location theory, in which the economic theory of business firm behavior is applied to gain insights into location decisions, is concerned with all aspects of location decisions rather than with the particular significance of taxation. It does provide important insights into the role of taxation in location decisions, however, and helps to place taxation, including workmen's compensation taxes, in its proper perspective. Location theory merely provides hypotheses or ideas about a firm's actual behavior. This chapter first summarizes location theory as it relates to the basic question of whether state and local tax differences affect location decisions, and then it presents the findings of investigators who have surveyed the question over the past thirty years.

Location Theory and Locational Tax Differences

Location theory assumes that firms try to choose the location that maximizes total profit.[1] Since total profit depends on both total revenue and total cost, useful hypotheses can be derived about a firm's behavior by investigating how these elements vary at different locations. Any factor that affects a firm's revenue and cost and varies from one location to another can be regarded as a determinant of location, even though it may be only partly responsible for the final decision. Thus, state and local tax differences, to the extent that they affect total profits at alternative locations, help to determine location decisions. But how much?

The most significant locational determinants are likely to be those that have the largest effect on total revenue or cost. As pointed out in chapter 5 and elsewhere, market considerations are most important in affecting revenue, while access to major productive inputs—raw materials, labor, and power—is most likely to affect costs. Transportation costs will also have an important effect on the total cost. Some firms may be sensitive to amenities—climate, cultural activities, or environment—for the benefit of their executives and employees. For some types of businesses, retail, insurance, and service firms, a location near their customers or clients may be essential. Other firms may not be restricted in this way, but the costs of transporting their final product may require that they locate near their markets, especially if that product has low value relative to its weight. Some, such as ore processors, need to locate near sources of raw materials to avoid high transport costs. Still other firms, like apparel manufacturers, may find that their profits are sensitive to labor costs and that they must locate in areas with low wages and surplus labor.

In general, firms or industries can be classified by their orientation— toward markets, raw materials, labor, power, or amenities, according to how important these factors are in their location decisions. Firms that have no strong orientation are often classified as footloose; their productive inputs and transportation expenses will cost about the same no matter where they locate.

For firms strongly oriented to markets or to particular sources of productive inputs, state and local tax differences probably will be only a minor factor in the location decision, simply because other considerations have a greater impact on profit. Taxes are probably more significant for footloose firms, which are not restricted to particular locations and can choose from among many communities.

But even footloose firms or firms not restricted to particular locations by other considerations probably are not strongly affected by state and local taxes when they make location decisions because such taxes are usually only a minor part of the total cost of doing business. Also, tax rates may not vary much within a geographical area (table 11.1). For example, while rates may vary greatly between the northeastern and southeastern United States, within each region the variation will be much smaller. If the communities under consideration are all within a single state, state taxes will not vary with location and will not affect the ultimate decision. Even if possible sites lie in a general area extending over several states, state taxes may not significantly affect the decision because, as the Advisory Commission on Intergovernmental Relations has pointed out, states tend to keep their tax structures and rates in line with those of neighboring states to maintain their competitive position (Advisory Commission on Intergovernmental Relations 1967). Thus offering tax concessions to attract industry, even if successful, will produce only short-lived advantages if other states follow suit.

Furthermore, although tax rates can vary considerably (especially between cities and rural areas), tax differences among local governments may be offset by differences in the quantity and quality of public services available. The amount of taxes a firm pays does not necessarily coincide with the value of the benefits it derives from the public services, but there is often a correlation between tax rates and the quantity or quality of these services. If police and fire protection, garbage collection, and water supply, for example, are not provided by the community, the firm probably will have to provide these services itself. In addition, a firm's executives will be concerned about the quantity and quality of such services as public education and recreation facilities, both for themselves and for the firm's employees and their families. Thus, low taxes may not actually mean lower costs at all, but more likely may be associated with the failure of the community to provide services valued by the firm. Even if the value of the benefits it receives from the public services does not equal its tax payments, a firm may find that other benefits of locating in an urban rather than a rural area offset higher tax rates, so that high urban taxes alone do not necessarily result in the out-migration or decline of firms.

Another reason that state and local taxes, including workmen's compensation taxes, may have only minor significance in location decisions is that they are deductible on federal income taxes, and local taxes are deductible on state income taxes. For corporations with a taxable net income over $25,000, the federal provision for deducting state and local taxes reduces the tax differences by almost half, and local differences are reduced even further by state deductibility provisions. Finally, some firms can shift the burden of taxes either to their consumers in the form of higher prices or to their factors of production, such as labor, so that higher taxes may not reduce their total profit in the end.

Location theory suggests, then, that for most firms the major determinants of location are likely to be market considerations or access to productive inputs (including labor, raw materials, and power) because these factors have the greatest impact on total profit. For most firms, tax differences are less important determinants because they have a small effect on total profit, are partly offset by income tax deductibility, and are often offset by other considerations, such as local amenities and the quality of public services.

Empirical Studies of Taxation's Effect on Industrial Development

Most research on industrial location decisions focuses on the factors that location theory suggests are fundamental: markets, raw materials, and labor supply.[2]

The most common approach of research on the effects of state and local taxation is to survey, through either questionnaires or personal interviews, business executives whose firms have decided on locations. Another way, often referred to as the tax bill approach, calculates total tax bills at alternative locations for hypothetical or real firms. Still another method analyzes firms' cost components and evaluates the relative importance of taxes. Other research has used econometric techniques or statistical correlation to analyze economic data on firm location and other variables, including tax rates. Most of the research has studied the location decisions of manufacturers rather than retail, wholesale, and service

Table 11.1. State and Local Taxes, 1976

State	Local property tax revenue per capita (dollars)	State tax revenue per capita (dollars)	Total tax revenue per capita (dollars)	State corporate income tax rate on income over $25,000 (percentage)	State retail sales tax rate[c] (percentage)	Gasoline excise tax (cents per gallon)
Alabama	49	334	383	5[a]	4	7
Alaska	188	423	611	5.4[b]	—	8
Arizona	214	369	582	10.5	3	8
Arkansas	83	301	384	6	3	8.5
California	342	420	762	9	4.75	7
Colorado	208	379	587	5	3	7
Connecticut	331	357	689	10	7	11
Delaware	121	558	679	7.2	—	9
Florida	154	366	520	5	4	8
Georgia	137	340	477	6	3	7.5
Hawaii	144	621	765	6.435	4	8.5[f]
Idaho	154	325	479	6.5	3	9.5
Illinois	286	413	699	4	4	8
Indiana	236	311	547	3[d]	4	8
Iowa	234	356	590	8[e]	3	7
Kansas	258	314	573	6.75	3	8
Kentucky	87	354	441	5.8	5	9
Louisiana	79	417	496	4	3	8
Maine	281	317	597	7	5	9
Maryland	209	466	674	7	4	9
Massachusetts	384	383	767	8.33[g]	5	8.5
Michigan	263	416	679	—[f]	4	9
Minnesota	217	479	696	12	4	9
Mississippi	96	329	425	4	5	9
Missouri	173	329	502	5	3	7
Montana	306	281	587	6.75	—	7.75

Nebraska	235	284	345	4.12^e	2.5	8.3
Nevada	237	501	738	—	2	6
New Hampshire	278	205	483	7	—	9
New Jersey	379	304	683	7.5	5	8
New Mexico	97	387	484	5	4	7
New York	343	609	952	10	4	8
North Carolina	109	353	461	6	3	9
North Dakota	168	349	517	6	4	7
Ohio	192	305	497	8	4	7
Oklahoma	108	321	428	4	2	6.58
Oregon	250	320	570	6.5	—	7
Pennsylvania	154	461	615	9.5	6	9
Rhode Island	252	354	606	8	6	10
South Carolina	92	329	422	6	4	8
South Dakota	252	267	519	5.5^h	4	8
Tennessee	104	319	424	6	4.5	7
Texas	171	296	467	—	4	5
Utah	143	329	472	6	4	7
Vermont	276	385	661	7^i	3	9
Virginia	140	370	510	6	3	9
Washington	213	409	622	—	4.6	9
West Virginia	92	358	450	6	3	8.5
Wisconsin	267	429	696	7.9	4	7
Wyoming	263	327	590	—	3	8
District of Columbia	199	526	725	8	5	10

Source: Advisory Commission on Intergovernmental Relations 1977, table 432, and U.S. Department of Commerce, *Statistical Abstract of the United States, 1976.*

a 6% for financial institutions.

b Plus 4% surtax.

c Plus county taxes.

d Plus supplemental tax of 2.5% of net income.

e 10% on taxable income over $100,000.

f Single business tax replaced corporate income tax of 7.8%.

g Plus 14% surtax.

h Rate of 5.5% applies only to banks and financial institutions.

i 7.5% on taxable income over $250,000.

firms (which is not surprising in view of the overriding importance of market considerations in the location decisions of these tertiary-type firms).

Almost all the research strongly supports the idea that markets, sources of raw materials, and labor supply are the major determinants of location decisions and that state and local taxation has only a minor effect. Due (1961) reviewed seventeen studies of various types published between 1950 and 1960 that "suggest very strongly that the tax effects cannot be of major importance." He did, however, cite an interview study of 196 Massachusetts manufacturing firms in which 16 percent of the firms indicated that local taxes had influenced their location decisions (Strasma 1959) and another study in which 14 percent of the firms that moved out of New York City between 1947 and 1955 listed taxation as the major reason (Campbell 1958). He qualified his general conclusion by stating that "in some instances taxes can be the deciding factor if other factors balance; this is likely to happen in metropolitan areas or when a suitable area straddles a state border" (Due 1961, p. 171). Nevertheless, Due concluded that "state and local taxes represent such a small percentage of total costs that the cases in which they are controlling cannot be very significant."

Morgan (1964) reviewed seventeen studies (only one of which was included in Due's survey) that used questionnaires. All but one were published between 1951 and 1961. Sixteen studies found market considerations to be of primary significance, and ten also found labor and raw materials to be of primary significance. Only one study found that taxes were of primary importance. Morgan also reviewed studies that used personal interviews, with similar findings, except that "personal factors" ranked somewhat higher than in the studies that used questionnaires.

Stinson (1968) reviewed twenty-six studies of different types published between 1955 and 1966 to assess the impact of local tax concessions and public industrial financing programs. One study (Spiegelman 1964) found that over half the responding firms did not consider taxes in making their location decisions, and another study found that 80 percent of the respondents made the same reply (State of Oregon 1957). On the basis of seven other survey studies, Stinson (1968, p. 4) concluded that "it appears that less than 10 percent of the respondents thought that the tax situation in an area is important enough to consider as a major factor in the location of a new plant . . . and that even among those that consider taxes in deciding where to locate their plants, taxes do not strongly influence the decision."[3] From five studies that used the comparative tax-cost approach, he concluded that, although significant interstate and intrastate tax differentials do exist and may affect the growth of new firms, "tax costs are probably of secondary importance in the selection of a plant site" (Stinson 1968, p. 14).[4]

Among these five studies was one that compared the tax costs with other geographically variable costs (Fulton 1960). As Stinson summarized the study, "it appears that the geographical variation in costs for other factors, such as labor, transportation, and raw materials, is so much greater than the variation in tax costs, that the firm would seldom consider the tax burden of a particular area under normal circumstances . . . in many instances the increase or decrease in tax costs for a new location was less than five percent of total geographically variable costs of the firm" (Stinson 1968, p. 13).

Other industrial location studies surveyed by Poole (1970) found that state and local taxes, although often considered, are not a very significant factor in the ultimate decision.[5] For example, a survey of 503 manufacturing firms in six southwestern states showed that taxes ranked twenty-fourth in importance as a factor affecting location decisions.

Although most studies conclude that taxes are of little importance compared with factors such as markets, raw materials, and labor, Alyea (1967) in a review of studies on property tax inducements, argued that the empirical studies "have not proved that, *ceteris paribus*, tax incentives or other inducement considerations are not significant *marginal* factors in attracting business to a community." He cited Ross's (1953) finding that only 7 percent of the total value of investments by firms that received exemptions under a Louisiana program would not have been made in the absence of the program. Although the value of investments that would not have been made without the program amounted to less than half the total tax loss to Louisiana, the possibility remains that the total tax loss associated with such programs could be offset by additional employment and payrolls from the few investments legitimately attributable to the programs. The possibility is not so far-fetched as it may seem. Morgan and Hackbart (1974) concluded that the benefits associated with exemption programs could exceed their costs, even if the induced investment as a percentage of the total tax-exempt investment was low.

A study by the Advisory Commission on Intergovernmental Relations (1967) concluded that the relative importance of tax differences increases as the location decision process narrows the alternative location possibilities to particular jurisdictions within a region. Nontax considerations are important in the choice of a region, and no relationship exists between industrial growth and tax differences in neighboring states, largely because states are careful not to get "too far out of line" with their immediate neighbors. However, interstate tax differences, especially in property taxation, can become a "swing" factor in the final selection of a particular plant site.

The observation that state and local taxes can be influential in the final choice among locations that meet all other criteria is made frequently as a qualification to the finding that taxes are not a major determinant of location decisions. However, that observation is not supported strongly by empirical evidence. Most survey studies have found that relatively few firms even consider taxes in location decisions and even fewer are influenced significantly by them. This suggests that in most decisions taxes are not very influential even in the final stages of the decision process.

Similarly, though several studies conclude that taxes may play a significant role in where a firm decides to locate within a given metropolitan area (if its choices are a number of political jurisdictions with differing tax rates), the contention is neither persuasive nor supported by empirical evidence. These studies imply that firms are footloose within metropolitan areas and that profitability does not vary with location. In fact, the profitability of most firms in metropolitan areas may be significantly affected by their location, because the profitability of most retail and service firms is sensitive to their location relative to traffic patterns, shopping centers, and the geographic distribution of customers. Some firms must locate near others that provide essential services, and other firms still must locate near transportation facilities or highways. Unfortunately, only a few studies have attempted to assess the importance of taxes for intrametropolitan locations, and these have presented only weak or inconclusive results.[6]

Previous reviews have overlooked a study by Williams (1967) that computed average costs, with and without state and local taxes, for thirty-eight classes of manufacturing industries in Minnesota and compared Minnesota's rank among the states for each industry with and without state and local taxes. The study confirmed that Minnesota business taxes were relatively heavy but also found that state and local taxes were very minor as a percentage of the value of the state's shipments of manufactured goods (about 1 to 2 percent). The principal finding, however, was that even the complete exemption of Minnesota manufacturers from taxation, assuming other states did not change their taxes, would not greatly change Minnesota's rank among the states in terms of average costs: of the thirty-eight industries, the state ranking would be unchanged for eighteen; it would be improved by only one position for eleven industries and by two or more positions for only nine industries. Of course, smaller reductions in business taxes would have even less of an impact on the state ranking. Although these findings are tentative because of the statistical difficulties in measuring costs, Williams concluded that "it appears unlikely that tax reduction would lower costs sufficiently to induce a very large number of new plants to locate in the state" (p. 56).

A study by Revzan (1976), which used the tax-bill approach based on data from actual firms, found that the differences in tax rates between various states or local governments tended to result in only small differences in the total tax bills, which were calculated to include payroll taxes. Revzan found that although property tax rates varied significantly within North Carolina and between North Carolina and South Carolina, the differences in the total tax bills at alternative locations were relatively minor. Comparing total tax bills for hypothetical apparel manufacturers in two unincorporated areas and two urban areas (in North Carolina and South Carolina), Revzan demonstrated that the highest total tax bill (in Charlotte) would be only 1.6 percent higher than the lowest bill (in South Carolina). Although property taxes paid at the four locations differed substantially, the effect of these differences was sharply reduced by the deductibility provisions of federal and state corporate income taxes and by differences in the state tax structures.

Finally, a political economic analysis of states' job-creation business incentives by Harrison and Kanter (1978, p. 424) concluded that there is "no reason to expect that tax or related costside incentives—by themselves—generate new investment." They point out that if any segment of the business community is likely to be responsive, it would be those firms paying the lowest wages and employing the fewest workers.

The research reviewed in this chapter concludes generally that state and local tax differentials carry little weight in determining locational choices. Although individual studies or particular approaches are subject to criticism, the theoretical reasoning that supports the general conclusion and the consistency of the empirical findings (regardless of time period, geographical area, or approach used) make it difficult to challenge the conclusion. With a possible exception for intrametropolitan locations, the research has been extensive and thorough, and so the usual call for additional research seems inappropriate.

Why, then, does the belief that state and local tax differences are important still lead to state and local efforts to use tax concessions as attractions for industry? For several reasons, not the least of which is ignorance of the research evidence. The main reason perhaps is that both history and other considerations have permitted tax policy to be confused with basic economic realities. Over the past several decades, manufacturing firms have been strongly motivated to move out of central cities (to which they were earlier tied by transportation constraints) to suburban and rural communities and out of industrial states to less industrial states.

The growth of markets in the South and West, low wages and absence of strong unions in the South, changes in production methods, improvements in highways, the availability of electricity, better communications, and other economic factors have played a major role in this decentralization. But it also happens that tax rates are usually higher in the northeastern states than in the southern states, and higher in the central cities than in the suburbs. Therefore, industry location or relocation possibly has been mistakenly attributed to tax differences when other factors are the actual cause.

The belief that taxes are important is likely to be reinforced by attitudes of businessmen, who frequently complain about taxation and government interference, leaving the impression with state and local officials that taxes are more important in location decisions than they actually are. Usually a firm will come into contact with industrial developers or officials of a state or local government only after it has decided that the state or community meets its basic location criteria, in terms of markets, labor supply, or transportation costs. Discussions between the firm and officials, including industrial developers, are then likely to be concerned with matters within the purview of those officials, such as taxes. The firms will naturally want information about taxes or want to negotiate assessments or concessions. Thus, even though taxes are not a major factor in the location decision, officials, under pressure by state and local industrial and economic developers are likely to get the opposite impression from their discussions with firms. Furthermore, state and local officials, who have responsibility for attracting industry but little or no control over such fundamental locational determinants as markets and labor supply, may offer tax and financial inducements, over which they may have some control, and then feel obligated to justify their actions.

The policy implication of research on industrial location decisions is simple and straightforward: Tax concessions to industry are not likely to be very effective in attracting industry. Although tax concessions or a tax system favorable to business may occasionally cause a firm to choose one location over another, the benefits from these few cases must be weighed against the total costs of tax concessions, many of which may be enjoyed by firms whose location decisions were not made on that basis.

Notes

1. For a further review of location theory, see William Alonso, "Location Theory"; Edgar M. Hoover, *The Location of Economic Activity*; or David M. Smith, "A Theoretical Framework for Geographical Studies of Industrial Location."

2. For a summary of this research and a discussion of issues, see Leonard J. Wheat, *Regional Growth and Industrial Location.*

3. The seven studies were as follows: Thomas Bergen and William Eagen, "Industrial Aid Bonds"; Henry Hunker and Alfred Wright, *Factors of Industrial Location in Ohio*; T. E. McMillan, Jr., "Why Manufacturers Choose Plant Locations vs. Determinants of Plant Locations"; Eva Mueller and James Morgan, "Location Decisions of Manufacturers"; and Business Week Research Report, *Plant Site Survey.*

4. The five studies were as follows: Maurice Fulton, "Michigan's Tax Structure and Its Influence on Economic Development"; State of Oregon *Report*; J. A. Stockfish, *A Study of California's Tax Treatment of Manufacturing Industry*; Washington State Department of Commerce and Economic Development and Washington State Tax Commission, *Industrial Tax Loads in Competing States*; and Ronald J. Wonnacott, *Manufacturing Costs and the Comparative Advantage of United States Regions.*

5. See Business Executives' Research Committee, *Factors Affecting Industrial Location in the Southwest.* See also U.S. Department of Commerce, *Basic Industrial Location Factors*; Irene Hanning, *How North Dakota Taxes Industry*; James E. Chapman and William H. Wells, *Factors in Industrial Location in Atlanta, 1946–1955*; and Warren E. Mueller, "Industrial Location Decisions."

6. See, for example, Sharon G. Levin, "Suburban–Central City Property Tax Differentials and the Location of Industry"; and Roger W. Schmenner, summarized in *Proceedings of the Sixty-sixth Annual Conference on Taxation*, pp. 528–33. In addition, central city—suburban property tax differentials may not be as large as a comparison of tax rates might indicate. In a study of location in Boston, Hamer found that, whereas tax rates suggest that the tax burden of firms in Boston is 2.5 to 4 times higher than in the suburbs, after assessment practices are taken into account the differentials are reduced considerably. He estimates a 5 percent property tax rate for Boston compared with an average of 4 percent for the suburbs (1973, pp. 45–48).

Part 4
Financing Community
Development

Chapter 12
Nongovernment Financing
of Industry

For a majority of manufacturing entrepreneurs the problem of obtaining adequate financing for their industrial ventures is surpassed only by problems of assessing the market potential for their product lines and selecting suitable plant locations with their attendant requirements of market accessibility and material, labor, and utility availability. Obtaining adequate financing, though, remains an important problem because the period of time required to negotiate and complete loan arrangements is generally much longer than that for the financing of other types of ventures, because the amount of capital needed is substantially greater than for other ventures and fewer sources are available that can finance the total loan requirements of an industrial firm. Industrial loans frequently involve joint participation by several different lending sources and thus the methods of financing are considerably greater and more complex than for other types of land use (Kinnard and Messner 1971; Murray 1964).[1] Usually different types of loans are arranged for the various aspects of the venture: land purchase, site development, building construction, machinery and equipment, start-up expenses, working capital, and capital to support inventory and receivables—each of which may be financed by a separate source that specializes in the specific types of loan required.[2] Unlike most other ventures, lending sources are likely to emphasize the credit rating and character of industrial borrowers more than the collateral used to secure the loans[3] because industrial real estate and equipment are more specialized in their uses and, hence, have a more limited resale market. Consequently, the ease of securing industrial loans frequently depends upon the degree to which the real estate and equipment can be used for other purposes.

Because many types of financing methods are available for industrial development and also a multitude of sources for such funds, only the most commonly used methods and sources will be discussed here. This chapter will discuss nongovernment finance sources and methods. The companion chapter (chapter 13) will outline available federal, state, and local government financing methods and sources that have practical value to most industrial and economic developers.

Equity Funds

Since large amounts of capital are required in industrial development ventures, such undertakings usually need some investment funds from outside the local money market. The large amount of capital also requires commitments on the part of three, rather than two, types of investors: the entrepreneurs themselves, equity investors, and lenders.

Equity represents the amount of money invested in the industrial firm without debt obligation, as opposed to the amount invested that carries a debt obligation. Equity investors, who normally include the entrepreneurs, are the owners of the industry. They exercise control over its management and assume most of the risks and rewards associated with ownership. The amount of equity held in an industry by its owners and the assets representing the equity (after eliminating questionable receivables and slow-moving or obsolete inventory) is of major importance to prospective lenders as they try to determine the degree of risk in lending more money to the firm. The greater the amount of equity the owners have in the firm, the lower will be the business worries and interest costs and the greater will be the owner's borrowing capacity and expansion capability.

Equity in a business can be obtained in essentially three ways: (1) subordinated debentures, (2) preferred stock, and (3) common stock. Subordinated debentures take the form of debt obligations and entail the same interest costs as other conventional debt obligations.[4] They differ from conventional debt obligations because the subordination tends to make this money more like additional equity than additional debt as far as creditors are concerned. Preferred stock provides the money that supports debt, but this method carries more risk than debt obligations, whether of the subordinated or conventional type. It is "preferred" over common stock because the investor is granted certain rights to dividend distributions and to the firm's assets if it should be liquidated. Common stock also provides debt-supporting equity money, but with the greatest degree of risk to the investor.

Subordinated Debentures

Investors in subordinated debentures may be private individuals; venture finance companies; pension and profit sharing trusts, foundations, insurance companies, and university endowments; or investment trusts.

Individuals, because of their tastes, interest, and tax status, like to invest money in promising industrial ventures. Almost every sizable community has among its population some such individuals. Others anywhere in the country look for promising situations in which they can make investments at an early stage in the development of the firm with as little risk as possible.[5] Private investors are looking for a good return on their investment, coupled with the partially or totally tax-free income flow through long-term capital gains. Since they also want to conserve their capital for other ventures, they probably want to lend money to an industry on a subordinated debenture basis so that they can be paid back out of the firm's earnings without having these earnings treated as taxable dividends. In many cases individual investors want detachable warrants, by which they have the option to purchase stock in the future at some specified price, as the medium for realizing their capital gains.[6]

Individual investors also may be attracted to investments that can be charged off annually against personal income taxes in order to reduce tax liabilities. This can be accomplished either by starting the venture as a limited partnership or a joint venture or by creating a corporation having no more than ten stockholders and electing to have it taxed as a partnership. Using these business organization techniques, individuals change their status from long-term investors primarily interested in transforming ordinary income into capital gains income to operator-investors. Operator-investors have the further tax advantage of offsetting their ordinary income liability by deducting certain expenses and allowances associated with the venture's operation in addition to the capital-gain advantages of long-term investors. However, no single investment method is appropriate for all private investors, since individual objectives and tax positions differ.

Venture finance companies prefer to invest by purchasing stock or subordinated debentures in small corporations with growth potential.[7] They most often invest in firms that have established markets for their products but need additional equity money for expansion or to make the firms more attractive for public financing. Sometimes, not so often anymore, they invest in firms that are developing new product lines. Since the financial rewards need to be in keeping with the risks involved, venture financing companies are interested in investments that they forecast will appreciate three to five times within five to ten years.

At first, venture finance companies were interested only in financing firms with new production processes or products. Later they broadened their portfolios to include all types of growth industries. Today these companies are interested primarily in making investments to new or growing industries. They are not interested in financing processes or products that are still in the inventive or experimental stage, since it is too difficult to assess the merits until the products are converted into proven or operational prototypes. Also excluded is investing in firms whose sole purpose is to provide services. Ventures outside the continental limits of the United States are usually not supported by these companies.

Because small investments take as much time as large ones, venture finance companies have generally found that very small investments are not practical. Investments frequently range between $500,000 and $1,000,000, although some are as little as $50,000. Small investments are likely to be approved, for example, when first-round seed money is needed to prove the value of a process or product and an agreement is drawn up whereby additional capital will be invested if the value is established.

New and small growing firms usually need management assistance as much as capital. Venture finance companies frequently consider it impractical to invest in such firms unless their involvement will grant them an equity interest large enough so that they can exercise an important role in decisions made by the firm—not necessarily control, but definitely a voice in the firm's management and direction. If management has not yet proven its ability, the venture company will want a larger degree of control in order to safeguard its investment.

Pension and profit-sharing trusts, foundations, insurance companies, and university endowments also provide opportunities for industrial firms to obtain equity funds.[8] These sources accumulate huge pools of capital and therefore they have considerable funds to invest. Such organizations typically pursue a fairly conservative investment policy, providing either secured or unsecured money only to larger, more well-established firms. Securities placed with these institutions may be common stock, preferred stock, subordinated debentures, or other debt securities. Frequently, the institutions want long-term debt securities that give them safety and assurance of income on their investment, together with a kicker that allows conversion of the debt into common stock or, more frequently, warrants that permit them to buy common stock at a fixed price far into the future, even after their money has been repaid. Occasionally, however, some institutions depart from their usual policy and make an investment-letter purchase of stock in a growing company to provide expansion funds in the hope of substantial capital appreciation. At other times some will actively look for somewhat more venturesome, long-term, unsecured loans on which they can obtain warrants or other equity kickers that can provide capital appreciation rewards in the future.

Investment trusts are primarily interested in seasoned stocks.[9] However, a number of investment companies will occasionally make an investment-letter purchase of a block of stock in a going growth company to provide it with expansion capital. In this way the trusts hope to bolster their investment portfolios through the rewards of substantial capital appreciation.

Preferred and Common Stock

The sale of preferred stock is another method of obtaining additional equity capital, but this kind of transaction is reserved almost exclusively for industries whose common stock is traded publicly; therefore it does not really represent a major method used to provide equity funds for a firm that desires to remain privately owned. At times, however, preferred stock may be sold to the management of a privately owned firm or to friends of management. The use of preferred stock as a financing vehicle carries a dividend requirement that must be met before any dividends are paid to the common shareholders. Usually a cumulative dividend requirement prevails, meaning that all unpaid preferred dividends must be paid before any common dividends can be issued. Although there is no requirement that preferred dividends must be paid, quite often certain rights accrue to preferred shareholders if they are not, such as the right to elect the firm's directors.

The sale of common stock to the public is the last major method of obtaining equity capital for industrial development. This method is not always readily available, especially in the case of small firms. If the requirements of going public may be harmful to the firm, sale of common stock is inadvisable. But for many firms it is usually the only practical way to get a substantial amount of additional equity capital in order to improve the firm's credit rating.

A firm must fulfill or be willing to fulfill a number of requirements before its stock will be considered for sale on the public market. First, the net earnings or the potential net earnings should be great enough to justify a public sale. Some of the larger investment houses are interested only in companies that show an after-tax profit of about $1,000,000, while some of the smaller houses, including regional underwriters, will consider only firms whose potential after-tax earnings, within a few years, would reach a level of $500,000. However, it is the many smaller underwriting houses with local networks of offices or close contacts with other dealers that are the most likely to undertake the sale of stock for small industrial firms. Whether they will do so depends upon the second requirement: that the industrial firm have a growth rate or potential growth rate higher than its industry as a whole. A third requirement is that the owner-managers be willing to operate under public scrutiny. An industrial firm interested in selling its stock to the public must provide unqualified audits prepared by a recognized independent CPA firm for at least the preceding three years. A prospectus must also be prepared, which outlines in detail the operations of the firm, its history, management characteristics including salaries, and the competitive environment in which the firm operates.[10] A final requirement that needs to be considered is the degree to which public disclosure may affect the ability of the firm to conduct its operations. Since the firm's financial condition, earnings, operating figures, and other information, to some extent, are a matter of public record, entrepreneurs should not consider going public unless they are confident that their firm's prospects are good enough to withstand inspection by their competitors and the investing public. The entrepreneurs must also realize a further disadvantage of going public: the ownership of the firm becomes diluted, which can be reflected in interference from outsiders, reducing the flexibility and control of the initial entrepreneurs.

The cost of going public also must be given serious consideration. In addition to stock sales commissions, legal fees, accounting fees, printing costs, stock certificate lithograph costs, Securities and Exchange Commission registration fees, federal issue and transfer tax fees, Blue Sky filing fees and expenses, and registrar and transfer agent fees must be paid. For small issues between $500,000 and $2,000,000, for example, costs can be especially high. The underwriter's compensation coupled with legal fees, audit expenses, and so forth can run as high as 15 to 20 percent of the total issue. Consequently, going public is far more expensive than either the sale of debt or preferred stock.

Underwriting houses use three different kinds of agreements to underwrite the sale of securities: (1) on a best effort, (2) all or none, or (3) firm commitment basis. The best-effort basis is not really an underwriting and is the weakest kind of selling agreement. It is merely an undertaking by an underwriting house to use its best effort to sell the stock issue. The underwriting house will neither guarantee that the stock will be sold nor will it undertake to purchase unsold securities itself. Under the all-or-none arrangement, the underwriting house agrees to sell the entire issue or return the money to investors who have already purchased the securities. The pressure is therefore on the underwriting house to make a substantial sales effort and to purchase the balance of the securities itself, if need be, after having sold a certain portion in order to avoid canceling the entire sale and losing its commission. The firm-commitment basis is a true underwriting, in which the underwriting house agrees to purchase a specified number of shares and relies upon its ability to resell them to the public. This is the only way in which an industrial firm can be sure of getting additional equity money without an underwriting failure appearing on its record.

Borrowed Funds

Borrowed funds entail a debt obligation whereby the borrower is required to pay principal and interest over a specified period of time; if these payments are not made, certain rights accrue to the lender. Debt obligation methods of financing industrial development may be either secured or unsecured. Secured debt is supported by collateral such as chattel mortgages on equipment, accounts receivable or inventory, stocks and bonds, real estate mortgages, and life insurance up to the cash value of the policy.[11] Unsecured debt, on the other hand, is supported by the credit reputation of the industrial firm and is usually measured by the income the firm is capable of generating, coupled with the risk involved in obtaining that income in the future.

Secured-Debt Loans

Loans secured by some form of collateral come from numerous sources: insurance companies, pension and profit-sharing funds, commercial banks, savings and loan associations, commercial finance and factoring companies, commercial mortgage companies, and real estate investment trusts.

The most prevalent methods of securing loans are through (1) real estate mortgages, construction, and leasing; (2) sale-leaseback financing; (3) equipment financing and leasing; and, in the case of more risky ventures, (4) commercial finance and factor company financing methods.

The *real estate mortgage* is the most common method of securing a loan (Bryant 1962). The amount of the loan is based upon the appraisal value of the land and building(s) used as the collateral, and it generally ranges from one-third to three-fourths of this appraisal. Mortgage loans are for terms of between ten and twenty-five years and provide for equal monthly payments of principal and interest over the life of the loan, as in the typical residential mortgage. Lenders prefer multipurpose manufacturing plants and warehouses rather than single-purpose structures, which cannot be easily converted to other uses. The location of the structure and the ability of the industrial firm to make payments are other items evaluated by mortgage lenders. The lender will examine the audited statements of an industry for about the past five years and base his loan decisions, in large part, on the firm's assets and liabilities, profits and losses, and reconcilement of net worth. Because of this, long-term mortgage loans are usually not available to new industries, since these firms have no "track record" for lenders to evaluate. Therefore, unless a new industry has a substantial portion of its equity funds invested in fixed assets, it will have to lease its plant facilities from real estate property owners. The largest single mortgage loan source has been the insurance companies that deal with the industrial firm either directly or through a mortgage banker or broker. Most institutional lenders, though, prefer to deal with mortgage bankers or others who specialize in this type of lending, since they possess appraisal and research capabilities to evaluate loan decisions. Other important sources of mortgage money include pension and profit-sharing funds, savings and loan associations, commercial banks, and real estate investment trusts.

Construction loans provide funds to build plant facilities and are closely allied to mortgage loans (Winston 1965). These loans are secured and usually require a commitment whereby the permanent mortgage loan will be financed by the lender of the construction loan. That is, the lender who provides the construction loan is quite often the permanent mortgage lender. Construction loan money is advanced in stages based upon the progress of the project, and upon its completion, permanent finance arrangements go into effect.

Real estate lease financing is another method of plant financing with some of the characteristics of mortgage loans. Under a lease financing arrangement for an industrial plant the real estate title remains in the hands of the lessor or owner of the property. The owner usually assumes all the risks, taxes, insurance, maintenance, and other costs of ownership as in the conventional lease, although some of these costs can be transferred to the industrial firm through the lease agreement. Initial lease terms typically last for twenty years, and property owners expect to recover their principal over this initial term at a given rate of return. Quite often lease agreements will feature renewal options with much lower rental payments. In highly industrialized areas, though, leases for efficient multipurpose buildings may be arranged with initial terms of less than twenty years. Whether it is better to own or lease plant facilities is a matter that merits careful review. Among the factors that should be evaluated in making this decision are the relative costs of different financing methods, the economic life of the facility for the particular industry, and the expected value of the property at the end of the initial lease term. Another point is that in determining an industry's credit rating, sophisticated investors and lenders analyze leases as debt when evaluating the firm's financial statements. The auditing profession also requires that leases be capitalized on the balance sheet, showing the property as a fixed asset and the capitalized lease obligation as a long-term debt.

Sale-leaseback financing is another method of providing needed plant facilities, closely allied to conventional lease methods (Korb 1971). In a sale-leaseback, an industrial firm sells its property outright to an institutional or private investor and receives a long-term lease to assure its continued occupancy. Initial leases usually run for a term of twenty to thirty-five years, with renewals for additional periods determined by negotiation. In this lease arrangement, the industrial firm assumes all the risks, taxes, insurance, maintenance, and other costs of ownership. The investors who put up the money take title to the property and get a lease commitment that assures the return of their money over the initial lease term at an adequate interest rate or other charge for the use of their money. In addition, the investors receive a kicker in the form of the residual value of the property or continued rentals after the initial lease term. New construction, as well as already existing facilities, can be financed by the sale-leaseback method. In new construction, the industrial firm usually builds to its own specifications, and the investor-purchaser agrees to buy the building and lease it back upon completion, provided that it meets the prearranged specifications. Small and large industries can take advantage of this method of financing. To qualify, they need a past history of profits and a rising sales trend. Hence, this method is not available to new industries. Major weight is given to the firm's credit standing, earnings record, management ability, and growth rate compared to the industry as a whole. The investor-purchaser is primarily interested in the credit rating of the industrial firm and not in the real estate. The location and quality of the real estate, though, is an important factor evaluated by investor-purchasers in their decision to negotiate a sale-leaseback agreement. The poorer the location, the better must be the credit rating of the tenant industry. Since general-purpose manufacturing plants again are favored over special-purpose ones, rental costs on special-purpose factory buildings tend to be higher. Sale-leaseback financing sources are numerous and include insurance companies, pension and profit-sharing trusts, and foundations. These investors are primarily interested in buying properties worth from $300,000 up. Private individuals may be found for properties valued at less than this amount.

Several *equipment financing* methods are available whereby either presently owned or newly purchased equipment is pledged as security for the loan.[12] The equipment pledged must usually be general purpose in its use and transportable from the property. Title to the equipment may be vested in the lender or in the industrial firm, in which case a lien is placed on the equipment by the lender until the loan is repaid. Equipment loans usually have an intermediate-term maturity (one to six years), based upon a period considerably shorter than the minimum productive life of the equipment. The most important methods used are the installment plan purchase, chattel mortgage loan, and lease agreement.

Under an installment plan purchase the industrial firm obtains physical possession of the equipment but does not obtain title until the loan is paid. A note and a conditional sales contract are signed and a monthly repayment schedule is set up to amortize the total loan balance in equal payments.[13] Under the chattel mortgage method the industrial firm pledges as security either new or valuable used equipment to which it holds an unencumbered title. A formal agreement and note are drawn whereby the industrial firm gives the lender a chattel mortgage on the equipment. Most loans made on chattel mortgage security are small, ranging from $1,000 to $10,000 on equipment in small industrial firms. Larger finance companies, however, will sometimes make substantial loans of between $25,000 and $250,000 or more. For such large loans the industrial firm must also pledge its accounts receivable and/or inventory as securities along with its equipment. Leasing equipment is an increasingly important financing method because it allows an industrial firm to conserve its capital for other uses. Instead of laying out cash or borrowing to purchase equipment, a firm can acquire the use of office and production equipment by obligating itself to pay regular rentals over a specified period of time, usually three to five years, and use its cash or borrowing power for additional working capital or for other purposes. However, by leasing its equipment the firm has fewer fixed assets than if it has purchased the equipment, and the obligation to pay rent is just as definite as the obligation to pay interest and amortize debt. But as a practical matter some lenders tend to regard equipment rentals payments as operating costs rather than as debt so that the leasing of equipment has less effect on the future borrowing capacity of the firm than does the purchase of equipment. Also to be evaluated before the decision to purchase or lease equipment is made are the relative tax gains to be achieved under each method. Rentals paid for equipment are deductible operating costs on tax returns. Money laid out for its purchase is not deductible, but over the life of the equipment can be charged off by depreciation allowances.

Commercial finance and factor company financing may be obtained by industrial firms with credit ratings less acceptable to commercial banks and other more conservative lending sources. These companies advance funds to industrial firms by purchasing the sales accounts of some of their customers and securing the receivables as collateral. For the degree of risk involved they charge an interest rate (usually higher than the going bank rate) on the amounts of sales credited to the accounts they purchase and, to protect their money, almost always take on the responsibility of the clerical work associated with the accounts. For this additional clerical work—credit checking, collection, and bookkeeping—the companies charge a commission, which is also scaled to the amount of sales credited to the purchased accounts. An advantage gained by industrial firms divesting themselves of this clerical work is that they can concentrate more completely on production and sales activity. Since many companies in the commercial finance field are also engaged in factoring, it is easy to confuse the two. Factoring involves the assumption of the credit risk on accounts purchased from industrial firms and the acceptance of the bookkeeping and collection responsibilities for the resulting receivables. In contrast to factoring, commercial finance companies do not guarantee against credit losses on sales to customers. Because of the added risk assumed in guaranteeing against credit failures, factoring companies usually charge a higher interest rate for their services than do finance companies. In a sense finance and factoring companies do not "lend" money, but by the purchase of some of a firm's sales accounts they provide revolving working capital to industries whose capital positions are insufficient for commercial banks to grant them needed credit lines. However, it is frequently the commercial banks that refer such industries to finance and factoring companies, and it is also the commercial banks that lend the needed money to the finance and factoring companies to advance to the firms. This practice is considered good business because the main purpose underlying commercial finance or factor-company financing is that industrial firms can be brought back to better business health and become better credit risks for commercial banks and other conventional lending sources. The decision to advance money needed by an industrial firm is based, among other things, upon the character and ability of its management, its diversification and past performance, the quality of the accounts pledged as security, and the ability of the firm to operate at a profit if the money is made available to it.

Unsecured-Debt Loans

Unsecured loans may be obtained from several sources, although the most prevalent lenders for this type of money are insurance companies and commercial banks. A wide range of maturities is available, from extremely short terms to terms of twenty to thirty years, with the more common methods of financing being long-term loans, interim-term loans, and short-term revolving credit and seasonal bank loans.

The *long-term loan* is of major interest to manufacturing firms, since industrial development usually involves financing of a permanent nature. The most prevalent lender of this type of money, as in the mortgage money market, is the life insurance company. These institutions have the ability to make loans from $250,000 to several hundred million dollars, with final maturities anywhere from ten to thirty years. These loans are made on an unsecured basis and heavy emphasis is placed on evaluating the financial strength of the industry because lenders expect to be repaid from the firm's future earnings or cash flow, rather than through the liquidation of its assets. Because the past earnings record is a good indicator of future prospects, new firms or firms with losses have difficulty in obtaining loans from insurance companies.

Long-term loans provided by insurance companies generally require equal annual or semiannual payments of principal plus interest over the life of the loan and have restrictions or penalties on early retirement of the debt. Interest rates are determined by the size and term of the loan and the degree of risk involved, and they remain fixed over the life of the borrowing. Even though unsecured, this type of loan generally imposes certain additional restrictions on the financial activities of the firm, including provisions that establish: (1) a requirement that a specified working capital level be maintained, (2) a limitation on additional long-term debt, (3) a requirement that short-term loans be paid up completely for a certain number of days each year, (4) a limitation of dividend payments to a percentage of net income, (5) a limitation on the amount of long-term lease obligations, and (6) other restrictions that apply to specific industrial firms. A violation of any of these covenants would put the industrial firm in default; and, unless the restriction were waived or modified, the lender would have the right to demand immediate payment of the loan. While these restrictions may be disadvantageous to the firm, the main advantage of long-term financing is that the loan is not restricted to the value of the industry's property, and, if the firm's credit is satisfactory, it is possible to borrow enough to cover its entire financial requirements. Another advantage that accrues from the spacing of payments over a long term is that the firm is thus enabled to grow at a more comfortable pace. A further residual advantage is that once a relationship is established with an insurance company, it is easier to obtain additional money when the industry's long-term financial needs increase.

Although not all industrial firms have balance statements or earning records to support long-term, unsecured debt, as already pointed out, this does not mean that there are no sources of long-term funds for these firms. Some insurance companies will provide loans to firms with good future growth prospects and earnings. However, in those cases insurance companies or other lenders want more than just simple interest for the use of their money because, in reality, a portion of the borrowed money is a substitute for equity funds. To obtain additional money, therefore, the lenders will require either additional interest from the firm, based upon a percentage of its future earnings or warrants giving them the option to purchase the firm's stock in the future at a specified price.

Interim-term loans are unsecured borrowings arranged primarily by commercial banks for industrial firms whose financial needs are for a somewhat shorter time period than long-term loans—a maximum of ten years, but more often three to five years. A loan agreement similar to that drawn with an insurance company, although probably not as restrictive on the repayment of principal before maturity, is required. If the industrial firm is small or even medium sized, though, the bank may require the principal owners themselves to endorse the loan agreement. Larger firms can usually avoid personal endorsements, unless their credit ratings indicate a sufficient degree of risk. Also, in the case where an industrial firm has debt obligations to its officers, stockholders, and others, it is customary that the bank require these creditors to subordinate their claim to the bank's claim by signing a subordination agreement that provides payment of the bank's loan before those of the other creditors and first claim to the firm's assets in the case of its liquidation.

Occasionally banks will participate with insurance companies on long-term loans, taking the early maturities. For instance, on a fifteen-year loan for $12 million a bank may take the first five years, or $4 million. The advantage to the industrial firm is that the involvement of the bank would probably make the interest rate over the life of the loan somewhat lower.

A revolving-credit loan gives an industrial firm the ability to borrow money up to a specified sum during a specified period, perhaps two to three years. During this time the loan can vary in amount, fluctuating both up and down with a nominal commitment fee of 0.5 percent paid by the firm on the unused loan commitment. At the end of the revolving period the industry has the option of converting the outstanding balance into a term loan to be paid back to the lender in equal installments over a period of three to five years. This financing method appeals to industrial firms that find it difficult to determine their exact loan requirements but want to assure the availability of sufficient funds. Revolving-credit loans are used primarily for industrial expansion, but they can be used for new developments as well. They are generally not used to finance land and buildings, but rather to cover machinery and equipment, start-up costs, and working capital. Commercial banks have the biggest role in providing these unsecured loans.

A short-term seasonal bank loan is the proper type of financing for industrial firms that need working capital to support the seasonal buildup of receivables and/or inventories. Such unsecured loans are usually extended for a year at a time, and it is expected that they will be completely retired each year for a period between thirty to sixty consecutive days. Again, commercial banks are the main financing sources.

While there are numerous nongovernment sources and methods for financing industrial development, most are interested in the potential risks and profits of investing in a venture. The major objective of nongovernment investors is to assure a high degree of safety for the funds they advance. A second objective is to realize a profit on the advanced funds. Government sources of financing also want to assure a high degree of safety for the funds they advance. More important objectives, however, are to "promote the general welfare" in backward, underprivileged, or problem areas and to reduce dependence upon specific locations for strategic capital goods or inputs. In order to spread social benefits more equitably or to maintain national security, government finance sources are not interested in profits and so will advance, or guarantee, funds for industrial firms exhibiting greater potential risk, as long as they fulfill specific public policy objectives. The following chapter will outline the major sources and methods of government financing available to industrial firms fulfilling these objectives.

Notes

1. See especially Kinnard and Messner: chap. 5, "Industrial Real Estate as an Investment"; chap. 8, "Industrial Real Estate Lending"; chap. 9, "Equity and Lease Financing of Industrial Real Estate"; and chap. 10, "Industrial Real Estate Leases."

2. Receivables are the outstanding accounts of the firm's customers and are listed as assets, since they represent money owed to the firm.

3. New firms or small, growing firms have not had sufficient time to establish substantial credit ratings or adequate earning backgrounds and find it extremely difficult to obtain loans until such "track records" are established. It is more practical for such companies to occupy multiple-use buildings as tenants.

4. A subordinate debenture holder is in a secondary credit position to a more preferred creditor who has been granted a prior claim.

5. Industrial ventures seeking individual lenders should enlist the services of an industrial real estate broker, mortgage banker, mortgage correspondent, or mortgage company.

6. A detachable warrant is an instrument issued by a firm giving the holder the right to purchase capital stock at a fixed price. A capital gain is the profit realized from the sale of capital investments, including real estate or stock. For federal tax purposes, only 40 percent of the income realized from a long-term capital gain is taxed. Ordinary income, on the other hand, is fully taxed.

7. The leading venture finance companies are Rockefeller Brothers, Payson and Trask, Clarke Estate, Henry Sears & Company, William A. M. Burden & Company, Fox-Wills & Company, all of New York; T. J. Mellon and Sons of Pittsburgh; and American Research and Development Corporation of Boston.

8. There are thousands of employee trusts, university endowments, and foundations, and any of them can, on occasion, make investments.

9. Atlas Corporation, Lehman Corporation, and Putnam Growth Fund are a few well-known investment trust companies.

10. To complete a public offering, it is necessary to meet the requirements of the Securities Act of 1933 and the Securities (Blue Sky) Laws of the state in which the securities are to be sold. If the securities are to be offered to more than twenty-five persons, registration with the United States Securities and Exchange Commission is necessary, unless it is an intrastate offering only or the offering is priced at $300,000 or less.

11. A chattel mortgage is a lien against any movable or immovable property (except real estate) as security for a loan.

12. If presently owned equipment is pledged as security, the borrowed money can be put to other uses, in many cases providing funds for the firm's expansion.

13. Amortization is the process of gradually liquidating a debt by a series of periodic payments to a creditor.

Chapter 13
Government Financing
of Industry

Government loans have helped numerous small industrial firms get started, expand, grow, and prosper. The loans, provided by all levels of government, have been used by firms to construct, expand, or convert facilities; purchase or lease buildings and equipment; or obtain materials or working capital. This chapter will outline available federal, state, and local government financing and briefly discuss financial forecasting.[1]

Federal Government Funds

The federal government alone has nineteen separate agencies supervising over ninety different programs that can fund industrial development ventures. But because of the way federal government funding occurs, not as many real options are available as it might seem from the number of programs. The most important programs are those funded by the Small Business Administration (SBA), the Economic Development Administration (EDA) in the Department of Commerce, and the Farmer's Home Administration (FMHA) in the Department of Agriculture.

Small Business Administration Loans

SBA loans are made for two purposes: to enhance competition within the nation by strengthening the small business sector of the economy and to promote balanced economic growth through planned community development (U.S. Small Business Administration, n.d.). Special attention is given to loans that aid in the elimination of urban poverty and the upgrading of depressed rural areas. By law, SBA loans cannot be made to firms that can obtain adequate funds from banks or other private sources. Firms must therefore seek private financing before applying to SBA; this means that a firm's loan application must be turned down by a local bank, or two local banks in a city of more than 200,000 people. Firms receiving SBA loans, as well as other federal loans, must also agree that they will not discriminate among employees on the basis of sex, race, color, or national origin and that they will comply with environmental protection standards. Industries planning to relocate from one area to another are not eligible for SBA loans if the move will create or aggravate unemployment problems at the former location of the firm.

For loan purposes, SBA defines a small business as one that is independently owned and operated, is not dominant in its field, and meets a specific size limitation developed for each type of industry. A manufacturing firm is considered small if its average employment in the preceding four calendar quarters did not exceed 250 persons, including employees of any affiliates. A firm is considered large if its average employment is more than 1,500 persons. Hence, firms with employment greater than 250 but less than 1,500, and at times even greater than 1,500, need to consult SBA for the specific size limitation for their particular type of industry.[2]

SBA has three loan programs available for industrial development purposes: the 501 State Development Company (SDC) Loan Program, the 502 Local Development Company (LDC) Loan Program, and the 7-A Business Loan Program.[3] SBA interest rates for direct loans and their portion of participation loans are about two percentage points below the prime rate. Banks are allowed to set their own interest rates on guaranteed loans and their portion of participation loans and to make adjustments in their interest rates every six months, up to two percentage points above prime rates.

The 502 local development company loan program is the most important of the three programs for local industrial development purposes. Its primary goal is to assist community development efforts. Under this program, SBA loans, whether direct or participation, are advanced to industrial firms through a legally incorporated local development organization composed of a minimum of twenty-five stockholders, of which 75 percent must be living or doing business within the community.[4] The 502 funds can never be loaned directly to a firm by SBA, nor can SBA guarantee a direct bank loan to a firm under the 502 program. All funds advanced to assist industrial firms must be through a local development corporation. The loans may be used by the local development corporation to assist an industry in financing the acquisition, construction, modernization, or expansion of industrial plants, including associated site improvements (grading); and for engineering, architect, legal, and accounting fees. Money acquired through these loans may also be used to purchase land, machinery, or equipment but not to provide working capital or to repay debt except interim debt incurred in the construction of the buildings involved in the project. Loans are secured by a lien on the fixed assets acquired by the loan, and maturities may be for as long as ten years, except those portions used for construction that may have a maturity of up to twenty-five years. The local development corporation is usually required to provide at least 20 percent of the cost of a project from its own funds but not less than the amount that the cost exceeds the appraised market value.[5]

Several methods are used by which 502 funds can be advanced. When private financing is not available to a firm on reasonable terms, the SBA can guarantee up to 90 percent or $500,000 (whichever is less) of a direct bank loan made to a local development company that is to be used to assist the firm. The SBA guarantees that the bank will lose no more than 10 percent of the loan. The bank, in turn, is able to sell the guaranteed portion of the loan as United States government–backed securities, if it chooses, to improve its liquidity position.

In cases where a firm's entire loan requirement is not obtainable from a private lending source or where a guaranteed loan is not available, the SBA can advance funds directly to a local development corporation for use on a participation basis with a bank and the local development corporation. Industrial firms are able to obtain as much as 100 percent financing of their fixed assets under this method if their loan requirements are within $1,425,000, although a more practical limit would be $1,250,000. This is because the SBA could conceivably advance 35 percent of the required funds up to a legal maximum of $500,000. Including bank and local development corporation participation amounting to $925,000, a $1,425,000 loan could therefore be financed.

SBA can participate in project financing, in several ways, one of which could be for a local development corporation to sell third mortgage bonds to provide an equity base of 10 percent of the loan. The bonds could be locally sold common stock or notes requiring that interest be paid to holders on a semiannual or annual basis. SBA could participate by lending up to 35 percent of the loan and be in a second mortgage position although it requires only that the local bonds not be retired any sooner than it takes the firm to repay the SBA funds advanced to them through the local development corporation. A bank could then participate by advancing the remainder of the loan, or a maximum of 55 percent. As long as the bank's portion of the loan is greater than 40 percent, it can obtain a first mortgage position and rapid amortization of the funds it advances. Another way in which SBA can participate in industrial development is for the local development corporation to build and equip a plant for an industrial firm with funds borrowed directly from SBA. The LDC could then lease the facility to the firm on a net lease basis.[6] The firm can occupy the property for the term of the loan or for a period of five years after its disbursement, whichever is longer. The firm can have the option to buy the property at any time for one dollar plus a sum equal to its outstanding debt obligations. If the industrial firm wants to hold title to the property, the local development corporation can relend the borrowed SBA funds to the firm and accept a promissory note and mortgage that gives the firm clear ownership when paid. In all cases the local development corporation assumes the credit risk of the firm and is responsible for the amortization of the SBA funds.

The *7-A Business Loan Program*'s primary goal is to strengthen the small business sector of the economy by providing funds either directly to a small business firm or by guaranteeing up to 90 percent (subject to a $350,000 limitation in most cases) of a direct bank loan to a firm. Since 95 percent of the funds available under this program are guaranteed funds, most loans are made on a guaranteed basis. SBA will consider making a direct loan to an industry under this program only when other forms of financing are not available, and these loans will not usually exceed $100,000. Under this program, also, SBA can advance loans on a participation basis with a bank by lending funds directly to a firm. The bank lending the greater share of the loan would obtain a first mortgage, but in the event of foreclosure both lenders would share in the collateral and losses in proportion to the amount of their investments.[7] The 7-A loans can be used for the same purposes as the 502 program, except that they can also be used to provide working capital to the firm. Interest rates and loan maturities are similar to those provided under the 502 program with the addition that working capital loans are usually limited to terms of less than six years. Participation by a local development corporation is not required to obtain 7-A funds.

Economic Development Administration Loans

EDA loans and grants are made for upgrading economically depressed areas by providing financial assistance that will result in the creation of permanent jobs and higher incomes for the area's inhabitants. Two programs are of interest for industrial development purposes—the Business Development Assistance Program and the Public Works and Development Facilities Program.

Under the *Business Development Assistance Program* either direct or guaranteed loans can be made available to an industrial firm planning to expand or locate plant facilities within a specific EDA-designated area, provided that it is a type of company that is consistent with the approved economic development plan for the area. Even so, no assistance will be provided to firms planning to relocate facilities from one area to another except in the case of a firm that is expanding facilities in an EDA area while continuing operations at their normal level of employment at the existing location. Neither will EDA assist industrial firms producing product lines for which there is sufficient plant capacity to meet existing and long-range demand for the lines.[8]

As in the case of SBA loans, a firm must seek private financing before applying for an EDA loan and must be turned down by at least two commercial banks. The venture should also not be eligible for SBA funds because of loan limits or other reasons. Unlike SBA, EDA does not have a restriction on the size of the firm because it is primarily interested in the number and types of new jobs the industry will create. Also unlike SBA, there is no established ceiling on the amount of money EDA may lend to an industry, except that assistance is generally limited to not more than $10,000 of EDA investment for every new job created or saved.[9] In terms of capital investment per worker, in effect, this means that EDA can participate in a major way only in projects that are highly labor intensive— but only in a very minor way in capital-intensive ones. EDA provides both direct and guaranteed loans that can be used for the same purposes as SBA programs, except that EDA provides direct working capital loans up to the full amount required by an industrial firm.[10] Loans are secured by liens on the usual forms of collateral and extend for terms determined by the useful life of the assets, except those portions of loans used to finance plant buildings that have maturities of up to twenty-five years. Working capital loans are usually limited to terms of not more than five years. Interest rates on EDA direct and participation loans are determined by the cost of federal government borrowing and are reviewed quarterly. As such, they tend to be higher than SBA rates, which are regulated by Congress. Banks are allowed to set their own interest rates on guaranteed loans and on their portion of participation loans. Their rates must be consistent with the going rates for loans that involve an equivalent degree of risk.

EDA requires that at least 15 percent of the total funds required by a venture be in the form of equity or a subordinated loan to be repaid and amortized no faster than the funds advanced to the firm by EDA. The industrial firm itself must provide two-thirds (or 10 percent) of this equity share and the state or local development corporation must provide a one-third (or 5 percent) share of the equity.[11] Depending upon the nature of the firm, EDA can provide direct loans to finance up to 65 percent of the cost of its required fixed assets. This maximum legal limit will be reduced by the amount of financing that private lenders are willing to invest in the venture. Private lenders can obtain first-mortgage positions and request rapid amortization of the funds they advance. For example, on a twenty-five-year loan for $10 million a bank may take the first five years (or minimum required private investment) for $2 million, and EDA and the local development corporation, the last twenty years for $8 million.[12] EDA will also guarantee loans from private lenders or leases for building, machinery, or equipment up to 90 percent of the amount owed on obligations it has backed. As in other general credit requirements loan applicants must be of good character, show ability to operate the firm successfully, and, above all, demonstrate that the requested loan is a sound investment.

The *Public Works and Development Facilities Assistance Program* can benefit industrial development activities by helping to reduce a firm's capital outlay and operating costs in communities that take advantage of the grants and loans provided under the program. To benefit from the program (which provides external economies to the industry) requires a good deal of cooperation between the firm and local community leaders. The program provides direct and supplementary grants and loans to communities only for purposes such as the construction or upgrading of industrial parks, utilities, streets and access roads; water and sewage facilities, primarily serving industrial and commercial users; port facilities for industrial expansion; regional airports; skill centers for the training or retraining of employed and underemployed adults; certain tourist facilities and other facilities to stimulate economic development. In addition, EDA will provide technical assistance to the community to help plan its development program.

Farmers Home Administration Loans

FMHA loans and grants are made to improve the economic and environmental climate of rural areas by creating and maintaining employment opportunities and providing essential community facilities. Of major importance for industrial development purposes are the business and industrial (B&I) loan program and the community facilities program.

All funds advanced under the *B&I loan program* are guaranteed loans covering up to 90 percent of the borrowed principal and its accrued interest, except that insured loans can be obtained in special circumstances.

FMHA does not provide direct loans to industrial firms, as do SBA and EDA. For this and other reasons industrial borrowers are advised to seek SBA or EDA financing if they are eligible before turning to FMHA for assistance. Unlike other federal loan programs this one has no requirement that the firm be turned down by private lending sources to be eligible for assistance. Neither is participation by a local development corporation required. To qualify, an industrial firm must be planning to locate in an area that is not within the outer boundary of a city having a population greater than 50,000 inhabitants, or its immediately adjacent urbanized or urbanizing area having a population density of more than 100 persons per square mile. Even so, priority is given to firms locating in open country, rural communities, and towns of 25,000 persons or less. Like EDA and SBA loans, these give no assistance to relocating industries if the move will aggravate unemployment conditions at their previous locations, if their production is likely to exceed demand, if they are likely to practice discrimination in their employment, or if they fail to comply with environmental protection standards.

FMHA guaranteed loans may be used to finance construction, modernization, or expansion of buildings; to purchase land, buildings, materials, machinery or equipment; and to provide start-up money, working capital, and certain interest payments, fees, and debt payments. Loans will not be made to guarantee lease payments or loans made by other federal agencies. Maximum maturities may be up to twenty-five years on land, buildings, and permanent fixtures; up to fifteen years on machinery (depending on its useful life); and up to seven years for working capital. Interest rates are negotiated between the industrial firm and the lender and can be fixed or variable. Variable rates have no established lower or upper limits and can be changed on a quarterly basis. FMHA requires that the industrial firm provide at least a 10 percent equity share in the venture; new firms, however, are required to have a larger equity share.

The *Community Facilities Program* provides loans and grants that can help industrial firms lower their unit costs of production. An explicit reason for providing funds under this program is to make small communities more attractive for industrial and economic development. FMHA can provide financial assistance to public bodies and sometimes to nonprofit organizations in places up to 10,000 persons for industrial parks (including land, buildings, parking areas, and access roads); fire protection; medical clinics; ambulance service; water, sewage, and solid-waste-disposal systems and extensions; streets, including curbs and gutters; economic development plans, and other such purposes. Communities of less than 5,500 persons are given priority assistance if they need to improve their water and sewage systems.

State and Local Funds

During the past few decades state and local governments have expanded rapidly to provide financial assistance to promote industrial development (Bridges 1965; Stinson 1967). Four main types of assistance programs have resulted. Two of these, state industrial finance authorities and local industrial bond financing, provide funds obtained from public sources. The other two, statewide development corporations and local development corporations, are quasi-public in nature and advance funds acquired primarily from private sources.

State Industrial Finance Authorities

State industrial finance authorities include two different types: one guarantees industrial loans made by private lenders, and the other makes direct loans of state funds to industrial firms. In the past, state finance authorities have provided most of their assistance to small and medium-sized firms. Sixty percent of the loans have been made to firms employing less than two hundred workers; and over 90 percent, to firms having less than five hundred workers. About half the loans are made to firms already established in the state, another third are made to entirely new firms, and the remainder are made to firms relocating from outside the state.

State loan guarantee authorities usually guarantee the repayment of first-mortgage loans advanced by private lenders, but not second- or third-mortgage loans. States pledge their credit as backing for the loans and usually provide reserve funds to pay claims in case of default. Guaranteed loans have maturities up to twenty-five years, and the advanced funds are used primarily to purchase land and finance the construction of plants. Loans are insured up to 90 percent of the land and plant costs. Local development corporations can provide a subordinated loan to finance the remaining 10 percent of the cost of the project; in some states this is mandatory. Guaranteed loans have averaged $500,000 and more in the past. States having guaranteed loan programs charge an annual insurance fee equal to about 1 percent of the outstanding loan balance. The insurance fee when added to the lender's interest rate still makes the cost of these loans somewhat less than those that high-risk firms could obtain from commercial lenders, if the loans were available in the first place.

Some *state direct loan authorities* restrict their loans to ventures that can be financed jointly with federal government agencies, while others limit loans to ventures located in labor surplus areas. Others, however, have no such restrictions. Loan funds are acquired through legislative appropriations or sales of tax-exempt bonds, or they are borrowed from the state treasury. States restricting their loans to joint participation with federal agencies provide 5 to 10 percent of the cost of the project. States financing loans jointly with conventional lending sources advance from 25 to 50 percent of the project cost. Typically, local development corporations are required to participate with the state by providing between 5 and 25 percent of the industry's needed financing. The loans are used to finance fixed assets, primarily land and plant costs, and have maturities of from ten to twenty years. Some states provide direct loans at slightly lower interest rates than those of conventional lenders, so that industrial firms may find it cheaper to borrow from the state authority if the opportunity is available.

Local Industrial Bond Financing

Through the sale of industrial bonds local governments in every state have the authority to finance the purchase of land and the construction of manufacturing plants for resale or lease to industries (Pugh 1971).[13] Some local governments can advance funds for machinery and working capital as well. The industry agrees to lease the property for a period ranging from ten to twenty-five years, paying all costs incident to the use of the real estate (net lease). The net rental paid by the firm is equal to an amount that will retire the bonds over the lease term—usually just sufficient to cover the debt's principal and interest and the maintenance of the property. In some cases the firm has the option to purchase the facilities at a price based upon a formula tied to the amortization of the debt. Or the firm may be required to buy a portion of the bonds. The interest income received by the bond holder may be exempt from federal income taxes (except for bonds held by the firm or any individuals with a substantial financial interest in the firm), and the facilities themselves may be exempt from state and local property taxation as long as they are publicly owned.

Two types of industrial bonds are used; some states permit only general obligation bonds, others authorize only revenue bonds, and still others allow both. General obligation bonds are secured by the taxation power of the government issuing the bonds, while revenue bonds are secured by the industrial property acquired by the bond sale. Because of this, investors prefer general obligation bonds over revenue bonds, which have no real guarantee of payment from the government that issues them. General obligation bonds are usually used to finance small to medium-sized firms, whereas revenue bonds finance a number of large firms in addition to smaller ones. The typical maturity of both types of bonds is up to twenty-five years, although terms up to forty years are not uncommon. Interest rates on general obligation bonds are about 1 to 1.5 percent below conventional rates, depending upon the credit rating of the government issuing the bonds. Those on revenue bonds are similar but can be higher, depending upon the credit rating of the firm financed by the bonds. Hence, the cost savings over the lease term may be considerable. For example, in comparing the cost of financing by corporate debentures at 9 percent with the cost by industrial bonds at 7.5 percent for a twenty-year term on a $5,000,000 issue payable in monthly installments, a savings of $1,129,594 is realized, since the total interest paid by the corporate bond financing arrangement would be $5,796,712, while that paid by the industrial bond financing would be $4,667,118—a 24 percent savings or an average annual savings of about $56,500.

Because of federal tax laws economic developers need to be aware of the Internal Revenue Service (IRS) guidelines that determine the tax-exempt status of revenue bonds—that is, the amount of tax-exempt bonds that can be issued to finance a project. The guidelines are based upon the capital expenditures and location of the plant. Bonds issued to finance pollution abatement equipment certified by the IRS, regardless of its cost, are tax exempt. Also, no tax-exempt bonds can be issued to assist in the financing of projects costing over a total of $10 million, except for pollution abatement equipment; or if the project is supported by a HUD Urban Development Action Grant, $10 million can be financed through tax-exempt bonds and up to $20 million through conventional financing. In other cases industrial firms can choose to adopt either of two guidelines. Guideline "A" places a limit of $1 million on the tax-exempt bonds that can be issued in any year in a county to finance land, buildings, and equipment for any individual firm. Guideline "B" places a limit of $10 million on all capital expenditures made by an individual firm (as determined by IRS) in a county over a six-year period. Under Guideline "B" all capital expenditures made by a firm in a county for three years prior to the date of the bond issue would be subtracted from the $10 million to determine the maximum amount of the tax-exempt issue. If a firm had capital expenditures totaling $2 million in a county for the three years prior to the issue, tax-exempt bonds could be sold for amounts up to $8 million. In the following three years no capital expenditures could be made if the maximum allowed issue was sold. If bonds of $2 million had been issued, the firm's capital expenditures during the following three years could not exceed $6 million. If a firm had no capital expenditures for three years prior to the date of issue, bonds up to $10 million could be sold, but capital expenditures during the following three years could not exceed $1 million. In both cases, if the maximum allowed capital expenditure limitation was exceeded in the following three years, the bond holders would have to pay income tax on the interest they received, and the IRS would require that all outstanding bonds be retired by the firm, including the costs of all prepayment penalties. Also, once a firm has chosen whether to use Guideline "A" or Guideline "B," it may not change that decision.

Statewide Development Corporation Loans

State business development or credit corporations are chartered by states to help finance high-risk ventures that exhibit promise of success. Although state-chartered, the corporations are privately financed organizations formed by public-spirited individuals and businesses interested in advancing the prosperity and economic welfare of their states. The main function of these corporations is to provide high-risk loans to small manufacturing firms that are recommended by commercial finance institutions. A high proportion of the loans are made to firms already established within the state, and the remainder are evenly distributed among newly established firms and those relocating from outside the state. In most states firms must show evidence that their loan application has been refused by at least one commercial finance institution before applying to the SDC. In most states also, loans are made to local development corporations.

State development corporations rely upon four main sources for their funds: (1) sale of stock to members, (2) credit lines pledged by member financial institutions or individuals, (3) SBA 501 loan funds, and (4) their own funds accumulated from retained earnings. The sale of stock provides the equity base for the state development corporation, and stockholders neither expect nor receive anything more than token dividends for the shares they purchase. Most SDCs have sold less stock than they have been authorized to issue, so that the money received from stock sales is not the main source of their funds. The main source is money advanced by member commercial lending institutions that are permitted by law to pledge a small percentage of their capital (about 1 to 2.5 percent) as credit to finance loans made by the SDC. The commercial lenders usually charge an interest rate of 0.5 to 1 percent above the prime rate for short-term loans extended to SDCs. Funds made available through the SBA's 501 SDC loan program are governed by the same requirements as those available through the LDC 502 loan program. The amount of funds available to SDCs from their retained earnings depends primarily upon how long they have been in existence. This amount is usually at least equal to the amount of funds available from the sale of stock.

Most state development corporation loans are made to purchase land or to provide buildings and equipment. A good number, though, are made to provide working capital to expand production and employment. Most loans are for amounts less than $500,000 and have interim maturities of five to ten years, although fifteen-year terms are not uncommon. SDCs charge interest rates of from 3 to 5 percent above the prime rate, considerably less than what high-risk firms would have to pay if they borrowed from commercial lenders. Frequently, also, SDCs participate with other lenders in advancing funds and they accept the later maturities. Promising industrial firms, lacking sufficient credit ratings for conventional financing, are directed to the SDC by commercial lenders. Once the degree of risk has been reduced through funds advanced by the SDC, commercial lenders are able to advance funds to the venture by taking the early maturities. Loans are generally paid on a monthly basis, with either variable payments covering a fixed amount of principal plus accrued interest or level payments including both principal and interest. Loans are secured by collateral such as liens on real property, machinery and equipment, assignments of life insurance policies, pledges of stock or bonds, and personal guarantees.

Local Development Corporation Loans

Local development corporations in the nation, which number in the thousands, may be called industrial development commissions, industrial development corporations, committees of 100, industrial development foundations or community development corporations. Most have been established in the past two or three decades and are organized as nonprofit corporations. Others are profit corporations, and still others are charitable trusts. A large number were either promoted or established by local chambers of commerce, and many today still operate directly under chamber of commerce supervision. Despite their large number, many LDCs are not active or are substantially less active than they could be. The requirements of federal programs that mandate participation by a legally incorporated local development corporation in order that federal loans be obtained by industrial firms, though, should result in greater activity by LDCs (U.S. Department of Commerce 1970).

To be eligible for participation in federal loan programs the LDC must be a corporation with a minimum of twenty-five stockholders or members, of whom 75 percent must live or do business in the LDC's constituent area, whether it be a community, city, or county. No more than 25 percent of the ownership or control of the LDC may be held by a single individual or his affiliates having a pecuniary interest in a project to be developed. The LDC can be either a profit or a nonprofit organization. If it is a profit organization, the rate of net return to its stockholders is limited to the prevailing interest rate that would be charged by other lenders if they were to invest in the project. In addition, loans made by profit LDCs are subordinate to all other lenders of the total project funds.

Local development corporations receive the bulk of their funds from private sources. Initial capital is raised by the sale of capital stock, memberships, or debt securities to local residents and other individuals or to firms doing business in the community. Other funds come from contributions or gifts of cash or kind (e.g., land) from residents and private charitable foundations. Sometimes grant funds are made available to the LDCs with "no strings attached" from state or federal agencies, EDA, FmHA, model cities or urban renewal programs, for example. Other LDC funds are borrowed from banks, insurance companies, federal government agencies, state development corporations, and private lenders. Usually these loans are secured by the personal endorsements of the LDC's principals, members, or stockholders. Still other funds are obtained from state finance authorities, often for an amount equal to a moderate percentage of the total project cost.

Funds raised by local development corporations are used for a variety of purposes, primarily to finance the construction of industrial plants built to the specifications of individual firms. The plants are leased to the firms at net rentals that enable the LDCs to retrieve their funds plus a moderate amount of interest over lease terms of ten to twenty-five years. In most cases industrial firms are given purchase option leases with rental payments accepted as installment payments for the purchase of the property. Other LDC funds are used to provide loans to industrial firms for the purchase of land, plants, and equipment, for plant construction and modernization, and for working capital. Some LDCs use their funds to purchase existing vacant plants or to construct shell plants for eventual lease or sale to anticipated firms. Other funds are used to take options on or to purchase desirable sites for sale to industrial firms. A small amount has been used to purchase stock in industrial firms.

Local development corporations, as already discussed, often finance projects jointly with commercial lending institutions, state finance authorities, state development corporations, and SBA and EDA. In most cases the LDCs provide loans of from 5 to 25 percent of the total project cost and accept the later maturities.

Financial Forecasting

Before seeking funds for industrial development, entrepreneurs need to determine the total amount of financing required. Lenders will need not only this information, but also a good deal more knowledge about the firm before they can evaluate loan requests. Entrepreneurs should be prepared to justify their request by providing lenders with information on (1) the nature of the product to be manufactured, its past market history, and future prospects; (2) the location, size, and share of the market to be supplied by the firm and the location, size, and general growth pattern of the firm's competition; (3) processing methods, utility and material requirements and sources, plant facilities and layout, and labor by skill level needed to manufacture and sell the firm's product; (4) ownership, sales and management experience, duties, affiliations with other firms, and any necessary patents or licenses required to manufacture the product; and (5) all capital and production costs, as well as anticipated profits.

Once the total amount of costs is determined, it is important for the entrepreneurs to prepare financial forecasts, for five years, to determine the amount of financing required and also the type of financing that would best fit the future cash flow of the firm. For example, because of the difference in interest rates, it would not be advisable to finance on a long-term basis if the cash flow indicated that the firm had the ability to repay shorter-term loans. To finance on a short-term basis would not be appropriate if the forecast indicated that it would place a strain on the capability of the firm to repay.

Large firms usually have a staff skilled in conducting financial forecasts. Smaller firms, on the other hand, are unlikely to have individuals adequately trained in financial forecasting and will need to obtain outside assistance. Most large commercial banks have corporate financial service staffs that are able not only to prepare forecasts, but also to suggest alternative methods of financing to meet the firm's objectives. The commercial banks also assist firms in financial planning using computerized projection models to facilitate mathematical computations and to make it easier to judge the impact of alternative estimates of sales and profit levels. However, lenders will expect management to demonstrate a basic understanding of their projections and how they were developed and to be able to explain and substantiate the validity of the major premises upon which the projections are based. Projections are so basic to the planning of a project that some lenders may view a working knowledge in this area as an indication of the ability of management to operate the proposed plant successfully. It is important that they include realistic provision for all start-up and operating costs until the plant reaches the break-even point.

Notes

1. For additional discussion on this topic, see Kinnard and Messner 1971, chap. 17, "Aids to Industrial Development."

2. Regardless of the number of employees, an industry, along with its affiliates, may qualify if its assets total less than $9 million, its net worth is less than $4 million, and its average net profit (after federal income taxes for the two preceding years) was less than $400,000.

3. The 501 SDC program is similar to the 502 LDC program and therefore need not be discussed here.

4. No more than 25 percent of the control of the LDC may be held by an individual with a pecuniary interest in the industrial project being assisted.

5. Local development corporation funds are raised by (1) the sale of stock, memberships, or debt securities; (2) contributions or gifts from individuals, businesses, foundations, or public bodies; or (3) loans from individuals, banks, insurance companies, or state lending authorities.

6. Rental payments are accepted as installment-purchase payments if the firm has an option to buy the facilities.

7. The combined participation would be subject to the $350,000 limitation, and the bank's share could be advanced on an SBA guaranteed basis.

8. Other ineligible manufacturing activities include those producing alcoholic beverages and apparel and garments within the textile industry.

9. The $10,000 investment per job created or saved is considerably less than the average United States cost of new plant facilities per worker in recent years, which has been over $30,000 per worker. Consequently, industrial firms seeking major loan participation from EDA will probably have to lease their plant facilities.

10. Actually, to receive a working capital loan the firm must be in operation and have existing working capital of at least 15 percent of its total working capital requirements.

11. EDA may waive the 5 percent community share in cases involving extreme economic distress (or in ventures involving Indian tribes) and allow the industrial firm or some other nonfederal source to provide the community's 5 percent equity share.

12. Under the $10,000-per-job loan limitation established by EDA, this $10,000,000 project would have to employ at least 650 workers.

13. In a few cases state government approval of a project is required before local bonds can be issued. In some cases, also, the state government is responsible for issuance of the bonds.

Part 5
Community
Development
Strategies

Chapter 14
Planning and Organizing
for Development

The key to the successful implementation of an economic development program lies in its planning and organization. For this reason one of the most important tasks of the professional developer is planning the community's economic development program. Since industrial development is largely a promotion and sales activity in a very competitive market, the first thing a developer must do is become thoroughly apprised of the advantages and disadvantages of the community as a location for industry. His task includes finding out the community's attractive features and being able to present them, along with factual data supporting them, to industrial prospects. It also requires recognizing the unattractive features and finding ways to improve those that are within the province of the community to change. Even though the community is very large in the minds of the people that live there, in reality it is only one of thirty thousand towns and cities or three thousand counties in one of fifty states in the country. When a prospect enters the state and the local area is fortunate enough to receive a visit, the community becomes like a piece of merchandise, which will be examined alongside others for attractiveness, quality, fit, and price. The community does not get a second chance to make a good first impression, so it is important that it be well prepared and the developer organized and as efficient and knowledgeable as possible. With objective information about the local area the developer is able to plan a program that realistically promotes the community's assets to specific types of industry that are likely to have an interest in what it has to offer.

This chapter provides some guidelines for promoting local industrial development. It first discusses the need of fostering good relationships among individuals interested in the community and briefly outlines how they can be organized to promote development. It then describes the characteristics of ideal industrial sites and methods of securing them for industrial development purposes. The chapter also describes the types of objective data sought by industrial prospects and other developers interested in the local area.[1]

Organizing for Community Development

A successful community economic development program requires teamwork. Teamwork is dependent on the development of good relationships (1) between the local developer and local public officials, community leaders, and business managers, (2) between the local developer and other developers serving the local area, and (3) between the local developer and potential industrial prospects.

Community Leaders

The involvement of the community's public officials, business managers, and other local leaders is essential for a successful development effort, for these are the people from whom the developer and the industrial prospect will gather most of their information about the community, its business climate, and its labor climate. They are also the people whose positions make them best able to correct barriers to development in the community, such as inadequate sewer or water supply, shortage of adequate industrial sites or properly zoned sites, lack of local consensus on development goals, or a negative attitude toward development. Since many prospects are likely to want to interview officials with the public administrative department, school department, public works department and planning department as well as such people as utility, bank, plant and personnel managers, the industrial developer should meet with each to discuss his role in the community development process and to become better acquainted. The association between the developer and community leaders must be such that the developer can call them on short notice to meet with industrial prospects. To be sure, the developer must know to which leaders the prospect should be directed and to which he should be steered away from if possible. To assure a more successful development undertaking, community leaders should be rehearsed on the kinds of information prospects are likely to need so that they can present the data thoroughly and accurately when called upon to do so.

The development of a community depends to a large extent on the interest and ability of its local leadership. To encourage development and to solve community problems, local officials, business managers, and other leaders need to participate in organizing and implementing the community development program (Preston 1976, chapters 3 and 4; Fernstrom 1974, chapter 8). Many such programs throughout the country have influenced where industrial plants have located and can serve as a guide to other communities.[2] The most successful provide a structure to help local leaders prepare their communities for overall development. A typical successful program attempts to involve local leaders in the following activities:

1. Establish a local, nonprofit development corporation to promote the program and to receive and disburse funds in order to take title to or acquire options on industrial sites and buildings or erect "spec" buildings.

2. Perform a comprehensive community information review, acquiring, compiling, and publishing current and total economic, industrial, commercial, social, and government information about the community.

3. Design and publish an up-to-date community promotion brochure.

4. Develop at least four bona fide industrial sites and exercise sufficient control over them so that they can be sold to a desirable industrial prospect at a predetermined price. (Towns served by rail should have at least two sites where rail service is feasible.)

5. Conduct a cleanup, fix-up campaign to improve the attractiveness of the community and its quality of life and involve a broad spectrum of the local people in the program.

6. Appoint a special committee that will be responsible for visiting existing industry and attentive to assisting in the expansion of these plants as well as in helping new firms. This committee is also responsible for conducting an ongoing promotional program to provide specific information on the contributions of existing industry. This effort can be in the form of newspaper articles and advertisements, speeches, billboards, and radio and television commercials.

7. Appoint a well-trained, articulate economic development team (with alternates) to be equipped with the information vital in dealing with the industrial prospects who visit their community.

Industrial Developers

Most of the industrial prospects who come into a state will, at some time, contact either the *state development agency* or the *state chamber of commerce*. For this reason it is important for the local developer to establish and maintain close relationships with these organizations and provide them with current community and site/building data for their files. It is also a good promotional idea to invite the developers from such organizations to the community for an on-the-spot briefing and a look at what the community has to offer. *Railroads, banks, chambers of commerce, and utility companies* have been in the industrial development business for years and can be a major source of prospects for the community. A periodic personal visit with representatives that serve the area is most important and the local developer should promote good relationships with them just as if they were bona fide industrial prospects in their own right. Many industries today have turned the task of locating new facilities over to a *consultant firm*. It is important, therefore, for developers to establish relationships with those who are constantly looking for sites for industrial clients. In major cities these consultants are listed under "Management Consultants" or "Plant Location Consultants" in the yellow pages of the telephone directory. The developer should contact consultants to offer them up-to-date community and site data for their files. Although most will refuse, those who accept information should be listed as valuable prospect sources.

Local developers can follow several guidelines to insure better relations with other public and private developers serving the local area.

1. If the local developer has a problem with assembling certain information or in knowing what procedures to follow, he should contact other developers serving the community for assistance. They can usually provide information or advice on how to compile the necessary data, prepare promotional materials, and deal with prospects or community and business leaders.

2. The local developer should send accurate, up-to-date copies of all development literature to other professional developers serving the local area, especially all relevant community data and available-site and building data.

3. The local developer should reply promptly to requests for information from other developers serving the community. The information should be accurate and up to date. If the local developer cannot provide all the requested information immediately, he should send what is available, along with an explanation. If it is not possible for the community to meet a specific requirement of a prospect, the local developer should reply promptly with an explanation.

4. If the local developer needs information from a state agency in order to respond to a request from a prospect, to compile community data or to prepare promotional literature, he should contact the state development agency, which usually has good relations with other state agencies and can obtain information more quickly and easily than the local developer.

5. When the local developer is contacted by a prospect, other developers actively serving the community should be informed. Informing

other professional developers gives them confidence in the local developer and time to prepare in case they are called upon to meet the prospect.

6. The local developer should maintain the confidentiality of all prospects who request it even when dealing with other developers or public officials.

7. The local developer should prepare community officials and business managers to meet prospects and other industrial developers that may choose to interview them to obtain additional information about the community's ability to meet an industry's requirements.

8. The local developer should inform other developers serving the area when a new industry locates in the community or plans to locate there.

9. The local developer should make arrangements for industrial developers serving the area to speak periodically to the local community development organization and local service clubs about economic development programs, trends, and practices. Keeping such groups informed of economic development efforts helps to promote good public relations and support for the local program.

10. The local developer should participate in area, state, and regional (if not national) professional development organizations, programs, workshops, and activities to become better acquainted with other developers and new methods and techniques of promoting local economic development.

Industrial Prospects

Regardless of the effort spent in planning the economic development effort, the community can easily lose an industry if the local developer does not establish good relationships with potential prospects (Fernstrom 1974, chapter 18). The developer should respond to all requests for information as quickly and accurately as possible. If the information is not readily available, the developer should inform the prospect and make every effort to quickly compile and forward it. Copies of all correspondence between the developer and prospects should be carefully filed for reference, as should notes on all conversations, both person-to-person and by telephone.

Industrial prospects require two types of information—community data and site/building data. The data need to be constantly checked for accuracy. Therefore, it is important that the developer be meticulous in collecting and updating data. Numerous prospects have been lost because of incorrect, out-of-date, or misleading information. In addition to data about the local area's relative location, population, and climate, assembled community data should include information on (1) community facilities (educational, religious, medical, shopping, and recreational), (2) government activities (police protection, fire protection, zoning ordinances, and building codes), (3) communications (newspapers, radio, television, telephone, and mail), (4) transportation (highways, railroads, motor freight carriers, airports and air service, bus service, and waterways), (5) utilities (electricity, water, sewage, gas, and other fuel), (6) financial institutions, (7) labor (available male and female workers, high school dropouts and graduates, extent of unionization, history of work stoppages, and unemployment rate), (8) local and state taxes (property and nonproperty taxes and rates), (9) major employers (manufacturing and nonmanufacturing), and (10) available industrial properties (land and buildings). A community data form (fig. 14.1) is not only useful in outlining the type of data that are important to industrial prospects and other developers, but it also provides a standardized format that can be prepared as a finished data document to be distributed to prospects.[3] Much of the data pertaining to the community can be extracted from government and other publications but other data can be acquired only within the community from public officials and surveys conducted by the local developer.

When a prospect visits the community on an inspection visit, the developer should have carefully planned every minute of the visit and have conducted a dress rehearsal with staff members and other community leaders that the prospect may choose to visit. Such small details as personally selecting the hotel room and having current newspapers and magazines placed in the room should not be overlooked. Maps of the roads the prospect will travel to see the community and industrial sites, and a list of the people (and their titles) that the prospect will meet should be ready for him upon arrival.

Selecting and Securing Industrial Sites

Despite the relative importance of the different plant location factors, if a suitable industrial site is not available in the local area even the most desirable community is not going to be able to attract industry. The various parcels of vacant land that exist in all communities give the impression that numerous sites exist and that many are available for industrial use. Much vacant land, however, may be unable to meet the requirements of an industrial site. For example, community-enacted zoning ordinances may have restricted the use of most vacant land for other purposes. An industrial prospect wants clear evidence (*not* a verbal assurance) that the community has industrial sites available that fit the requirements of his plant. Failure to provide this evidence can be harmful to the community's

Figure   14.1 Community Data Form

State_____Community_____County_____

Compiled by_____

LOCATION   EDUCATION

Nearby Metropolitan City	Distance in Miles		Number of Schools	Number of Teachers	Grades	Number Enrolled

Elementary _____		_____	____	_____

_____ _____

Junior High_____		_____	____	_____
(or middle school)				

Average Elevation   _____   High School_____   _____ ____ _____

Private and_____		_____	____	_____

POPULATION   Parochial

1980 1970 1960 1950   Vo-Tech   _____

County ____ ____ ____ ____   College(s) _____

City   ____ ____ ____ ____   (state or private)

Libraries: Number _____   Total Volumes_____

Estimated Present   MEDICAL
  Population (30 mi.) _____   Hospitals: Number _____   Beds _____

Clinics: Number _____   Beds _____

CLIMATE   Doctors: _____   Dentists_____
                Annual   Monthly
                Average   Average   RECREATION FACILITIES (Public)

Temperature _____ January _____

                         July   _____   Bowling   _____   Ball Field   _____

Annual Average Rainfall   Indoor Movie   _____   Swimming Pool _____
              (inches)_____
Annual Average Snowfall   Outdoor Movie   _____   Tennis Court _____
              (inches)_____   YMCA   _____   Golf Course   _____

Prevailing Winds _____   YWCA   _____   Amateur Theatre_____

Auto Race Track _____		Skating Rink	_____

Number of Parks _____Local_____Other_____

COMMUNITY FACILITIES   Other Recreation Facilities

Churches (Number): Protestant _____   (country club, auditorium, museums, etc.)

  Catholic____Jewish___Other_____   _____

Number Motels_____ Total Rooms_____   _____

Number Hotels_____ Total Rooms_____   _____

Number Shopping Centers_____   _____

COMMUNICATIONS

Newspaper(s) _____

  Daily (D)_____ Weekly(W)_____

Radio Station(s)_____

Television Station(s)_____

Distance to Station(s)_____

Cable Television_____ Channels_____

Telephone Service_____

Telegraph Service_____

Post Office_____(Class)

GOVERNMENT

Type of Government_____

Police Dept. Personnel: (full time)_____

Fire Dept. Personnel: (full time)_____

               (volunteer)_____

  Equipment_____

  Fire Insurance Rating_____

  Service Provided Industry beyond Corpor-

    ate Limits or by County_____

Planning Commission: Yes ( ) No ( )

Industrial Plan Approval: Yes ( ) No ( )

Zoning Regulation: Yes ( ) No ( )

FINANCIAL INSTITUTIONS

	Number	Total Assets
Banks	_____	_____
Savings and Loan Associations	_____	_____
Plant Financial Assistance		
Available	Yes ( ) No ( )	

UTILITIES AND SERVICES

  Electricity

Power Supplier(s)_____

_____

Power Distributor(s)_____

_____

  Water

Name of Supplier_____

Source_____

Maximum Daily capacity_____GPD

Peak Load_____GPD

Storage Capacity: Overhead_____Gals.

               Ground_____Gals.

  Sewers

Storm Sewer: Yes ( ) No ( ) Coverage ____%

Sanitary Sewer: Yes ( ) No ( ) Coverage ____%

Treatment Plant: Type_____

Capacity_____GPD Present Load ____%

Solid Waste Disposal _____

  Natural Gas

Gas Supplier(s)_____

Gas Distributor(s)_____

  Other Fuels

Fuel Oil Distributor(s)_____

Coal Source _____

LP Gas Distributor(s)_____

LABOR ANALYSIS

Radius of Labor Drawing Area_____

Est. Available: Males____Females____

Annual Number High School Graduates_____

Work Stoppages in Last 5 Years_____

Manufacturing Workers in Unions_____%

Unemployment Rate   _____%

Right-to-Work Law Yes ( ) No ( )

Wage and/or Labor Survey
  Available Yes ( ) No ( )

TRANSPORTATION

Highways Serving Area_____

Distance Nearest Interstate
Interchange to City Limits_____

Railroads

Name_____

Piggyback Service_____

Frequency of Switching Service_____

Motor Freight Carriers

Name	Terminal Facilities (or miles to nearest)
_____	_____
_____	_____
_____	_____
_____	_____
_____	_____

Air

Nearest Airport _____

Runway Length_____ Surface_____

Commercial Service _____

Bus Service

Name_____

Intracity Service Yes ( )   No ( )

Parcel Service _____

Waterways

Nearest Navigable Waterway and Channel Depth

_____
_____

Port Facilities_____

TAXES (tax year 19____)

Manufacturers Real Property

	Rate/ $1000 (Actual Value)	Assess. Ratio	Effective in City	Rate out of City
City	$____	____%	$_____	$_____
County	$____	____%	$_____	$_____
School	$____	____%	$_____	$_____
State	$____	__ _%	$_____	$_____
OTHER	$____	____%	$_____	$_____

Effective Rate/$1000 Actual
Value: $_____ $_____

Avg. % Increase last 5 years _____

Local Non-Property

Type	City	County
Inventory (yes)	_____	(yes)_____
Machinery-Equip. (yes)	____	(yes)_____
Retail Sales (yes)	_____	(yes)_____
Income(wage) (yes)	_____	(yes)_____

State Taxes

Type	Rate	Type	Rate
Corporate Income	___%	Retail Sales	____%
Intangibles	___%	Indv. Income:	
		Minimum Rate	____%
		Maximum Rate	____%

Gasoline _____¢ Gal.

AVAILABLE INDUSTRIAL PROPERTIES

Name	Size (acres)
_____	_____
_____	_____
_____	_____
_____	_____
_____	_____
_____	_____
_____	_____
_____	_____

MAJOR EMPLOYERS

Name	Product or Service	Employees Male	Female	Year Established Here	Union
_____	_____	_____	_____	_____	_____
_____	_____	_____	_____	_____	_____
_____	_____	_____	_____	_____	_____
_____	_____	_____	_____	_____	_____
_____	_____	_____	_____	_____	_____
_____	_____	_____	_____	_____	_____
_____	_____	_____	_____	_____	_____
_____	_____	_____	_____	_____	_____
_____	_____	_____	_____	_____	_____
_____	_____	_____	_____	_____	_____
_____	_____	_____	_____	_____	_____
_____	_____	_____	_____	_____	_____

FOR ADDITIONAL INFORMATION CONTACT:

Name_____

Organization_____

_____

Address_____

Phone_____

Footnotes

economic development efforts. Consequently, it is important that the industrial developer maintain accurate, up-to-date information on a wide variety of available sites in his area to accommodate the varying needs and interests of different industrial prospects. The sites should vary in size, shape, location, utility service, and transportation mode access: rail and nonrail, but also air or water ports if available (Preston 1976, chapters 7 and 8; Fernstrom 1974, chapter 16).

Characteristics of the Ideal Industrial Site

Before establishing an inventory of the potential industrial sites in the community, the industrial developer should consider the characteristics of an ideal site.

Size and shape. The ideal site is a parcel of land having a regular shape and distinctive property lines, attractive surroundings, and no potential for depreciating property values. The size of the lot depends on the type of manufacturing operation and the particular company's attitude. During the past few decades relatively large sites have been selected to allow for employee parking, loading space, landscaping, and future expansion. A rule of thumb on the size of an ideal site in more rural areas is "ten times the size of the building." However, an inverse relationship operates between the land cost and the building area–site area ratio: the higher the land cost, the lower the ratio. In built-up urban areas the ratio of land to building area is closer to 1.5:1. Energy conservation measures incorporated into zoning ordinances may reduce the ratios in the future.

Topography and soils. The site should be comparatively level with enough slope to provide good drainage, well above the all-time flood level (a minimum of ten feet), and well drained. If the site does not meet these criteria, the topography should be such that the site can be altered by grading to provide adequate drainage at a minimum cost. Cleared land, requiring a minimum amount of grading, provides the ideal site. The amount of clearing and grading required directly determines its cost. The industrial developer should remember that the cost of a site to a prospect includes both the land cost and the land preparation cost. It is recommended that the industrial developer have someone familiar with grading operations estimate the land preparation costs for selected sites and include this estimate in the site's information. Contour maps of the site should be obtained and made available to prospects. Quite often these maps are available for ten- or twenty-foot intervals; the smaller the interval, the better. The most useful is the two-foot-interval site map, which enables the prospect to determine the exact amount of earth to be moved before construction can begin. In a few extraordinary cases an industrial prospect may be interested in a hilly or sloping site for aesthetic or architectural reasons.

The industrial developer should know the characteristics of the soil on the site when he recommends it to a prospect. If soil test reports are not available on the site, soil classification maps and reports from the Soil Conservation Service and test borings that may be available for nearby property can be used. It is important that the prospect know as much as possible about the load-bearing and drainage characteristics of the soil because of their effect on site preparation and construction costs.

Utilities. The industrial site must have adequate water and sewer service adjacent to it. The water line and pressure should be of sufficient capacity and quality to meet the prospect's requirements and be approved by the underwriters in the area who handle factory insurance. A site with inadequate pressure can be improved by building a standpipe or a combination storage-pumping system to meet the insurance requirements. But the ideal site already possesses adequate water service to meet most requirements. The same is true of sewer service. The collection line should be large enough to handle whatever needs the prospect has, and the treatment plant that serves the site should be able to handle the plant's discharged waste. In the case of river sites, on-site packaged waste treatment plants can be used when approved by the appropriate government agencies. The ideal site has natural gas service, even though it may be available in only a few areas of the country and in limited quantities. The developer should confirm the availability of gas, if any, and the conditions of supply. Electric power, of course, is important for all operations. For some plants it is the most important utility. Reliable electric service is essential. The sites should be close to a transmission line, since many plants, particularly large ones, are served directly from that source. A site is not considered ideal unless it is close enough to a transmission line or substation that it can be adequately served with a minimum amount of cost and trouble. Since some manufacturing plants require dual electric service for protection against interruptions, some sites should be located close to two or more separate electric feeder lines. Telephone service, the availability of which is often assumed, is also important, and the developer should confirm that it is feasible to get industrial-type service to the site. This point is especially significant because many firms use telephone lines for data processing linkups with other plants and offices.

While a site must be adequately served by utilities, it is also important that no easements cross the property. A power, gas, or sewer line running across a piece of land could add considerable cost to the site. Construction cannot take place on these utility lines; if a prospect does purchase such a site, the lines will have to be relocated at a substantial cost to the prospect. The industrial developer should also be alert to any restricted areas designated by government agencies in the community. The purposes for which property can be used adjacent to such areas may also be restricted.

Transportation facilities and access. The ideal site should face a good highway providing easy access to the interstate highway system to facilitate the travel of employees, customers, and salesmen and the shipping of supplies, equipment, and products. If the site is not situated on a highway, arrangements for an access road should be made before the location is recommended to a prospect, perhaps in the form of an agreement with public officials to provide the road if the site is developed for industrial use. Motor freight service should be available at all sites, and the ideal site should be located close to one or more motor freight terminals. The ideal rail site has a spur line along the back of the property to avoid conflict with the plant's highway access. For sites a short distance from a railroad it may be feasible for an industry to construct its own spur or siding and switching facilities. Generally, the requirements for serving a site with rail limit the curvature of the track to twelve degrees and the grade to two degrees (or about 106 feet per mile). Railroad site developers would be willing to confer on the feasibility and cost of providing rail service to a particular site. The prospect would have to take into account the cost of providing the rail service as part of the overall site cost. Sites located close to a commercial airport or within easy access to one of the approximately 46,000 smaller airports are desirable, not only for travel by executives and sales personnel, but also for rapid delivery of certain materials, products, and replacement parts. In communities located close to navigable ports or streams, sites upon which dock loading facilities can be constructed should be included in the inventory of potential industrial sites.

In metropolitan locations, access to public transportation is an important consideration in selecting ideal industrial sites, and this factor will become even more crucial in the future for many industrial sites, depending upon the availability and price of petroleum and upon local energy conservation measures enacted to reduce commuter travel.

Zoning, insurance rates, and taxes. Proper zoning is an important characteristic of an ideal industrial site. Correct zoning provides protection to industries for the continual operation of their business at the particular location, as well as protection for the property's value. Fire insurance ratings should be obtained for each site. These ratings are based upon the fire protection equipment and available water that may exist or be extended to the site. The amount of tax paid on the site and its assessed value should also be ascertained and should be reasonable in comparison to surrounding properties. A piece of land that sells for a very low price may not be as good a value as one with a higher price. That judgment has to be made by the industrial developer during the process of selecting sites for documentation and presentation to prospects. Ideal sites are very difficult to locate. The actual evaluation and selection process is one of comparing different sites and making compromises and trade-offs with the ideal site standards in order to select the one closest to ideal.

Securing Available Industrial Sites

After a parcel of land that has the desired characteristics has been located, the next step is to confirm the availability of the site. In many instances sites or parcels of land that have been shown to industrial prospects have later turned out to be unavailable. The industrial developer should be aware that a parcel of land, no matter how ideal, is not an industrial site if it is not available for sale. Thus one of the tasks that needs to be done when evaluating and selecting sites is to determine whether a site owner will make his land available for industrial development at a definite price. Sometimes—for example, when the land is part of an estate—the developer, in order to accomplish this, will have to contact several owners who either own a single parcel of land jointly or several parcels individually. Naturally, a site should have a clear title, or a clear title should be obtainable without complications. Industrial developers must try to exercise some degree of control over industrial sites that they believe desirable to assure that the sites will be available at a fixed price when a prospect arrives. Several methods may be used to control industrial sites.

The verbal option. The simplest method of controlling industrial sites, although not the most desirable, is the verbal option: a statement from the landowner to the developer making the owner's land available for a designated period of time at a fixed price. For example, the owner may be willing to sell the land at a certain price for a period of two years, after which a new price would have to be negotiated to cover a new period of time. The verbal option is often referred to as "a gentleman's agreement" and is not legally binding.

The letter of intent. A more effective method than the verbal option for controlling the availability of a site is the letter of intent, a letter written to the industrial developer by the property owner briefly describing the site and stating the owner's intention to make the land available for industrial development for a specific period of time at a specific price (fig. 14.2). The letter can also include (1) the right of refusal against

Figure   14.2 Letter of Intent to Sell

```
Area Development Corporation
P. O. Box 0000
Raleigh, North Carolina  27610

Re:  Industrial Option on 200-acre tract of land at the intersection of
     U.S. Highway #70 and State Road #1836, as described in Deed Book
     787, Page 275 of the Wake County, N.C. Registry

Gentlemen:

     This letter of intent constitutes my firm option to sell all of the above
land, for industrial use, at a selling price of $750.00 per acre.  This option
shall remain in effect until such time as I shall notify you with a 30-day written
cancellation notice.  This letter also grants the above-named addressee the right
of first refusal to acquire this land for industrial development.

                         Yours very truly,
```

a purchase under certain conditions, (2) a written notice of the cancellation of the agreement, and (3) a price escalation clause whereby the price of the land is increased by a certain percentage (usually fixed to the area's average annual increase in land prices) on a specific date each year. It is debatable whether the letter of intent is legally binding, but this has proven a very flexible and inexpensive way of assuring a site's availability.

The land sale option agreement. One of the most effective methods of controlling sites is a written legal sales option agreement, which can be as complex or as simple as needed. A brief and very popular version of this is the short-form option agreement (fig. 14.3), which consists of one page with space for the necessary endorsements by the landowner(s) and notary. This form of option is popular because it is a simple, straightforward, legal and binding document. The legal sales option specifies a definite price for the land and covers a definite period of time. The property owner usually receives some compensation that is negotiated, based on the selling price of the land and the length of the option term. Sometimes a prospect likes a particular site not under option and requests that it be controlled for a stated period of time. This is entirely similar to but should not be confused with the option agreement. In this case an option form must be negotiated to reflect the terms that have been agreed upon by the landowner(s) and the agent representing the industrial prospect. Legal options of this type are recorded in the county register of deeds office and take the property off the market during the period of time specified in the option.

Outright site ownership. The most conclusive method of controlling industrial sites is by outright ownership of the land, which can be accomplished by private and public sources, depending on state and local laws regulating the use of public funds for such purposes. Certainly, only the most ideal industrial sites should be acquired by this method (unless other suitable sites are available at extremely favorable prices). A popular way of purchasing sites at the community level is through the formation of local development corporations. These legal entities can be established as profit or nonprofit organizations to support the local industrial development effort by purchasing and inventorying sites, constructing and leasing plant buildings, and promoting the community to potential prospects, among other activities (see chapters 13 and 15). Outright ownership is the most effective way of controlling sites, but it is also the most expensive and must be evaluated with this in mind.

Regardless of which method of control is used, it is important that the industrial developer be fully aware of the site's availability and the conditions under which it is available, when it is shown to a prospect. In

Figure   14.3 Option Agreement

THIS OPTION AGREEMENT made by_____
and his wife, _____, herein called the "Owners" and
_____, herein called the "Optionee":

W I T N E S S E T H:

In consideration of $_____, the receipt of which is acknowledged,
the Owners give the Optionee an option to buy the land hereinafter described upon
the following terms and conditions:

(1) The land subject to this option is described as follows:

(Continued on reverse side)

(2) The total purchase price to be paid is $_____and shall
be paid as follows:

(Continued on reverse side)

(3) The period within which this option may be exercised for the consideration above stated begins with the date hereof and ends at midnight on
_____, 19____. If however, Optionee pays or tenders to owner in cash or
by check the additional sum of $_____ on or before midnight on
_____, 19____, the period with this option may be exercised will, in
consideration therefor, be thereby extended to end at midnight on _____,
19____.

(4) If this option is not exercised all the consideration given for it
shall be retained by the owners. If this option is exercised, all such consideration
shall be applied on the purchase price, and the owners agree to execute a deed
prepared by Optionee at his expense and deliver same to the Optionee or his
assigns conveying a good and sufficient title to the above described real property
in fee simple with covenants of general warranties, except:

(Continued on reverse side)

(5) If this option is exercised, all taxes and insurance will be prorated
as of the date of closing and the Owners will give possession_____.

(6) It is mutually agreed between the parties hereto that this option may
be assigned, and Optionee shall have the right to enter in and upon the land herein-
above described for the purpose of making surveys, for engineering and other appropriate purposes needed for the evaluation of the premises.

IN WITNESS WHEREOF, the Owners have hereunto set their hands and seals
this _____, 19_____.

_____   _____
          WITNESS   OWNER   (SEAL)

_____   _____
          WITNESS   OWNER   (SEAL)

order to assure availability and to avoid embarrassment and the possible loss of the prospect, one of the practical methods of control described above needs to be used.

Presenting Industrial Sites to Prospects

After confirming the availability of a site and taking action to exercise some measure of control over it, the next step is to prepare a site data form (fig. 14.4). The data form documents all the characteristics of the property that are of interest to most industrial prospects, including (1) location of the site (maps), (2) size and shape (plats and air photos), (3) cost (letters of intent or options), (4) topography (contour maps), (5) grading requirements, (6) susceptibility to flooding, (7) drainage features, (8) the load-bearing capacity of the soil, (9) depth of the water table, (10) zoning, (11) adjacent land uses and current use of the site, (12) buildings and encroachments, (13) tax rate and fire insurance rating, (14) transportation facilities (rail, highway, etc.), and (15) utilities serving the site (electricity, gas, water, sewer, and telephone). All information on the data form should be expressed in relation to the site; for example, the site is fifteen miles from the nearest airport or 2,500 feet from the nearest sewer line.

Of considerable importance are the graphic materials that are a part of the documentation. These have to be compiled from a number of sources and prepared by the developer for presentation to interested prospects. The graphics usually consist of a plot map, county or municipal road map, topographic map, and aerial photographs. A soil classification map, geologic map, floodplain map, utility map, land use map, and zoning map are useful additions. The plot map is a scale drawing of the site showing its exact boundaries and the location of features such as the closest roads and highways, utility and rail lines, and waterways. Base maps for drafting plot maps can be obtained from the city or county tax assessor's office. Other plot map information can be obtained from the water, sewer, electrical, and other engineering departments serving the local area. Most of the other maps can be obtained from either the state or local highway department or the city or county manager, engineering, or planning office. If not available from these sources, some of the necessary materials can be obtained from the United States Geological Survey (USGS) in Washington or from authorized agencies in each state. These maps should show the location of the site clearly either by drawing directly on them or by using a transparent overlay.

Aerial photographs are an important part of the documentation, since they show not only the site but large adjacent areas as well. Such physical

Figure   14.4 Site Data Form

<u>PREPARED BY</u>

    Name

    Date

    Office

    District

<u>NAME</u>

    Site Identification

<u>LOCATION</u>

    State

    County

    Municipality

    Town Limits Distance from Site

    Town Limits Direction from Site

    Other Districts

    (school, fire, township, etc.)

<u>DESCRIPTION</u>

    Total Acreage

    Estimated Cleared Acreage

Will Owner Sell Portion of Site?

    Minimum Acreage Owner Will Sell

Would Adjacent Land Be Available?

North Boundary

(property owners, rail, highways,
  rivers, etc.)

                     length   ft.

East Boundary

                     length   ft.

South Boundary   _____

                                                  _____length_____ft.

West Boundary   _____

                                                  _____length_____ft.

Describe Present Land Use   _____
                                                  (agricultural, idle, timber, etc.)

Describe Site Contour as You
  See It   _____
                                                  (rolling, level, draws, etc.)

Is Contour Map Available?   _____

  Map Available from   _____

  Total Elevation Difference   _____ft.
                                                  (actual or estimated)

Is Site Subject to Flood?   _____

  Percentage of Site Subject to Flood   _____

  Describe Natural Drainage   _____
                                                  (creeks, draws, slopes, etc.)

Describe Artificial Drainage   _____
                                                  (ditching, piping, highways, etc.)

Describe Type of Soil   _____

  Have Soil Test Bearings Been
  Made on the Site?   _____

AVAILABILITY

  Present Owner(s) Name   _____

                    Address   _____

                    Name   _____

                    Address   _____

                    Name   _____

                    Address   _____

Local Contact(s) Name   _____

                 Address   _____

                 Name   _____

                 Address   _____

                 Name   _____

                 Address   _____

Describe Written Option or
Commitment Given   _____

Describe Oral Option or
Commitment Given   _____

   Date of Option   _____

   Option Expiration Date   _____

   Option Holder /Name   _____

                 Address   _____

Will the Owner or Present
Option Holder Give an Option
to an Industrial Client?   _____

   What Time Limit Would Be
   Placed on Such an Option?   _____

*   *   *   *   *   *   *   *   *

Total Site Price   _____

   Price per Acre   _____
                                         (on total or partial tract)

Is Site Price Firm in Your
Estimation?   _____

Date Site Priced   _____

*   *   *   *   *   *   *   *   *

Is Site Zoned?   _____

  What Zoning Authority?   _____

  Present Zoning Proposals   _____

Present Annexation Proposals   _____

Other Restrictions   _____
                                      (right-of-way, setback, etc.)

WATER

  Is Municipal Water Available ?   _____

    Distance to Nearest Line   _____

    Line Size   _____ in.

    Static Pressure on Line   _____ psi.

    Residual Pressure on Line   _____ psi.

    Distance to Nearest 8" Line   _____

    Estimated Cost to Extend an 8"
    Line per Linear Foot in Area   _____

    What Provisions for Paying Costs
    Could Be Expected?   _____

    Municipal Total Capacity   _____ gpd.

    Municipal Excess Capacity   _____ gpd.

    Treated Ground Storage
    Capacity   _____ gal.

    Treated Elevated Storage
    Capacity   _____ gal.

  Planned Improvements   _____

    Estimated Completion Date   _____

    New Capacity   _____ gpd.

  *   *   *   *   *   *   *   *   *

Average Well Diameter in Area _____ in.

Average Well Depth in Area _____ ft.

Average Well Yield in Area _____ gpm.

*   *   *   *   *   *   *   *   *

Name of River or Stream _____

Distance from Site _____

Direction from Site _____

Direction of Flow _____

Average Flow _____ gpd.

Average 7-Day Minimum Flow _____ gpd.

Location of Gauging Station _____

Classification of Stream _____

Flood Stage Elevation M.S.L. _____ ft.

SEWER

Is Municipal Sewerage Available? _____

Distance to Line _____ ft.

Line Size _____ in.

Estimated Cost to Extend per
Linear Foot in the Area _____

What Provisions for Paying
Cost Could be Expected? _____

Type of Municipal Treatment
System _____

Municipal Total Capacity _____

Municipal Excess Capacity _____

*   *   *   *   *   *   *   *   *

What Type of Individual (on site)
Sewer Systems Are Now Being
Used in the Area?

                                          (septic, emhoff, etc.)

    Distance to Nearest Disposal
    Area

                                            (creek, river, etc.)

TRANSPORTATION

    Highway(s) Adjacent to Site

        Interstate Highways in Area   distance   mi.

        U.S. Highways in Area   distance   mi.

                                                distance   mi.

                                                distance   mi.

        State Highways in Area   distance   mi.

                                                distance   mi.

                                                distance   mi.

*   *   *   *   *   *   *   *   *   *   *

    Railroad(s) Adjacent to Site

        Railroad(s) in Area   distance   mi.

                                                distance   mi.

        Is a Spur Track on the Site?

        Does the Lay of the Land Look
        as if a Spur Track Is Feasible?

        What Is the Estimated Elevation
        Difference between the Rail
        Track and the Usable Portion
        of the Site?

        Nearest Piggyback Service

*   *   *   *   *   *   *   *   *   *

Commercial Airport in Area   _____ distance _____   mi.

  Airlines Serving   _____

                                                 _____

                                                 _____

  Total Flights per Day   _____

  Number of Runways   _____

  Longest Runway Length   _____   ft.

  Charter Service Available   _____

*   *   *   *   *   *   *   *   *

Nearest Local Airport   _____ distance _____   mi.

  Number of Runways   _____

  Longest Runway Length   _____   ft.

  Runway Paved   _____ length _____   ft.

  Runway Lighted   _____

  Navigational Aids   _____

  Services Available   _____

*   *   *   *   *   *   *   *   *

Navigable Waterway in Area   _____ distance _____   mi.

  Channel Depth   _____   ft.

Deep-Water Port(s) in Area   _____ distance _____   mi.

UTILITIES

  Electric Supplier   _____

    Nearest Distribution Line   _____ distance _____   ft.

    Voltage   _____ kv _____   phase

    Nearest Transmission Feeder   _____ distance _____   mi.

Voltage   kv

Territory Assignment Status   _____

                               (negotiated, commission-ordered, etc.)

*   *   *   *   *   *   *   *   *

Natural Gas Supplier   _____

  Nearest Transmission Line   _____distance_____ ft.

  Nearest Distribution Line   _____distance_____ ft.

  Size of Line   in.

  Pressure of Line   psi.

*   *   *   *   *   *   *   *   *

Telephone Service Supplier   _____

GRAPHICS CHECKLIST

Topo Maps   _____

                               (attach or state from where available)

Aerial Photos   _____

                               (attach or identify)

Copy of Soil Test Data   _____

                               (attach or state from where available)

Attach Map(s) of Area Showing:

_____Site Location (clearly and accurately)

_____Highways Location

_____Rivers Location

_____Electric Lines Location

_____Natural Gas Lines Location

Attach Site Plat or Sketch Showing:

_____Site Boundaries

_____Site Dimensions

_____Scale Notations

_____North Directional Mark

features as drainage ditches, cleared and wooded areas, highways and trails, wet areas, and apparent property lines reveal a great deal about a site. The exact property lines should be drawn on the photograph with a grease pencil for the site's easy identification. Aerial photos can usually be obtained from the county agricultural extension office, the local planning office, or the state or county Agricultural Stabilization and Conservation Service Office of the United States Department of Agriculture (USDA). In a few parts of the country no USDA photographs are available.

Some communities may choose to develop an industrial park or planned industrial district, which is a large tract of land that can be subdivided as different industries decide to locate there. The property should have all the characteristics of the ideal industrial site, including installed utilities, highly accessible highway and rail connections, and finished grading. The cost of land is generally quite high in such districts, and room for expansion is limited, since the average land area–building area ratio is about two to one. Most such districts are designed to accommodate light industry interested in occupying ten acres or less. For this reason the districts are apt to be more appealing to small manufacturers than large ones, which can operate more effectively on raw industrial land. As part of the site inventory, the industrial developer should have all the necessary details about any industrial districts or parks in the local area.

From time to time industrial buildings become available for sale or lease in the community. An available building can be an asset if it is located on land that possesses many of the ideal site characteristics. The ideal building is the shell type, which can be modified to meet the requirements of a potential industry. The industrial developer should keep an appropriate data form on any such buildings in his area and make sure to check on their availability every ninety days. Blueprints of the building are important, but general information on its floor area, ceiling height, floor weight-bearing capacity, and other construction characteristics should definitely be kept on file along with other site characteristics. In presenting available buildings to industrial prospects the developer should be sure that the plant is as attractive as possible—the inside should be clean and the outside grounds reasonably well kept. The developer should also have the electricity turned on and be familiar with the location of the light switches, heating plant, fuse boxes, and the like. The developer should be prepared also for inclement weather and other emergencies. He should have appropriate rainwear in the back of his car, including boots and umbrellas, for both himself and the prospect(s). He is also wise to carry a shovel, heavy pruning shears, small telescoping pennants to identify the outlines of the site, and a long tape measure.

While some of the data about a site or an available plant building remain the same, other information can change from time to time, and so an annual update of the data form is warranted. An accurate, well-documented site description with effective graphics can enhance the credibility of the industrial developer in the mind of the prospect, whereas incomplete, incorrect, or out-of-date information can be detrimental to the community's development effort.

Notes

1. For additional information on organizing for industrial and community development, see Fernstrom 1974 and Preston 1976.

2. Examples of these community programs are (1) Arkansas Community Development Program—a project of the state chamber of commerce with cooperation from the University of Arkansas, the State Industrial Development Commission, and local chambers of commerce; (2) the All-Kentucky City Award, conducted by the state chamber of commerce; (3) the Mississippi Merit Program, conducted by the Mississippi Economic Council; (4) the Louisiana Alert Program for municipal development, cosponsored by the state and local chambers of commerce; (5) the North Carolina Governor's Award Program, sponsored by the North Carolina Divisions of Economic Development; (6) the South Carolina GREAT (Governor's Rural Economic Achievement Trophy) TOWN Program, sponsored by the South Carolina State Development Board; and (7) the California Congress for Community Progress Program, sponsored by Pacific Gas and Electric Company.

3. This form has been endorsed by the American Industrial Development Council, Inc., the Southern Industrial Development Council, and the Industrial Development Research Council. On the form, under the Manufacturer's Real Property Tax, the figure needed in the "Rate per $1,000" column is the millage expressed in terms of thousand-dollar units. Many millage rates are expressed in terms of "rate per $100." If so, multiply this figure by ten. The *assessment ratio* is the percentage applied to the actual value or market value of the manufacturer's property, and it varies widely. In some instances, state tax commissions may set the assessed value of the manufacturer's property. Express all percentages to the nearest percent, i.e., 10, 29, 56, etc. The *effective rate* (both in and out of the city) is the product of the millage rate per $1,000 times the assessment rate. For instance, if the rate per $1,000 is $18 and the assessment rate is 50 percent, the effective rate would be $9 per $1,000 actual value. Express all figures in dollars and cents.

Chapter 15
The Systematic Approach
To Development

This chapter combines many of the individual concepts and methods discussed in the previous chapters into a systematic approach to industrial development (Sweet 1970). The systematic approach is called a *selective development program* because it concentrates staff energy, money, and research on attracting and retaining the industry that has the greatest potential for meeting the economic needs of a state's or region's local communities.

Selective development is an alternative to the traditional "shotgun" approach to area development, which fires a broadside of high-powered promotional advertising and development efforts, hoping to attract industry—any industry—to the community. The shotgun approach is expensive and inefficient in a decade of intense, sophisticated competition among states and regions for economic development. And that approach may not attract or develop the kind of industry that meets the needs and goals of the local community. The selective development program described here matches a community's resources and economic development goals with the needs and requirements of industries. The program enables area developers at the state and local level to target their efforts on industries whose needs can realistically be met by a specific community.

The selective development philosophy and tools can be used at the state level or modified and adapted for use by the local area developer. When used at the state level, it focuses on the needs and resources of local communities or regions within the state. Inevitably, the geographic focus for this systematic approach is a county or multicounty urban or rural region. Regardless of the geographic area covered, the term community will be used in this discussion. Many of the techniques described can be employed by a one-man development program on a limited budget. Other tools require more sophisticated techniques, larger budgets, and more manpower.

A selective development program asks three basic questions about a region's or community's economic development: Where are we now? Where should we be going? How do we get there? The approach begins with an initial definition of development objectives and proceeds through a systematic review of the community's resource base (fig. 15.1).

Assuming that the community has decided to develop or redirect its economic development program, the initial effort must involve a definition of goals for the program. These goals or objectives can best be specified after a thorough review of the community's current industrial economy and its strengths and weaknesses for future economic growth. The selective development program uses three techniques—the industrial monitoring system, the community-industrial attitude census and the regional resource analysis—to find out where the community is now.

The program's second phase develops an analytic framework using either a manual tool (the screening matrix) or a computer analysis (the regional potential model) to determine where the community should be going. Both tools help to identify target industries for future location in the community or resident firms that should be encouraged to expand. The matrix or the model enables local area developers to balance the industries the community hopes to attract against what the community can offer.

In the program's third phase, a marketing strategy is developed to sell target industries on locating or expanding in the community. The marketing program develops the action step or implementation phase of the systematic approach and responds to the basic question, "How do we get there?"

Identifying Community Development Goals and Resources

In the first stage of the selective development program, participating community groups define their objectives for an industrial development effort. This initial step is crucial because it helps determine the direction the program should follow and the types of prospect industries that will be emphasized. Although many objectives are overlapping or virtually reinforcing, others can lead to quite contradictory results. Examples of development objectives that have been stated by various agencies include (1) increase in wage levels, (2) increase in total employment, (3) de-

Figure   15.1 The Selective Development Program

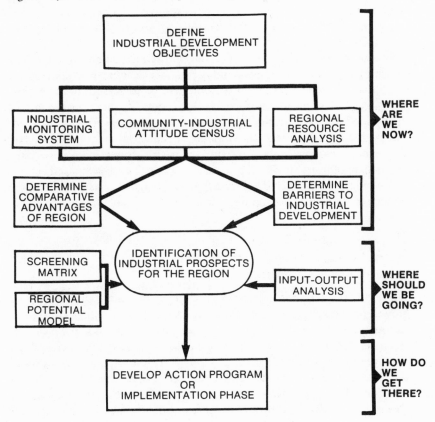

velopment of greater employment stability, (4) utilization of existing labor pool, (5) increase in tax revenues received, (6) reduction in out-migration of skilled workers and youths, (7) using industrial linkages in the region, and (8) upgrading of types of industries in the region.

Objectives such as higher wage levels and reducing out-migration may be achieved by similar types of industries. But a desire for higher wage levels may be inconsistent with the objective of increasing total employment. Regardless of which objectives are adopted, these goals must be clearly identified during the first phase of the research program. The industrial monitoring system, the community-industrial attitude census, and the regional resource analysis provide the basic information necessary for program organizers to develop a clear statement of goals based on the review of the community's resources, its comparative advantages and the barriers to economic development, and the attitudes of the citizens in the community.

Industrial Monitoring System

The industrial monitoring system is a means of identifying sources of growth or stagnation within a business community. The monitoring system identifies a community's strengths and weaknesses for industrial development from the point of view of industrial management. It attempts to survey every business that has expanded, relocated, shut down, or consolidated. The survey results give resident management's opinions of community strengths and weaknesses as an environment for development. The strengths identified by a resident firm can be used to market the area to a new firm with similar needs. The survey results can also be used to develop a list of target industries based on those firms that have already successfully located or expanded in the community.

The major tool for the survey is the Inventory of Business and Industrial Change questionnaire (appendix A to this chapter), which can be adapted for use by state or local area developers. Mailing lists for the form are developed from publications like state or local business directories, state development agency reports, newspaper clippings of expansion, relocation, or closing announcements, and other state agency industry reports. At the local level, mailing lists can be developed from the local chamber of commerce directory or a state-level business directory.

Another monitoring technique for the local area developer is a thorough analysis of correspondence from firms interested in locating in the area. Incoming letters can suggest what kinds of industry are attracted to the community and what those firms see as assets for developments.

State and local communities that have used the industrial monitoring system discover that about 60 to 80 percent of the state's or community's future economic growth will be generated by the expansion of resident firms. Based on an assessment of where they are, many of these communities have shifted the major emphasis of their economic development programs to "retention-expansion," or servicing the needs and stimulating expansion of resident business.

Community-Industrial Attitude Census

The community-industrial attitude census is one way of determining what local leaders think of their community and what kind and degree of industrial development is needed and wanted. In the selective development program, the census is conducted on a county or multicounty basis.

Specifically, the census identifies county problems and unique strengths as well as goals for industrial development. The census can identify barriers to progress that are severe enough to require solutions before any type of industrial development program can be continued. Such problems include inadequate sewer or water supply, shortage of adequate industrial sites, inadequate knowledge of sites, inadequately trained labor pool, lack of local consensus on goals, or negative local image. The census can also be used to involve the community, particularly the business leadership, actively in developing or rethinking an industrial development program. Such involvement is essential for a successful development effort. Like industrial monitoring, the census may show that a community needs a retention-expansion program for resident business, as well as a program to attract new firms.

The census requires more manpower and a larger budget than industrial monitoring. The basic procedure is as follows: First, the local development group reviews recently developed, comprehensive master plans or overall economic development plans for the community. These plans are a starting point for identifying economic development goals. Second, the group develops a list of one hundred to five hundred names and addresses of "community leaders." The list may be developed specifically for the census or may be an existing list of key members of the chamber of commerce and other local organizations. Local publicity can expand the list with volunteer participants. Third, the group drafts a cover letter and prepares census forms, and self-addressed return envelopes (appendix B). Fourth, the local development group mails the census. For maximum response, the group should arrange for local publicity to coincide with the form mailing. Follow-up calls are often necessary. Finally, the group tabulates the census returns and summarizes the results.

Regional Resource Analysis

The final step in the first phase of the program is to evaluate the resource base of the community. Resources are the major determinant of the community's comparative advantages and thus attract the new investments required for economic growth and development. A wide variety of natural, human, and institutional resources must be evaluated, as well as existing industrial structure and other related services (fig. 15.2). In contrast to the first two steps of this phase, which involved community or industrial surveys, the information for the resource analysis is available primarily in published census volumes and other data sources that provide an objective overview of the community's resource base. (Many of the more useful data sources are listed in the annotated bibliography at the end of this chapter.)

The review of a community's natural resources can be divided among local, environmental, and basic resources. The *locational* resources reveal the community's proximity not only to suppliers but also to markets that would be served by the industries under investigation. These markets may range from a primarily local orientation to one that is regional, multistate, or national in scope. The second type of natural resources are *environmental* in nature and include the climate of the area, recreational opportunities, and other physical amenities that are significant to industry in attracting and keeping high-caliber employees. The amenities of the community are particularly important in attracting industries of the footloose type, which are not tied to an extractive or other significant locational resource. The third category of natural resources has generally been labeled as *basic* resources, such as nearby minerals, forest products, agricultural products, and available industrial water and energy supplies. Data for assessing these natural resources are readily available in a state almanac or other publications on mineral, agricultural, and forest resources published by state agencies or as part of the United States census. A search of the local public library or university library will provide other sources.

Human resources are significant in varying degrees to all types of industries and must be thoroughly evaluated in an industrial development program. This evaluation must include information on the educational background, skill level and experience, employee performance, wage levels, and other selected measures of interest to potential industries.

Closely associated with human resources are the *institutional resources* of the community, which serve as both a training ground for employees and an idea-producing sector for industrial innovations. Emphasis is usually placed on educational institutions such as vocational or technical schools, colleges and universities, and other specialized facilities within

Figure 15.2 Regional Resource Analysis in Industrial Development Research

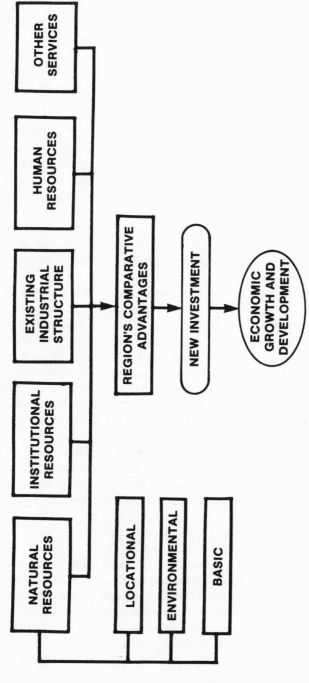

or nearby the community. However, it is also important to identify research and development activities under way in the community as part of private research institutes or those affiliated with universities or other research organizations. State and federal government facilities can also provide valuable input as part of a community's industrial resource base.

Another resource that is worthy of emphasis in this analysis phase is the area's *existing industrial structure*. The existing industrial base is considered a resource because these industries are potentially important suppliers or consumers of a new industry's products and services. The industries consume not only raw materials, but also significant quantities of components and semi-finished goods purchased from other manufacturers. Therefore, it is important to make note of the materials flowing among these companies and their current level of importing materials from outside the area. The term *industrial linkage* is often used for these relationships; this concept will be a major part of the discussion of the second phase of the systematic approach. From the point of view of economic development, much manufacturing exists to supply and to buy from other manufacturers and commercial establishments. As such, industrial facilities are just as truly resources as are raw materials like iron ore and coal.

The final resource that must be evaluated is a wide variety of *services*, such as transportation and warehousing, communications, wholesale and retail trade, finance and insurance, and medical services. These are the support services essential to a community and must be available not only to the companies considering the community for location but also to the workers and employees in these companies. They provide a valuable support function, and critical levels of availability are essential for the success of a total economic development effort.

Data for this type of analysis are available from the United States Census Bureau publications, *County Business Patterns*, *County-City Data Book*, various state publications, input-output tables, and a wide variety of printed resources available to the analyst (see bibliography).

Determining Comparative Advantages and Barriers

The resource analysis and surveys provide the basic information to identify the overall goals that should be established for the community's economic development program, and to assess its comparative advantages, as well as some of the barriers to future economic growth and development. It is comparative advantages that promote new investment and lead to the attraction of new industry or the expansion of existing industry. At the same time, the exploration of barriers to industrial development provides targets for future public policy or private development efforts. These barriers or comparative disadvantages are handicaps to attracting new industry to the community. It is essential that a successful development effort seek to minimize their impact on industrial development.

This completes the first step in the selective development process—answering the question, Where are we now? The report that is prepared from this review provides an assessment of the local community's resources, attitudes, comparative advantages, and barriers. The report serves not only as a basic community orientation and economic review, but also as a vehicle for community workshops and economic development seminars aimed at increasing the awareness of local public officials and business leaders concerning the current state of economic affairs in their community.[1] The next challenge is to use this information to provide direction to future economic development efforts.

Selecting Target Industries

The second major step in the systematic approach to industrial development addresses the question, Where should we be going? This effort builds on the information base that has been developed in the first phase of the program and begins selectively to identify target industries that could be attracted to or expanded in the area under study. A development program does not have the time or the financial resources for a shotgun-type targeting effort. The myriad of potential industry targets could quickly overwhelm a developer, for there are more than four hundred four-digit Standard Industrial Classification (sic) manufacturing industries alone and thousands of possible companies within these industries. The selective approach seeks to target specific industries rather than to cast out a net in hopes that a prospect or two might be landed.

A typical response of many industrial development organizations seeking direction for their programs—most of which are not equipped with large research staffs—is to retain the services of a consultant. While there are many highly qualified consultants in this field, it is important to note that many techniques can be applied by a small development staff that will assist in the targeting effort and guide program development activities. Techniques for identifying potential industrial prospects can use information from local public or university libraries or by purchasing a number of inexpensive data sources.

Two techniques that can be used by developers to identify target industries will be discussed: one relatively simple—the screening matrix—and a more sophisticated, computerized one—the regional potential model. Both use information developed in an input-output analysis.

Input-Output Analysis

A successful industrial developer must have both a good understanding of the geographic area for which the program is being developed and a general appreciation of the operations of an industrial economy. The first phase of the selective approach provides essential information on the specific region. (An understanding of how a regional economy operates can be obtained by reviewing chapter 2 of this book.)

One of the best tools available to the industrial developer for describing the interaction and interdependence of industrial activities within a regional or national setting is a set of input-output tables. A simplified example of an input-output table is shown in chapter 2 (tables 2.5 and 2.6). By reading down any given column, a developer can identify the source from which a particular industry purchases its inputs—the raw materials, utilities and energy resources, unfinished or intermediate products, and other supplies and services—that it combines with its own contribution (value added) to create its own output. At the same time, by reading across the row, a developer can identify the markets to which the industry sold its output. The most readily available source of input-output data of this type is in the *Survey of Current Business*, published by the United States Department of Commerce.[2] These tables describe the national economy in terms of eighty-five economic categories, with the level of detail in the manufacturing sector at primarily the three- and four-digit (sic) industrial classification.[3] While these tables are for the national level, it is possible to locate tables that have been constructed for specific states and regions.

A survey of eighty-three input-output studies conducted on a regional, state, or national level pointed to the wide variety of applications for this type of analysis in industrial development programs (Draper 1968), mentioning most often the following.

1. *Forecasting output.* The most frequently mentioned use was to forecast the growth of output, and in turn, employment by industry in the region. Input-output can be used to determine the implications of projected gross production on the various sectors of the economy.

2. *Valuation of exports.* Using the export-base theory, the tables can be used to determine those industries exporting goods and services to other regions. The tables indicate those industries for which the region has a competitive advantage, as revealed by exports from the region to other regions.

3. *Import substitutions.* The tables can be used to identify local markets that are presently being supplied by imported goods and services.

This information can demonstrate the need for substituting local or regional industry in place of externally supplied goods and services.

4. *Intermediate exports.* The tables can be used for analysis of forward integration of existing manufacturers. If the raw materials are available in the region for production of intermediate products, significant industrial potential can be identified that will meet the needs for intermediate products outside the region under study.

5. *Identification of linkages.* Identification of industrial linkages can be obtained between prospect industries and the industries located in the region. In contrast to intermediate exports, these are intermediate products produced in the region to meet the needs of existing regional industries. A *forward linkage* refers to a movement of intermediate products as inputs to another industry's production. It might also be noted that a forward linkage could be movement of a product directly to the consumer market. A *backward linkage* would tie a prospect industry to an existing industry producing intermediate products that the prospect industry utilizes.

6. *Other uses.* Input-output tables can also be used for impact studies such as the effect of a specific new industry on the region's economy. Furthermore, the tables can be used for program planning of various kinds.

While input-output tables have many potential uses a number of specific examples should clarify some of the simpler applications of the technique (Miernyk 1965).

The input-output table for the United States published in the *Survey of Current Business* (1974) can be valuable in identifying three types of linkages: a backward or supplier linkage, a forward linkage *to an intermediate market*, and a forward linkage *to a final-consumer market*.

For example, let us use the input-output table for analysis of a backward linkage with the paperboard containers and boxes industry as the potential target industry. The *Survey of Current Business* assigns this industry an I/O identification number of 25. It is necessary to convert the I/O number to an SIC number. The conversion table indicates that this industry is comparable to SIC 265. The major supplier linkage in this case is with the paper and allied products industry (I/O 24 or SIC 26). Forty percent of the industry's total input or 64 percent of the intermediate input comes from this single source. The detailed input-output table shows that 88 percent of the single input comes from the paperboard mills industry (I/O 24.03 or SIC 2631). Thus the backward linkage for the prospect industry is clearly identified.

It is also possible to explore the forward linkage of the paperboard containers and boxes industry to intermediate markets. Of the total output from this industry, 97 percent is destined for intermediate markets. The three largest intermediate markets emerge when reviewing the input-output table: food and kindred products (28 percent—I/O 14 or SIC 20); paper and allied products (6 percent—I/O 24 or SIC 26, except containers —265); and drugs, cleaning, and toilet preparations (6 percent—I/O 29 or SIC 283 and 284).

Another example is the forward linkage to a final consumer market. To illustrate, the footwear industry (I/O 34 or SIC 314) sends 86 percent of its final output directly to the consumer market. Thus, an evaluation of this prospect industry would also require an evaluation of the final markets available in the community and within an appropriate shipping area as revealed in the *Census of Transportation*.

Obviously, in using the container industry as a potential target industry, the backward or forward linkages evident in the community and its surrounding area, based on the industry analysis completed in phase I, will determine whether this potential industry deserves further review as a target or candidate industry.

The Screening Matrix

Using the background information on input-output, it is possible to proceed to the actual targeting of industries. One approach that can be used is the screening matrix, a tool for identifying industries that have the greatest potential for location or expansion in a community. This approach tests each candidate industry, listed by SIC number, against a set of screening criteria designated by the industrial developer. The selected criteria can emphasize the community's priorities for new development opportunities, as well as the needs and requirements of an individual industry. A sample matrix format is shown in figure 15.3. It is important that the local area developer select criteria that fit the specific community. Each criterion is weighted, admittedly on a subjective basis, according to the community's priorities that have been identified in the first phase of the selective development process. In the sample matrix (fig. 15.3), the following criteria were utilized: industry growth rates, wage levels, raw material availability, linkages to intermediate industries, markets, labor supply, energy requirements, and port orientation.

Candidate industries. Since there are over four hundred SIC manufacturing industries, it is desirable to select from this total number a smaller, more manageable list of industries that can be evaluated in greater detail. In the sample screening matrix, the criteria of industry growth rates and

Figure 15.3 Sample Screening Matrix

	CRITERIA																
	HIGH GROWTH INDUSTRY	WAGES		MATERIALS			LINKAGES		MARKETS		LABOR						
INDUSTRY 4-DIGIT SIC	HIGH GROWTH INDUSTRY	VERY HIGH	HIGH	GENERALLY IN REGION	PARTIALLY FOUND IN REGION	MOST IN REGION	PARTIALLY IN REGION	MOST LINKS ELSEWHERE	REGIONAL	NATIONAL	PROFESSIONAL	SKILLED	SEMI SKILLED	LABOR INTENSIVE	ENERGY – NATURAL GAS USAGE	PORT ORIENTATION	TOTAL
WEIGHT	10	10	5	6	3	8	5	2	3	5	2	4	6	5	8	2	
2611 PULP MILLS	X		X	X		X			X			X				X	38
2732 BOOK PRINTING	X		X	X			X			X			X	X	X		50
2911 PETROLEUM REFINING	X	X					X		X		X	X				X	36
3541 MACHINE TOOLS	X		X					X		X	X	X		X	X		41
3673 ELECTRON TUBES	X		X					X		X		X		X			31
3831 OPTICAL LENSES	X		X					X		X	X	X			X		36

wage levels were used to develop the list of industries for the left vertical column. However, depending on local development goals and objectives, other criteria may be used to select the candidate industries for detailed review.

Projected industry growth rates. The future growth potential of an industry is a key factor in analyzing industry development potential. Fast-growing industries are seeking new locations or expansion opportunities. In many analyses, industrial growth rate is determined by past performance alone. Many sources that forecast future industrial growth potential are available for use in analyses of this type. For example, the *U.S. Industrial Outlook* provides an excellent series of articles on future industry growth prospects. Using projected industry growth rates as a criteria avoids the backward-oriented slant of most traditional targeting methods. Most industries demonstrating high growth are also above average in productivity increases, total employment, and investment in research and development, and become good development prospects. It is also wise to determine the industries that are growing more rapidly in the community's region of the country than in the nation as a whole. In this way the chance of successfully attracting an industry can be enhanced.

Wage levels. If an "income gap" exists between the local community or area and other parts of the United States, a major development goal may be to create more and higher-paying jobs. Industries can be screened to find those that have demonstrated wage and salary levels above the national average. Pertinent data are located in the *Census of Manufacturers* and *County Business Patterns.* The sample matrix identifies two groups within the general wage criteria: high wages (industries paying wages at average to 25 percent above average national industrial wages) and very high wages (25 percent or more above national average industrial wages).

The remaining criteria in the horizontal column—raw material availability, industrial linkages, markets, labor supply, energy requirements, and port orientation—help to identify industries most suitable for the community. The input-output data provide the basic source of information for these criteria.

Raw material availability. Candidate industries are screened according to the degree to which needed materials are available in the community's general area. Two criteria are used: (1) industries heavily dependent on raw or unfinished materials and (2) raw materials (minerals, agricultural products, forestry products, primary metals) that are available in the region. The input-output tables are excellent sources for identification of the dependence of an industry on these various basic materials. The industry's requirements are evaluated against the availability of the materials in the area and a determination made as to whether most (over 75 percent) or only part (50 percent) of the materials are located in the area.

Industrial linkages. Existing industries in an area (normally those within the maximum commuting range of the community) are potential suppliers or purchasers of the intermediate products produced by a new industry. Likewise, a new industry may be linked to an existing industry to supply intermediate products or purchase semi-finished products. Candidate industries are screened to find the degree to which they have a linkage with existing industry in the area. If suppliers and/or intermediate markets for candidate industries exist within or near the community, the argument is much stronger for its location there. If the candidate industry would have to go outside the area for suppliers and intermediate markets, an industrial linkage cannot be used as an argument for its location or expansion in the community. Again, the input-output table is an excellent source of data on the candidate industry's potential linkage, to either suppliers or intermediate markets.

An entry based on this evaluation is made in the screening matrix for each industry reviewed. Each candidate industry is evaluated to determine if most (75 percent or more), partial (50 percent to 75 percent), or few (less than 50 percent) of the linkages exist in the area.

Markets served. A large market usually means a greater number of jobs, higher wage rates, and higher product value for a given industry. Candidate industries are therefore screened to identify those that serve final consumer markets on a regional or national basis. Transportation economics plays a critical role in determining the markets that can be served. Food and other related manufacturing industries are more likely to serve a regional market, while the printing and electronics industries serve a national market. The *U.S. Census of Transportation* is used to determine the extent to which an industry serves a regional or national market. For example, if 90 percent of an industrial commodity reaches its final destination within three hundred miles, the industry is primarily serving a regional market.

Labor supply—skill level. In the screening matrix example, the labor requirements of candidate industries are divided into three categories:

1. professional—industries with a higher than average proportion of nonproduction employees—that is, scientists, engineers, and technicians;

2. skilled—industries requiring a higher-than-average proportion of skilled and specialized production workers;

3. semi-skilled—industries requiring higher-than-average proportion of semi-skilled production workers.

These data can be developed from the *U.S. Census of Population.* Some industries require a combination of these identified characteristics and are given more than one score in the matrix.

Labor supply—intensity. An evaluation may be made of the level of labor intensity of industry in communities that have significant levels of surplus labor. In labor surplus communities industries with high levels of labor intensity will be attractive for local development efforts. The criterion utilized in this example is value added per employee, which provides an index of the concentration of jobs in the candidate industry and can be calculated by using *U.S. Census of Manufacturers* data. In the example, those industries with above-average levels of labor intensity were identified.

Energy requirements. Energy availability has become an extremely important factor in the location of industrial prospects. While industries can be evaluated on a wide variety of energy uses, the community under study in the example was short on natural gas supplies. Thus the screening factor evaluated the use of natural gas and identified those with low requirements.

Port orientation. Candidate industries that would benefit from the use of the port facilities in the sample community under study for transportation of materials and products are identified by this criterion. Data on transportation by mode are obtained from the *U.S. Census of Transportation*, and those with above-average use of water transportation (and port facilities) can thus be identified.

Weighting criteria. As stated earlier, the criteria are given weights so a composite score can be calculated. In the sample, the highest weights are given to the high-growth and very-high-wage industries. Since linkages are also very important, industries with most of the linkages found in the area were given the second highest rating, along with those that required little natural gas. In the example, since the area had a surplus of semi-skilled labor, a higher score was given to industries able to utilize these semi-skilled workers. The remainder of the weighting system is self-explanatory.

After the weights are determined and the analysis completed, an indication of the relative attractiveness of the screened industries for the particular community or area can be gleaned from the resulting list of industries, ranked according to their potential for location in the community. Using the scores, industries with the highest development potential can be identified. The lower the score, the lower the potential of that industry's locating in the community. Scores for a specific industry cannot be interpreted on an individual basis, but the ranking process identifies high-, medium-, and low-priority targets.

The results of the screening matrix can help industrial developers focus on those industries that best match the needs and resources of the community. The screening matrix is a relatively simple tool for answering the question, Where should we be going? It is a flexible approach using criteria that can be selected for each economic development program and using data from readily available sources to complete the analysis.

The next step in the screening process is to assemble as much relevant information on that target industry as possible to aid the developer in further evaluation of the candidate industry. For example, the top prospect industry in the example was book printing (SIC 2732). A profile of the book printing industry should be developed that includes data on employees per establishment; average hourly wage; land area per establishment; percentage of shipments by rail, motor carrier, and water; natural gas, fuel oil, and water use per establishment; water discharge per establishment; forward linkages; backward linkages; percentages of work force that are professional, skilled, and semi-skilled (see chapter bibliography for appropriate data sources). With this detailed profile, one can then develop a marketing strategy directed at specific companies within the target industry.

Regional Potential Model

The regional potential model (RPM) is a computer system for matching the needs or requirements of individual industries or groups of industries with the assets or resources of a multicounty region and determining where these needs and assets are most compatible (Sweet 1971). The major purpose of this matching process is to identify those industries that, when seeking locations for new facilities, are most likely to be attracted to a specific region. This knowledge enables industrial development groups in the county to approach companies in these industries on a selective development basis. The RPM is a more sophisticated tool for answering the question, Where should we be going?

Many computer models for industrial location identify only optimal locations. In the site selection process, however, most decision makers evaluate and select from a set of satisfactory alternative locations, not optimal alternatives. It is generally agreed that industrial location decision making is a two-step process: first, a desired region is identified; second, the specific community and site is selected. The RPM is aimed at simulating that first step. A region can refer to a multistate geographic area or a multicounty unit. In some cases the region is a labor market area ranging from one to several counties.

In developing the regional potential model, a set of relevant industrial location factors was selected that define what industries seek in a regional location and also what attributes a region must have to attract an industry. Many empirical studies have attempted to identify through survey techniques or case studies the most important factors in the location decision (chapter 5). In most of these studies, the traditional factors of marketing, raw materials, transportation, labor, and utilities are frequently mentioned as most important. Thus, the computer model uses these factors to assess an industry's needs and compares them with a region's resources (fig. 15.4).

In the model each industry is evaluated on fifteen characteristics, which include the industry's orientation to the intermediate and consumer markets; each industry's requirements for raw materials, intermediate or semi-finished manufactured products, and other services; the industry's orientation to shipping products by rail, highway, or water; and the requirement of the average plant in each specific industry for workers with various skill levels (as evaluated by educational attainment). Similarly, each region is evaluated in terms of the intermediate and consumer market potential within an accessible radius of the region; suppliers available to a plant potentially locating in the region, including raw materials, intermediate or semi-finished products, and other services; distance to the nearest interstate highway, rail line, and port from a central point in the region; and the available labor force in the region by educational level.

The RPM lists and describes the candidate industries considered, the four-digit SIC code for each, and, most important, an index number indicating how well each industry is likely to satisfy its four major needs in the community considered. In some cases, industries previously regarded as "natural" or obvious candidates for location do not measure up as well as anticipated against the hard, analytical test of the RPM. Very often, industries that local community leaders felt would fit in very well have proved to be economically infeasible. The RPM provides lists of target industries realistically matched to community resources. Thus, the model also offers a "feedback" function or a method of reconciling differences between what the community sees as its assets and industry's more realistic and unemotional view of those assets.[4]

The regional potential model and the screening matrix are two techniques for targeting potential prospect industries for the selective development program. This discussion has set the stage for the third and final phase of the selective approach to industrial development.

Prospecting for Target Industries

The first two phases of the selective development program identify an area's comparative advantages and target industries that can contribute to

Figure 15.4 The Regional Potential Model

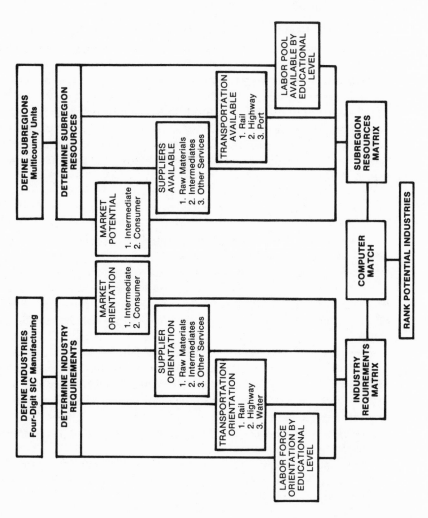

the economic development in a specific community. Success or failure in actually attracting these industries to a community depends on the marketing program; first, converting industry targets into specific company targets; then selling the target companies on locating or expanding in the community; and finally selling them on a specific site.

If a community decides to utilize a selective approach to industrial development, that approach should also apply to the marketing phase. Marketing tools like advertising and direct mail can be designed with the "rifle" strategy in mind to form the final phase of the program, How do we get there?

The Community Brochure

The first step in a selective development marketing strategy should be the development of a community brochure. The brochure has two purposes— to provide general information about the community and to arouse enough interest in the community to induce a specific request from a manufacturing or commercial prospect for more detailed information. Phase I of the program develops the type of information included in the brochure.

However, since the community brochure does not usually give an industrialist enough information to assess the community properly in light of his particular requirements, it should be supplemented by other information more specifically directed to the interest of prospects (see community data form in chapter 14).

Experienced developers offer the following advice for preparing the brochure:

1. Do not concentrate too much on the visual effects of printing and photographs because the experienced businessman looks for pertinent information, not window dressing.

2. Do not fill the brochure with indiscriminate facts that make it so voluminous that it is unreadable.

3. Design the brochure to be neat and compact, containing only specific facts and a limited number of pertinent illustrations.

4. Size the brochure to fit a standard envelope or file folder and to be light enough to mail economically.

5. Concentrate on communicating the relevant facts on unique advantages of the community instead of making boastful generalities.

6. Refer to existing companies in the community, both new firms and those that have been operating there for a long period of time.

7. Use only the most up-to-date statistics.

8. Be certain that art work and illustrations look professional. No art work at all is preferable to bad art work.

9. Direct the brochure toward a specific audience.

10. State clearly the name, address, and phone number of your organization.

Numerous factors are involved in the decision to locate or expand industrial facilities. To industry, the trends and intensity of statistical changes are more important than data for a particular year. A summary of details that the average site seeker needs is listed below:

1. *Availability of labor*: number and sex of workers; skills; unemployment, by skill and sex; population size and age distribution.

2. *Proximity to markets*: market locations, size of markets, distance to major markets, buying power, competition, trends.

3. *Transportation*: rail, truck, air, water; routes (name, number, type); transportation companies (name, size); shipping distance; shipping time; schedules.

4. *Sites and buildings*: property data, costs, availability, zoning, surrounding property use.

5. *Financing programs*: private funds available; community, state, and federal financing assistance.

6. *Proximity to materials*: nearest major sources, by-products of neighboring firms.

7. *Taxes*: local rates and trends, area rates and trends, state taxes, special assessments, unemployment compensation rates, sources.

8. *Water*: availability, cost, quality, mineral content, sources.

9. *Power and other utilities*: company names with addresses, availability, rates, voltages, pressures, line sizes.

Trade Associations and Publications

Whether the development group in a community elects to take a broad or a selective approach to development, contacts with trade associations and trade publications will be productive. For the community targeting on a few selected industries, in-depth data can often be obtained from the executive secretaries of the trade associations representing those industries. Directories or lists of national trade associations are available in most public libraries.

Listings of trade associations include the full name and address of the association, telephone number, name of the executive secretary, number of active company members, year of initiation, and, in some cases, names of trade publications published by the association and dates and places of annual conventions.

When making telephone, personal, or letter contact with trade associations, the developer should find out the names of the leading trade publications published by outside companies, which are directed toward the trade association's membership. In most cases, one publication is generally recognized as fundamental to the industry because it contains most of the pertinent data about national conventions and trade shows, as well as statistical data, lists of companies in the industry, and related information.

After targeting several particular industries, the development group should subscribe to the trade publications directed toward the particular industry of interest. In this way it will be possible—at a very low cost—for the community to "keep up" with the activities within a particular industry: Who is expanding? Who is merging? Who is out looking for new sites? Who are the most likely prospects? During the process of monitoring activities of the target industry, the developer can also compile data on potential target companies within that industry.

Often this kind of continued surveillance or monitoring of a particular industry results in early "leads" and opportunities to respond, to promote a community, and actually to conduct site tours before competing communities are even aware of a particular company's interest.

Direct-Mail Campaigns

A major part of the marketing phase in the selective development approach is the use of direct mail. The direct-mail form of promotion is viewed as the most selective, since the development group can pick its targets and make an effort to attract only the selected industries or services. A survey of senior executives of "blue chip" manufacturing companies, conducted by a federal reserve bank, investigated the receptivity of these executives to several promotional techniques and concluded that, if managed correctly, the direct-mail approach is more effective than any other type of advertising. The direct-mail method provides absolute control by the promoter, and the success of the campaign can be measured by the rate of response.

The following points should be considered in preparation of a direct-mail letter.

1. Keep the letter brief and concise, containing only enough detail to encourage the recipient to seek further information.

2. Tailor the letter specifically to a particular class of prospects.

3. Direct the letter to various levels of command. Since most execu-

tives' mail is screened by secretaries, sending enough copies to various levels of command should bring the letter to the attention of the right individuals.

4. Include the three essentials: the eye-catcher, the facts, and the offer.

5. Make sure that the eye-catcher—the first sentence—has the strength to save the letter from being deposited in the wastebasket. One of the best items on which to touch is corporate profits. Data for these opening sentences may be obtained from the first two phases of the program. Some examples of this approach are:

"If your net profit is now under 7% you will be interested in . . ."

"A $5-million, unserved market is available to you in _____ county!"

"Why is one of your competitors in _____ county?"

6. Once interest has been aroused, put in a few facts. Include only prime facts and figures on several location factors, such as markets, transportation, available energy supplies, and available skilled labor. The letter should be no longer than one page.

7. Employ short, simple sentences.

8. A major purpose of the letter is to encourage further action, so tell the recipient specifically what you want him to do: send for a brochure, fill out a checklist, or look forward to a personal phone call from a development leader.

9. Make the desired response as convenient as possible for the executive. If he is supposed to send for more material, enclose a stamped, self-addressed return postcard.

The second phase of the selective development program identified specific industries of interest to the community. The direct-mail phase will require that these industry targets be converted to specific company targets. Complete lists of companies within a four-digit SIC industry can be obtained by using any number of data sources such as the *Million Dollar Directory* and *Register of Corporations, Directors, and Executives*. Some of these listings are also available on computer tape.

Rather than contacting the entire list of firms with the same general letter, it is desirable to group the companies by size or location. Different letters can be drafted for different company groups and the responses monitored in an attempt to identify the most effective approaches. Continual monitoring of prospect companies is important and can best be accomplished through compilation of company annual reports, trade publications, and other financial and business publications. Also, the *F & S Index of Corporations and Industries* and the *Business Periodicals Index* provide excellent sources of information on companies throughout the country and world that are indexed by SIC (see chapter bibliography).

Development Trips

One of the often-used techniques of attracting industrial prospects to a particular area is the so-called development trip, or a trip by developers to the corporate offices of prospective industries. Obviously, development trips to large cities are costly. For this reason, it is often not possible for smaller communities to arrange and sponsor development trips. However, the small community or county has allies or representatives who can accept this responsibility for them, such as members of state development agencies. Selected personnel within these agencies periodically make development trips to major cities throughout the United States and Canada, as well as abroad.[5] Smaller, more selective trips may be productive for development groups in individual communities if they concentrate contacts on executives and firms in specific industry categories that seem most appropriate for the communities represented.

Advertising and News Releases

Advertising in nationally or regionally distributed magazines or newspapers is the most frequently used method of attracting industrial prospects to a community. But the cost of advertising in certain classes of publications is quite high. Consequently, it may be difficult to justify these costs when the rate of response is relatively low.

Again, the selective approach to development can make advertising more economical and effective. Advertising space in specialized trade publications with smaller circulations is usually far less expensive than in high-circulation publications like the *Wall Street Journal*, the *New York Times*, or *Fortune* magazine.

Carefully phrased advertisements placed in the basic publications of selected industries can be effective. If the advertisement employs the precise language of the industry to which it is directed, the readers will get the impression that the advertisers—the communities—are familiar with the industry and its problems and may be better able to respond to the industry's needs.

The news release offers two advantages in industrial development work: it is free, and it is often more effective to have a third party—in this case, a newspaper or radio/television station—speak favorably of a product or a community than for the company or community to act as its own spokesman.

Because many news releases must compete for the attention of the editor/director, the development group should prepare and distribute releases on legitimate news only. Examples of legitimate release material include research reports or photographs and announcements of ground breakings for new plants and vocational schools. The key to making the front page or business column is quality in contrast to quantity. The best place to begin publicity is at the local level to inform area citizens; increased local knowledge and awareness of community assets and accomplishments often result in greatest support from the local citizenry in general. Also, to be successful, it is essential that the local development group maintain local support for the program. Good local news coverage is one way of keeping the general public informed of local development efforts.

Site Tours

Clearly the major objective of all advertising and promotion is to attract interested industrial prospects to the community for further contact and discussion. Rarely, if ever, are site selection decisions made until at least a representative group of company officials has visited the community, talked with community leaders, and actually toured potential sites. Community leaders should make certain, in these meetings, that leaders with backgrounds in areas of interest to visiting company representatives are introduced to those individuals. Bankers should talk with corporate financial officers, real estate people should talk with their counterparts, and journalists should talk with public relations people.

Industrial site seekers ask for specifics such as the chemistry of the local water supply, tax assessment rates, and foundation subsoil characteristics—questions that demand careful and detailed answers. So that members of the development team are at all times prepared to answer questions from prospects, a central facts book that includes more data than the community brochure should be available and kept up to date in a form ready for quick reference. The fact book should include at least:

1. site descriptions, photographs, and specifications,
2. aerial maps, industrial zoning data,
3. labor supply and characteristics,
4. service rates,
5. local and regional marketing information and supplier services,
6. business climate data, and
7. basic economic data.

If the industrial prospect is generally pleased with the specific community, finding that the community or region meets its location needs, then it is essential that community leaders be in a position to offer the prospect an adequate selection of specific sites. The site may be fully developed, including all buildings and utilities, it may be partially developed, or it may be undeveloped acreage.

In presenting a fully developed site to an industrial site seeker, the developer should be prepared to explain why the site is not in use and to emphasize those features that might be most appealing to the prospect. To be attractive to the industrial prospect, the partially developed or undeveloped site should have good soil conditions and nearby transportation connections and adequate utilities.

A thorough description of a site involves more than simply the location, size, and approximate cost of the site. Community leaders should, in the early stages of planning the industrial development program, make an industrial site survey of their community. An ideal site survey team might include the mayor or other local officials, a representative of a local planning agency, a zoning commission representative, an engineer, the tax assessor, a local industrial realtor, an official of the chamber of commerce or development agency, representatives of the utilities companies, and officials of firms already located in the area.

Site information, compiled through a site survey, should include the following:

1. exact ownership, size, availability, and asking price of the property;
2. physical characteristics of the property—topography, soil composition, drainage, and load-bearing characteristics;
3. service and access roads and highways, utilities and their availability and proximity, current taxes, assessment, liens, easements, and zoning;
4. types of industries considered most suited to the sites the community has to offer;
5. which organizations have information concerning the site and/or surrounding areas.

The general attitude of the local development people who serve as hosts to visiting site seekers is very important. An attitude of provincialism or hostility to outsiders quickly alienates site seekers, who then turn to more hospitable communities. Visiting prospects should be informed of local recreational activities such as golf, swimming, and fishing. Whether tourist or cultural facilities figure directly in the economic development plan or not, these facilities are important to the long-term future of a community's industrial development effort.

Follow-Up

Locating an industrial prospect is not simply a process of establishing a development program and waiting for prospects to beat a path to the community or a one-shot direct-mail letter or a single development trip visit. Industrial development at the community level means continued community involvement; it means periods of low industrial activity; it means building industry and company prospect files; and, most of all, it means hard work.

Only communities with a unique set of extremely desirable characteristics can afford simply to wait for opportunities to host prospects who venture into the community. Most communities find that their characteristics are no better than, and perhaps inferior to, those of neighboring, competing communities. Consequently, in order to achieve real success in industrial development activities, communities need to act, rather than react or respond; they must aggressively seek prospects to bring into the community.

Some community leaders, in attempting to justify inadequate follow-up or initiative, contend that an image of over-aggressiveness degrades the community in the eyes of industry and reduces its "bargaining position." This is a risk that a marketer of any product or service must take. Community leaders must carefully evaluate individual situations and determine precisely what level of response and effort is warranted in each case.

Retention-Expansion

Based on an assessment of where it is now and where it should be going, a local community may decide to focus its economic development activities on the retention and expansion of resident industry, an emphasis that demands a different marketing strategy.

One approach to retention-expansion at the local level might be the creation of a municipal, countywide, or regional organization to retain and encourage expansion of resident industry, assist new industries to locate, prepare the community for new industrial growth, and take advantage of all available federal and state funds to assist economic development.

Such a commission should be composed of members of the community improvement corporation or similar group and representatives of the community's elected government leaders, labor sector, management groups, academic community, minority groups, and the general public.

The organization's responsibilities might include the following:

1. establish policy and develop a broad-based plan for the community's economic and industrial development,

2. insure that the community takes advantage of available federal and state funds and programs to assist in economic development,

3. carry overall responsibility for implementing retention-expansion, site development, and outside sales programs.

The organization could then create two working committees: retention-expansion and site development. The retention-expansion (R&E) committee might be assigned the following functions:

1. establish a continuing program of person-to-person contact between the committee and area industries. An "account executive" approach could be designed to provide continuous communication between the committee and businessmen.

2. develop an "early warning system" to help the committee determine which resident firms are experiencing problems and might need assistance in remaining or expanding in the community.

3. work to improve the local economic, political and social climate to provide for the retention and expansion of job opportunities in the community.

Such a communitywide R&E effort should tie in with and take advantage of similar efforts at the state level. A second approach to retention-expansion particularly suited to a large, developed metropolitan area is the creation of a special volunteer task force of business, civic, labor, and local government leaders to help deter plant closings and out-of-town relocation of resident firms.

Such an approach can include an advertising campaign to explain task force services and establishment of a "hot line" to put resident businessmen in touch with experts who can help solve R&E problems, such problems as manpower availability and training, union-management relations, street and plant security, government regulations, environmental protection, taxes, market expansion, and state and federal financial assistance. The community as a whole can be encouraged to support the R&E effort by alerting the task force to firms that may be planning to move out.

Notes

1. It might be noted that much of the data compiled in the first-phase analysis can be of value in preparing federal grant applications for funds to support local economic development efforts.

2. See, for example, U.S. Department of Commerce, "The Input-Output Structure of the U.S. Economy."

3. This table will suffice for most industrial development applications. However, for the developer wishing to pursue input-output analysis in greater detail, the U.S. Department of Commerce also publishes a set of tables with a 367-category breakdown.

4. For further discussion of the regional potential model and examples of specific applications see David C. Sweet, "Development and Application of an Industry Potential Model"; David C. Sweet et al., *Appalachian Selective Develop-*

ment Program; and Richard J. Darwin, "Geography, Economic Development and Spatial Policy."

5. Ideally, participants in state-sponsored development trips should be impartial, not favoring one section of the state over others. However, trip participants naturally favor those specific communities seeking industrial development that cooperate most fully by providing the maximum and best information available about their communities.

Appendix A

Inventory of Business and Industrial Change

Please complete and return
to:

_____

_____

_____

DIRECTIONS:
If your company experienced a change (new business in _____ expansion, relocation, consolidation, temporary shutdown, closing, move-out, or other
type of change that would have an effect upon the economy of _____)
during 19____ please complete page 1. On pages 2 through 4, complete ONLY the section that deals with the type of change in which this facility was involved.

Company Name_____

Address of the Facility
Involved in the Change_____

City_____ Zip Code_____ County_____

Previous Address (if applicable)_____

_____

Type of Business at the
Facility Involved in a Change_____

If a Manufacturer, List
Products of this Facility_____

THE CHANGE AT THE ABOVE FACILITY INVOLVED:

(Where there is a choice, please underline
the appropriate word.)

Yes

____ New construction.

____ Lease or purchase of existing
     facility.

____ Sale or loss of existing facility.

____ Incorporation of existing company.

____ Addition or loss of equipment.

____ Addition or loss of employees.

____ Pollution control.

____ Other: (explain)_____

_____

_____

1. Amount of new capital
   expenditures or losses: $\pm$ $_____

2. Number of added
   or lost jobs: $\pm$ _____

3. Added or lost
   work area: $\pm$ _____sq. ft.

(Please mark with an asterisk (*) any of
 the above figures that are estimated.)

Date operations began (or closed) following the completion of the change:

_____

FORM COMPLETED BY:

_____
name   title   phone

SECTION A: NEW FIRMS

Yes

_____   1. This is a newly formed _____ company.
_____   2. This is an out-of-state company starting business in _____.
            The company is based in, or moved from _____, and has no
                                                   state or county
            other facilities located in this state.

(If you checked "yes" for either of the above, please answer the following
questions.)

a. Why did you decide to open a facility in _____?

_____

_____

_____

_____

_____

b. Why did you choose the particular area of _____ in which
    you located?

_____

_____

_____

_____

SECTION B: EXPANSIONS

Yes

_____   1. This company, currently doing business in _____, is ex-
            panding a _____ facility.

_____   2. This company, currently doing business in _____, is
            opening a new _____ plant site. All other _____
            plant sites remain in operation.

(If you checked "yes" for either of the above, please answer the following
questions.)

a. Why did you expand your operation in _____ rather than in
    some other county or state?

_____

_____

_____

_____

_____

b. Why did you choose the particular area of _____ in which you
    expanded?

_____

_____

_____

_____

SECTION C: RELOCATIONS

Yes

___   1.   This company, currently doing business in _____ , is relocating.

The facility at _____is being or was closed
              address

and the operations moved to _____
                         address

a. Why did you leave the address in which your facility was formerly located?

_____

_____

_____

_____

_____

b. Why did you choose the address to which you moved?

_____

_____

_____

_____

SECTION D: CONSOLIDATION OF FACILITIES

Yes

___   1.   This company, currently doing business in _____ , is con-
       solidating its facilities.

The facility(ies) at _____ was/were
                 address

closed and the operation(s) moved to a plant in operation at _____

_____.

(If the consolidation involved more than is described here, please use an additional
page to describe fully.)

a. Why did you consolidate your facilities?

_____

_____

_____

_____

b. Why did you choose the particular location in which you consolidated your
    facilities?

_____

_____

_____

_____

SECTION E: TEMPORARY SHUTDOWNS, WORK SLOWDOWNS, AND LAYOFFS

Yes

___   1. This facility is temporarily shut down.

___   2. This facility is experiencing a work curtailment or slowdown.

___   3. This facility is laying off some of its employees.

(If you checked "yes" in one of the above, please complete the following.)

a. Please explain the reason for the above action. _____

_____

_____

_____

_____

b. When do you expect to resume normal operations at this facility? _____

_____

SECTION F: MOVE-OUTS AND CLOSINGS

1. This company is moving (has moved) out of _____. The
    facility at _____was closed and the oper-
                          address
    ations moved to_____

    _____
                               city   state or country

    a. Why did you choose the particular place to which you relocated?

        _____

        _____

        _____

        _____

        _____

        _____

2. This_____ company is going (has gone) out of

    business _____

    b. Why did you cease operations in _____? _____

        _____

        _____

        _____

        _____

        _____

        _____

Appendix B

Community Industrial Attitude Census

A. CLASSIFICATION DATA:

Please answer the following questions by placing an "X" in the appropriate box
or filling in the information requested. Your responses to these and all questions will be treated in confidence.

1. How long have you lived in this county?

a.___ 0-2 years d.___ 10-20
b.___ 3-5   e.___ 21+
c.___ 6-10

2. Age:

a.___ under 25   d.___ 45-54
b.___ 25-34   e.___ 55-64
c.___ 35-44   f.___ 65 and over

3. Sex:

a.___ Female   b.___ Male

4. Race:

a.___ Black   c.___ White
b.___ Other

5. Educational attainment:

a.___ less than   d.___ 13-15
      8 years   e.___ 16
b.___ 9-11   f.___ 17+
c.___ 12

6. Occupation:

a.___ laborer   e.___ proprietary
b.___ profes-   f.___ technical
      sional   g.___ other (explai
c.___ clerical   _____
d.___ administrative

7. Place of work: Name of city or village_____

8. Place of residence: Name of city or village_____

9. Major community activities and offices held, if any:_____

B. COUNTY PROBLEMS, ASSETS, AND DEVELOPMENT:

Please express your opinions on the subjects listed below in the appropriate spaces.

1. What do you consider to be the primary problems of your community?

2. What do you consider to be the greatest assets of your community?

3. What do you consider to be important accomplishments in your county in the past five years?

4. What individuals do you feel were most responsible for these accomplishments: How?

5. Which organizations were the most helpful in achieving these accomplishments? How?

6. What individuals and/or groups do you feel hindered the development of your county most? How?

7. Please name specific types of industries or services you would like to see developed in your county. If you cannot name specific industries, please try to describe basic characteristics of an industry or industries you would like to see in your county.

8. Please name specific industries or services your would not like to see developed in your county. If you cannot name specific industries, please try to describe basic characteristics of an industry or industries you would not like to see in your county.

C. COUNTY DEVELOPMENT POLICIES

Please indicate if you agree with the following statements by checking Agree, No Opinion, or Disagree.

Agree   No Opinion   Disagree

1. Land use zoning controls are an effective way to protect property values.

2. Annexation makes good sense for better public services in rural areas.

3. County agencies can better handle countywide needs (e.g., public utilities) than a local agency.

4. The following are desirable capital improvements which should be financed through county bond issues:
    a) construction of recreational facilities

    b) construction of improved airport facilities

    c) construction of additional hospital facilities

    d) purchasing land for industrial parks

    e) expansion of water and sewer systems for industrial use

    f) low-income housing projects

5. Establishment and enforcement of environmental protection (air, water pollution, etc.) standards should be the responsibility of:
    a) federal agencies

    b) state agencies

    c) county agencies

6. Industrial development should be influenced by local efforts.

7. One countywide organization should be responsible for industrial development.

8. Industrial development should be determined only by market forces.

D. COUNTY INDUSTRIAL DEVELOPMENT GOALS AND OBJECTIVES

The major goal of an industrial development program should be to:

		Agree	No Opinion	Disagree

1. attract companies which can take advantage of the existing industrial base.

2. attract companies which will diversify the existing industrial base.

3. retain and expand existing companies.

4. attract any industry willing to locate in the county.

5. encourage manufacturing industries.

6. encourage service industries.

7. encourage extractive industries (e.g., mining and lumbering).

8. attract defense and space-oriented industries.

9. stress the attraction of branch plants.

10. encourage the attraction or formation of locally managed business.

11. place major emphasis on the recreation and tourism potential of this county.

12. attract industries which use relatively more machines than people (capital intensive).

13. attract industries which use relatively more people than machines (labor intensive).

E. VOLUNTEERED COMMENTS ON ANY OF THE FOREGOING

(Please key to specific question and part. Attach additional sheets if needed.)

Appendix C

Annotated Bibliography of Selected Sources of
Data for Industrial Development Research

Dun & Bradstreet, Inc. *Million Dollar Directory*. New York: Dun & Bradstreet, annual. Alphabetic listing of firms with number of employees, sales, SIC, and names of officers.

H. W. Wilson Company. *Business Periodicals Index*. New York: H. W. Wilson Company, annual. Current articles appearing in business publications by subject. A new index would be available by approximately the middle of June.

Predicasts, Inc. *F & S Index of Corporations and Industries*. Cleveland: Predicasts, Inc., annual. Listing for each industry (arranged by SIC), news report citations of articles appearing in business-oriented periodicals, and alphabetic listing of citations by firm.

Standard and Poor's Corporation. *Register of Corporations, Directors, and Executives*. New York: Standard and Poor's Corporation, annual. Alphabetic listing of corporations with number of employees, sales, products, SIC, and names of officers.

U.S. Bureau of the Census. *Annual Survey of Manufacturers. Statistics for States, SMSAs, Large Industrial Counties, and Selected Cities*. Washington, D.C.: U.S. Government Printing Office, annual. Following data available for substate areas: number of employees, payroll, number of production workers, production man-hours, production payroll, value added by manufacture, cost of materials, value of industry shipments, and new capital expenditures.

U.S. Bureau of the Census. *County and City Data Book*. Washington, D.C.: U.S. Government Printing Office, 1979. Detailed information by city, county, and SMSA on the following subjects: area population, birth and death rates, education, labor force, families, income, social security and public assistance, housing, presidential vote, government finances, banking, manufacturers, retail trade, wholesale trade, mineral industries, agriculture.

U.S. Bureau of the Census. *County Business Patterns.* Washington, D.C.: U.S. Government Printing Office, annual. Number of employees, taxable payrolls, and number of firms by four-digit SIC for each county and each SMSA.

U.S. Bureau of the Census. *Census of Governments. Guide to the 1977 Census of Governments.* Washington, D.C.: U.S. Government Printing Office, 1979. Lists, with examples, of the hundreds of tables available in the various volumes of the *Census of Governments.* Among the general categories for which local government data are available: number of employees, taxable and other property values, assessment–sales price ratios, property tax rates, school district finance, special district finance, state payments to local governments, finances of county governments, municipal and township government finance, and employee retirement systems.

U.S. Bureau of the Census. *Census of Housing. Housing Characteristics for States, Cities, and Counties.* Washington, D.C.: U.S. Government Printing Office. 1972. Data for counties and SMSAS on structural and plumbing characteristics, equipment and financial characteristics, and fuels and appliances used in the area housing stock.

U.S. Bureau of the Census. *Census of Manufactures, 1977. Area Series.* Washington, D.C.: U.S. Government Printing Office, 1979. Categories available from the Annual Survey of Manufactures (see above), treated in greater detail in the Census of Manufacturers. Data are available by SIC within each county or SMSA.

U.S. Bureau of the Census. *Census of Population, 1970. Characteristics of the Population.* Washington, D.C.: U.S. Government Printing Office, 1972. Data for SMSAS on educational, occupational, and employment status; worker mobility; family income; mobility; commuting; and veteran status; fertility and family composition; and detailed characteristics of experienced unemployed workers. For non-SMSA counties, data on age by race and sex; educational and family characteristics; income; occupation; employment; earnings; and detailed economic characteristics of rural farm vs. nonfarm population.

U.S. Bureau of the Census. *Census of Retail Trade, 1977. Area Series.* Washington, D.C.: U.S. Government Printing Office, 1979. The following data for SMSAS, counties or cities with 500 or more establishments, and cities or counties with 2,500 or more inhabitants: number of establishments, type of business organization, sales, payroll, and number of employees—all by detailed type of business.

U.S. Bureau of the Census. *Census of Selected Service Industries, 1977. Area Series.* Washington, D.C.: U.S. Government Printing Office, 1979. The following data for SMSAS, counties with 300 or more service establishments, and cities with 300 or more establishments: number of establishments, type of business organization, receipts, payroll, and number of employees—all by detailed type of business.

U.S. Bureau of the Census. *Census of Transportation, 1977. Commodity Transportation Survey—Area Statistics.* Washington, D.C.: U.S. Government Printing Office, 1979. For each "production area" (generally includes five to ten contiguous counties), the following data: tons of shipments and means of transport for commodities originating in the production area by SIC by regional destination, distribution of an area's shipments by distance shipped by SIC, and distribution of an area's shipments by SIC by weight of shipment.

U.S. Department of Commerce. *Area Economic Projections 1990.* Washington, D.C.: U.S. Government Printing Office. Population, earnings by industry (two-digit SIC), total personal income, and employment projected for 1980 and 1990 by SMSA, Bureau of Economic Analysis (BEA) economic area, and state. Published every five years.

U.S. Department of Commerce. Domestic and International Business Administration. *U.S. Industrial Outlook.* Washington, D.C.: U.S. Government Printing Office, annual. Estimated on an annual basis and projected for 1985: volume of shipments, total employment, production workers, value added, value added per production worker man-hour, value of shipments, value of imports, and value of exports—all by four-digit SIC for the United States. Each set of industry data accompanied by a narrative summary of the major business developments and future prospects for each hundred major industries.

U.S. Department of Labor. *Handbook of Labor Statistics.* Washington, D.C.: U.S. Government Printing Office, annual. Index on the cost of living for twenty-three SMSAs, by cost of food, housing, apparel and upkeep, transportation, health and recreation, and an overall index. Also, data on employment status of the population in thirty SMSAs by race and sex, detailed employment and earnings characteristics by industry, labor turnover rates by industry, work stoppages by industry, and occupational illnesses and injuries by industry.

U.S. Water Resources Council. *OBERS Projections.* Washington, D.C.: U.S. Government Printing Office. Population, earnings by industry (two-digit SIC), total personal income, and employment projected for 1980, 1985, 1990, 2000, and 2020 by SMSA, BEA economic area, water resources regions and subareas, and state.

Selected Bibliography

Advisory Commission on Intergovernmental Relations. *Significant Features of Fiscal Federalism*. Vol. 2. Washington, D.C.: U.S. Bureau of the Census, 1977.

————. *State-Local Taxation and Industrial Location*. Washington, D.C.: Advisory Commission on Intergovernmental Relations, 1967.

————. *The Problem of Special Districts in American Government*. Washington, D.C.: U.S. Government Printing Office, 1964.

Allaman, P. M., and Birch, D. L. *Components of Employment Change for Metropolitan and Rural Areas in the United States by Industry Group, 1970–72*. Working Paper 8. Cambridge, Mass.: Joint Center for Urban Studies of MIT and Harvard University, 1975.

Alonso, William. "Location Theory." In *Regional Policy: Readings in Theory and Applications*, edited by John Friedmann and William Alonso. Cambridge, Mass.: MIT Press, 1975: 35–63.

Alyea, Paul E. "Property Tax Inducements to Attract Industry." In *Property Taxation USA*, edited by Richard W. Lindholm, pp. 139–58. Madison: University of Wisconsin Press, 1967.

American Law Institute. *A Model Land Development Code: A Final Text and Commentary*. Philadelphia: American Law Institute, 1976.

Andrews, Richard N. L. "Impact Statements and Impact Assessments." In *Management and Control of Growth*, vol. 3, edited by Randall W. Scott, pp. 148–56. Washington, D.C.: Urban Land Institute, 1975.

Barro, Stephen M. *The Urban Impacts of Federal Policies*. Vol. 3, *Fiscal Conditions*. Santa Monica, Calif.: Rand Corporation, 1978.

Batra, R., and Scully, Gerald W. "Technical Progress, Economic Growth, and the North-South Wage Differential." *Journal of Regional Science* 12 (1972): 375–86.

Bell, Thomas L. "Central Place as a Mixture of the Function Pattern Principles of Cristaller and Losch: Some Empirical Tests and Applications." Ph.D. dissertation, University of Iowa, 1973.

Bergen, Thomas, and Eagen, William. "Economic Growth and Community Facilities" *Municipal Finance* 19 (May 1961) : 146–50.

Berry, Brian J. L. *Metropolitan Area Definition: A Re-evaluation of Concept and Statistical Practice.* Working Paper 28. Washington, D.C.: Bureau of the Census, 1968.

————, and Horton, Frank E. *Urban Environmental Management.* Englewood Cliffs, N.J.: Prentice-Hall, 1974.

Borchert, J. R. "American Metropolitan Evolution." *Geographical Review* 57 (1967) : 301–23.

————, and Adams, R. B. *Trade Centers and Trade Areas of the Upper Midwest.* Upper Midwest Economic Study, Urban Report no. 3. Minneapolis: University of Minnesota, 1963.

Bradfield, M. "Necessary and Sufficient Conditions to Explain Equilibrium Regional Wage Differentials." *Journal of Regional Science* 16 (1976) : 247–55.

Bridges, Benjamin, Jr. 1965a. "State and Local Inducements for Industry: Part I." *National Tax Journal* 18 (1965) : 1–14.

————. 1965b. "State and Local Inducements for Industry: Part II." *National Tax Journal* 18 (1965) : 175–92.

Bryant, Willis R. *Mortgage Lending.* 2d ed. New York: McGraw-Hill, 1962.

Bureau of Economic Analysis. *Long Term Economic Growth Trends.* Washington, D.C.: Bureau of Economic Analysis, 1977.

Business Executives Research Committee. *Factors Affecting Industrial Location in the Southwest.* Norman, Okla.: University of Oklahoma, 1947.

Business Periodicals Index. New York: H. W. Wilson Company, annual.

Business Week Research Report. *Plant Site Survey: A Study of Business Week Subscribers.* New York: McGraw-Hill, 1964.

Campbell, A. K. "Taxes and Industrial Location in the New York Metropolitan Region." *National Tax Journal* 11 (1958): 195–218.

Center for Urban Studies, University of Chicago. *Mid-Chicago Economic Development Study.* Vol. 2, *Technical Analysis and Findings, Economic Development of Mid-Chicago.* Chicago: Center for Urban Studies, 1966.

Chapin, F. Stuart, Jr. *Urban Land Use Planning.* Urbana: University of Illinois Press, 1965.

Chapman, James E., and Wells, William H. *Factors in Industrial Location in Atlanta, 1946–1955.* Atlanta: Georgia State College, 1958.

City of San Diego Planning Department. *San Diego's Industry, 1969–1990: A Planning Analysis.* San Diego: City of San Diego Planning Department, 1970.

Cowen, David G. "Dynamic Aspects of Urban Industrial Location." Ph.D. dissertation, Ohio State University, 1971.

Cramer, D. B. *Changing Location of Manufacturing Employment.* New York: National Industrial Conference Board, 1963.

Cumberland, John H., and Korbach, Robert J. "A Regional Interindustry Environmental Model." *Regional Science Association Papers* 30 (1973): 61–75.

Daggett, S., and Carter, J. P. *Structure of Transcontinental Rail Rates.* Berkeley: University of California Press, 1947.

Damstadter, Joel. *Conserving Energy: Prospects and Opportunities in the New York Region.* Baltimore: Johns Hopkins University Press, 1975.

Darwin, Richard J. "Geography, Economic Development and Spatial Policy." Ph.D. dissertation, Ohio State University, 1974.

Domestic and International Business Administration, U.S. Department of Commerce. *U.S. Industrial Outlook.* Washington, D.C.: U.S. Government Printing Office.

Doodan, J. "Commuting Zones within Appalachia." Unpublished paper. Columbus: Ohio State University, 1972.

Draper, C. R. "Input-Output Studies and Industrial Development." *AIDC Journal* 13 (1968): 47–53.

Due, John F. "Studies of State-Local Influences on Location of Industry." *National Tax Journal* 14 (1961): 163–73.

Dun and Bradstreet, Inc. *Million Dollar Directory.* New York: Dun and Bradstreet, Inc., annual.

Dunshee, Donald G. "A Methodology for Conducting a Labor Availability Survey in a Standard Metropolitan Statistical Area." *AIDC Journal* 5 (1970): 29–47.

Estall, R. C. *New England: A Study of Industrial Adjustment.* New York: Praeger, 1966.

Federal Water Pollution Control Administration. *Industrial Waste Guide on Thermal Pollution.* Washington, D.C.: Federal Water Pollution Control Administration, 1968.

Fernstrom, John R. *Bringing in the Sheaves.* Corvallis: Oregon State University Extension Service, 1974.

Filani, M. O. *Changing Patterns of Central Places and Functional Regions: Temporal and Spatial Dynamics of Air Traffic Flow in the United States.* University Park, Pa.: Pennsylvania State University, 1972.

Finkler, Earl. *Nongrowth as a Planning Alternative: A Preliminary Examination of an Emerging Issue.* Chicago: American Society of Planning Officials, 1972.

———. *Nongrowth: A Review of the Literature.* Chicago: American Society of Planning Officials, 1973.

Friedlander, Stanley L. *Regional Economic Development and Federal Legislation.* Washington, D.C.: Economic Development Administration, U.S. Department of Commerce, 1976.

Fuchs, V. R. *Changes in the Location of Manufacturing in the United States since 1929.* New Haven: Yale University Press, 1962.

———. "Hourly Earnings Differentials by Region and Size of City." *Monthly Labor Review* 90 (1967): 22–26.

Fulton, Maurice. "Michigan's Tax Structure and Its Influence on Economic Development." In *Taxes and Economic Growth in Michigan,* edited by Paul W. McKracken. Kalamazoo: W. E. Upjohn Institute for Employment Research, 1960.

Gadsby, Dwight M. *Secondary Impacts of Public Investment in Natural Re-*

sources. Washington, D.C.: Office of Economic Research Service, U.S. Department of Agriculture, 1968.

Gold, N. N. "The Mismatch of Jobs and Low-Income People in Metropolitan Areas and Its Implications for the Central-City Poor." In *Population Distribution and Policy*, 5:441–86. Washington, D.C.: Commission on Population Growth and the American Future Research Reports, 1972.

Goldfarb, R. S., and Yezer, A. M. J. "Evaluating Alternative Theories of Intercity and Interregional Wage Differentials." *Journal of Regional Science* 16 (1976): 345–63.

Goodstein, M. E. "A Note on Urban and Nonurban Employment Growth in the South, 1940–1960." *Journal of Regional Science* 10 (1970): 397–401.

Gruen, Gruen and Associates. "The Impacts of Growth: An Analytical Framework and Fiscal Example." In *Management and Control of Growth*, vol. 2, edited by Randall W. Scott, pp. 512–33. Washington, D.C.: Urban Land Institute, 1975.

Hamer, Andrew M. *Industrial Exodus from Central City.* Lexington, Mass.: Lexington Books, 1973.

Hanna, Frank A. *State Income Differentials.* Durham, N.C.: Duke University Press, 1959.

Hanning, Irene. *How North Dakota Taxes Industry.* Bismarck, N.D.: State of North Dakota Economic Foundation, 1947.

Hansen, Niles M., ed., *Growth Centers in Regional Economic Development.* New York: Free Press, 1972.

Harris, Chauncy D. "The Market as a Factor in the Localization of Industry in the U.S." *Annals of the Association of American Geographers* 44 (1954): 315–48.

Harris, Curtis C., Jr., and Hopkins, Frank E. *Locational Analysis.* Lexington, Mass.: Lexington Books, 1974.

Harrison, Bennett, and Kanter, Sandra. "The Political Economy of States' Job-Creation Business Incentives." *Journal of the American Institute of Planners* 44 (1978): 424–35.

Heaton, Tim B., and Fuguitt, Glenn V. "Nonmetropolitan Industrial Growth and Population Change." Paper presented at Annual Meeting of the Association of American Geographers, New Orleans, La., 1978.

Hirschman, A. O. *The Strategy of Economic Development.* New Haven: Yale University Press, 1958.

Hoch, I. "Income and City Size." *Urban Studies* 9 (1972): 299–328.

Hoover, Edgar M. *An Introduction to Regional Economics.* 2d ed. New York: Alfred A. Knopf, 1975.

———. *The Location of Economic Activity.* New York: McGraw-Hill, 1948.

Howard, William C. "The Staffing Experience of a New Industrial Plant: A New Technique for Determining Manpower Availability and Characteristics." *AIDC Journal* 9 (1974): 1–29.

Hunker, Henry L. *Industrial Development: Concepts and Principles.* Lexington, Mass.: Lexington Books, 1974.

———, and Wright, Alfred. *Factors of Industrial Location in Ohio.* Monograph 119. Columbus: Ohio State University, 1963.

Huntington, Hillard, and Kahn, James. "Regional Industrial Growth and the Price of Energy." Working paper 76-WPA-35. Washington, D.C.: Federal Energy Administration, 1976.

Industrial Council of the Urban Land Institute. *Industrial Development Handbook*. Community Builders Handbook Series. Washington, D.C.: Urban Land Institute, 1975.

Isard, Walter. "Interregional and Regional Input-Output Analysis: A Model of a Space-Economy." *Review of Economics and Statistics* 33 (1951): 318–28.

————, and Coughlin, Robert E. *Municipal Costs and Revenues Resulting from Community Growth*. Wellesley, Mass.: Chandler Davis, 1957.

————, et al. *Methods of Regional Analysis*. Cambridge, Mass.: MIT Press, 1960.

Kaiser, Edward J.; Elfers, Karl; Cohn, Sidney; Reichert, Peggy A.; Hufschmidt, Maynard M.; and Stanland, Raymond. *Promoting Environmental Quality through Urban Planning and Controls*. Socioeconomic Environmental Study Series. Washington, D.C.: Office of Research and Development, U.S. Environmental Protection Agency, 1974.

Karaska, Gerald J., and Bramhall, David F. *Locational Analysis for Manufacturing: A Selection of Readings*. Cambridge, Mass.: MIT Press, 1969.

Kinnard, William N., Jr., and Messner, Stephen D. *Industrial Real Estate*. 2d ed. Washington, D.C.: Society of Industrial Realtors, 1971.

Kirk, Alan G., II. "Federal Environmental Regulation: Impact on Land Use." In *Management and Control of Growth*, Vol. 3, edited by Randall W. Scott. Washington, D.C.: Urban Land Institute, 1975.

Kocher, Douglas J., and Bell, Thomas L. "The Effects of Work Place-Residence Separation and Ride Sharing on Employee Absenteeism: Survey and Pilot Study." *The Professional Geographer* 29 (1977): 272–77.

Korb, Irving. *Real Estate Sale-Leaseback: A Basic Analysis*. Rev. ed. Washington, D.C.: Society of Industrial Realtors, 1971.

Lampard, Eric E. "The Evolving System of Cities in the United States: Urbanization and Economic Development." In *Issues in Urban Economics*, edited by H. S. Perloff and L. Wingo, Jr. Baltimore: Johns Hopkins University Press, 1968.

Ledebur, Larry C. *Issues in the Economic Development of Nonmetropolitan United States*. Washington, D.C.: Office of Economic Research, U.S. Department of Commerce, 1977.

Leontief, Wassily W. "The Structure of the U.S. Economy." *Scientific American* 212, no. 4 (1965): 25–35.

Leopold, Luna B., et al. "Evaluating Environmental Impact: A Procedure." Geological Survey Circular 645. Washington, D.C.: U.S. Government Printing Office, 1972.

Levin, Sharon G. "Suburban-Central City Property Tax Differentials and the Location of Industry: Some Evidence." *Land Economics* 1, no. 4 (November 1974).

Longabaugh, Robert J. T. "Cost-Revenue Implications of Various Industrial Land Use Patterns." Master's thesis, University of North Carolina, 1960.

Lonsdale, Richard E. "Two North Carolina Commuting Patterns." *Economic Geography* 42 (1966): 114–38.

————. "Rural Labor as an Attraction for Industry." *American Industrial Development Council Journal* 4 (1969): 11–17.

————, and Browning, Clyde E. "Rural-Urban Locational Preferences of Southern Manufacturers." *Annals of the Association of American Geographers* 61 (1971): 255–68.

————, Kinworthy, J. C.; and Doering, T. R. "Attitudes of Manufacturers in Small Cities and Towns of Nebraska." Unpublished paper. Lincoln, Nebr., 1976.

McCarthy, Kevin F., and Morrison, Peter A. "The Changing Demographic and Economic Structure of Nonmetropolitan Areas in the United States." *International Regional Science Review* 2 (1977): 123–42.

Mace, Ruth. *Industry and City Government.* Chapel Hill, N.C.: Institute of Government, 1963.

Mack, Pamela C. "Federal Environmental Laws: Piecemeal Land Use." In *Management and Control of Growth*, Vol. 3, edited by Randall W. Scott. Washington, D.C.: Urban Land Institute, 1975.

McMillan, T. E., Jr. "Why Manufacturers Choose Plant Locations vs. Determinants of Plant Locations." *Land Economics* 41, no. 3 (August 1965): 239–46.

Mandell, L. *Industrial Location Decisions: Detroit Compared with Atlanta and Chicago.* New York: Praeger, 1975.

Marshall, F. R. "Some Rural Economic Development Problems in the South." *American Economic Review* 62 (1972): 209.

Metropolitan Washington Council of Governments. *Energy Consumption in the Metropolitan Area.* Washington, D.C.: Metropolitan Washington Council of Governments, 1975.

Miernyk, William H. *Elements of Input-Output Analysis.* New York: Random House, 1965.

Morgan, William E. "The Effects of State and Local Tax and Financial Inducements on Industrial Location." Ph.D. dissertation, University of Colorado, 1964.

————, and Hackbart, Merlin M. "An Analysis of State and Local Industrial Tax Exemption Programs." *Southern Economic Journal* 41, no. 2 (October 1974): 201–5.

Moriarty, Barry M. "The Distributed Lag between Metropolitan Area Employment and Population Growth." *Journal of Regional Science* 16 (1976): 195–212.

————. "Manufacturing Wage Rates, Plant Location, and Plant Location Policies." *Popular Government* 42 (1977): 48–53.

————. "Population and Employment Shifts within Regional Hierarchies of Cities." *Proceedings of the Association of American Geographers* 7 (1975): 155–59.

————. "Unexplained Residuals in North-South Wage Differentials Models." *Journal of Regional Science* 18 (1978): 105–8.

Morrisset, I. "The Economic Structure of American Cities." *Papers and Proceedings of the Regional Science Association* 4 (1958): 239–56.

Moss, Laurence I. "Energy Conservation in the U.S.: Why? How Much? By

What Means?" *Energy Conservation Training Institute.* Washington, D.C.: Conservation Foundation, 1976.

Mueller, Eva, and Morgan, James. "Location Decisions of Manufacturers." *Proceedings and Papers of the American Economics Association* 52 (May 1962): 204–17.

Mueller, Warren E. "Industrial Location Decisions." *Oklahoma Business Bulletin* 26, no. 6 (June 1959): 1–4.

Muller, Peter O. *The Outer City: Geographical Consequences of the Urbanization of the Suburbs.* Commission on College Geography Resource Paper. Washington, D.C.: Association of American Geographers, 1976.

Muncy, Dorothy A. *Industrial Land Development.* Technical Report no. 2. Baltimore: Baltimore Regional Planning Council, Maryland State Planning Commission, May 1959.

———. "Planning Guidelines for Industrial Park Development." *Urban Land* 29, no. 12 (December 1970).

Murray, Thomas F. "Financing Industrial Real Estate." *Advanced Course in the Technique of Real Estate.* Washington, D.C.: Society of Industrial Realtors, 1964.

Myrdal, Gunnar M. *Economic Theory and Under-Developed Regions.* London: Duckworth, 1957.

National Conference Board. "Educational Attainment and the Work Force." In *Road Maps of Industry.* New York: The Conference Board, 1972.

Naylor, Thomas H., and Clotfelter, James. *Strategies for Change in the South.* Chapel Hill: University of North Carolina Press, 1975.

Nelson, Kathryn P., and Patrick, Clifford H. *Decentralization of Employment during the 1969–1972 Business Cycle: The National and Regional Record.* Oak Ridge, Tenn.: Oak Ridge National Laboratories, 1975.

New York Division of Housing and Community Renewal and Urban Renewal Administration. *Industrial Renewal: Determining the Potential and Accelerating the Economy of the Utica Urban Area.* New York: U.S. Housing and Home Finance Agency, 1963.

North, D. J. "The Process of Locational Change in Different Manufacturing Operations." In *Spatial Perspectives on Industrial Organization and Decision-Making,* edited by F. E. I. Hamilton. New York: John Wiley, 1974.

North, Douglas C. "Location Theory and Regional Economic Growth." *Journal of Political Economy* 63 (1955): 243–58.

North Carolina State Energy Division. *Energy Conservation in North Carolina—1973.* Raleigh, N.C.: State Energy Division, 1975.

Office of Management and Budget. *Catalog of Federal Domestic Assistance.* Washington, D.C.: Superintendent of Documents, 1975.

Owen, W. *The Accessible City.* Washington, D.C.: Brookings Institution, 1972.

Parker, Francis H. "Regional Imperatives and Managed Growth." In *Management and Control of Growth,* vol. 3, edited by Randall W. Scott, pp. 284–92. Washington, D.C.: Urban Land Institute, 1975.

Polenske, Karen R. *Shifts in the Regional and Industrial Impact of Federal*

Government Spending. Washington, D.C.: Economic Development Administration, U.S. Department of Commerce, 1969.

Poole, Richard W. "An Approach for Evaluating the Impact of State-Local Taxes on Industrial Location." *New Mexico Business* 23, no. 6 (June 1970): 5–11.

Pred, Allan R. "The Intra-Metropolitan Location of Manufacturing." *Annals of the Association of American Geographers* 54 (1964): 165–80.

————. *The Spatial Dynamics of U.S. Urban Industrial Growth, 1800–1914: Interpretive and Theoretical Essays.* Cambridge, Mass.: MIT Press, 1966.

Predicasts, Inc. *F and S Index of Corporations and Industries.* Cleveland, Ohio: Predicasts, Inc., annual.

Preston, Richard. *Principles of Industrial Development.* Wenham, Mass.: AIDC Educational Foundation, 1976.

Pugh, Olin S. *Industrial Aid Bonds as a Source of Capital for Developing Regions.* Columbia, S.C.: University of South Carolina Bureau of Business and Economic Research, 1971.

Regional Economic Analysis Division. "Work-Force Migration Patterns, 1960–1973." *Survey of Current Business* 56 (1976): 23–26.

Revzan, L. H. "Tax Policy and Industrial Location Decisions." *Popular Government* 41, no. 3 (1976): 10–14.

Ross, William D. "Tax Exemptions in Louisiana as a Device for Encouraging Industrial Development." *Southwestern Social Science Quarterly* 34 (June 1953): 14–22.

Rostow, W. W. *The Stages of Economic Growth.* Cambridge, Mass.: MIT Press, 1960.

Schaenman, Philip S., and Muller, Thomas. "Land Development: Measuring the Impacts." In *Management and Control of Growth*, vol. 2, edited by Randall W. Scott, 494–500. Washington, D.C.: Urban Land Institute, 1975.

Schmenner, Roger W. *Proceedings of the Sixty-sixth Annual Conference on Taxation, 1973, Toronto.* Columbus, O.: National Tax Association, Tax Institute of America, 1974.

Scully, Gerald W. "The North-South Manufacturing Wage Differential, 1869–1919." *Journal of Regional Science* 11 (1971): 235–52.

Shenkel, William M. "The Economic Consequences of Industrial Zoning." *Land Economics* 40, no. 3 (August 1964): 255–65.

Smith, David M. *Industrial Location: An Economic Geographical Analysis.* New York: John Wiley, 1971.

————. "A Theoretical Framework for Geographical Studies of Industrial Location." *Economic Geography* 42, no. 2 (April 1966): 95–113.

Smolin, Harlan. "The Structure and Pattern of Commuting in Central Ohio." Master's thesis, Ohio State University, 1974.

Spiegelman, Robert G. "Locational Characteristics in Footloose Industries." *Land Economics* 40 (February 1964): 79–86.

Standard and Poor's Corporation. *Register of Corporations, Directors, and Executives.* New York: Standard and Poor's Corporation, annual.

State of Oregon. *Report of the Legislative Interim for Study Committee*. Salem, Oreg.: State of Oregon, 1955–57.

Stinson, Thomas F. *The Effects of Taxes and Public Finance Programs on Local Industrial Development*. Agricultural Economic Report 133. Washington, D.C.: Economic Research Service of the U.S. Department of Agriculture, 1968.

————. *Financing Industrial Development through State and Local Governments*. Agricultural Economic Report 18. Washington, D.C.: Economic Research Service of the U.S. Department of Agriculture, 1967.

Stockfish, J. A. *A Study of California's Tax Treatment of Manufacturing Industry*. Sacramento: California Economic Development Agency, 1961.

Strasma, J. D. *State and Local Taxation of Industry*. Boston: Federal Reserve Bank of Boston, 1959.

Struyk, Raymond J., and James, Franklin. *Intrametropolitan Industrial Location: The Pattern and Process of Change in Four Metropolitan Areas*. Lexington, Mass.: Lexington Books, 1975.

Sulvetta, Anthony J., and Thompson, Norman. *An Evaluation of the Public Works Impact Program (PWIP)*. Washington, D.C.: Economic Development Administration, U.S. Department of Commerce, 1975.

Sweet, David C. "Development and Application of an Industry Potential Model." Ph.D. dissertation, Ohio State University, 1970.

————. "Identifying Industrial Potential." *AIDC Journal* 6, no. 1 (January 1971): 71–76.

————. "The Systematic Approach to Industrial Development Research." *AIDC Journal* 5 no. 2 (April 1970): 21–32.

————, et al. *Appalachian Selective Development Program*. Publication 72-37/RP-216. Washington, D.C.: Appalachian Regional Commission, 1973.

Taaffe, Edward J.; Garner, Barry J.; and Yeates, Maurice H. *The Peripheral Journey to Work*. Evanston, Ill.: Northwestern University Press, 1963.

————, and Gauthier, Howard L. *Geography of Transportation*. Englewood Cliffs, N.J.: Prentice-Hall, 1973.

————, and King, Leslie J. "Networks of Cities." Unit 3, *High School Geography Project*. Washington, D.C.: Association of American Geographers, 1966.

Thompson, A. A. "Industrial Revenue Bonds and Regional Development." *Review of Regional Studies* 1, no. 1 (1969): 185–210.

Till, Thomas. "The Extent of Industrialization in Southern Non-Metropolitan Labor Markets in the 1960's." *Journal of Regional Science* 13 (1973): 453–61.

Toffler, A. *Future Shock*. New York: Random House, 1970.

Tremaine, J. Richard. "Implementing Environmental Policies: A Systematic Approach to Specific Site Review." In *Management and Control of Growth*, vol. 3, edited by Randall W. Scott. Washington, D.C.: Urban Land Institute, 1975.

Ullman, Edward L.; Dacey, Michael F.; and Brodsky, Harold. *The Economic Base of American Cities*. Seattle: University of Washington Press, 1971.

U.S. Bureau of the Census. *Annual Survey of Manufacturers: Statistics for States, SMSA's, Large Industrial Counties, and Selected Cities*. Washington, D.C.: U.S. Government Printing Office, 1977.

————. *Census of Housing: Housing Characteristics for States, Cities, and Counties.* Washington, D.C.: U.S. Government Printing Office, 1970.

————. *Census of Manufactures.* Washington, D.C.: U.S. Government Printing Office, 1958, 1967, 1972.

————. *Census of Population: Characteristics of the Population.* Washington, D.C.: U.S. Government Printing Office, 1870, 1900, 1910, 1920, 1930, 1940, 1950, 1960, 1970.

————. *Census of Population Subject Reports: Mobility for States and the Nation.* Washington, D.C.: U.S. Government Printing Office, 1973.

————. *Census of Population Subject Reports: Occupation by Industry.* Washington, D.C.: U.S. Government Printing Office, 1972.

————. *Census of Retail Trade: Area Series.* Washington, D.C.: U.S. Government Printing Office, 1977.

————. *Census of Selected Service Industries: Area Series.* Washington, D.C.: U.S. Government Printing Office, 1977.

————. *Census of Transportation: Commodity Transportation Survey—Area Statistics.* Washington, D.C.: U.S. Government Printing Office, 1977.

————. *County and City Data Book.* Washington, D.C.: U.S. Government Printing Office, annually.

————. *County Business Patterns.* Washington, D.C.: U.S. Government Printing Office, annually.

————. *Guide to the 1977 Census of Governments.* Washington, D.C.: U.S. Government Printing Office.

U.S. Bureau of Labor Statistics. *Handbook of Labor Statistics, 1972.* Bulletin 1735. Washington, D.C.: U.S. Government Printing Office, 1972.

U.S. Department of Commerce. *Area Economic Projections 1990.* Washington, D.C.: U.S. Government Printing Office.

————. *Basic Industrial Location Factors.* Washington, D.C.: U.S. Government Printing Office, 1947.

————. *Industrial Location As a Factor in Regional Economic Development.* Washington, D.C.: U.S. Government Printing Office, 1967.

————. "The Input-Output Structure of the U.S. Economy." *Survey of Current Business.* Washington, D.C.: U.S. Government Printing Office, 1974.

————. *The Local Economic Development Corporation: Legal and Financial Guidelines.* Washington, D.C.: U.S. Government Printing Office, 1970.

————. *Statistical Abstract of the United States.* Washington, D.C.: U.S. Government Printing Office, 1975, 1976, 1977, 1978.

U.S. Department of Labor. *Handbook of Labor Statistics.* Washington, D.C.: U.S. Government Printing Office, annual.

U.S. Office of Economic Opportunity. *Catalog of Federal Programs for Individual and Community Development.* Washington, D.C.: U.S. Government Printing Office, 1965.

————. *The Vice President's Handbook for Local Officials: Guide to Federal Assistance for Local Government.* Washington, D.C.: U.S. Government Printing Office, 1968.

U.S. Office of Management and Budget. *Project Notification and Review for*

Federal and Federally Assisted Programs and Projects. Circular no. A-95. Washington, D.C.: U.S. Government Printing Office, n.d.

U.S. Small Business Administration. *Loan Sources in the Federal Government.* Bulletin 52. Washington, D.C.: U.S. Government Printing Office, n.d.

————. *SBIC Financing for Small Business.* Bulletin OPI-13. Washington, D.C.: U.S. Government Printing Office, n.d.

U.S. Water Resources Council. *OBERS Projections.* Washington, D.C.: U.S. Government Printing Office, n.d.

————. *The Water-Use Data Book.* Washington, D.C.: U.S. Government Printing Office, 1969.

Vaughan, Roger J. *The Urban Impacts of Federal Policies.* Vol. 2, *Economic Development.* Santa Monica, Calif.: Rand Corporation, 1977.

Vernon, Raymond. "Production and Distribution in the Large Metropolis." *American Academy of Political and Social Science* 314 (1959): 15–19.

Wallace, L. T., and Ruttan, V. W. "The Role of Community in Industrial Location." *Papers of the Regional Science Association* 7 (1961): 133–42.

Wallman, Nathaniel, and Bonem, Gilbert W. *The Outlook for Water Quality and National Growth.* Baltimore: Johns Hopkins University Press for Resources for the Future, Inc.

Walsh, Stuart Parry. "Twelve Common Mistakes in Industrial Land Development." *Urban Land* 22, no. 6 (June 1963): 1, 3–4.

Washington State Department of Commerce and Economic Development and Washington State Tax Commission. *Industrial Tax Loads in Competing States.* Olympia, Wash.: Washington State Department of Commerce and Economic Development, 1963.

Wheat, Leonard J. *Regional Growth and Industrial Location: An Empirical Viewpoint.* Lexington, Mass.: Lexington Books, 1973.

Widner, Ralph R. "State Growth and Federal Policies: A Reassessment of Responsibilities." In *Management and Control of Growth,* vol. 3, edited by Randall W. Scott, pp. 403–9. Washington, D.C.: Urban Land Institute, 1975.

Williams, William V. "A Measure of the Impact of State and Local Taxes on Industry Location." *Journal of Regional Science* 7, no. 1 (1967): 49–59.

Winston, Carey. "Mortgage Financing of Industrial Construction." *The Appraisal Journal* (October 1965): 1–4.

Wonnacott, Ronald J. *Manufacturing Costs and the Comparative Advantage of United States Regions.* Minneapolis: University of Minnesota Upper Midwest Economic Study, 1963.

Yaseen, Leonard C. *Plant Location.* New York: American Research Council, 1956.

Zelinsky, Wibur. "Has American Industry Been Decentralizing: The Evidence for the 1930–1954 Period." *Economic Geography* 38, no. 3 (1962): 251–89.

Ziehr, Charles. "The Importance of Incentives on the Location of Manufacturing in South Carolina." Master's thesis, University of South Carolina, 1975.

Index